THE
PLANT
SELECTOR

Brian Davis

WARD LOCK

A WARD LOCK BOOK

First published in the UK 1997
by Ward Lock
Wellington House
125 Strand
London
WC2R 0BB

A Cassell Imprint

Distributed in the United States
by Sterling Publishing Co., Inc.
387 Park Avenue South, New York, NY 10016–8810

A British Library Cataloguing in Publication Data block for
this book may be obtained from the British Library

ISBN 0 7063 7567 X

Printed in Hong Kong by Dah Hua

PHOTOGRAPH ACKNOWLEDGEMENTS
All pictures supplied by Brian Davis except for the following:
Jerry Harpur: p.1 (Designer: Mark Rumary, Yoxford,
Suffolk; Garden: Kettle Hill, Blakeney), p.7 (Designer: Susan
Whittington, London),p.10 (*top*) (Great Dixter, Northiam,
East Sussex), p.10 (*bottom*) (Wollerton Hall, Shropshire),
p.11 (Dolwen, Clwyd, Wales), p18; **Andrew Lawson**: pp.6, 8,
12, 15, 20; **Clive Nichols**: p.23 (Hadspen, Somerset)

Frontispiece: *Lilies add elegance and scent to any garden.*

CONTENTS

How to Use This Book   4
Symbols and Abbreviations   5

Planting Styles   6
Formal   6
Informal   7
Wild   8
Cottage Garden   8

Creative Planting   9
Colour   9
Size, Shape and Form   11
Year-round Effect   14
Scent in the Garden   15
Putting it All Together   16

Practical Aspects   17
Site and Aspect   17
Soil   18
Plant Selection   19
Maintenance   19

A–Z DIRECTORY   23
Trees   24
Shrubs   40
Climbers   98
Roses   116
Perennials   130
Ornamental Grasses   179
Hardy Ferns and Palms   185
Bamboos   189
Bulbs, Tubers and Corms   191
Alpines   209
Biennials   221
Conifers   225

Index   235

HOW TO USE THIS BOOK

The world of gardening and plants is forever changing, and almost any would-be definitive statement is likely to be contradicted almost as soon as it has been made. That said, however, the plants included in the directory entries in this book have been chosen on the basis of my own personal observations over many years, and they take into account all the possible factors that can influence a plant's performance.

The selection included in the directory covers those plants that are worth considering first in a planting scheme, whatever its size. There are, however, many thousands of varieties available within the various genera, and you may come across different named varieties in your local garden centre or nursery. Here *The Plant Selector* can help. You may well find the genus or even the species described in its pages, even though the actual variety is not mentioned. It is safe to assume that the conditions of those included will be largely the same as those of related plants that are not included.

The heights, spreads and flowering times indicated for each plant are based on the best average conditions that can be expected in any given planting location. They assume that the recommended cultivation processes, such as pruning, are undertaken and carried out as suggested. Soil conditions are fundamental to success, and a failure to take these into consideration when plants are chosen and planted will inevitably lead to disappointment. The most important factor to be considered before purchasing any plant is the alkalinity or acidity of your garden soil. Inexpensive testing kits are obtainable from garden centres and suppliers, and if, after testing, you find that the conditions in your garden are wrong, move on, using *The Plant Selector* to identify another suitable plant.

There are a number of ways in which you can use *The Plant Selector* to find the plant best suited to your requirements. Each will start you on a trail of investigation and, eventually, selection.

Simply dipping into the text from time to time may make you aware of interesting plants with which you were not previously familiar. You may come across plants with good general garden value or find one that will fulfil a specific task or fill a gap that you have identified in your garden.

Alternatively, you may already have a particular plant in mind, and the text will enable you to ensure not only that it will suit the circumstances existing in your garden but that you provide it with the correct growing conditions and cultivate it in the right way. Finally, there is the possibility that you will find an alternative variety that will produce better flowers or foliage or some other feature that will suit your garden.

The Plant Selector comes into its own when you are searching for a specific plant. If, for example, you wanted a plant of a particular height for your garden, by working through the entries you can identify those that might achieve the desired height over the time span you have in mind and draw up a short list of possible purchases.

Next, you can look at, say, the foliage and flowers to determine whether they would fit into your overall plan, taking into account when they flower and their colour. Are the flowers large or small, are they single or scented, or are they borne in clusters? Is the foliage evergreen or deciduous? Are the size, colour and shape right for the position you want to fill? A plant's habit of growth is important if it is to be used with other plants, and this information is also included. Finally, you need to consider if the aspect, hardiness and soil conditions prevailing in your garden will suit the plants on your short list. If any of these factors suggest that the plant will not thrive in your garden, simply move on to the next on the list.

Once you have chosen a plant that fulfils your needs and will grow in your garden, check to see if there are any tips about purchasing - whether container-grown plants are to be preferred, for example. All plants included in the text are readily available from nurseries and garden centres.

You may need or would like to propagate your own plants, and if this is the case, the best technique is shown under 'Needs'. Some plants are very difficult to propagate, and these are shown as requiring commercial propagation. In these instances it is better to purchase the selected plant rather than to try to grow it yourself.

Finally, if a plant has special cultivation requirements – pruning, for example – this information is included to cover the life of your selected plant. Wherever possible, follow these suggestions; they will help to avoid later problems.

SYMBOLS AND ABBREVIATIONS

The following symbols and abbreviations are used in the plant directory:

▲   Interesting overall plant shape

❀   Good flower colour and form

❦   Interesting foliage colour or shape

SI   Season of interest

SC   Scented flowers or foliage

E   Evergreen

D   Deciduous

♛   Royal Horticultural Society Award of Garden Merit

❄   Minimum temperature that can be tolerated

Z   North American hardiness zone. These are:

1	below -45°C
	below -50°F
2	-45 to -40°C
	-50 to -40°F
3	-40 to -34°C
	-40 to -30°F
4	-34 to -29°C
	-30 to -20°F
5	-29 to -23°C
	-20 to -10°F
6	-23 to -18°C
	-10 to 0°F
7	-18 to -12°C
	0 to 10°F
8	-12 to -7°C
	10 to 20°F
9	-7 to -1°C
	20 to 30°F
10	-1 to 4°C
	30 to 40°F
11	above 4°C
	above 40°F

Plant dimensions are given as height (H) and spread (S)

PLANTING STYLES

Planting styles are very much a matter of personal taste, and each of us will have our own ideas about what constitutes an ideal garden. Styles themselves, however, can vary over time, and they may, in any case, be influenced or even determined by existing planting within a garden or by the conditions in terms of factors such as soil type and climate that obtain in a particular area.

It takes time for many plants to achieve their full potential and for the effect of a particular plant or group of plants to create the impression intended. Planning from the outset is important, however, not only to impose your chosen style but to make sure that the plants needed to create a particular style have the space in which to develop. Failing to consider the ultimate height and spread of plants leads to more mistakes in creating a garden than any other, and putting such errors right can be costly if you have to move or remove a large tree or shrub.

Formal

A formal garden depends on there being very clear lines within a geometric layout. Even when these regimented patterns are established, it is important to select plants that can carry forward the theme. In most cases the choice will be of plants that are grown for their overall specimen shapes, which can be maintained for many years to come.

The distinct geometric shape of the hedging and perennials in strong colours successfully blend to create this formal style.

The backbone of any formal planting is hedging or edging, which creates the lines of the pattern to which plants are added to infill. Hard landscaping, such as the inclusion of paths, walls and formal pools, can have a role to play in the overall formal concept, and such a garden would not be complete without at least one vista with a focal point. This can be provided by a garden ornament or a carefully selected specimen plant.

It is possible to create a formal garden by using only a few types of plant – perhaps as few as two or three – which are often set in grass or paving. Conifers and evergreen shrubs feature high in the lists of plants used in these gardens, and they can be supported by perennial plants with strong shapes or large foliage such as yuccas and phormiums.

Many formal gardens are based on a colour theme, such as all blue, red or white flowers, and foliage can also be used to emphasize or even impose a colour, with all silver, all gold or even red being among the most often planted.

Formal gardens might also include avenues, walkways and arches, and plants that can be used to line such features, as well as those that are suitable for hedging and edging and for use as specimen plants are identified in the directory.

Informal

Although an informal garden sounds as if it is simply the opposite of a formal planting scheme, many of the same rules apply to both. Without a structure and planting plan, informal gardens may simply look a mess. Hedges, for example, are still needed to protect and divide, although in an informal garden they need not always be formally clipped and shaped.

Informal gardens often include a wider range of plants than formal gardens, but these plants must be carefully selected so that each plant or group of plants blends with its neighbours in terms of colour, form and, most importantly, size. Too often a beautiful small plant is dominated by the planting of an overpoweringly large neighbour.

The aim of an informal garden is to provide a display of plants that flows smoothly from one point to the next, providing shape and a harmony of colour for as long a period as possible during the year. As in a formal garden, a colour theme can be used, and one of the most popular is to base the planting scheme on plants with pastel shades in their flowers.

Yellow Narcissus *contrasts crisply with the blue* Pulmonaria *in this loosely informal planting.*

Wild

A wild garden is not one in which the owner has walked away and allowed the area to become a wilderness or jungle. The intention is to have a garden in which individual plants or groups of a single variety of plant can grow to show off their full potential of shape, size, flower and foliage colour. Such plants normally stand alone in grassy areas, which are cut only once a year in mid-summer after the seeds of annual and biennial plants have fallen so that they can provide new plants for the next flowering year. The picture is completed by bulbs that are allowed to naturalize in the grass, with snow-drops *(Galanthus)* and daffodils *(Narcissus)* being the best choices.

Not all plants are suitable for wild gardens. The major considerations must be that they are robust and will achieve an overall size that allows them to withstand the competition that exists in such a garden.

Cottage Garden

The cottage garden is, perhaps, the most difficult to create and almost impossible to plan, for it relies on having a natural, long-established look. The true cottage garden is built up over many years, with the gardener introducing plants almost by whim. Some will survive, others die, but in the end those that remain create the desired effect.

Looking at established cottage gardens may help us to find the secret of plant selection to achieve the effect. When the traditional cottage garden is analysed, it will be found that the plants most often found are those with pastel colouring to their flowers. The main plants used are roses and perennials, such as delphiniums and lupins, supported by biennials, like hollyhocks *(Alcea rosea)*, which in many cases become perennial. These carry the planting display through summer and into autumn, when the fruits of plants such as Chinese lanterns *(Physalis)* come into their own. In spring, colour is supplied by bulbs, including aconites *(Aconitum)*, snow-drops *(Galanthus)*, daffodils *(Narcissus)* and tulips *(Tulipa)*, supported by biennials such as forget-me-nots *(Myosotis)* and polyanthus *(Primula)*.

CREATIVE
PLANTING

Colour

The importance of colour in gardening cannot be over-stated. When the colours we see are harmonious and right, we feel happy or contented; when the reverse is the case, we feel unhappy or uncomfortable. As gardeners we can control the colours we have around us, and, by the skilful use of different plants, we can achieve different effects at will.

Hot summer days can be cooled down by the white flowers of *Philadelphus* and the blues of delphiniums. The pinks of camellias in spring hint at the warm days of summer to come, while the bold flame reds, yellows and oranges of the autumn foliage of *Acer* and *Cotinus* can furnish us with memories of warm colours to carry us through winter to what seems a far-off spring. Yellow, gold and white plants can be used as focal points to create vistas that add the illusion of space and distance, and these include the winter stems of birch *(Betula)* or the golden foliage of the cut-leaved elder *(Sambucus racemosa* 'Plumosa Aurea'*)*. Such plants can also be used brighten up a dull, uninteresting or dark corner by reflecting what little winter light there is available.

The white-variegated foliage of *Cornus alba* 'Elegantissima' or the gold leaves of *Cornus alba* 'Spathii' can also be used to bring alive a gloomy area, and the effect can be heightened when planted with the purple foliage of *Berberis thunbergii* f. *atropurpurea* (barberry) or one of its varieties.

Dark green foliage can be used to show off paler colours, and the foliage of *Osmanthus* 'Burkwoodii' is ideal for the task, with the added bonus that there are scented white spring flowers. Warmth can be introduced by planting pink tulips, while pink roses of any type have the same effect on the dullest of summer days.

Silver and grey plants, such as santolina (cotton lavender) and artemisias, are the ideal foil for most other colours, and they can be introduced to create buffer zones between strong colours, such as reds and blues, and to provide somewhere for the eye to rest.

Seasons change, and so do the sources of colour. In spring, summer and autumn there are so many that we tend to take them for granted. In autumn we look for the colour of the leaves and also of ripening fruits and berries, such as those of cotoneasters and pyracanthas (firethorn). The importance of evergreens, such as elaeagnus and photinias, in providing colour in winter is often overlooked, and *Jasminum nudiflorum* (winter jasmine) offers yellow winter flowers. When it is planted with the red-fruiting *Cotoneaster horizontalis* (fishbone

Aconites and crocus provide bright colour in spring and herald the warm days of summer to come.

Although very similar in colour, colchicum and Petunia 'Purple Wave' have contrasting shapes and flower size and complement each other.

This combination of plants in soft pastel colours has a charm of its own.

cotoneaster) it makes a unique display. Combinations cannot always be planned and some of the happiest colour effects are achieved by accident.

Colours can be used as garden features in their own right – edging a path with the blue and grey of catmint (*Nepeta*) or a rose border with the yellow-green of *Alchemilla mollis* (lady's mantle) are good examples.

The use of background goes hand in hand with plant colour. Planting a tree where it can be silhouetted by a blue sky can intensify the flower or leaf colour many times over.

Flowers not only offer colour but also scent, and when the two coincide, the effect of each can be heightened. The appreciation of a particular fragrance is always a personal matter, and what gives pleasure to one may not be detected by another. It is worth remembering, too, that some plants, especially roses and lilies, are expected to be fragrant. In fact, this is not always the case, and if scent is important to you, check that the variety you are proposing to plant is, in fact, scented.

In addition to the pleasures that colour and scent bring us, we should not forget that we can include in our gardens plants that will attract butterflies and other beneficial insects. In autumn moths are attracted by blue flowers, and *Ceanothus* (Californian lilac) and *Caryopteris* (blue spiraea) are often covered by moths in their endless search for nectar. Not only do planting

schemes that positively encourage insects play their part in conserving wildlife, but they also encourage a natural ecosystem to develop in our gardens.

To enjoy colour and scent in the garden, it is first necessary actually to grow the appropriate plants. This may seem obvious, but many gardens, even those apparently well designed, do not look exciting or stimulating simply because the number and balance of the plants in them have not been thought through and acted upon.

Size, Shape and Form

No matter how much careful planning and planting have gone into your garden, it can all be to no avail if the ultimate sizes of the plants have not been considered, and this means the width or spread of the plants, not just their height. The overall shape and form of every plant must be taken into account, for they will largely determine the final effect of the planting, particularly the way it appears in winter. Height and spread can be used to advantage when you want to provide sentinel effects in borders or to highlight a gateway or path.

The ultimate size and shape of all mature plants can be predicted with some accuracy. These dimensions may be reached within one or two years, as with perennials such as *Acanthus spinosus* (bear's breeches), or it may be many years or even generations before a plant reaches its maximum height and spread. The beautiful blue cedar, *Cedrus libani* ssp. *atlantica* 'Glauca Pendula', for example, will take generations to achieve its full height and spread, but it will need the space in which it can grow and develop.

In all the entries in the directory there is an indication of the average height and spread that is to be expected from any given plant over a given number of years. The information about the height and spread of plants that is included in this, as in most gardening books, is based on experience and observation, and it is, by and large, accurate. However, it is worth bearing in mind that a plant's development will always be influenced by the conditions in which it is grown. Soil type, weather conditions, cultivation techniques and geographical location will all play their part. A willow *(Salix)* growing in a dry soil will possibly grow less well, and fail to achieve the height and spread that it would have done on its preferred, moist soil.

Different soil types will also provide the plant with different levels of nutrition, and the different conditions will influence growth rates and the overall size of the plant. Poor, impoverished soils will reduce growth levels

Varied tones of red and purple are merged here to give a warm effect.

and overall performance. The soil may be of a kind that physically restricts root development – if *Agapanthus* are grown on heavy clay soils, for example, their thick, fleshy roots will not be able to develop to the full. Adding large amounts of organic material to the soil can help overcome this problem and aid the roots in their development. Clay soils tend to have a high moisture content, and they are, therefore, colder than lighter soils, and this will slow down the overall rate of growth of the plant. Soils that have a high sand content, on the other hand, will be warmer but lacking in moisture, which can make it difficult for plants to find the nutrients they require.

The alkalinity and acidity of the soil may enhance or depress growth rates if the individual plants are like rhododendrons and azaleas, which require a specific soil – in their case, an acid soil. If they are planted on an alkaline soil, they will often grow and struggle for a number of years, but in the end they will never reach their expected potential and may even die.

Weather conditions will provide more or less moisture in the form of rain, which in turn will increase or restrict growth levels. Cold, wet springs will result in the late growth of a plant. Wind and snow may physically damage the structure, and snow must be removed, especially from conifers, if at all possible. Persistent wind from one direction may, notably in coastal areas, distort the overall shape and therefore the size. Cultivation, most particularly poor planting preparation, may slow down the rate of development, often to the point of eventually killing a plant. Pruning in order to encourage the flower production of a shrub will not reduce the overall height but, of course, that used to shape or contain foliage shrubs will. Feeding and watering will improve growth rates, as will mulching and general weed control, but they cannot change the probable ultimate dimensions of any plant.

The speed at which the plant matures is important in the overall design of a planting. Where in the text this is shown as one measurement – as with, say, snowdrops (*Galanthus*) – the plant can be expected to achieve that height in its first year of growth. The ultimate size of plants such as shrubs, trees, conifers and climbers is shown as the average dimensions reached between the first five and ten years. Some trees, of course, may grow on to even greater heights, and where this is the case an indication of the predicted size at maturity is given. For many trees, maturity is achieved after several years, and in most cases between 40 and 60 years.

Foliage that has interesting shape and texture, like the Hydrangea aspera *and* Eryngium giganteum *shown here, adds an extra dimension to plants.*

Height is only one of the dimensions that must be considered. Spread is, in many ways, even more important when a garden is being planned. Planting too close at the outset will lead to overcrowding, which not only reduces the plant's overall performance and appearance, but is also like to cause damage or distress to adjacent plants. In addition to these problems, overplanting is often a waste of money.

When climbers or wall shrubs are being sited it is important to remember that the plants will have a certain amount of forward spread, and if such a plant is in a narrow border next to a path, it can impede easy passage when the plant is fully developed. A *Garrya elliptica*, for example, can spread forward by as much as 2m (6ft) in as little as two or three years, and reducing such a plant by pruning will substantially diminish its overall effect.

Blending the shapes and sizes of all the plants in a garden is crucial to the overall design and the effect that can be achieved. However, planting architectural conifers so that they grow together should be avoided. Thinking ahead about their eventual size can avoid future damage and disappointment. An overplanted group of conifers is one of the saddest sights in gardening. Planting each one in the first place so that it has room to develop and using some other low-growing or relatively short-lived plant such as heathers between each overcomes the sparse, underplanted effect that results by correctly spacing the important plants at the outset.

A plant with a spreading habit can be used to really good effect in the planning of a garden, as can carpeting, pyramidal or mound-forming plants. When colour and texture are associated with shape and size, you have a very wide palette of plants to chose from and one that will allow you to achieve almost any effect in your garden design. Unfortunately, only rarely are all these factors taken into consideration at the early, planning stages, and the true potential of many of the plants used is seldom achieved.

Even when a planting scheme is thoroughly researched, the results may be disappointing, and this is usually because of time. As we have already noted, plants can take many years to reach a useful shape and size and to produce their full display potential. One solution to this problem is to intersperse slow-growing plants with quicker, maybe shorter-lived perennials, so that a long-term effect can be achieved without any gaps in the planting being apparent while the main plants grow to maturity. These fillers must be carefully chosen. Avoid any with an invasive habit or that are likely to work against the required overall effect.

Year-round Effect

Every gardener's ambition should be to introduce plants that provide something of interest in the garden every day of the year. This aspiration can be achieved with just a little research into the many plants that are described in *The Plant Selector*.

If you have sufficient space, it is possible to have a plant flowering every day of the year, and although this might be desirable, flowers are not the only, nor even the main, attraction of many plants.

A characteristic that is often overlooked but that can bring year-round interest is the overall shape of the plant. If you plant, say, a pyramidal conifer where it can be seen from a distance, it can offer interest in the darkest days of winter. Planting a pair of shaped conifers to show off a entrance or highlight a exit makes a garden feature in its own right. A bold carpet planting or a plant that tumbles down a bank or wall can be pretty whether in flower or not, and even the twining effect of a climbing plant like wisteria as it makes its way skywards to cover even greater areas can be spectacular. Winter flowers are always a delight, of course, but winter stems and the effect of winter sunlight can be as startling and attractive as any summer flowers. Management by pruning is required to produce the best stems, but it is worth the effort.

Evergreen foliage of all kinds has always been important because it brings solidity and structure. Dark green foliage helps to show off other, lighter types, and many flowering plants can be seen to their best against a dark backdrop. In winter the stems of birch *(Betula)* stand out wonderfully against a background of dark green conifers. Gold- or silver-variegated evergreen plants can add colour and interest in their own right throughout the year, but in winter they come into their own, catching whatever winter sunshine there is and providing interest in the form of colour, contrast and shape. Finally, the value of evergreen plants to wildlife, especially as safe roosting places and, later, nesting sites for birds should never be underestimated.

As spring unfolds in the garden, leaf shape and form begin to reveal themselves. Delicate new leaves open, bringing freshness and dainty shapes in such variety that it seem as if the patterns and colours are unlimited. These are followed by flowers, which never fail to amaze with their diversity of colours, shapes, scents and forms.

From giant trees to the smallest of alpine plants, the garden is seen at its best as spring turns into the gentle mellow days of summer. By now the foliage is mature, with evergreens showing off their cloaks of new leaves, providing shade from the sun and shelter from the rain. As summer passes, flowers begin to give way to the first signs of interesting and attractive autumn fruits and seeds. Autumn is more unpredictable. Sometimes late sunshine highlights unexpected beauties, while the increasingly bare stems and branches of deciduous shrubs and trees reveal their underlying shapes. There are still a few flowers, mostly blue and smaller now that winter approaches.

The stars of autumn are, of course, the many coloured fruits and autumn leaf colours that can be among the most spectacular sights of the whole garden year. The fruits can range from the graceful seedheads of grasses like *Stipa gigantica* to the bold yellow, red or orange displays of a pyracantha. There are the red-orange hips of roses, such as *Rosa moyesii*, or the unusual dark pink spindles of *Euonymus europeaus* 'Red Cascade'. Foliage colours range from the orange-red leaves of *Acer palmatum* to the all-yellow leaves of *Acer platanoides*, which bring a sunny look to the autumn garden.

As these leaf displays fall and we collect them to turn to compost, we begin to think about winter and the start of the displays that will mark the beginning of the garden year all over again.

Scent in the Garden

Of all the joys that a garden can offer, scent must top most people's lists. It is, however, a very personal and individual pleasure, Different people perceive and appreciate different scents in different ways and to different degrees.

Remember that scents do not come only from flowers. Leaves are often aromatic, especially when crushed or brushed against, and even some stems are subtly scented.

In summer many plants blend their scents – a rose garden in full summer has a unique scent that is quite different from the scents of the individual roses. Such a perfume can be almost overpowering in its intensity. But scent is an attribute of other seasons than summer. On a cold winter's day the scent of scent of a *Mahonia japonica* or a winter-flowering *Daphne mezereum* will lift the spirits.

The dramatic autumn colours of the Rhus typhina *will be remembered long into the winter.*

Putting it All Together

Putting together all the various elements can be a daunting prospect. Preparing the ground and planting a single plant is straightforward task, but when a large group or even the entire garden is to be planted, the work can seem impossible. However, there are some simple guidelines to follow that can eliminate must of the worry and reduce the effort.

First, draw up a simple scale plan of the garden or border to be planted. On this outline plan draw circles to represent plants to be planted. At the back large circles will show where large plants will go, medium sized circles will go in the centre, and small ones at the front. Make sure that the circles are drawn to scale and that they cover the whole of the area of the plan to be planted. If you are planning an island bed – that is, one surrounded by lawn – make sure that the largest plants are in the middle, with the smallest ones all around the edges.

With most plantings the larger plants will be planted singly, the medium sized ones in threes of one variety and the smallest ones in threes or fives. Keeping these bold planting numbers is important if the border is not to look uninteresting when it reaches maturity.

Next, place a sheet of tracing paper over the plan. Use *The Plant Selector* to find the names of the plants you want to include in your scheme, and write them on the tracing paper in the appropriate place. The advantage of using tracing paper is that if everything goes wrong and you do not like the end result, you can simply tear it up and start again without having to go to the trouble of redrawing the plan and circles.

Take the heights, spreads and the colours of foliage and flowers into account and group and position the plants according to their expected performance in the garden. The picture will slowly emerge, and you will be able to add the finishing touches, allowing each plant and its companions to have their own spaces. As a reminder, you may wish to make a note on the plan of details of cultivation, particularly pruning, to help you while the plants mature.

PRACTICAL ASPECTS

Site and Aspect

The factors that most influence the ways in which a plant develops in a garden are the plant's hardiness, and the site and the aspect of the garden – that is, the amount of sun and shade and the possibility of physical damage by wind if no support is provided. A plant's hardiness is possibly the most important of the three, and it is judged not just by the plant's ability to withstand winter cold but also the degree to which it might be damaged by spring frosts.

When you are choosing plants, you must consider the micro-climate of the site. Does your garden face the morning sun, in which case overnight frosts will clear more quickly and it will soon warm up, or does it receive sun in the afternoon? Is it in a frost pocket, where the plants will be subjected to more frosts than gardens only a short distance away? Is the garden sheltered by near-by buildings? Do these buildings funnel cold winds or are there windbreaks that will protect all or part of the garden? Wind intensifies the effects of cold by driving it at greater force into the tissue of the plant, and evergreens suffer most in this respect.

All these factors affect the amount of time a plant is exposed to levels of cold that can cause damage to the stem, foliage or, less often, the roots. In the directory each entry includes a minimum temperature that can be tolerated by any plant. If a plant is particularly prone to damage by spring frosts – as are hydrangeas and pieris, for example – this is indicated in the text.

Closely related to the levels of cold that a plant can tolerate is the amount of water in the soil. The roots of plants such as camellias can be suffocated by too high levels in the surrounding soil, and this is particularly so in winter, when they use less than in summer. Surprisingly perhaps, too much sun can also cause problems. Plants with very thin leaf skins or membranes can be damaged in strong sunlight because the fluids within the leaf simply boil and damage the leaf cells, causing scorching and the death of the leaf. If this happens to too many leaves, the entire plant may die. Such delicate plants must be grown where they will receive adequate shade, at least between 11 o'clock in the morning and 3 o'clock in the afternoon during the summer months. *Acer palmatum* varieties and many golden-leaved shrubs are most affected by the problem.

Wind, heavy rain and snow can take their toll of plants, and if any plant is likely to be damaged in this way, this is noted in the directory. It is important to support and protect these plants if their beauty is not to be lost just when they are at their best. Garden centres and suppliers stock several useful items that can help you, ranging from stakes to lightweight fleece to protect tender plants from frosts. Twigs of shrubs such as hazel and layers of straw around the roots can also be used, and these often provide all the additional support and protection that is required.

Soil

While the aspect of your garden will affect the way your plants develop, even more important is the soil. Almost every plant requires a specific type of soil if it is to thrive, with a level of moisture and organic material that is ideal for it alone. Fortunately, of course, many plants tolerate a range of conditions on either side of the ideal, but a few do not, and those plants that will grow only in specific soil conditions are noted in the directory.

The most important factor influencing the success of a planting scheme is the acidity or alkalinity of the soil – that is, the level of calcium (chalk or lime) in the soil. Those plants that are known or may be suspected of resenting alkaline types of soil are clearly identified in the text, and if you know that your soil is alkaline, it is probably best not to attempt to grow the plants, no matter how much acid soil you try to introduce. It is sometimes possible to grow these plants in containers, provided you use a lime-free compost and use rain water for watering.

Snow, wind and heavy rain can take their toll on plants.

The moisture level of the soil is also important. Some plants are known to require a well-drained soil because their roots are unable to withstand waterlogging. You may be able to improve the drainage by adding sand; however, if your soil is very heavy, even this may not guarantee success. Some plants, on the other hand, thrive in high levels of moisture, and if your soil is light and free-draining, adding organic material to the soil in the form of well-rotted farmyard manure or garden compost will be necessary. Some plants require the presence of large quantities of organic material in the ground so that their fleshy root systems can pass through the soil. If the roots of such plants are restricted, they will not grow and the plant itself will not thrive.

Plant Selection

Once you have made your choice of plant, having considered site, aspect and soil conditions in your garden, check to see if any recommended planting time is indicated.

When you are choosing plants at a nursery or garden centre look for bushy plants with foliage that shows no sign of distress or of pests or disease. This is usually not a problem with a reputable supplier, but it is always wise to check. It is also worth asking locally for recommended nurseries. Plants are available in so many places these days, not just at garden centres and nurseries, but if you want properly named varieties and healthy stock, it is worth seeking out a specialist nursery.

Some plants are bought while in flower, and this is sometimes the best time to buy and plant. Look out for strong, well-established plants. If a plant is identified as being slightly tender, delay planting until all spring frosts have passed, keeping it under the protection of a greenhouse or other suitable cover until it can be safely put in the garden.

The range of plants that is available is very wide, and new varieties are appearing all the time. No single nursery or garden centre could possibly stock them all, especially those of a seasonal planting nature, such as roses, but once you have made your choice, search around until you find the variety you want.

Maintenance

Without good gardening practice all the effort that you have put into selecting the right plants for your garden plan will have been wasted. No garden plant will grow and perform to its full potential without help, and planting, pruning, feeding, watering and general maintenance are equally important.

Planting should really be described as soil preparation, for the actual planting is a very small part of the process. Even if you are one of the very lucky minority of gardeners who have perfect soil, the soil must be prepared so that the plant's roots have free passage through it and are not restricted in any way. If the roots are prevented from growing by compacted ground or by dryness or waterlogging, they will fail to penetrate their immediate boundaries, and, in turn, the plant itself will fail to grow and may ultimately die.

Every plant needs to obtain a cocktail of nutrients from the soil. In many cases there are only very small amounts of each nutrient in any given area of soil, and even when the gardener adds extra fertilizer, the plant has to seek out these nutrients from a very large area. It is essential that the soil is broken up to enable the plant's roots to pass easily through it. Before planting, therefore, use a garden fork and spade to dig the whole area to a depth of 50cm (20in), although when you do this, you must make sure that the top 25cm (10in) or so of topsoil is always kept on top of the subsoil.

For a single plant dig a hole 1m (about 3ft) across, first removing the topsoil and, if necessary, turf to a depth of 25cm (10in) and storing this on a board alongside the hole. Then the lower 25cm (10in) – more if you can – should be dug over and a good quantity of organic material added. Add some more organic material to the removed topsoil before it is returned to the planting hole.

If you need to prepare a larger area and cannot cope with the double digging by hand, you might want to hire a mechanical mini-digger. The principle is the same, however: remove the topsoil from a trench across the area to be dug and store it close to the far end of the area being prepared but not actually on it. The trench needs

Good soil preparation is vital for gardening success.

to be at least 50cm (20in) wide and, of course, to be only 25cm (10in) deep. As with the preparation for a single plant, organic material is added to both levels. The next trench is dug and the soil thrown forwards, into the first. Trench after trench is dug, until all the area is covered. The soil from the first trench is used to fill the last. The soil is now ready for planting, and it is a simple matter to dig a hole in the prepared soil that is large enough to accommodate the roots of the plant, with a few centimetres (inches) to spare all round. Return the soil around the sides of the roots and gently firm it in.

Trees should always be provided with a strong stake that reaches to just below the lowest branches. Secure the tree to the stake with two adjustable, plastic tree ties to prevent the stem or branch rubbing against the stake, which can cause a wound through which diseases can enter.

If you are planting in spring or summer you should water all new plants thoroughly. If you are planting in the autumn and it has been particularly dry, you will also need to water the new plant. After autumn or winter planting the plant may require refirming after severe frosts, which can raise the plant out of the soil and expose the roots, causing severe damage.

After planting, always label the new plant or make a note on your original plan so that you have a reminder of any specific aftercare, such as pruning, that will be necessary.

Pruning can range from simply cutting away the dead topgrowth of perennials to the more specialized care required by some shrubs and roses. The pruning of perennials should be done at the right time. In autumn, cut all topgrowth to within 30cm (1ft) of ground level; do not cut it to ground level until spring. This routine means that the topgrowth that is left over winter will be tidy yet provide some protection in very cold weather for the plant that is just below the surface of the soil.

Shrubs may require more specialist pruning, and this is described in the directory, especially when the pruning method and time affect the plant's flowering potential. There are two main methods. The first involves the removal of one-third of the total growth. Once the plant has been planted more than three years, each year after that one-third of the total number of shoots, choosing the oldest, should be removed after flowering to as close to ground level as possible. This may seem drastic but the rewards outweigh the effort of doing it and ensure that the majority of growth is two or three years old and, therefore, the best flowering. A few shrubs are pruned like this in spring to improve their foliage, and this is noted in the directory.

The second method involves cutting back all the previous year's shoots to within a few centimetres (inches) of their origin in early to mid-spring. This may, again, appear drastic but the reward in terms of the numbers and the size of flowers will repay the work. With silver-leaved plants hard cutting back, where recommended, is best carried out once signs of new growth are seen emerging from the old shoots in spring. If no pruning is recommended, the plant does not require any and may even resent it.

Feeding helps to ensure that all the nutrients a plant will require are freely available to it. But applying the right type and at the right rate and time is important. Like all the chemicals you use in the garden, fertilizers must be clearly labelled and stored safely out of the reach of children. They must be applied at the rates shown on the packet. Use bonemeal in autumn and early winter because it takes six months to break down and become available in the soil. A general-purpose fertilizer is best applied in early to mid-spring, because it takes about six weeks to become available to the plant. Finally, a liquid fertilizer can be used from early to mid-summer, because these take about six days to be of benefit to the plant. You could use all three, but any one on its own will help, and applications of a general-purpose fertilizer in the form of granules is probably the most effective. Do not apply fertilizers of any kind after mid-summer (except bonemeal) because this can lead to tender growth which will make the plant vulnerable to winter cold.

No fertilizer can work unless there is adequate water in the soil. If the soil around plants dries out the plant's roots cannot take in the nutrients required, and the plant will die. Adding quantities of organic material to the soil at planting time will aid the soil's ability to retain water, and applying a layer of organic material to the surface of the soil in winter will help capture and store water for the plant through spring and summer.

As we have already noted, if plants are added to the garden in a dry period they will need regular watering after planting until they have become established, and this can take several months. You must also remember to water new plants regularly in times of drought, even if this is in spring or autumn.

Follow these simple rules and your garden will reward the effort you have put into it with flowers, foliage and form all year round.

A–Z DIRECTORY

ACER NEGUNDO
Aceraceae
BOX ELDER,
ASH-LEAVED MAPLE

▲ ❀ ❦ SI spring–summer
H 5 yrs 4m (13ft)
S 5 yrs 3m (10ft)
H 10 yrs 5m (16ft)
S 10 yrs 4m (13ft)
❀ -10°C (14°F)
Z 2–9

A tree with interesting foliage, this is a good choice for gardens both large and small. All forms respond to being cut back hard in spring, so their size can be further reduced if needed. All the variegated forms are interesting, but the pink and white *A. n.* 'Flamingo' is particularly attractive.

Soil All soil types, except extremely dry
Aspect Full sun or light to mid-shade
Habit Round-topped tree on long or short stem
Leaf Deciduous, light green leaves, 15–20cm (6–8in) wide and long, with 3–5, sometimes to 9, leaflets, slightly pendulous; some variegated forms
Flower Sulphur yellow, hanging, fluffy in spring
Use As a specimen tree for small areas
Needs Propagate by seed or commercial layering or grafting. Can be pruned hard back and will regrow in same season to reach original size as long as it is cut from the time of planting
Varieties *A. negundo* green-leaved form • *A. n.* 'Auratum' golden-yellow foliage • *A. n.* 'Elegans' (syn. *A. n.* 'Elegantissimum') bright, yellow-edged variegated foliage • *A. n.* 'Flamingo' ♀ pale to rosy pink variegated leaves at tips of all new growth • *A. n.* 'Variegatum' (syn. *A. n.* 'Argenteovariegatum') broad white leaf margins

ACER NEGUNDO
'FLAMINGO'

ACER PLATANOIDES
Aceraceae
NORWAY MAPLE

▲ ❀ ❦ SI spring–autumn
H 5 yrs 5m (16ft)
S 5 yrs 4m (13ft)
H 10 yrs 10m (32ft)
S 10 yrs 8m (26ft)
❀ -15°C (4°F)
Z 3–7

Among the most showy of large ornamental foliage trees, the species has a wide range of leaf colour, all exaggerated in autumn. The trees are largely trouble free, but make sure they have enough room to grow.

Soil Any; tolerates high alkalinity
Aspect Full sun to light shade
Habit Round-topped tree
Leaf Deciduous, light green, soft-textured, hand-shaped and 5-lobed leaves, 15–20cm (6–8in) wide and long; lobes are pointed and slightly toothed; purple and variegated forms
Flower Small, green-yellow, erect clusters in spring
Use As specimen tree for large gardens; ideal for avenues when planted 12m (39ft) apart; can be pollarded (cut back) if required
Needs Propagate *A. platanoides* from seed, named varieties by grafting or budding
Varieties *A. platanoides* 'Columnare' upright habit, light green foliage • *A. p.* 'Crimson King' (syn. *A. p.* 'Goldsworth Purple') ♀ dark purple foliage, purple winged fruit in autumn • *A. p.* 'Drummondii' ♀ light green to grey-green foliage, with primrose-yellow variegation on leaf edge • *A. p.* 'Globosum' smaller growing, very round top, green foliage, useful as a garden feature • *A. p.* 'Laciniatum' light to mid-green, deeply cut foliage • *A. p.* 'Royal Red' new foliage wine-red, ageing to purple-red • *A. p.* 'Schwedleri' ♀ red to purple-red new growth, ageing to green

ACER PLATANOIDES
'CRIMSON KING'

ACER PSEUDOPLATANUS

Aceraceae
SYCAMORE, GREAT MAPLE, SCOTTISH MAPLE

▲ ❀ ❦ SI spring–autumn
H 5 yrs 5m (16ft)
S 5 yrs 4m (13ft)
H 10 yrs 10m (32ft)
S 10 yrs 8m (26ft)
✳ -15°C (4°F)
Z 3–7

ACER PSEUDOPLATANUS 'BRILLIANTISSIMUM'

This species is often underestimated, but it has much to offer, whether in its wild form or as one of the more ornamental varieties that are now available. Many are small, and others are among the most compact of trees. In autumn almost all produce a display of yellow foliage.

Soil Any soil type; tolerates high alkalinity
Aspect Full sun to light shade
Habit Large spreading tree to tight, mop-headed tree
Leaf Deciduous, grey-green to mid-green, some purple or variegated, 5-lobed, deeply veined leaves, 10–15cm (4–6in) across; most are green in spring, others bright pink or purple
Flower Light green and scale-shaped, borne in hanging racemes in spring
Use As a screening tree or as an individual specimen; ideal for large avenues when planted at distances of 12m (39ft)
Needs Propagate *A. pseudoplatanus* from seed; named varieties are commercially grafted or budded
Varieties *A. pseudoplatanus* 'Atropurpureum' (purple sycamore maple) ♀ purple-green foliage with purple undersides • *A. p.* 'Brilliantissimum' (shrimp-leaved maple) ♀ small growing, clusters of green-red flowers • *A. p.* 'Leopoldii' ♀ grey-green to mid-green foliage, splashed yellow • *A. p.* 'Prinz Handjéry' large growing, new foliage splashed pink • *A. p.* 'Simon-Louis Frères' new foliage splashed white and rose-pink, older leaves splashed white • *A. p.* 'Worley' (golden sycamore, golden sycamore maple) ♀ new foliage lime green to yellow, ageing to golden-yellow

ACER RUBRUM

Aceraceae
RED MAPLE

▲ ❀ ❦ SI autumn
H 5 yrs 5m (16ft)
S 5 yrs 3m (10ft)
H 10 yrs 10m (32ft)
S 10 yrs 6m (20ft)
✳ -15°C (4°F)
Z 3–9

ACER RUBRUM

Few trees can compete with this North American tree for autumn colour. Even during the rest of the year, the leaves are attractive, as is the smooth, dark grey bark of the trunk and branches. The species needs space to grow to its full potential, and it must be in acid soil. The overall shape is upright, but as they achieve maturity the branches sweep downwards gracefully.

Soil Neutral to acid; dislikes alkaline soil
Aspect Tolerates light shade but prefers full sun
Habit A large tree with a graceful habit
Leaf Deciduous, triangular, 3- or 5-lobed and hand-shaped leaves, 15–20cm (6–8in) long and wide, with coarsely toothed edges, dark green upper surfaces and blue-white undersides
Flower Pendent, thick clusters of attractive red, scale-like flowers in spring
Use As a large tree for large gardens, either singly or in groups; can be used for avenue planting at distances of 12m (39ft)
Needs Propagate *A. rubrum* from seed; named varieties are commercially grafted onto rootstocks of *A. rubrum*
Varieties *A. rubrum* the main form planted • *A. r.* 'October Glory' ♀ an improved form • *A. r.* 'Scanlon' ♀ upright habit, needs a truly acid soil to do well

ACER
Aceraceae
SNAKE-BARK MAPLE

▲ ❀ ❦ SI winter–autumn
H 5 yrs 3m (10ft)
S 5 yrs 1.5m (5ft)
H 10 yrs 5m (16ft)
S 10 yrs 3m (10ft)
❊ -10°C (14°F)
Z 3–9

ACER GROSSERI VAR. HERSII

Few other trees offer such interesting winter features as the snake-bark maples, but the autumn foliage colours should not be overlooked either, as they can compete with those of any of the better known stars of autumn. These acers must be planted in the right soil if later problems are to be avoided.

Soil Requires moisture-retentive soil high in organic material
Aspect Full sun to light shade
Habit Forms a neat, small, round-topped tree
Leaf Deciduous, grey-green to mid-green, excellent display of orange, yellow and bronze autumn colours; hand-shaped, 5–10cm (2–4in) long and wide, with toothed edges
Flower Short, pendent racemes of green to yellow-green flowers in spring
Use As individual specimen trees for winter stem effect or for group planting; interesting feature when grown on a trunk or as a low-branching shrub
Needs Propagate by seed or by commercial layering or grafting
Varieties *A. capillipes* ♀ bark purple-red to coral-red when young ageing to purple with white veining • *A. griseum* ♀ not truly a snake-bark maple but has very attractive mahogany-brown winter stems • *A. grosseri* var. *hersii* (Hers's maple) ♀ green to grey-green marbled bark • *A. pensylvanicum* (moosewood, striped maple) ♀ bright green young shoots, ageing to grey-green with white-striped veining • *A. rufinerve* ♀ white-striped winter bark

---

AESCULUS
Hippocastanaceae
CHESTNUT

▲ ❀ ❦ SI spring–autumn
H 5 yrs 10m (32ft)
S 5 yrs 7m (23ft)
H 10 yrs 20m (64ft)
S 10 yrs 12m (39ft)
❊ -15°C (4°F)
Z 3–8

AESCULUS INDICA

The diversity and range of forms of chestnut are not always appreciated. The coloured flowers and the attractive summer and autumn foliage contribute to an interesting, if very large tree, while in autumn the fruits of *Aesculus hippocastanum* are collected by children as conkers.

Soil Any except extremely wet or dry
Aspect Full sun to light shade
Habit Stout branches often form a goblet-shaped or round tree
Leaf Deciduous, large, hand-shaped leaves, light to dark green in spring and summer, yellow-brown in autumn
Flower Upright panicles of white, yellow, pink or red in spring or summer
Use As specimen tree for large gardens; useful for avenue plantings at distances of 12m (39ft); *A. pavia* as a small, compact, flowering tree or large shrub for medium to large gardens
Needs Propagate from seed or by commercial budding or grafting
Varieties *A.* × *carnea* 'Briotii' ♀ large, dark red-pink flowers • *A. flava* (sweet buckeye) ♀ yellow to pale yellow florets borne in upright panicles • *A. hippocastanum* (horse chestnut) ♀ white flowers patched red at base produced in large conical panicles • *A. h.* 'Baumannii' (syn. *A. h.* 'Flore Pleno') large, double, white flowers • *A. indica* 'Sydney Pearce' upright panicles of white florets blotched with yellow and red • *A. pavia* (red buckeye) ♀ bright red florets

ALNUS
Betulaceae
ALDER

▲ ❀ catkins ♥ SI all year
H 5 yrs 6–6.5m (20–22ft)
S 5 yrs 2.5m (8ft)
H 10 yrs 10–12m (32–39ft)
S 10yrs 5m (16ft)
❄ -15°C (4°F)
Z 5–7

ALNUS CORDATA

Alders are often planted near water or in moist areas, but their ornamental attributes are often overlooked. Even the native forms, grown *en masse* in the right place, have interest. The cut- or golden-stemmed forms add variety and interest, making them worth planting provided they are in the right type of soil.

Soil Acid or alkaline, but prefers moist soil; dislikes very dry conditions
Aspect Full sun to light shade
Habit An upright main stem; some forms have pendulous branches
Leaf Deciduous, dark green and oval, with shiny upper surfaces and light grey-green undersides, some finely indented; good yellow autumn foliage
Flower Brown catkins, opening to yellow in spring, followed by brown nuts in autumn and winter
Use As an individual specimen tree or in group plantings
Needs Propagate from seed or by layering
Varieties *A. cordata* (Italian alder) ♀ brown catkins, opening to yellow • *A. glutinosa* 'Aurea' bright golden-yellow foliage • *A. g.* 'Imperialis' ♀ light green, deeply cut, almost lacerated foliage • *A. incana* (grey alder) scaly, brown catkins opening to yellow • *A. i.* 'Aurea' golden shoots, foliage and catkins when young • *A. i.* 'Laciniata' light green foliage, deeply cut and lacerated • *A. i.* 'Pendula' weeping branches, dark green, silver-backed foliage • *A. rubra* (syn. *A. serrulata*) new shoots red, catkins larger and longer

---

ARBUTUS
Ericaceae
STRAWBERRY TREE

▲ ❀ ♥ SI all year E
H 5 yrs 1m (3ft)
S 5 yrs 1m (3ft)
H 10 yrs 2m (6ft)
S 10 yrs 2m (6ft)
❄ -5°C (23°F)
Z 8

ARBUTUS UNEDO

The common name aptly describes the fruit of this slow-maturing tree. Interestingly, the flowers, which hang in small clusters like waxy lily-of-the-valley blooms, are borne in autumn a whole year before they turn into fruit. Therefore, each autumn the tree bears both flowers and fruit at the same time, both set off by the attractive, dark evergreen foliage.

Soil All types, except extremely alkaline; requires high levels of organic material
Aspect Full sun to light shade
Habit Bushy, moderately slow, attractive winter stems
Leaf Evergreen, dark green leaves with paler undersides and purple shading and veining
Flower Pure white or pink-tinged, waxy, cup-shaped, pendent flowers in autumn, followed a year later by yellow-red, strawberry-like fruit
Use As a free-standing specimen shrub and, eventually, a small tree
Needs Propagate from seed or semi-ripe cuttings taken in early summer
Varieties *A. andrachne* (Grecian strawberry tree) dark red to cinnamon-coloured peeling bark • *A.* × *andrachnoides* ♀ (Killarney strawberry tree) cinnamon-red branches • *A. menziesii* (madrona) ♀ smooth, peeling bark, revealing light red to terracotta underbark • *A. unedo* ♀ abundant white or pink flowers, followed by bright red, edible fruit • *A. u.* 'Quercifolia' dark green, dissected foliage with purple undershading to veins • *A. u.* f. *rubra* dark pink flowers

BETULA
Betulaceae
BIRCH

▲ ✦ ❦ SI all year
H 5 yrs 6m (20ft)
S 5 yrs 1.5m (5ft)
H 10 yrs 10m (32ft)
S 10 yrs 1.5m (5ft)
✳ -15°C (4°F)
Z 2–6

**BETULA UTILIS VAR.
JACQUEMONTII**

The stems of the birch need little description, except to say
that in addition to white, orange, yellow, brown and even
pink variations can be found. The foliage, too, differs widely
with variety. Cut and purple-leaved forms are available.

Soil Tolerates a wide range of conditions
Aspect Full sun to light shade, but prefers full sun
Habit Upright, feathery, coloured stems
Leaf Oval, from 1–8cm (½–3in) long, depending on variety;
grey-green, light green or purple, with good yellow autumn
colour; some forms have attractive, dissected variations
Flower Round to oval female catkins, opening to yellow
stamens in spring
Use As individual specimens or planted in closely grouped
formations less than 1–1.5m (3–5ft) apart for coppice effect
Needs Propagate by commercial grafting, layering or seed
Varieties *B. albosinensis* var. *septentrionalis* (Chinese red
birch) ♀ bark colours orange-brown through yellow-orange
to orange-grey • *B. ermanii* (gold birch) orange-brown bark,
ageing to cream-white • *B.* 'Jermyns' ♀ very white stems,
oval foliage • *B. pendula* (silver birch, common birch,
European white birch) ♀ white stems • *B. p.* 'Purpurea'
(purple-leaved birch) bright purple foliage ageing to purple-
green, purple catkins and fruit • *B. p.* 'Tristis' ♀ lobed
foliage, good autumn colour • *B. utilis* (Himalayan birch)
oval foliage, yellow catkins • *B. u.* var. *jacquemontii* ♀
pure white stems, with large areas of brown peeling bark,
large catkins

CARAGANA
**Leguminosae/
Papilionaceae**
PEA TREE, PEA SHRUB

▲ ✦ ❦ SI spring–summer
H 5 yrs 2m (6ft)
S 5 yrs 2m (6ft)
H 10 yrs 4m (13ft)
S 10 yrs 4m (13ft)
✳ -18°C (0°F)
Z 2–9

**CARAGANA ARBORESCENS
'WALKER'**

This very graceful tree is native to Siberia, so its hardiness is
not in doubt. The main form is rarely grown, but the
varieties deserve inclusion in any planting scheme. They vary
from small to medium sized trees, some of which are weeping.

Soil Any soil conditions; tolerates high alkalinity
Aspect Prefers full sun but tolerates light shade
Habit Basic form round-topped, others weeping; all are
moderately slow growing
Leaf Deciduous, light green leaves, with some yellow autumn
colour, are produced in pairs and grouped 4–6 together, oval
or narrow, thin, strap-like and lance-shaped; their soft
texture gives a cloud-like effect
Flower Small, yellow, pea-shaped flowers, borne in clusters
of up to 4 on thin stalks in mid-spring
Use As a small specimen tree; the attractive spring flowers,
foliage and habit are suitable for any size of garden
Needs Propagate from seed for basic form; named varieties
by commercial grafting onto rootstock of *C. arborescens*
Varieties *C. arborescens* (Siberian pea tree) tall, round-
topped tree, light green foliage, yellow flowers • *C. a.*
'Lorbergii' ♀ semi-pendulous habit, grey-green, strap-like
leaves give a hazy appearance • *C. a.* 'Pendula' weeping
habit, round, grey-green foliage • *C. a.* 'Walker' very small,
weeping tree, soft, strap-like foliage with yellow flowers, can
be grown in a container

CARPINUS
Corylaceae
HORNBEAM

▲ ❀ ❦ SI all year
H 5 yrs 4m (13ft)
S 5 yrs 2m (6ft)
H 10 yrs 8m (26ft)
S 10 yrs 6m (20ft)
❄ -25°C (-13°F)
Z 3–5

CARPINUS BETULUS

Although the hornbeam is a common tree, there are several varieties that warrant attention when you are looking for a feature tree for the garden, especially one with an upright habit. The green foliage is interesting, but in autumn the yellow coloration is exceptionally attractive.

Soil Tolerates almost any soil conditions
Aspect Full sun to medium shade, but prefers full sun
Habit Round-topped or pyramidal tree with a medium rate of growth
Leaf Deciduous, oval to ovate, light grey-green leaves, ageing to bright green
Flower Hanging catkins, 4–8cm (1½–3in) long, in spring
Use As a small to medium tree for medium or large gardens, as individual specimens, shaped and pruned features, or in large, tall hedges on stilts when trained horizontally
Needs Propagate from seed; named varieties are commercially grafted
Varieties *C. betulus* ♀ the basic form makes a round-topped tree, but seedlings can be used as a hedge when planted at distances of 50cm (20in) • *C. b.* 'Columnaris' slender, upright, pyramidal habit • *C. b.* 'Fastigiata' (syn. *C. b.* 'Pyramidalis') ♀ narrow, upright branches • *C. b.* 'Quercifolia' (oak-leaved hornbeam) round-topped tree with interestingly shaped foliage • *C. b.* 'Pendula' weeping form with interesting growing habit • *C. b.* 'Purpurea' (purple-leaved hornbeam) upright habit

CATALPA
Bignoniaceae
INDIAN BEAN TREE

▲ ❀ ❦ SI spring–autumn
H 5 yrs 5m (16ft)
S 5 yrs 5m (16ft)
H 10 yrs 9m (30ft)
S 10 yrs 9m (30ft)
❄ -10°C (14°F)
Z 4–5

CATALPA BIGNONIOIDES

The giant leaves, large white flower spikes and long bean pods make this a spectacular tree. Native to North America, it has found a place in many gardens as a specimen and shade tree of distinction.

Soil Tolerates acid and alkaline conditions but requires high organic content and constant access to moisture, although dislikes waterlogging
Aspect Golden- and purple-leaved forms require full sun; green-leaved varieties tolerate light shade; foliage may be damaged by late spring frosts
Habit Upright when young, becoming round-topped and spreading with age
Leaf Deciduous, very large oval, yellow, grey-green or purple leaves with yellow autumn colour
Flower Upright panicles of white, bell-shaped flowers with yellow markings in throats in summer, followed by long, grey-green seedpods in autumn
Use As a large-leaved shade tree in medium sized and large gardens
Needs Propagate green-leaved varieties from seed or by layering; purple- and golden-leaved varieties are normally commercially grafted. Can be cut back hard and will reshoot
Varieties *C. bignonioides* ♀ light green foliage, white flowers • *C. b.* 'Aurea' ♀ broad, large, golden-yellow leaves • *C. b.* 'Variegata' large, grey-green leaves, edged with gold • *C. × erubescens* purple foliage, white flowers • *C. speciosa* grey-green foliage, white flowers

CERCIS
Leguminosae/ Caesalpiniaceae
JUDAS TREE, REDBUD

▲ ❀ ☙ SI spring
H 5 yrs 1.5m (5ft)
S 5 yrs 1.5m (5ft)
H 10 yrs 3m (10ft)
S 10 yrs 3m (10ft)
❆ -10°C (14°F)
Z 5–9

CERCIS SILIQUASTRUM

As if by magic each spring, from bare stems appear teardrop-like purple flowers. These flowers are meant to represent the tears Judas shed after he had betrayed Jesus. The foliage is interesting, as is the overall spreading shape of this low-growing tree. A good plant for gardens both large and small, it takes time to show to the best. There are species from both North America and Asia.

Soil Prefers neutral to acid soil but tolerates moderate alkalinity
Aspect Prefers light shade but tolerates full sun to medium shade
Habit A low- and slow-growing, spreading tree
Leaf Deciduous, broad kidney-shaped purple-green leaves with a blue sheen and yellow autumn colour; one variety has all-purple leaves
Flower Numerous purple-rose to pink or white flowers, 1–2.5cm (½-1in) long, are borne as leaves begin to open
Use As free-standing large shrub or small tree; can be successfully fan-trained against a large wall
Needs Propagate from seed or by layering
Varieties *C. canadensis* (eastern redbud) pale rose-pink flowers • *C. c.* 'Forest Pansy' ♀ heart-shaped, deep purple leaves • *C. chinensis* purple-pink flowers • *C. c.* 'Avondale' an improved form with darker flowers and more compact habit • *C. siliquastrum* (Judas tree, love tree) ♀ purple-rose flowers • *C. s. f. albida* pure white flowers, scarce

CRATAEGUS
Rosaceae
THORN, HAWTHORN

▲ ❀ ☙ SI spring–autumn
H 5 yrs 4m (13ft)
S 5 yrs 2m (6ft)
H 10 yrs 6m (20ft)
S 10 yrs 4m (13ft)
❆ -25°C (-13°F)
Z 4–9

CRATAEGUS LAEVIGATA 'PAUL'S SCARLET'

These small trees can be used in a wide range of situations. There are two types to look out for: the European forms, which have masses of, normally, double flowers in white, pink or dull red, and the Oriental forms, which bear larger, single, white flowers. Both produce fruit.

Soil Most soil conditions except very dry
Aspect Full sun to medium shade but prefers light shade
Habit Round-topped tree; moderately slow to establish
Leaf Deciduous, oval leaves, light, mid-green or grey-green
Flower Clusters of single or double, white, pink or red
Use Oriental forms in medium sized and large gardens or for avenues planted at distances of 10m (32ft); European forms as small round-topped trees for all types of gardens; can be severely pruned to control or shape
Needs Propagate by commercial budding or grafting
Varieties *C. crus-galli* (cockspur thorn) Oriental type, flat-topped tree of spreading habit, slightly less height, good autumn colour, white flowers, red fruit • *C. laciniata* (syn. *C. orientalis*) Oriental type, dark grey-green, cut-leaved foliage, white flowers, dull orange fruit • *C. laevigata* (syn. *C. oxyacantha*) European type, single, white flowers • *C. l.* 'Paul's Scarlet' (syn. *C. l.* 'Coccinea Plena') ♀ European type, double, dark pink to red flowers • *C. l.* 'Plena' European type, double, white flowers • *C. l.* 'Rosea Flore Pleno' ♀ European type, double, pink flowers • *C.* × *lavalleei* 'Carrierei' Oriental type, semi-evergreen, good autumn colour, white flowers, red fruit

DAVIDIA INVOLUCRATA

Cornaceae
HANDKERCHIEF TREE

▲ ❀ ❦ SI summer
H 5 yrs 2m (6ft)
S 5 yrs 1.2m (4ft)
H 10 yrs 6m (20ft)
S 10 yrs 3.5m (12ft)
❈ -5°C (23°F)
Z 5–6

DAVIDIA INVOLUCRATA

One of the most elegant of summer-flowering trees, not only because of its overall shape and foliage but also because of the large, handkerchief-like flowers that adorn its branches. It can, however, take as long as 15 years to reach flowering size. Spring frosts are the main problem, often killing the flowers and damaging the foliage, but the risk is worth taking. The eventual size means that this is a tree suitable only for the larger garden, where it can achieve its full potential.

Soil Does best on deep soil high in organic material; tolerates moderate alkalinity
Aspect Prefers light shade but tolerates medium shade to full sun
Habit Slow to establish then quick to grow into a pyramid shape
Leaf Deciduous, large, oval, deeply veined leaves, with mid-green upper surfaces and white-felted undersides; tooth-edged and pointed; 6–15cm (2½–6in) long and 5–6cm (2–2½in) wide; yellow autumn colour
Flower Small black flowers, flanked by two broad, oval, pure white leaves, 6–15cm (2½–6in) long, which act like flower petals to attract insects
Use As a large, summer-flowering tree in medium sized and large gardens
Needs Propagate by commercial layering
Varieties *D. involucrata* ♀ is the only variety normally grown

EUCALYPTUS

Myrtaceae
GUM TREE

▲ ❀ ❦ SI all year E
H 5 yrs 5m (16ft)
S 5 yrs 2m (6ft)
H 10 yrs 10m (32ft)
S 10 yrs 4m (13ft)
❈ -5°C (23°F)
Z 5–9

EUCALYPTUS GUNNII

This Australian tree has found a home in many gardens, although its hardiness can be suspect in cold areas. Its height and fast rate of growth are often underestimated, which can lead to some expensive removal problems. It is almost unique in that it can be cut to ground level and will regrow very quickly.

Soil Prefers light, well-drained soil but tolerates a range of conditions
Aspect Full sun to light shade but prefers full sun
Habit Upright and fast-growing; trunks and major stems can have ornamental bark that is useful in winter
Leaf Evergreen, round to oval, broadly lance- or kidney-shaped leaves; young foliage ranges from glaucous-blue, through white to bronze; adult foliage grey-green, light green or dark shiny green depending on variety.
Flower White to yellow tufts in summer
Use As ornamental foliage tree or large shrub in large to medium sized gardens. Useful for flower arranging
Needs Propagate from seed
Varieties *E. coccifera* (Tasmanian snow gum) ♀ glaucous-blue, round to oval juvenile foliage, grey-green, lance-shaped adult foliage, yellow flowers • *E. gunnii* (cider gum) ♀ the main variety planted, also possibly the hardiest, blue-green adult and juvenile foliage • *E. parvifolia* (Kybean gum) ♀ blue-green leaves to 15cm (6in) • *E. pauciflora* ssp. *niphophila* (snow gum) ♀ attractive trunk patched with green, grey and cream, large, leathery, grey-green leaves

FAGUS
Fagaceae
BEECH

▲ ❀ ❦ SI spring–autumn
H 5 yrs 4m (13ft)
S 5 yrs 3m (10ft)
H 10 yrs 8m (26ft)
S 10 yrs 8m (26ft)
❅ -15°C (4°F)
Z 4–8

**FAGUS SYLVATICA
'PURPUREA PENDULA'**

Beech has always been a favourite tree with gardeners, and rightly so, but sadly, the many beautiful varieties with interesting foliage variations and forms are often overlooked by potential planters.

Soil Any soil type; tolerates high alkalinity
Aspect Full sun to light shade but prefers full sun
Habit Round, upright or weeping, according to variety; slow to become established then quick to grow, slowing with age
Leaf Deciduous, oval leaves, light green, yellow, bronze or purple, with slightly toothed edges, 5–13cm (2–5in) long
Flower Small, yellow-green to green-brown flowers, followed by brown nuts
Use As a standard tree for large gardens, as coppice or for an avenue when planted at distances of 12m (39ft); can be grouped to form a windbreak or trained horizontally
Needs Propagate by seed or by commercial grafting
Varieties *F. sylvatica* (common beech, European beech) ♀ green leaves bronze-yellow in autumn • *F. s.* 'Dawyck' (syn. *F. s.* 'Fastigiata'; dawyck beech) ♀ narrow, upright habit, glossy, bright green foliage, a purple form is available • *F. s.* 'Pendula' (weeping beech) ♀ rounded, glossy green foliage • *F. s.* 'Purpurea Pendula' (weeping purple beech) bright purple-red foliage in spring, ageing to bronze-purple • *F. s.* 'Riversii' (Rivers' purple) ♀ large, dark purple foliage • *F. s.* 'Rohanii' slow growing, very dark purple • *F. s.* 'Zlatia' (golden beech) bright yellow spring growth, ageing to lime green

FRAXINUS
Oleaceae
ASH

▲ ❀ ❦ SI spring–summer
H 5 yrs 6m (20ft)
S 5 yrs 2m (6ft)
H 10 yrs 10m (32ft)
S 10 yrs 4m (13ft)
❅ -18°C (0°F)
Z 3–8

**FRAXINUS EXCELSIOR
'JASPIDEA'**

This common tree is often overlooked when a specimen is being chosen for the garden. It is fair to say that the wild form, *F. sylvestris*, is a little uninteresting, but there are many fine varieties worth considering, and the weeping form makes a real garden feature, both when young and as a mature specimen.

Soil Any soil type
Aspect Full sun to mid-shade but prefers full sun
Habit Upright, becoming spreading; a weeping form is available
Leaf Deciduous, oval to pinnate leaves, to 30cm (1ft) long depending on variety, normally light green but some variegated with white; yellow autumn colour
Flower Short racemes of fluffy white, cream-coloured or green-yellow flowers
Use As shade trees for medium to large gardens; good for avenues when planted at distances of 12m (39ft)
Needs Propagate by seed or by commercial grafting
Varieties *F. angustifolia* 'Raywood' ♀ purple autumn foliage • *F. excelsior* (common European ash) ♀ large green foliage, invasive roots • *F. e.* 'Jaspidea' ♀ yellow to golden-yellow stems with distinct black buds in winter, good yellow autumn colour, fluffy white flowers, plant against a dark background • *F. e.* 'Pendula' ♀ weeping form of wild type, very architectural habit • *F. ornus* (manna ash, flowering ash) ♀ grey-green foliage with shallow toothed edges, large, fluffy, off-white flowers in early summer

GLEDITSIA
**Leguminosae/
Caesalpiniaceae**
HONEYLOCUST

▲ ❀ ❦ SI summer
H 5 yrs 4m (13ft)
S 5 yrs 2m (6ft)
H 10 yrs 8m (26ft)
S 10 yrs 4m (13ft)
❄ -10°C (14°F)
Z 4–9

**GLEDITSIA TRIACANTHOS
'SUNBURST'**

The delicate foliage and colour make this a useful tree, and this is reinforced by its moderate size and good growth habit. Because it is mainly grown as a foliage tree, its reluctance to flower is not a drawback.

Soil Prefers deep, well-drained soil, high in organic material, but tolerates limited alkalinity to fully acid types
Aspect Full sun to light shade
Habit Upright at first, becoming more spreading in time; slow to moderate rate of growth; stem are sometimes armed with spines
Leaf Deciduous, pinnate or bipinnate, light green leaves with a glossy sheen, to 20cm (8in) long, with up to 32 leaflets, 2.5cm (1in) long; golden-yellow- and purple-leaved varieties
Flower Green-white male flowers are borne in hanging racemes, 5cm (2in) long; often shy to produce flowers
Use As a moderately large, tall shade tree for medium sized or larger gardens; green, golden and purple varieties can be grown as small ornamental trees in any moderately sized garden
Needs Propagate from seed; varieties are commercially grafted
Varieties *G. triacanthos* taller than the cultivars, green foliage • *G. t.* f. *inermis* (thornless honeylocust) small, round, mop-headed tree with delicate, light green, pinnate leaves • *G. t.* 'Rubylace' spreading habit, purple to purple-green foliage • *G. t.* 'Sunburst' ♀ the main form planted, beautiful bright golden-yellow, pinnate foliage and new shoots

LABURNUM
**Leguminosae/
Papilionaceae**
LABURNUM, BEAN TREE

▲ ❀ ❦ SI spring
H 5 yrs 4m (13ft)
S 5 yrs 2m (6ft)
H 10 yrs 4–6m (13–20ft)
S 10 yrs 3m (10ft)
❄ -15°C (4°F)
Z 5–6

**LABURNUM × WATERERI
'VOSSII'**

This well-loved flowering tree has a long pedigree of good flower production but only since the introduction of *L.* 'Vossii'. On earlier forms the flowers were small and poorly coloured. Today, *L.* 'Vossii' s still the best variety to plant, and seeing the tree trained as an archway or fanned on a wall is an unforgettable experience.

Soil Any soil conditions; tolerates high alkalinity
Aspect Full sun to light shade but prefers full sun
Habit Upright when young, spreading with age; moderately slow growing
Leaf Deciduous, 3-fingered, grey-green to dark or olive green leaves, to 8cm (3in) long; yellow autumn colours
Flower Long hanging racemes of deep yellow pea flowers followed by green pods; the seeds are poisonous
Use As a small to medium sized feature for medium to large gardens; can be trained to cover archways and walkways or as a climber on north- or east-facing walls; is also used as a bush, standard tree or in weeping form for containers
Needs Propagate *L. alpinum* from seed; *L. a.* 'Pendulum' and varieties are commercially grafted
Varieties *L. alpinum* almost evergreen, late yellow flowers • *L. a.* 'Pendulum' good weeping form, reaching only about 3m (10ft) • *L.* × *watereri* 'Vossii' ♀ racemes of numerous deep yellow to golden-yellow pea flowers to 30cm (1ft) long

LIQUIDAMBAR
Hamamelidaceae
SWEET GUM

▲ ❀ ❦ SI autumn
H 5 yrs 4m (13ft)
S 5 yrs 2m (6ft)
H 10 yrs 8m (26ft)
S 10 yrs 4m (13ft)
❄ -10°C (14°F)
Z 6–9

LIQUIDAMBAR STYRACIFLUA

Although the foliage, corky stems and overall shape of this tree are attractive, the real season of interest is in autumn, when the green foliage of spring and summer gives way to a dazzling display of orange and dark red, which emphasizes the tree's pleasing pyramidal shape.

Soil Prefers moist soil, high in organic material, but dislikes waterlogging; although tolerates high alkalinity, autumn colours may be less intense
Aspect Full sun to light shade but prefers full sun
Habit Upright, pyramidal form, slow to become established then fast to grow, slowing down when large. The corky bark is best seen in winter
Leaf Deciduous, green, hand-shaped leaves, with 3 or 5 fingers, 8–15cm (3–6in) wide and 13–20cm (5–8in) long, turning orange or scarlet in autumn
Flower Small, inconspicuous flowers
Use As a moderately compact, pyramidal tree, providing autumn colour and interesting architectural shape, in medium or larger gardens
Needs Propagate from seed, by layering or by grafting
Varieties *L. formosana* (Formosan gum) slightly more tender • *L. styraciflua* excellent orange-red autumn colour • *L. s.* 'Aurea Variegata' golden-yellow splashed variegation • *L. s.* 'Lane Roberts' ♀ non-corky bark, dark wine-red autumn colours • *L. s.* 'Pendula' weeping habit • *L. s.* 'Variegata' cream-white margins on grey-green leaves • *L. s.* 'Worplesdon' ♀ corky bark, good autumn colours

LIRIODENDRON
Magnoliaceae
TULIP TREE

▲ ❀ ❦ SI spring–summer SC
H 5 yrs 3.5m (12ft)
S 5 yrs 2m (6ft)
H 10 yrs 7m (23ft)
S 10 yrs 4m (13ft)
❄ -10°C (14°F)
Z 5–9

LIRIODENDRON TULIPIFERA

An elegant, very large tree that can achieve noble proportions over a hundred years or so. The interestingly shaped foliage provides good yellow autumn colour, and 25 years, to the day, after planting it will produce an abundance of large, spectacular, tulip-shaped flowers.

Soil Most soil conditions except very dry
Aspect Prefers full sun but tolerates limited light shade; golden-variegated forms must have full sun to maintain coloration
Habit Upright, spreading slightly with age; fast growing once established but slowing with age
Leaf Deciduous, large, 3-lobed leaves, 5–20cm (2–8in) long, light green or with golden variegation; good yellow autumn colour
Flower Fragrant green and yellow flowers, consisting of 6 upright petals and 3 spreading sepals with numerous stamens, resembling a tulip flower
Use As a specimen tree in large gardens
Needs Propagate from seed or by layering
Varieties *L. chinense* (Chinese tulip tree) similar to main form but may be less hardy • *L. tulipifera* ♀ the main form planted, grey-green foliage, green and yellow flowers • *L. t.* 'Aureomarginatum' ♀ bold yellow to green-yellow leaf margins • *L. t.* 'Fastigiatum' ♀ thick, upright columnar tree with good foliage colour and flowers, useful feature tree

MALUS
Rosaceae
FLOWERING CRAB APPLE

▲ ❀ ❦ SI spring SC some
H 5 yrs 4m (13ft)
S 5 yrs 4m (13ft)
H 10 yrs 6m (20ft)
S 10 yrs 3m (10ft)
❄ -15°C (4°F)
Z 4–9

MALUS FLORIBUNDA

A star of spring, when an abundance of white or pink flowers is borne on small to medium sized trees. Later in the year the coloured fruit can be made into crab apple jelly.

Soil Most soil conditions but dislikes waterlogging
Aspect Does best in full sun to very light shade
Habit Round-topped tree with a moderate growth rate
Leaf Deciduous, oval, tooth-edged leaves, 5cm (2in) long, green or wine-red, depending on variety
Flower White, pink-tinged white or wine-red flowers, 2.5–4cm (1–1½in) across, borne singly or in multiples of 5–7, followed by ornamental or edible fruit
Use As ornamental flowering trees with edible fruit
Needs Propagate some from seed; most are grafted or budded
Varieties *M.* × *adstringens* 'Simcoe' attractive purple-pink flowers • *M. floribunda* green foliage, masses of pink flowers • *M.* × *gloriosa* 'Oekonomierat Echtermeyer' (syn. *M.* 'Echtermeyer') arching habit, purple foliage, flowers and fruit • *M. hupehensis* ♀ fragrant, soft pink-white flowers, yellow-red fruit • *M.* 'John Downie' ♀ green foliage, conical, bright orange fruit • *M.* × *robusta* 'Red Sentinel' ♀ green foliage, white flowers, red fruit • *M.* × *r.* 'Red Siberian' ♀ green foliage, white flowers, red fruit • *M.* 'Royalty' best purple-red leaf form, dark red fruit • *M. transitoria* ♀ pink-white flowers, rounded yellow fruit • *M. tschonoskii* ♀ upright habit, good autumn colour, white flowers • *M.* × *zumi* 'Golden Hornet' (syn. *M.* 'Golden Hornet') ♀ white flowers, bright yellow fruit

MORUS
Moraceae
MULBERRY

▲ ❀ ❦ SI spring–summer
H 5 yrs 3.5m (12ft)
S 5 yrs 1.2m (4ft)
H 10 yrs 5m (16ft)
S 10 yrs 2.5m (8ft)
❄ -10°C (14°F)
Z 3–5

MORUS NIGRA

This excellent feature and shade-providing tree has been grown in gardens for many centuries, mainly for its edible fruit. The tree's ability to grow fast when young and slow with age and to take on an aged appearance very quickly is one of its merits.

Soil Moist, deep, well-drained soil, high in organic material
Aspect Does best in full sun but tolerates light shade
Habit Quick growing at first, but slows with age; round-topped or weeping, depending on form
Leaf Deciduous, oval, grey-green leaves, lobed or un-lobed; good yellow autumn colour
Flower Very short green male or female catkins followed by black or red fruit
Use As an architectural fruiting tree, ideal for medium sized or large gardens, except for the weeping *M. alba* 'Pendula', which can be grown in a smaller space
Needs Propagate by hardwood cuttings taken in early winter
Varieties *M. alba* (syn. *M. bombycis*; white mulberry) fastest growing type, large, oval light green leaves, red fruit, may be tender in cold areas • *M. a.* 'Pendula' weeping form, delightful garden subject with bold, large leaves • *M. nigra* (common mulberry, black mulberry) ♀ good black, sweet fruit in all areas, good garden tree in sufficiently large space

TREES

POPULUS
Salicaceae
POPLAR

▲ ❁ ❦ SI spring–autumn
H 5 yrs 4m (13ft)
S 5 yrs 2m (6ft)
H 10 yrs 10m (32ft)
S 10 yrs 4m (13ft)
❁ -15°C (4°F)
Z 3

POPULUS ALBA

Poplars can grow too tall for all but the largest gardens, and great care must be taken with siting because of the potential ultimate size and the possible damage the roots can cause when they grow into drains and undermine walls, even leading to subsidence. In polluted and maritime areas, they can make good windbreaks and screens.

Soil Most soil types, including waterlogged conditions for part of the year
Aspect Full sun to medium shade; *P. alba* needs full sun
Habit Some upright, others spreading; very quick to mature
Leaf Deciduous, broad, oval with pointed ends, some yellow
Flower Yellow catkins on male plants in spring
Use As individual specimens or in avenues
Needs Propagate from hardwood cuttings in winter
Varieties *P. alba* (white poplar, abele) very fast and large growing, leaves with grey upper surfaces and white undersides • *P. a.* 'Richardii' bushy habit, forming large shrub, silver-white and yellow foliage borne at the same time • *P.* × *candicans* 'Aurora' fast growing, new foliage splashed white and pink, balsam scent • *P. lasiocarpa* (Chinese necklace poplar) ♀ interesting pyramidal shape, slow to mature, green leaves, 25cm (10in) or more long, can be grown in an average sized garden • *P. nigra* var. *italica* (*P. n.* 'Pyramidalis'; Lombardy poplar) ♀ very upright, fastigiate shape, silver foliage • *P. n.* 'Lombardy Gold' upright column, golden foliage in spring turning lime green in summer, good yellow autumn colour

PRUNUS
Rosaceae
FLOWERING CHERRY

▲ ❁ ❦ SI spring–autumn
H 5 yrs 3.5m (12ft)
S 5 yrs 2.5m (8ft)
H 10 yrs 7m (23ft)
S 10 yrs 3.5m (12ft)
❁ -15°C (4°F)
Z 2–9

PRUNUS 'TAIHAKU'

Truly the queen of spring-flowering trees, the range of size, shapes and colours makes this a welcome addition to a large number of gardens. Although it is not an especially large tree, it does need space to develop fully.

Soil Most conditions but resents poor soil
Aspect Does best in full sun but tolerates limited light shade
Habit Moderately fast growing, the habit depends on variety and includes spreading, upright, round-topped and weeping
Leaf Deciduous, oval, green leaves, often large; good autumn colour
Flower Single or double flowers, from white to deep pink
Use As ornamental tree; ideal for medium sized or large gardens
Needs Propagate by commercial budding or grafting
Varieties *P.* 'Accolade' ♀ large clusters of rich pink flowers • *P.* 'Amanogawa' (flagpole cherry) ♀ upright habit, pale pink flowers • *P. incisa* (Fuji cherry) early pink buds opening to white • *P.* 'Kiku-shidare-zakura' (flowering cherry) ♀ large, double, pink flowers • *P.* 'Kursar' ♀ red-bronze young foliage, early deep pink flowers • *P.* 'Pandora' ♀ early shell pink flowers to 2.5cm (1in) across • *P.* 'Shirotae' ♀ pure white fragrant flowers to 5cm (2in) across • *P.* × *subhirtella* 'Autumnalis' (winter cherry) ♀ white flowers • *P.* 'Taihaku' (great white cherry) ♀ single, pure white flowers • *P.* × *yedoensis* ♀ single pink-white flowers • *P.* × *y.* 'Perpendens' (Yoshino weeping cherry of Japan) weeping habit, single, pink-white flowers

PYRUS
Rosaceae
ORNAMENTAL PEAR

▲ ❀ ❦ SI spring–summer
H 5 yrs 3m (10ft)
S 5 yrs 2m (6ft)
H 10 yrs 5m (16ft)
S 10 yrs 4m (13ft)
❄ -15°C (4°F)
Z 3–9

PYRUS SALICIFOLIA
'PENDULA'

These ornamental pears make very good flowering and foliage trees.

Soil Any type but shows distress in extremely poor soil
Aspect Green forms tolerate moderate shade; silver-leaved varieties prefer full sun
Habit Moderately fast growing, round-topped, upright or weeping habit with interesting stems and bark
Leaf Deciduous, ovate to linear, sometimes round, green or silver-grey leaves, depending on variety
Flower White, single, cup-shaped florets in clusters, each to 4cm (1½in) across, followed by small, non-edible, brown fruit
Use As a free-standing ornamental tree in any size of garden; often grown as a feature plant
Needs Propagate by commercial grafting or budding onto rootstock of pear, quince or *P. communis*
Varieties *P. calleryana* 'Chanticleer' (callery pear) ♀ upright, dark, glossy green leaves until late autumn, white flowers, brown fruit, good feature tree • *P. communis* (common pear, wild pear) upright, green foliage, white flowers, interesting dark bark • *P. c.* 'Beech Hill' upright, attractive round, green foliage, white flowers, good sentinel tree for a feature • *P. nivalis* (snow pear) attractive round-topped tree, white to silver-grey, oval foliage, white flowers, brown fruit, silver stems • *P. salicifolia* 'Pendula' (weeping willow-leaved pear) ♀ mop-headed, narrow, lance-shaped, silver leaves to 5cm (2in) long, white flowers, brown fruit, silver-grey stems

RHUS
Anacardiaceae
SUMACH, SUMAC

▲ ❀ ❦ SI autumn
H 5 yrs 2m (6ft)
S 5 yrs 2m (6ft)
H 10 yrs 4m (13ft)
S 10 yrs 4m (13ft)
❄ -10°C (14°F)
Z 3–9

RHUS TYPHINA

A reliable and popular 'tree', which is truly a shrub but which has been given, in gardening, the status of tree because of its shape. The upright flowers, which look like red candles, are interesting, but it is the startling autumn foliage that is the real attraction.

Soil Any type
Aspect Full sun to light shade
Habit Suckering, sometimes invasively, the tree is upright when young and spreading with age; in tree terms, slow growing and short lived
Leaf Deciduous, light to mid-green, large, pinnate leaves, to 40cm (16in) long and 15cm (6in) wide, deeply toothed; excellent autumn colour of yellow, red and orange
Flower Green panicles on male forms and dark pink on female forms
Use Planted singly as a free-standing tree or large shrub; can be included in large shrub borders or, if pruned hard, mass-planted; on the regrowth the leaves are often as much as three times the size of the normal leaves
Needs Propagate from the freely produced root suckers
Varieties *R. glabra* 'Laciniata' (smooth sumach, vinegar tree) deeply cut, fern-like foliage, good orange, yellow and red autumn colours • *R. typhina* (staghorn sumach) good autumn colour, winter fruit borne in conical clusters, crimson ageing to brown • *R. t.* 'Dissecta' ♀ dissected leaves, pastel shades in autumn

ROBINIA
Leguminosae/
Papilionaceae
FALSE ACACIA

▲ ❀ ❦ SI spring–summer
H 5 yrs 3m (10ft)
S 5 yrs 2m (6ft)
H 10 yrs 6m (20ft)
S 10 yrs 4m (13ft)
❊ -10°C (14°F)
Z 5–9

**ROBINIA PSEUDOACACIA
'FRISIA'**

Pretty foliage and flowers and an interesting habit of growth
are the ideal qualities in a plant. Add to this a moderate size,
for the perfect garden tree – but not quite perfect, for
robinias are prone to structural wind damage in exposed
gardens. There is a wide range of flower colours.

Soil Most soil conditions except very wet
Aspect Full sun or very light shade
Habit Upright, becoming spreading with age
Leaf Deciduous, green or gold leaves; yellow autumn colour
Flower Racemes of pea-shaped, white or pink flowers are
borne in summer
Use As medium tree or large shrub for medium sized and
large gardens; most forms are suitable for small gardens
Needs Propagate from seed or by commercial grafting
Varieties *R.* × *ambigua* 'Decaisneana' green foliage, pale
pink flowers • *R. hispida* (rose acacia, moss locust) ♀ green
foliage, pink flowers • *R. h.* 'Macrophylla' interesting green
foliage, deep pink flowers • *R.* × *margaretta* 'Casque Rouge'
('Pink Cascade') green foliage, deep pink flowers •
R. neomexicana (syn. *R. luxurians*) green foliage, pink
flowers • *R. pseudoacacia* 'Bessoniana' quick growing, tall,
spreading habit, green foliage, white flowers • *R. p.* 'Frisia'
♀ golden foliage, white flowers • *R. p.* 'Tortuosa' contorted
stems, green foliage, white flowers • *R. p.* 'Umbrauculifera'
(syn. *R. p.* 'Inermis') mop-headed, very tight habit, green
foliage, shy to flower, a good feature tree • *R.* × *slavinii*
'Hillieri' ♀ green foliage, pink flowers

SALIX
Salicaceae
WILLOW

▲ ❀ ❦ catkins SI spring
H 5 yrs 6m (13ft)
S 5 yrs 6m (13ft)
H 10 yrs 8m (26ft)
S 10 yrs 7m (23ft)
❊ -15°C (4°F)
Z 5–10

**SALIX CAPREA
'KILMARNOCK'**

These are useful trees provided that there is sufficient space
for them to achieve their full potential. They are best planted
away from buildings, especially the drains.

Soil Any soil conditions; extremely tolerant of waterlogging
Aspect Full sun to medium shade
Habit Spreading or weeping
Leaf Deciduous, narrow, oval to lance-shaped, 8–15cm
(3–6in) long, and silver-grey, green or purple-green
Flower White, yellow or silver-white catkins are carried on
bare stems in early spring
Use As ornamental trees for winter stems and habit of
growth and for the display of catkins in spring
Needs Propagate by hardwood cuttings in winter
Varieties *S. acutifolia* 'Blue Streak' ♀ blue stems covered
in white down, yellow catkins • *S. a.* 'Pendulifolia' blue
stems covered in down, hanging purple leaves, yellow catkins
• *S. alba* var. *sericea* (syn. *S. alba* f. *argentea*, *S. a.*
'Splendens') silver-white foliage, small yellow catkins •
S. alba f. *vitellina* (syn. *S. vitellina*; golden willow) yellow
stems in winter • *S. alba* f. *vitellina* 'Britzensis' red stems
in winter • *S. babylonica* var. *pekinensis* 'Tortuosa' (syn.
S. matsudana 'Tortuosa'; Peking willow) attractive contorted
stems • *S. caprea* 'Kilmarnock' (syn. *S. caprea* var.
pendula) ♀ low, weeping habit, yellow catkins • *S. purpurea*
'Pendula' ♀ purple-blue foliage and catkins, weeping •
S. × *sepulcralis* f. *chrysocoma* (syn. *S.* 'Chrysocoma'; golden
weeping willow) weeping habit, golden stems

SORBUS
Rosaceae
MOUNTAIN ASH,
WHITEBEAM, ROWAN

▲ ❀ ❦ SI autumn
H 5 yrs 4m (13ft)
S 5 yrs 4m (13ft)
H 10 yrs 6m (20ft)
S 10 yrs 6m (20ft)
❄ -10°C (14°F)
Z 3

SORBUS AUCUPARIA

This genus consists of three main types of plant, which bring different attributes to the garden: whitebeams have silver-grey foliage and flowers and fruit; rowans or the mountain ash have flowers, fruit and autumn colour; and the Oriental types have attractive flowers, fruit and foliage.

Soil Most
Aspect Full sun to light shade
Habit Upright, some becoming round-topped
Leaf Deciduous, green or silver leaves, to 23cm (9in) long
Flower Clusters of white flowers in summer; fruit in autumn
Use As small, ornamental subjects in all gardens
Needs Propagate by seed, commercial grafting or budding
Varieties *S. aria* 'Lutescens' (silver whitebeam) ♀ bright silver-white foliage, white flowers, orange fruit • *S. a.* 'Majestica' ♀ large, oval, grey foliage, red fruit • *S. a.* 'Mitchellii' grey leaves, 20cm (8in) long, red fruit • *S. aucuparia* (rowan, common mountain ash) dark green, with grey sheen, red fruit • *S. a.* 'Fastigiata' (upright mountain ash) red fruit • *S. cashmiriana* (Kashmir mountain ash) ♀ white fruit • *S. commixta* 'Embley' (rowan) ♀ good autumn colour • *S. hupehensis* (Hupeh rowan) ♀ grey foliage, white-pink fruit • *S. h.* var. *obtusa* ♀ grey foliage, deep pink fruit • *S.* 'Joseph Rock' ♀ erect habit, yellow fruit • *S. sargentiana* (Sargent's rowan) ♀ large clusters of red fruit • *S.* × *thuringiaca* 'Fastigiata' upright habit, red fruit • *S. vilmorinii* ♀ small growing, small leaves, purple fruit

TILIA
Tiliaceae
LIME, LINDEN

▲ ❀ ❦ SI all year SC
H 5 yrs 4m (13ft)
S 5 yrs 2m (6ft)
H 10 yrs 8m (26ft)
S 10 yrs 4m (13ft)
❄ -15°C (4°F)
Z 3–5

TILIA × EUCHLORA

This elegant tree has become so much a part of the landscape that it is hardly noticed, which is sad, because there are many good varieties that can be used in the larger garden.

Soil Tolerates most soils
Aspect Full sun to light shade
Habit Upright, spreading with age and with an attractive weeping form
Leaf Deciduous, round to oval, light green young foliage, 10–17cm (4–7in) long and wide, with pronounced veining and grey undersides
Flower Dull white to yellow-green flowers, to 2.5cm (1in), are produced on short stalks and hang usually in groups of 3 but occasionally as many as 40
Use As a specimen plant in a large garden; can be trained for smaller gardens, either pleached as hedges or heavily pollarded; useful for avenues when planted 12m (39ft) apart
Needs Propagate from seed or by commercial layering, budding or grafting
Varieties *T. americana* (American lime, American basswood) dark green foliage • *T. cordata* (small-leaved lime) ♀ small, round, green leaves • *T.* × *euchlora* (yellow-twigged lime) ♀ yellow twigs in winter • *T.* 'Petiolaris' (pendent white lime, weeping silver lime) ♀ weeping habit • *T. platyphyllos* (broad-leaved lime) mid-green leaves with some red veining • *T. p.* 'Rubra' ♀ bright red stems in winter after pruning • *T. p.* 'Tortuosa' bold silver undersides to leaves • *T. tomentosa* 'Brabant' (silver lime) ♀ white underside to leaves

ABELIA
Caprifoliaceae
ABELIA

▲ ❀ ✿ SI summer–autumn
H 5 yrs 1m (3ft)
S 5 yrs 1m (3ft)
H 10 yrs 1.2m (4ft)
S 10 yrs 1.2m (4ft)
❄ -10°C (14°F)
Z 4–6

**ABELIA × GRANDIFLORA
'FRANCIS MASON'**

A plant for autumn, not only because of the leaf colour but because of the often scented flowers. The habit of growth means that it is suitable for a wide range of situations.

Soil Most, but shows signs of distress in dry, alkaline soil
Aspect Full sun to light shade; plant against a sheltered wall in exposed gardens
Habit Upright, becoming arching
Leaf Semi-evergreen, ovate, olive-green leaves with reddish shading or grey-green, yellow or white variegation, 2.5–6cm (1–2½in) long and 1cm (½in) wide
Flower Pink, white or pink-white petals form small, bell-shapes, 5mm (¼in) long and wide, borne in small cluster from summer through autumn; calyx is brownish-red and retained
Use As a specimen shrub or in a mixed planting; plant in a line, 75cm (30in) apart, for an informal hedge; fan-train
Needs Propagate from cuttings in winter or early summer. Prune in spring by removing one-third of the total number of shoots to ground level, removing the oldest shoots
Varieties *A. chinensis* taller growing, white to rose-tinted flowers • *A.* 'Edward Goucher' ♀ grey-green foliage, purple-pink flowers • *A. floribunda* ♀ grey-green foliage, cherry red flowers, 5cm (2in) long • *A. × grandiflora* ♀ dark green foliage, pink-white flowers • *A. × g.* 'Confetti' pink- and white-variegated foliage, pale pink flowers • *A. × g.* 'Francis Mason' ♀ gold-variegated foliage, pink to white flowers • *A. schumannii* grey foliage, lilac-pink flowers • *A. triflora* grey-green foliage, pink-tinged white flowers

ABUTILON
Malvaceae
FLOWERING MAPLE,
PARLOUR MAPLE

▲ ❀ ✿ SI summer
H.5 yrs 1.5m (5ft)
S 5 yrs 1.5m (5ft)
H 10 yrs 2m (6ft)
S 10 yrs 2m (6ft)
❄ -5°C (23°F)
Z 4–6

**ABUTILON VITIFOLIUM
'TENNANT'S WHITE'**

Not one of the hardiest of shrubs – and the golden-variegated form needs even more protection – but if the conditions are right it is very appealing and worth growing.

Soil Most, but dislikes very dry soil
Aspect A tender plant, therefore needs full sun and warmth
Habit Upright, becoming more spreading as it ages
Leaf Deciduous, ovate leaves, 5–10cm (2–4in) long, with toothed edges; olive green to purple-red or golden-variegated
Flower Medium sized, pendent, bell-shaped flowers with yellow or orange petals and red calyx
Use Can be fan-trained; needs support if grown free standing; suitable for containers outside or in a conservatory
Needs Propagate by cuttings in summer. Prune to shape in spring
Varieties • *A.* 'Kentish Belle' ♀ large orange-yellow flowers • *A. megapotamicum* ♀ green foliage, yellow-red flowers, hardiest form • *A. m.* 'Variegatum' yellow-variegated foliage, orange-yellow flowers, very tender • *A. × milleri* ♀ very large, dark green foliage, orange petals, crimson stamens • *C. × suntense* deep mauve flowers • *A. vitifolium* (syn. *Corynabutilon vitifolium*) grey-green, hand-shaped leaves, large, saucer-shaped, pale mauve flowers, after 5 yrs 4m (13ft) plus high, can be tender • *A. v.* var. *album* (syn. *C. vitifolium* var. *album*) white flowers • *A. v.* 'Tennant's White' (syn. *C. vitifolium* 'Tennant's White') ♀ white flowers • *A. v.* 'Veronica Tennant' (syn. *C. vitifolium* 'Veronica Tennant') deep mauve flowers

ACER
Aceraceae
JAPANESE MAPLE

▲ ❀ ❦ all year
H 5 yrs 1–3m (3–10ft)
S 5 yrs 1–3m (3–10ft)
H 10 yrs 1–5m (3–16ft)
S 10 yrs 1–5m (3–10ft)
❋ -10°C (14°F)
Z 5–9

**ACER PALMATUM
'BLOODGOOD'**

The Japanese maple is one of the most cherished of garden plants, and one that offers interest the whole year round. In addition to the ornamental stems and shape in winter, the foliage is attractive from spring until autumn.

Soil Moderately alkaline to acid; moist but not waterlogged
Aspect Very light shade out of strong sunlight and cold winds
Habit Upright to spreading
Leaf Deciduous, hand-shaped leaves, some dissected, 5cm (2in) wide and long, in green, purple, white-pink or gold
Flower Small, yellow-red hanging clusters in spring
Use As specimen plants; good subjects for containers although they can reach the dimensions of small trees
Needs Propagated by grafting. No pruning required
Varieties *A. japonicum* 'Aconitifolium' (syn. *A. j.* 'Laciniatum') ♀ green, indented leaves turn orange-red in autumn, to 1.20m (4ft) in 5 yrs • *A. j.* 'Vitifolium' ♀ green with plum then orange autumn colour, to 1.2m (4ft) in 5 yrs • *A. palmatum* green leaves turn orange-red in autumn, to 2m (6ft) in 5 yrs • *A. p.* f. *atropurpureum* deep purple leaves turn orange-red in autumn, to 2m (6ft) in 5 yrs • *A. p.* 'Bloodgood' ♀ red-purple leaves turn scarlet in autumn, to 2m (6ft) in 5 yrs • *A. p.* var. *dissectum* ♀ finely dissected green leaves turn brown-orange in autumn, to 1m (3ft) in 5 yrs • *A. p.* Dissectum Atropurpureum Group finely dissected purple leaves turn orange-red in autumn, to 1m (3ft) in 5 yrs • *A. shirasawanum* 'Aureum' (syn. *A. japonicum* 'Aureum') ♀ golden-yellow foliage, to 1m (3ft) in 5 yrs

---

AMELANCHIER
Rosaceae
SERVICEBERRY, JUNEBERRY, SHADBUSH

▲ ❀ ❦
H 5 yrs 3m (10ft)
S 5 yrs 3m (10ft)
H 10 yrs 5m (16ft)
S 10 yrs 5m (16ft)
❋ -18°C (0°F)
Z 5–9

**AMELANCHIER ×
GRANDIFLORA 'BALLERINA'**

One of the hardiest of shrubs, the amelanchier produces masses of spring flowers, which are followed by interesting small, red fruit in summer. The brilliant red-orange autumn colours are an added bonus.

Soil All but the most alkaline; dislikes drought or dry conditions
Aspect Full sun to light shade
Habit Bushy but can be trained into small tree
Leaf Deciduous, light green, ovate leaves, 4–8cm (1½–3in) long; orange-red autumn colour
Use As a solo plant or in a group; can be used in large shrub plantings; often trained and grown as a relatively short-lived tree; good for screening
Needs Well-prepared soil since, to grow well, it needs to sucker from the base. Propagate from rooted suckers. Pruning is rarely necessary. To form a tree tie one strong shoot to a cane or stake and remove remainder of shoots. Continue to tie in selected shoots until the desired height is reached, removing any side growths below the required height as they appear
Varieties *A. × grandiflora* 'Ballerina' ♀ compact habit, arching branches, large white flowers but may be shy to fruit • *A. lamarckii* ♀ the type species

ARALIA ELATA
Araliaceae
JAPANESE ANGELICA
TREE, DEVIL'S WALKING
STICK

▲ ❀ ❦ SI all year
H 5 yrs 2m (6ft)
S 5 yrs 1.5m (5ft)
H 10 yrs 3m (10ft)
S 10 yrs 2.5m (8ft)
❄ -10°C (14°F)
Z 4–9

ARALIA ELATA 'VARIEGATA'

Although it may be somewhat ungainly for mixed planting, as a solo or group feature, this plant is an excellent choice. The thorny stems have a rather menacing appearance, as one of the common names implies, but the large leaves have a luxuriant, tropical look. Aralias are not always available in garden centres and nurseries, and the golden-variegated form may be particularly difficult to find.

Soil Any, although poor soils may hinder growth rate
Aspect Prefers full sun but tolerates very light shade
Habit Very upright habit, with single non-branching, grey shoots; spines on stems can cause injury
Leaf Deciduous, pinnate, olive green to grey-green leaves, some forms with silver or gold variegation, very large, to 0.6–1.2m (2–4ft) long and almost 1m (3ft) wide
Flower Very large, to 60cm (2ft), upright panicles of white flowers with branching side panicles borne at the top of each mature shoot in late summer
Use As specimen plant in groups or solo
Needs Plant in an open space so that it can be viewed to the best advantage. Propagate *A. elata* from self-grown suckers; variegated varieties are commercially grafted. No pruning required
Varieties *A. elata* ♀ grey-green leaves • *A. e.* 'Aureo-variegata' more branching habit, golden-variegated leaves • *A. e.* 'Variegata' ♀ very attractive branching habit, leaves margined and blotched with cream, ageing to white variegation

AUCUBA JAPONICA
Aucubaceae
SPOTTED LAUREL

▲ ❦ SI all year E
H 5 yrs 1.2m (4ft)
S 5 yrs 1.2m (4ft)
H 10 yrs 1.8m (5ft 6in)
S 10 yrs 1.8m (5ft 6in)
❄ -10°C (14°F)
Z 7–10

**AUCUBA JAPONICA
'VARIEGATA'**

This tried and true evergreen was much loved by Victorians. Over the years, however, it fell from favour with gardeners, but now, as new varieties with more intense markings become available, its value in the garden is being reappraised.

Soil Any, including dry and alkaline soil
Aspect Tolerates very deep shade and dislikes full sun
Habit Bushy
Leaf Evergreen, dark, glossy green, lanceolate to oval leaves, some forms with different degrees of golden variegation, 8–20cm (3–8in) long and 2.5–8cm (1–3in) wide
Flower Sulphur yellow panicles in summer; varieties bear either male or female flowers; the latter also produce small, bright red fruit in late summer, which are retained in winter
Use As a specimen plant or in a group; for mixed shrub planting; for informal hedging when planted in a single line at distances of 1m (3ft); suitable for large containers
Needs Propagate from cuttings. Pruning not required and may be resented. Container-grown plants must be well watered
Varieties *A. japonica* female or male forms, green leaves • *A. j.* 'Crotonifolia' ♀ female, green leaves with bold gold spots • *A. j.* 'Gold Dust' female, golden-variegated foliage, red fruit • *A. j.* 'Goldstrike' female, bright golden-variegated leaves with red berries • *A. j.* 'Picturata' male, dark green leaves splashed with chrome yellow • *A. j.* 'Salicifolia' female, narrow, tooth-edged, dark green leaves, red fruit • *A. j.* 'Variegata' (syn. *A. j.* 'Maculata') female or male forms, leaves splashed golden and yellow

AZALEA
Ericaceae
DWARF, TALL AZALEA

▲ ❀ ❦ SI spring flowers, autumn foliage SC some E some
<u>Dwarf</u>: 5 yrs H 1m (3ft)
S 1m (3ft), 10 yrs H 1m (3ft)
S 1.2m (4ft) • <u>Tall</u>: 5 yrs
H 2m (6ft) S 2m (6ft), 10 yrs
H 2.5m (8ft) S 2.5m (8ft)
❀ -10 (14°F)
Z 5–8

AZALEA 'HINO-MAYO'

Little needs to be said of the beauty of these plants, which are, botanically, classified as rhododendrons, and bring colour and shape to the garden.

Soil Acid soil, high in organic material, is essential
Aspect Prefers light shade but tolerates full sun
Habit Dwarf forms are mound-forming; tall forms are bushy
Leaf Evergreen, semi-evergreen to deciduous, depending on variety, oval leaves, 2–8cm (¾–3in) long; evergreen foliage dark green; deciduous foliage mid-green with orange-red autumn colour; all foliage with silver reverse
Flower Small or large open bells, some scented, in a galaxy of colours in spring
Use Solo or in groups; in containers; dwarf cultivars in rock gardens; tall forms as hedges, planted at distances of 1m (3ft)
Needs Propagated commercially from summer cuttings. Pruning rarely required
Varieties <u>Dwarf</u> (all evergreen): *A.* 'Addy Wery' ♀ deep vermilion flowers • *A.* 'Hinode-giri' bright crimson flowers • *A.* 'Hino-mayo' ♀ clear pink flowers • *A.* 'Mother's Day' ♀ rose red flowers • *A.* 'Orange Beauty' ♀ salmon-orange flowers • *A.* 'Palestrina' ♀ pure white flowers • *A.* 'Vuyk's Scarlet' ♀ bright crimson flowers <u>Tall</u>: *A.* 'Berryrose' ♀ rose-pink flowers with yellow flush • *A.* 'Brazil' tangerine-coloured flowers • *A.* 'Fireball' deep red flowers • *A.* 'Gibraltar' ♀ flame-orange flowers with yellow flush • *A.* 'Persil' ♀ white flowers • *A.* 'Strawberry Ice' ♀ light pink flowers • *A.* 'Tunis' deep crimson flowers

AZARA
Flacourtiaceae
AZARA

▲ ❀ ❦ SI all year SC E
H 5 yrs 1.5m (5ft)
S 5 yrs 1.5m (5ft)
H 10 yrs 2.5m (8ft)
S 10 yrs 2.5m (8ft)
❀ -5°C (23°F)
Z 4–6

AZARA DENTATA

The bright evergreen foliage of this shrub, which can reach the proportions of a small tree, is surpassed only by the massed display of yellow flowers in spring. Azaras require careful positioning against a wall for protection, but before planting, remember the possible eventual size

Soil Most, but dislikes excessive alkalinity and waterlogging
Aspect Tolerates full sun to mid-shade; requires shelter in cold areas
Habit Normally produces limited numbers of upright shoots, which, in turn, produce side shoots to form a bushy column. After about 10 years the lower branches die or can be cut away to produce a multi-stemmed 'tree' shape
Leaf Evergreen, bright green to dark glossy green, ovate to oblong, leaves with felted undersides, 2.5–4cm (1–1½in) long
Flower Clusters of fragrant yellow flowers are borne in profusion during spring
Use As a free-standing shrub in sheltered, warm gardens; against a wall in more exposed locations; in very warm gardens can be used as a tall screen or informal hedge
Needs Propagate from cuttings in summer. Requires no pruning. Shelter is important in cold areas
Varieties *A. dentata* large tufts of yellow flowers • *A. lanceolata* light green leaves, mustard yellow flowers • *A. microphylla* ♀ very small, dark green leaves, yellow, vanilla-scented flowers • *A. m.* 'Variegata' small, cream-variegated leaves, sulphur yellow flowers • *A. serrata* light green, serrated leaves, yellow flowers

BERBERIS
Berberidaceae
BARBERRY

▲ ❀ ❦ SI all year E some
H 5 yrs 0.6–2m (2–6ft)
S 5 yrs 0.75–2m (30in–6ft)
H 10 yrs 1–2m (3–6ft)
S 10 yrs 1.5–3m (5–10ft)
❀ -10°C (14°F)
Z 4–10

BERBERIS DARWINII

Despite their spiky protection, these plants are worthy of consideration in any planting scheme. Many forms are evergreen, while others have coloured foliage; some produce fruit, but all bear flowers.

Soil Most soils but resents dryness
Aspect Full sun to deep shade depending on variety
Habit Forms bushy shrubs
Leaf Evergreen or deciduous, from light to dark olive green leaves; some forms with purple or gold foliage
Flower Pale yellow or white to gold or bright orange flowers
Use As an individual shrub or for mass-planting; makes an informal, thick hedge, planted at distances of 75cm (30in)
Needs Propagate from cuttings taken in midsummer.
Varieties Evergreen: *B. darwinii* (Darwin's barberry) ♀ double, bright orange flowers • *B. julianae* (wintergreen barberry) double, cup-shaped, lemon-yellow flowers • *B. linearifolia* narrow, dark green leaves, double, bright orange flowers • *B.* × *lologensis* narrow, dark green leaves, large, orange to bright orange flowers • *B.* × *stenophylla* ♀ narrow dark green leaves, double, yellow flowers
Deciduous: *B. thunbergii* f. *atropurpurea* red-purple foliage • *B. t.* 'Atropurpurea Nana' ♀ dwarf form, purple foliage • *B. t.* 'Aurea' medium height, golden foliage, grow in light shade • *B. t.* 'Golden Ring' gold-edged, purple foliage, white-red flowers • *B. t.* 'Red Pillar' upright habit, red to red-purple foliage, red-white flowers • *B. t.* 'Rose Glow' ♀ purple foliage turning variegated pink and white

---

BRACHYGLOTTIS
Asteraceae/Compositae
SENECIO,
SHRUBBY RAGWORT

▲ ❀ ❦ S all year E
H 5 yrs 75cm (30in)
S 5 yrs 75cm (30in)
H 10 yrs 1m (3ft)
S 10 yrs 1m (3ft)
❀ -10°C (14°F)
Z 4–6

BRACHYGLOTTIS DUNEDIN GROUP 'SUNSHINE'

The evergreen foliage and bright yellow summer flowers make this a favourite shrub with gardeners. It has to be decided how to prune, whether to go for the best foliage or summer flower display. Some species in this genus are now classified as *Senecio*.

Soil Well-drained, open soil; dislikes waterlogging
Aspect Full sun to very light shade
Habit Upright, branching and spreading with age
Leaf Evergreen, silver-grey, ovate leaves, 2.5–6cm (1–2⅜in) long, some with indented edges
Flower Clusters of yellow, daisy-shaped flowers in abundance in summer
Use At the front of shrub borders; for mass-planting; all forms make low, informal hedges when planted at distances of 40cm (16in)
Needs Propagate from cuttings taken in summer. Trim lightly each spring to keep healthy; once growth starts old, woody shrubs can be cut back hard in early spring and will rejuvenate from ground level; alternatively, one-third of the shoots (the oldest) can be removed in late spring
Varieties *B. cineraria* (syn. *Senecio cineraria*; dusty miller, silver groundsel) very white, felted, dissected leaves, tender • *B.* Dunedin Group 'Sunshine' (syn. *Senecio laxifolius*) ♀ ovate, silver-grey foliage • *B. leucostachys* (syn. *Senecio leucostachys, S. viravira*) silver-white, pinnate leaves, white daisy flowers, tender • *B. monroi* ♀ dark steel-grey leaves with wavy curling edges, yellow flowers

BUDDLEJA
Buddlejaceae
BUDDLEIA,
BUTTERFLY BUSH

▲ ❀ ❦ SI summer
H 5 yrs 1.5–3m (5–10ft)
S 5 yrs 2–3m (6–10ft)
H 10 yrs 2–3.5m (6–10ft)
S 10 yrs 2–4m (6–13ft)
❊ -10°C (14°F)
Z 5–10

**BUDDLEJA DAVIDII
'PINK BEAUTY'**

The butterfly bush – few other plants attract so many butterflies – is a fast-growing shrub. They grow quite large, so must be carefully sited if they are not to overpower other plants. Pruning is important to give the best flowers.

Soil Tolerates most but does best on rich, deep soil
Aspect Full sun to light shade
Habit Upright when young, spreading with age
Leaf Deciduous, broad, lanceolate leaves, 10–30cm (4–12in) long, light green, grey-green, or downy white to dark green; some white-variegated forms
Flower Long racemes or globe-shaped blooms, ranging from white, pink, yellow and lilac to deep purple in summer
Use Singly or grouped in mixed borders
Needs Propagate from cuttings in summer or winter. Cut previous year's shoots hard back in spring to 10cm (4in)
Varieties *B. alternifolia* (fountain buddleia) ♀ arching branches, lilac flowers, do not cut hard back • *B. davidii* 'Empire Blue' ♀ violet-blue flowers • *B. d.* 'Fascinating' lilac-pink flowers • *B. d.* 'Harlequin' creamy-white variegated leaves, rich purple flowers • *B. d.* 'Nanho Purple' purple-blue flowers • *B. d.* 'Peace' white flowers • *B. d.* var. *nanhoensis* f. *alba* dwarf habit, narrow green foliage, white flowers • *B. d.* 'Pink Beauty' deep pink flowers • *B. d.* 'Royal Red' ♀ long, arching branches, purple-red flowers • *B. d.* 'White Profusion' ♀ pure white flowers with yellow eyes • *B. fallowiana* var. *alba* grey leaves, white flowers • *B. globosa* (Chilean orange ball tree) ♀ globes of yellow flowers

BUXUS
Buxaceae
BOX

▲ ❀ SI all year E
H 5 yrs 1m (3ft)
S 5 yrs 1m (3ft)
H 10 yrs 2m (6ft)
S 10 yrs 2m (6ft)
❊ -25°C (-13°C)
Z 3–5

**BUXUS SEMPERVIRENS
'ELEGANTISSIMA'**

Whenever a neat, versatile evergreen is required this plant comes into its own. Box can shaped into topiary, used for low hedges or simply grown as a feature plant in its own right.

Soil Any
Aspect Full sun to deep shade
Habit Upright when young, becoming open then spreading with age
Leaf Evergreen, small, dark green leaves, slightly glossy on upper side, light grey on underside, round to ovate, 2.5–4cm (1–1½in) long; some gold- and silver-variegated varieties
Flower Fluffy, sulphur yellow flowers are borne in small clusters at each leaf axil on mature wood
Use As an evergreen in its own right or topiarized, plant 50cm (20in) apart for an attractive, low hedge; good in tubs and containers
Needs Propagate from cuttings taken in summer
Varieties *B. sempervirens* ♀ fluffy sulphur yellow flowers, good for hedging • *B. s.* 'Aureovariegata' (syn. *B. s.* 'Aurea Maculata') green leaves with bold gold mottling • *B. s.* 'Elegantissima' (syn. *B. s.* 'Silver Variegated') ♀ slow growing, neat habit, creamy-white variegation • *B. s.* 'Handsworthiensis' leaves round or oblong and larger, best form for hedging • *B. s.* 'Notata' (syn. *B. s.* 'Gold Tip') leaves lance-shaped to round, light to dark grey-green, gold tipped • *B. s.* 'Rotundifolia' larger, rounder, deep green leaves • *B. s.* 'Suffruticosa' (edging box) ♀ smaller leaves, very low, dwarf edging variety

CALLICARPA
Verbenaceae
BEAUTY BERRY

✿ ✿ SI autumn fruit
H 5 yrs 2m (6ft)
S 5 yrs 2m (6ft)
H 10 yrs 3m (10ft)
S 10 yrs 3m (10ft)
✳ -15°C (4°F)
Z 5–8

CALLICARPA BODINIERI VAR. *GIRALDII* 'PROFUSION'

Although the flowers of callicarpa are interesting, they are not attractive, and it is not until the round balls of purple or white fruit appear that the full beauty of the plant is seen. It is not a small shrub, but it has a neat shape and is best sited towards the back of the border where it comes into its own when the fruits appear. Strangely, it seems to fruit better when planted in twos and threes.

Soil Any except extremely alkaline
Aspect Full sun to light or medium shade
Habit Upright when young, becoming more branching with age, forming a spreading, round, open shrub of neat habit
Leaf Deciduous, broad, lance-shaped, light grey-green leaves, turning purple in autumn
Flower Clusters of small, lilac-pink flowers produced in clusters at each leaf axis on shoots more than one year old. Followed by bold clusters of purple or white fruits
Use As a late-flowering, autumn-fruiting shrub which when well established produces a spectacular display in groups or in mixed shrub borders
Needs Propagate from cuttings taken in summer. No pruning required; large shoots or limbs may safely be reduced if wished
Varieties *C. bodinieri* var. *giraldii* small, lilac-pink flowers, purple fruit • *G. b.* var. *g.* 'Profusion' ♀ improved form with large purple fruit • *C. japonica* 'Leucocarpa' (Japanese beauty berry) light green leaves, yellow autumn foliage, clusters of white flowers, white fruit

---

CALLISTEMON
Myrtaceae
BOTTLEBRUSH

▲ ✿ ✿ SI spring–summer E
H 5 yrs 2m (6ft)
S 5 yrs 1.5m (5ft)
H 10 yrs 3m (10ft)
S 10 yrs 2.5m (8ft)
✳ -5°C (23°F)
Z 4–9

CALLISTEMON CITRINUS 'SPLENDENS'

This native of Australia has captured the interest of gardeners for many years. It is not fully hardy, so care is required when growing it in all but the most sheltered of places. It is, in fact, an ideal plant for the conservatory. There are many other varieties than those listed below, but they are even more vulnerable to cold winters.

Soil Good, rich, acid soil; dislikes any alkalinity
Aspect Full sun; good in maritime areas
Habit Upright when young, becoming increasingly arching to form a graceful, wide-spreading shrub
Leaf Evergreen, narrow, light green, lance-shaped leaves, 2.5–4cm (1–1½in) long, often with red-orange shading or coloured veins
Flower Tufted, dense, brush-like spikes of red flowers followed by hard, brown cylinder-shaped clusters of fruit in autumn and winter
Use As a large, summer-flowering shrub for mild districts; as a large wall shrub; for a container in large conservatory
Needs Propagate from cuttings in late spring. No pruning required; remove old shoots occasionally to allow to rejuvenate from base
Varieties *C. citrinus* red bottlebrush flowers • *C. c.* 'Mauve Mist' mauve-pink flowers, more tender than type species • *C. c.* 'Splendens' ♀ brilliant red flowers • *C. pallidus* lemon-yellow flowers, tender • *C. speciosus* (Albany bottlebrush) Deep red flowers • *C. viminalis* (weeping bottlebrush) weeping habit, red flowers

CALLUNA
Ericaceae
SCOTS HEATHER, LING

❀ ❦ SI summer E
H 5 yrs 40cm (16in)
S 5 yrs 75cm (30in)
H 10 yrs 40cm (16in)
S 10 yrs 1m (3ft)
❄ -10°C (14°F)
Z 4–8

**CALLUNA VULGARIS
'PETER SPARKES'**

There is a wide range of flower colours and interesting foliage. Careful cultivation increases its life span.

Soil Acid soil essential; dislikes any alkalinity
Aspect Full sun but will tolerate very light shade
Habit Short, dense, upright, spreading to a low mound
Leaf Evergreen, small, lance-shaped, dark green to light green or yellow, gold and purple leaves, 1cm (½in) long
Flower Purple-pink, white, pink or purple, bell-shaped flowers on upright spikes in summer
Use As a summer-flowering, low carpeting, ground cover
Needs Propagate from cuttings taken in summer. Trim lightly after flowering with hand clippers
Varieties *C. v.* 'Aurea' gold foliage, single, purple flowers • *C. v.* 'Cuprea' golden foliage turning bronze, single, pale mauve flowers • *C. v.* 'Goldsworth Crimson' single, deep crimson flowers • *C. v.* 'H.E. Beale' double, bright rose-pink flowers • *C. v.* 'Joan Sparkes' good golden foliage, double, mauve flowers • *C. v.* 'Joy Vanstone' ♀ golden foliage, orange in winter, orange flowers • *C. v.* 'Kinlochruel' ♀ deep green foliage, double, white flowers • *C. v.* 'Peter Sparkes' grey-green foliage, double, pink flowers • *C. v.* 'Silver Night' silver-green foliage, single, purple-pink flowers • *C. v.* 'Spitfire' variegated yellow foliage, turning gold and orange, single, pink flowers • *C. v.* 'Tib' ♀ dark green foliage, double, rose-red flowers • *C. v.* 'Tricolorifolia' bronze-red foliage ageing to deep green, single, pink flowers • *C. v.* 'Winter Chocolate' cream foliage, single, purple-pink flowers

CAMELLIA
Theaceae
CAMELLIA

▲ ❀ ❦ SI spring E
H 5 yrs 1m (3ft)
S 5 yrs 1m (3ft)
H 10 yrs 2m (6ft)
S 10 yrs 2m (6ft)
❄ -10°C (14°F)
Z 8–10

**CAMELLIA 'ADOLPHE
AUDUSSON'**

This well-known relation of the tea plant needs little introduction. There are types with single, double or semi-double flowers in a wide range of colours.

Soil Acid to neutral; dislikes alkalinity
Aspect Does best in light to mid-shade
Habit Upright or spreading
Leaf Evergreen, dark, ovate to oblong leaves, with glossy green upper surfaces and grey-green undersides, 8–10cm (3–4in) long and 4cm (1½in) wide
Flower Large, cup-shaped flowers, single, semi-double, double, anemone or peony-shaped, in spring
Use Evergreen shrub for acid soils; good plant for tubs or containers; can be fan-trained on a sheltered wall
Needs Propagate from cuttings in summer. No pruning required
Varieties *C.* 'Adolphe Audusson' (*japonica*) ♀ semi-double, blood-red flowers • *C.* 'Arajishi' (*rusticana*) rose-red, peony-shaped flowers • *C.* 'Betty Sheffield Supreme' (*japonica*) semi-double, white, peony-shaped flowers with rose-pink or red edges to each petal • *C.* 'Cornish Snow' ♀ single, small white flowers • *C.* 'Donation' (× *williamsii*) ♀ clear pink, semi-double • *C.* 'Elegans' (*japonica*) ♀ large, peach-pink flowers • *C.* 'Mary Christian' (× *williamsii*) ♀ single, clear pink flowers • *C.* 'Mathotiana Alba' (*japonica*) ♀ double, white flowers • *C.* 'Mercury' (*japonica*) ♀ semi-double, deep crimson flowers • *C.* 'Tricolor' (*japonica*) ♀ semi-double, white flowers with carmine or pink strip

CARPENTERIA CALIFORNICA
Hydrangeaceae
CARPENTERIA

❀ ❦ SI summer SC E
H 5 yrs 1m (3ft)
S 5 yrs 1m (3ft)
H 10 yrs 1.5m (5ft)
S 10 yrs 1.5m (5ft)
❄ -5°C (23°F)
Z 4–9

CARPENTERIA CALIFORNICA

A gem of a flowering shrub when it is grown as a free-standing plant but is even better when against a wall. The bold white clusters of flowers, set off against the dark green foliage, are delightful. The way the foliage dies at the end of winter can be a little alarming, but it is quickly replaced with a new crop.

Soil Deep, rich soil; tolerates acidity and moderate amounts of alkalinity
Aspect Must be in full sun to flower and keep its shape
Habit Upright when young, becoming a mound-shaped shrub as it ages
Leaf Evergreen, broad, lance-shaped, light to bright green leaves, 5–10cm (2–4in) long, may turn brown as leaves die after winter and can be unsightly for a short time
Flower Medium to large, pure white, saucer-shaped flowers with yellow central anthers, borne in open clusters in early to midsummer
Use As an evergreen summer-flowering shrub for mild areas; can be fan-trained on a sunny wall in more exposed regions
Needs Propagate from cuttings taken in summer. May be cut back hard and will regenerate; remove one-third of shoots to ground level, choosing the oldest wood each spring to maintain health
Varieties *C. californica* 'Ladhams' Variety' larger flowers than type species

CARYOPTERIS
Verbenaceae
BLUE SPIRAEA, BLUE-BEARD, BLUE-MIST SHRUB

▲ ❀ ❦ SI summer
H 5 yrs 60cm (2ft)
S 5 yrs 75cm (30in)
H 10 yrs 70cm (27in)
S 10 yrs 75cm (30in)
❄ -5°C (23°F)
Z 5–9

**CARYOPTERIS × CLANDO-
NENSIS 'HEAVENLY BLUE'**

Resembling clouds of blue smoke, the autumn flowers give this plant a magical appearance, although its hardiness can be in question and correct pruning is essential. It can be grown as a single feature plant, but it looks even more spectacular in groups. The flowers attract swarms of beneficial insects, bees and butterflies.

Soil Any, especially alkaline
Aspect Needs full sun
Habit Upright but becomes spreading with age
Leaf Deciduous, grey-green, aromatic, lance-shaped leaves, 5–8cm (2–3in) long, with slightly toothed edges
Flower Tufts of blue to violet-blue flowers borne in clusters
Use For mixed or silver-grey borders; spectacular in mass-planting; makes a pretty low hedge planted at distances of 50cm (20in)
Needs Propagate from cuttings taken in summer. All previous season's shoots must be cut back to 5cm (2in) in mid- to late spring
Varieties *C. × clandonensis* 'Arthur Simmonds' light grey foliage, pale blue flowers • *C. × c.* 'Ferndown' deep grey foliage, dark violet to blue-violet flowers • *C. × c.* 'Heavenly Blue' ♀ more compact habit, mid-grey foliage, mid-blue flowers • *C. × c.* 'Kew Blue' grey-green foliage, clear blue flowers • *C. × c.* 'Worcester Gold' light blue flowers, grey flushed yellow foliage • *C. incana* (syn. *C. tangutica*; common bluebeard) violet-blue flowers, grey-green foliage

CEANOTHUS
Rhamnaceae
CALIFORNIA LILAC

▲ ❀ ❦ SI late summer–
autumn E some
H 5 yrs 1.5–2m (5–6ft)
S 5 yrs 2m (6ft)
H 10 yrs 2–3m (6–10ft)
S 10 yrs 2–3m (6–10ft)
❋ -10°C (14°F)
Z 3–8

CEANOTHUS 'ITALIAN SKIES'

These well-known spring- or autumn-flowering shrubs are not without their problems – they are prone to damage from cold – but they are worthy of a place in any large garden.

Soil Deep, rich soil; tolerates both acidity and mild alkalinity
Aspect Full sun but tolerates light shade
Habit Upright, forming round or fan-trained shrub
Leaf Deciduous forms: ovate, light to olive green leaves, 8–13cm (3–5in) long, tooth-edged; evergreen forms: light to dark green, mostly ovate, 1–4cm (½–1½in) long
Flower Deciduous forms: shades of blue or pink, 8–10cm (3–4in) long; evergreen forms: tufted flowers in shades of blue
Use Deciduous forms: as free-standing shrubs or fan-trained; as informal hedge at distances of 1m (3ft); evergreen forms: as fan-trained or free-standing shrubs
Needs Propagate from cuttings in summer. Prune deciduous forms hard back in spring
Varieties Deciduous: *C. × delileanus* 'Gloire de Versailles' ♀ large panicles of powder blue flowers • *C. × d.* 'Henri Defosse' large panicles of deepest blue flowers • *C. × d.* 'Topaz' ♀ indigo flowers • *C. × pallidus* 'Marie Simon' rose-pink flowers   Evergreen: *C. arboreus* 'Trewithen Blue' ♀ deep vivid blue flowers • *C.* 'Autumnal Blue' ♀ dark blue flowers • *C.* 'Burkwoodii' ♀ rich blue flowers • *C.* 'Cascade' ♀ powder blue flowers • *C. impressus* deep blue flowers • *C.* 'Italian Skies' ♀ dense clusters of bright blue flowers • *C.* 'Puget Blue' ♀ deeper blue flowers

---

CERATOSTIGMA
Plumbaginaceae
SHRUBBY PLUMBAGO

▲ ❀ ❦ SI autumn
H 5 yrs 60cm (2ft)
S 5 yrs 60cm (2ft)
H 10 yrs 1m (3ft)
S 10 yrs 1m (3ft)
❋ -5°C (23°F)
Z 3–7

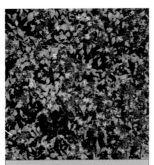

**CERATOSTIGMA
WILLMOTTIANUM**

This genus of autumn-flowering plants includes both shrubs and perennials, all with the deepest indigo flowers. The habit of the shrubby types is pleasing, as is the foliage on all types. As long as they are pruned, they will live for many years.

Soil Deep, rich and well drained
Aspect Does best in full sun; dislikes shade; in cold areas or gardens protect all types in winter
Habit Shrubby forms: bushy, sometimes spreading; perennial forms: creep by way of underground shoots
Leaf Deciduous, ovate, dark green leaves, with purple-red veining and shading, 2.5cm (1in) long and wide; some autumn colour
Flower Deep blue, saucer-shaped flowers, with yellow stamens, borne singly or in clusters, followed by attractive, fluffy, grey seedheads in autumn
Use As a specimen plant in areas such as large rock gardens; good at the front of mixed borders, alone or in groups; as an informal hedge planted at distances of 75cm (30in); shrub varieties are good in containers; perennial types best planted in isolation for best effect
Needs Prune all types hard back close to ground level in early spring. Propagate from summer cuttings
Varieties *C. griffithii* large, deep purple-blue flowers • *C. plumbaginoides* ♀ perennial type, deep blue flowers • *C. willmottianum* ♀ deep blue flowers

CHAENOMELES
Rosaceae
FLOWERING QUINCE,
JAPANESE QUINCE,
JAPONICA

❀ ✿ SI spring
H 5 yrs 2m (6ft)
S 5 yrs 2m (6ft)
H 10 yrs 3m (10ft)
S 10 yrs 3m (10ft)
❄ -15°C (4°F)
Z 4–8

**CHAENOMELES × SUPERBA
'PINK LADY'**

A well-known plant, as reliable and popular today as ever. A fine display of coloured flowers in spring is followed by yellow fruits in autumn, and these are retained into winter.

Soil Any, but prone to chlorosis in very alkaline areas
Aspect Full sun to heavy shade
Habit Bushy but can be fan-trained on walls
Leaf Deciduous, light to dark green, elliptic, 8–10cm (3–4in) long; some yellow autumn colour
Flower Single or semi-double flowers, shaped like apple blossom, are available in colours from white through pink, apricot and flame-orange to red; yellow apple- or pear-shaped fruits are borne in late summer and early autumn
Use Traditionally fan-trained on walls; can be grown as a free-standing specimen or as part of a mixed border
Needs Each spring take back all previous year's shoots to a flower bud just before the buds open. Propagate from summer cuttings. Fan-trained plants need support
Varieties *C. speciosa* 'Brilliant' bright red flowers • *C. s.* 'Cardinalis' crimson-scarlet flowers • *C. s.* 'Geisha Girl' semi-double, deep apricot flowers • *C. s.* 'Moerloosei' (syn. *C. s.* Apple Blossom) ♀ apple blossom pink flowers • *C. s.* 'Nivalis' white flowers • *C. s.* 'Simonii' low growing, deep red flowers • *C. s.* 'Snow' white flowers • *C. s.* 'Umbilicata' deep pink flowers • *C. × superba* 'Elly Mossel' bright scarlet flowers • *C. × s.* 'Fire Dance' orange-scarlet flowers • *C. × s.* 'Pink Lady' ♀ clear pink flowers • *C. × s.* 'Yaegaki' (syn. *C. speciosa* 'Chosan') low growing, semi-double, apricot flowers

CHIMONANTHUS PRAECOX
Calycanthaceae
WINTERSWEET

❀ ✿ SI winter SC
H 5 yrs 1.2m (4ft)
S 5 yrs 1m (3ft)
H 10 yrs 2m (6ft)
S 10 yrs 1.5m (5ft)
❄ -10°C (14°F) (not flowers)
Z 4–6

CHIMONANTHUS PRAECOX

These beautiful winter-flowering plants can take as long as six years to come into flower, but once they do, they are among the most attractive. The upright habit means that a winter-sweet can be planted towards the back of the border or behind other plants so that it can stand alone in winter when it is in flower. The fragrant flowers are normally hardy to -5°C (23°F), but in cold areas planting against a wall or fence may encourage flowering.

Soil Most soils, especially alkaline
Aspect Full sun, tolerates light shade; protection of a wall will encourage flowering
Habit Mainly upright with flowers at the top of the branches
Leaf Deciduous, light green to yellow-green, elliptic leaves, 8–17cm (3–7in) long; good yellow autumn colour
Flower Pleasantly scented, waxy, bell-shaped flowers in shades of yellow with purple anthers
Use Often rightly thought of as a wall shrub; can be used to good effect as a free-standing specimen plant; ideal for winter colour at the back of a mixed border
Needs No pruning required and may, in fact, be resented. Propagate from summer cuttings
Varieties *C. praecox* (syn. *C. fragrans*) fragrant, lemon-yellow flowers, the main form available • *C. p.* 'Grandiflorus' ♀ fragrant, deeper yellow flowers, stained red • *C. p.* 'Luteus' ♀ fragrant, bright yellow flowers

CHOISYA TERNATA
Rutaceae
MEXICAN ORANGE BLOSSOM

▲ ❀ ❦ SI all year SC E
H 5 yrs 1m (3ft)
S 5 yrs 1.2m (4ft)
H 10 yrs 2m (6ft)
S 10 yrs 1.8m (5ft 6in)
❄ -5°C (23°F)
Z 4–6

CHOISYA TERNATA

This has long been a favourite of gardeners, not only for its orange blossom scented flowers but also for the dark, glossy evergreen leaves. It is not, unfortunately, always as hardy as is usually thought, and in a hard winter may show signs of foliage damage.

Soil Does well on most soils except very alkaline
Aspect Full sun to deep shade; in deep shade foliage may be lighter green and form more open; may require protection in hard winters
Habit Round, uniform bushy habit
Leaf Evergreen, aromatic, dark green to yellow-gold, glossy, trifoliate leaves, 8–15cm (3–6in) long
Flower Single, white, orange-scented flowers borne in flat-topped clusters in early summer; sometimes a repeat flowering in autumn
Use As a specimen plant in groups or solo; good in mixed borders and containers; as an informal hedge planted at distances of 1m (3ft)
Needs Propagate in summer from cuttings. Prune each year by cutting back one-third of the total number of shots to ground level, choosing the oldest first
Varieties *C.* 'Aztec Pearl' ♀ very narrow, light green leaflets, scented, white flowers • *C. ternata* ♀ mid- to dark green leaves, clusters of scented, white flowers • *C. t.* 'Sundance' ♀ foliage yellow-green in spring, golden-yellow in autumn and winter, scented, white flowers in early summer, some repeat flowering

---

CISTUS
Cistaceae
ROCK ROSE

▲ ❀ ❦ SI summer E
H 5 yrs 0.6–1m (2–3ft)
S 5 yrs 0.6–1m (2–3ft)
H 10 yrs 0.75–1m (30–36in)
S 10 yrs 0.75–1m (30–36in)
❄ -5°C (23°F)
Z 4–6

CISTUS × PURPUREUS

This shrub may not always be hardy in bad winters, but this should not be a reason for not growing it. The display of summer flowers is reliable, and the plant is quick to establish.

Soil All except very wet
Aspect Full sun; requires protection in cold winters
Habit Shrubby; some forms are low growing
Leaf Evergreen, light green or grey leaves, glossy or with a grey downy covering
Flower Profusion of white through shades of pink to dark purple-pink flowers borne in summer
Use As solo plants or in groups in the mixed border; suitable for mass-planting; good in containers; as an informal hedge at distances of 75cm (30in)
Needs Propagate by summer cuttings. Shorten all flowered shoots by 50 per cent
Varieties *C. × aiguilarii* tall growing, grey foliage, large white flowers • *C. × a.* 'Maculatus' ♀ tall growing, glossy green foliage, white flowers with maroon blotches • *C. × corbariensis* low growing into wide mound, green leaves, small white flowers • *C. × cyprius* ♀ tall growing, glossy leaves, large white flowers • *C.* 'Grayswood Pink' low growing, grey foliage, pink flowers • *C.* 'Peggy Sammons' ♀ grey foliage, soft pink flowers • *C. × pulverulentus* 'Sunset' grey foliage, cerise-pink flowers • *C. × p.* 'Warley Rose' sage green leaves, cerise flowers • *C. × purpureus* ♀ green leaves, rose-crimson flowers • *C.* 'Silver Pink' grey foliage, silver-pink flowers

CONVOLVULUS CNEORUM
Convolvulaceae
SHRUBBY SILVER BIND-
WEED, SILVERBUSH

▲ ❀ ✿ SI all year E
H 5 yrs 50cm (20in)
S 5 yrs 60cm (2ft)
H 10 yrs 50cm (20in)
S 10 yrs 60cm (2ft)
❄ -5°C (23°F)
Z 7–10

CONVOLVULUS CNEORUM

The family connection should not be held against this pretty summer-flowering plant, and it should not be compared with its distant relative, the invasive field bindweed (*C. arvensis*). In no way spreading and with only its hardiness in question, *C. cneorum* deserves to be planted in many more gardens.

Soil Warm and well-drained but never completely dry
Aspect Must be in full sun in a sheltered part of the garden; winter protection important and covering with straw or protection fleece in the worst weather may help
Habit Low and bushy
Leaf Evergreen, oval and pointed leaves, 8cm (3in) long; light grey with an overall silver sheen
Flower Numerous large, white, trumpet-shaped flowers, to 4cm (1½in) long and 2.5cm (1in) wide at the mouth of the trumpet, are borne in summer
Use As a low-growing shrub for the front of a mixed border; good planted as a specimen or in a group; good in containers in both long and short term; in very favourable situations could be considered as a low hedge planted at distances of 50cm (20in)
Needs Trim back all shoots in mid-spring by up to 30 per cent of their length. Propagate from cuttings in summer
Varieties None

CORNUS
Cornaceae
DOGWOOD, CORNEL

▲ ❀ ✿ SI all year
H 5 yrs 1.5m (5ft)
S 5 yrs 1.5m (5ft)
H 10 yrs 2.5m (8ft)
S 10 yrs (8ft)
❄ -10°C (14°F)
Z 3–8

CORNUS KOUSA

This genus includes deciduous trees and shrubs, planted for their flowers, foliage and winter colour of their stems.

Soil *C. alba* and *C. mas*: moist; *C. alternifolia*, *C. controversa* and *C. kousa*: neutral to acid; *C. florida*: acid
Aspect Full sun to light shade, except *C. kousa* and *C. florida*, which prefer light shade
Habit *C. alternifolia*, *C. controversa* and *C. mas:* bushy; *C. florida* and *C. kousa:* tree-forming
Leaf Deciduous, oval leaves, 8cm (3in) long, green or with gold or silver variegation
Flower *C. alba*, *C. alternifolia*, *C controversa* and *C. mas:* clusters of white or yellow flowers in summer or winter; *C. florida* and *C. kousa:* white or pink bracts in summer
Use As part of mixed plantings; as specimen plants
Needs Cut back *C. alba* types hard back in spring; others require no pruning. Propagate *C. alba* by summer or winter cuttings; others by layering or commercial grafting
Varieties *C. alba* (red-barked dogwood) red stems, green foliage, white flowers and fruit • *C. a.* 'Aurea' golden foliage • *C. a.* 'Elegantissima' ♀ white-variegated foliage • *C. a.* 'Spaethii' ♀ gold-variegated foliage • *C. alternifolia* 'Argentea' ♀ tiers of white-variegated leaves • *C. controversa* 'Variegata' ♀ tall, tiers of white-variegated leaves • *C. florida* (eastern flowering dogwood) pink flower bracts • *C. kousa* (kousa) erect, white bracts • *C. kousa* var. *chinensis* ♀ autumn colours, white bracts • *C. mas* (cornelian cherry) ♀ yellow flowers in winter

CORYLOPSIS
Hamamelidaceae
COWSLIP BUSH,
WINTER HAZEL

▲ ❀ ❦ SI winter–early
spring SC
H 5 yrs 1–1.5m (3–5ft)
S 5 yrs 1–1.5m (3–5ft)
H 10 yrs 1–2.5m (3–8ft)
S 10 yrs 1–2.5m (3–8ft)
❅ -10°C (14°F)
Z 6–9

CORYLOPSIS SPICATA

When it is grown in the right soil conditions – it will not
tolerate alkaline soil – this can be one of the most beautiful of
winter-flowering plants, with its lovely green summer and
yellow autumn foliage, fragrant, yellow flowers in profusion
and a pleasing habit of growth.

Soil Neutral to acid; dislikes alkalinity
Aspect Light to medium shade
Habit Shrubby and gracefully spreading
Leaf Deciduous, light green to grey-green leaves, ageing to
light olive green; some forms have red-purple leaf stalks;
good yellow to yellow-brown autumn colour
Flower Cowslip-shaped, scented flowers in shades of yellow
are borne in winter and early spring
Use As a free-standing shrub; as part of woodland or winter-
flowering group; will grow in a large container
Needs No pruning required except for removal of any dead
branches that may appear. Propagate by layering in summer
Varieties *C. glabrescens* tall growing, large grey-green
leaves, large yellow flowers • *C. pauciflora* ♀ low growing,
good yellow autumn colour, primrose-yellow flowers, smallest
and possibly most attractive form • *C. sinensis* var.
calvescens f. *veitchiana* (syn. *C. veitchiana*) ♀ tall growing,
primrose-yellow flowers in long racemes • *C. sinensis* var.
sinensis (syn. *C. willmottiae*) tall growing, soft yellow flowers
• *C. s.* var. *s.* 'Spring Purple' tall growing, rich purple
stems, yellow flowers • *C. spicata* best of the tall-growing
forms, pale yellow flowers

CORYLUS
Corylaceae
HAZEL

▲ ❀ ❦ SI all year SC E
H 5 yrs 3m (10ft)
S 5 yrs 3m (10ft)
H 10 yrs 4m (13ft)
S 10 yrs 5m (16ft)
❅ -18°C (0°F)
Z 4–9

**CORYLUS AVELLANA
'CONTORTA'**

For centuries the easy-going hazel has been valued for both
its attractive form and for the nuts. Ornamental varieties
have widened the plant's appeal and use.

Soil Any
Aspect Full sun to moderately deep shade
Habit Upright, spreading with age
Leaf Deciduous, large, light to mid-green to gold and purple,
round leaves, 5–10cm (2–4in) long
Flower Male catkins yellow and 5–6cm (2–2½ft) long, female
catkins small, red and tufted in winter and early spring;
followed by edible nuts
Use As free-standing specimens or in mixed planting; for
avenues and walkways planted at distances of 2m (6ft); good
for screening; cut shoots to support other plants
Needs Prune hard back every 7 years to encourage new
growth. *C. a.* 'Contorta' is grafted and may produce straight-
growing basal shoots or suckers, which should be removed to
prevent regrowth
Varieties *C. avellana* (hazelnut) green leaves, yellow catkins
• *C. a.* 'Aurea' (golden-leafed hazel) lime green to soft
yellow, round leaves • *C. a.* 'Contorta' (corkscrew hazel,
Harry Lauder's walking stick, contorted hazel) ♀ branches
and leaves contorted • *C. a.* 'Heterophylla' (syn. *C. a.*
'Laciniata'; cut-leaved hazel) deeply lobed, grey-green leaves
• *C. maxima* (filbert) large light to mid-green leaves, edible
nuts • *C. m.* 'Purpurea' ♀ (syn. *C. m.* 'Atropurpurea',
purple-leaved filbert) large, deep purple leaves, purple catkins

SHRUBS

COTINUS
Anacardiaceae
SMOKE TREE

▲ ❀ ✾ SI summer–autumn
H 5 yrs 1.5m (5ft)
S 5 yrs 1.8m (5ft 6in)
H 10 yrs 3m (10ft)
S 10 yrs 3m (10ft)
❄ -10°C (14°F)
Z 5–10

**COTINUS COGGYGRIA
'ROYAL PURPLE'**

This genus of trees and shrubs is grown for it flowerheads, foliage and autumn colour. Each flowerhead actually consists of hundreds of very small, petal-less flowers on a web of fine stalks. Both the purple- and green-leaved varieties provide rich autumn colour

Soil Prefers rich, deep soil but tolerates most types
Aspect Full sun; green-leaved forms tolerate very light shade
Habit Bushy, slow to mature but increasing in growth rate in second and third years
Leaf Deciduous, ovate leaves, 4–5cm (1½–2in) long; in autumn green or purple leaves turn deep orange-red
Flower Large, open feather plumes of green or purple, 15–20cm (6–8in) wide and long, are borne in early autumn
Use As a specimen or in a shrub border; purple forms contrast with other coloured plants
Needs Propagate by layering. Cut back in spring to improve foliage (this means losing the flowers)
Varieties *C. coggygria* (syn. *Rhus cotinus*) ♀ green foliage, pink flowers • *C. c.* 'Foliis Purpureis' young leaves plum-red, turning to pale purple, good autumn colour, purplish-pink flowers • *C. c.* 'Notcutt's Variety' deep purple foliage, good autumn colour, pink-purple flowers • *C. c.* 'Royal Purple' ♀ deep purple leaves, purple-pink flowers • *C.* 'Flame' large green leaves, good autumn colour • *C.* 'Grace' greenish-red foliage with salmon autumn colour, pink flowers • *C. obovatus* ♀ (syn. *C. americanus*) large green foliage, perhaps best autumn colour of all, pink flowers

COTONEASTER
Rosaceae
COTONEASTER

▲ ❀ ✾ SI all year E some
H 5 yrs 0.6–4m (2–13ft)
S 5 yrs 1–5m (3–16ft)
H 10 yrs 0.6–6m (2–20ft)
S 10 yrs 1–6m (3–20ft)
❄ -15°C (4°F)
Z 5–8

COTONEASTER FLOCCOSUS

A very large group of plants, offering attractive flower, fruit and foliage and a range of sizes, from low mounds to almost full-sized trees.

Soil Most
Aspect Full sun to light shade
Habit Mound-forming or upright to tree-like
Leaf Dark green deciduous or evergreen, small, round to long, lance-shaped leaves
Flower White clusters in early summer on all forms
Use Almost all uses within a garden, depending on the variety planted
Needs Propagate by cuttings in summer. No pruning needed
Varieties Deciduous: *C. atropurpureus* 'Variegatus' (syn. *C. horizontalis* 'Variegatus') ♀ spreading habit, white-variegated leaves, autumn colour, red fruit • *C. divaricatus* bushy habit, glossy foliage, good autumn colour, red fruit • *C. horizontalis* (fish-bone cotoneaster) ♀ spreading habit, red fruit • *C. simonsii* ♀ upright habit, good autumn colour, red fruit, good for hedging Evergreen: • *C. buxifolius* bushy habit, red fruit • *C. dammeri* ♀ carpet-forming, red fruit • *C. floccosus*, tall, arching habit, narrow leaves, red fruit • *C. frigidus* 'Cornubia' ♀ tall, upright habit, red fruit • *C. microphyllus* ♀ mound-forming, purple fruit • *C. salicifolius* 'Pendulus' (syn. *C.* 'Hybridus Pendulus') spreading yet mound-forming habit, red fruit • *C. s.* 'Rothschildianus' ♀ tall, upright habit, yellow fruit • *C.* × *suecicus* 'Skogholme' creeping, red fruit

CRINODENDRON
Elaeocarpaceae
CRINODENDRON

▲ ❀ ❦ SI summer E
H 5 yrs 1m (3ft)
S 5 yrs 75cm (30in)
H 10 yrs 2m (6ft)
S 10 yrs 1m (3ft)
❄ -5°C (23°F)
Z 6–8

**CRINODENDRON
HOOKERIANUM**

Although it is not always easy to grow, because of its soil and environmental needs, this is a truly beautiful plant and is often grown to give the effect of an oriental-type garden. The dark foliage sets off the hanging lantern-shaped flowers to wonderful effect, and if you garden in a wet area and have acid soil, this is the feature plant for you.

Soil Must be acid; dislikes alkalinity
Aspect Full sun to light shade; suitable for coastal gardens if not exposed to strong winds; protect from cold in winter
Habit Upright, becoming more spreading with age
Leaf Evergreen, dark green, lance-shaped leaves, 4–5cm (1½–2in) long, with bright silver undersides
Flower Beautiful and interesting crimson-red or white lanterns hanging from the undersides of branches in summer
Use As a specimen shrub for acid gardens; good in association with dwarf rhododendrons, azaleas and heathers or as a specimen plant in association with water features; grow in a container for a limited time before planting out
Needs Propagate from cuttings in summer. No pruning required. Protect from cold in winter. Make sure it does not dry out in droughts
Varieties *C. hookerianum* (syn. *Tricuspidaria lanceolata*; Chile lantern tree) ♀ crimson-red, lantern-shaped flowers, best form to plant if only one can be grown • *C. patagua* (syn. *Tricuspidaria dependens*) white, bell-shaped flowers

CYTISUS
**Leguminosae/
Papilionaceae**
BROOM

▲ ❀ SI spring SC
H 5 yrs 0.75–2m (30in–6ft)
S 5 yrs 1–1.5m (3–5ft)
H 10 yrs 1–3m (3–10ft)
S 10 yrs 1.5–2m (5–6ft)
❄ -10°C (14°F)
Z 6–10

CYTISUS 'KILLINEY SALMON'

This is a large group of plants, with varieties in a wide range of colours, sizes and shapes. They can be relatively short lived and will probably need replacing after 10 years, when they tend to become unsightly and misshapen.

Soil Most but dislikes very thin, chalky soil
Aspect Full sun
Habit Strong, upright or spreading, but becoming branching and then woody with age
Leaf Comparatively few deciduous or evergreen, grey to silvery-grey or grey-green, lance-shaped leaves, 1–2cm (½–¾in) long and wide
Flower White, pink, red, amber, yellow, bronze or bright yellow, pea-shaped flowers are borne in spring
Use As a free-standing shrub for most shrub borders or for mass-planting
Needs Propagate from cuttings in summer. No pruning required
Varieties *C.* 'Buttercup' buttercup yellow flowers • *C.* 'Burkwoodii' ♀ deep red flowers • *C.* 'Criterion' brown-purple flowers • *C.* 'Hollandia' ♀ purple-red flowers • *C.* 'Killiney Salmon' red-salmon flowers • *C. multiflorus* ♀ small, white flowers • *C.* × *praecox* primrose-yellow flowers • *C.* × *p.* 'Albus' pure white flowers • *C.* × *p.* 'Allgold' ♀ golden-yellow flowers • *C.* 'Zeelandia' ♀ bicoloured pink and mauve flowers

CYTISUS BATTANDIERI
Leguminosae/ Papilionaceae
PINEAPPLE BROOM,
MOROCCAN BROOM

▲ ❀ SI spring SC E (semi)
H 5 yrs 3m (10ft)
S 5 yrs 2m (6ft)
H 10 yrs 5m (16ft)
S 10 yrs 4m (13ft)
❋ -5°C (23°F) to -10°C (14°F)
Z 4–8

CYTISUS BATTANDIERI

A somewhat gaunt specimen plant that needs space to show itself off to the best advantage. It is not reliably hardy, and in all but the warmest gardens it needs the protection of a wall.

Soil Most but dislikes very thin, chalky soil
Aspect Prefers full sun
Habit Strong, upright growth, becoming branching and spreading and then woody with age
Leaf Semi-evergreen, grey to silver-grey, pinnate leaves, to 10cm (4in) long and wide
Flower Long, upright, bright yellow, pineapple-scented panicles in early summer
Use As a free-standing shrub for mild areas or as wall shrub in colder localities; as a small tree in warmer areas
Needs Propagate from seed but best grafted on to *Laburnum vulgaris*. No pruning required
Varieties None

DAPHNE
Thymelaeaceae
DAPHNE

▲ ❀ ❦ S spring SC E
H 5 yrs 20–60cm (8–24in)
S 5 yrs 40–75cm (15–30in)
H 10 yrs 50–75cm (20–30in)
S 10 yrs 60–75cm (24–30in)
❋ -5°C (23°F)
Z 4–8

DAPHNE × BURKWOODII

This shrub has been grown for generations, largely for its perfumed flowers. It is worth risking losing a plant from the viruses that can kill any variety in order to enjoy the scent.

Soil Acid to neutral but tolerates alkaline soil provided it is rich in organic material
Aspect Prefers light shade but tolerates full sun
Habit Mostly bushy, but some spreading and a few upright
Leaf Evergreen or deciduous, green, oval to lance-shaped leaves, 1–2.5cm (½–1in) long
Flower Scented, creamy-white, pale pink to deep rose-pink flowers; the fruits are poisonous
Use As small specimen plant planted alone or in groups
Needs Propagate from cuttings in summer. No pruning
Varieties *D. blagayana* creamy-white flowers • *D. × burkwoodii* ♀ pale pink flowers • *D. × b.* 'Somerset' large pale pink flowers • *D. × b.* 'Somerset Gold Edge' gold-margined leaves, pale pink flowers • *D. cneorum* (garland flower) prostrate habit, rose-pink flowers • *D. c. f. alba* pure white flowers • *D. c.* 'Eximia' ♀ rose-pink flowers, crimson when in bud • *D. c.* var. *pygmaea* pink flowers • *D. c.* 'Variegata' cream-edged leaves, lighter pink, scented flowers • *D. collina* rose-pink flowers • *D. mezereum* (mezereon) upright habit, purple flowers in winter • *D. m. f. alba* small white to green-white flowers • *D. odora* 'Aureomarginata' purple-pink, trumpet-shaped flowers • *D. pontica* ♀ yellow-green flowers • *D. retusa* deep rose-purple flowers • *D. tangutica* ♀ purple-tinged, white flowers

DEUTZIA
Hydrangeaceae
DEUTZIA

▲ ❀ ❦ SI summer
H 5 yrs 1–3m (3–10ft)
S 5 yrs 1m (3ft)
H 10 yrs 1–3m (3–10ft)
S 10 yrs 1–2m (3–6ft)
❄ -25°C (-13°C)
Z 5–9

DEUTZIA SCABRA 'PLENA'

Few other shrubs produce as much flower as this shrub, and the autumn colours on some are a bonus to the display.

Soil Moist, well fed, tolerates high alkalinity
Aspect Full sun to light shade
Habit Mostly upright, becoming very branching with age
Leaf Deciduous, olive-green, ovate, 4–10cm (1½–4in) long
Flower Short panicles of bell-shaped flowers in shades of white or pink through to purple-pink
Use For borders or group plantings, free standing
Needs Propagate from cuttings in summer or winter. Remove one-third of shoots after flowering
Varieties *D.* 'Contraste' panicles of star-shaped, semi-double, soft lilac-pink flowers • *D.* × *elegantissima* panicles of rose-pink flowers • *D.* × *e.* 'Rosealind' ♀ single, deep carmine-pink flowers in short panicles • *D.* × *kalmiiflora* pink to flushed carmine flowers • *D. longifolia* 'Veitchii' ♀ clusters of single, lilac-pink flowers • *D.* 'Magicien' single, white-edged, mauve-pink flowers with purple reverse • *D.* × *magnifica* double, pure white flowers • *D. monbeigii* single, star-like, white flowers • *D.* 'Mont Rose' single to semi-double, rose-pink flowers • *D. ningpoensis* (syn. *D. chunii*) single flowers, pink outside, white within • *D. pulchra* pure white flowers • *D.* × *rosea* 'Carminea' ♀ rose-carmine flowers with paler shading • *D. scabra* 'Candidissima' double, pure white flowers • *D. s.* 'Plena' double, rose-purple flowers with white shading • *D. s.* 'Pride of Rochester' double, white flowers

ELAEAGNUS
Elaeagnaceae
ELAEAGNUS

▲ ❀ ❦ SI all year SC E
H 5 yrs 1.2m (4ft)
S 5 yrs 1.2m (4ft)
H 10 yrs 2m (6ft)
S 10 yrs 2m (6ft)
❄ Deciduous: -10°C (14°F);
  Evergreen: -15°C (4°F)
Z 3–7

ELAEAGNUS PUNGENS 'MACULATA'

Among the finest of foliage plants, both evergreen and deciduous forms can reach the height of small trees in time. Although they are often hidden by the foliage, the flowers, which are produced in autumn, have a pleasant scent.

Soil Most but unhappy on extremely alkaline or dry soils
Aspect Full sun to deep shade but may be more lax in shade
Habit Upright when young, becoming very twiggy and dense with age and forming an upright shrub or round bush; after 20 years can form a small tree
Leaf Evergreen or deciduous depending on variety, oval or lance-shaped, 5–15cm (2–6in) long, grey-green, or gold or silver variegated
Flower Small, inconspicuous, strongly scented, sulphur yellow flowers in late summer to autumn
Use As a specimen plant or in a mixed shrub border; good in a container in the short term; evergreen forms as a hedge planted at distances of 75cm (30in)
Needs Propagate from cuttings in summer. Shorten shoots by 50 per cent in spring to keep bushy
Varieties Deciduous: *E. angustifolia* ♀ lance-shaped, bright silver leaves • *E. commutata* (syn. *E. argentea*) silver foliage Evergreen: *E.* × *ebbingei* grey-green leaves • *E.* × *e.* 'Gilt Edge' ♀ gold-margined leaves • *E.* × *e.* 'Limelight' gold-splashed leaves • *E. pungens* 'Dicksonii' holly-like leaves with bright gold margins • *E. p.* 'Goldrim' gold-splashed leaves • *E. p.* 'Maculata' ♀ dark green leaves with central gold patches • *E. p.* 'Variegata' cream-white-margined leaves

EMBOTHRIUM COCCINEUM
Proteaceae
CHILEAN FIREBUSH

▲ ❀ ❦ S late spring E
H 5 yrs 2m (6ft)
S 5 yrs 1m (3ft)
H 10 yrs 4m (13ft)
S 10 yrs 2m (6ft)
❄ -10°C (14°F)
Z 4–8

**EMBOTHRIUM COCCINEUM
LANCEOLATUM GROUP**

Given the right soil and aspect, this South American shrub can be one of the most spectacular plants in a garden, often reaching the dimensions of a small tree. When it is in flower it gives the impression of being covered with brightly coloured birds, and it should be planted against a dark background so that the brilliant flowers can be fully appreciated.

Soil Deep, rich, peaty and moisture-retentive soil; dislikes alkalinity
Aspect Does best in a lightly shaded woodland clearing or similar position; needs winter protection until over 2m (6ft) tall to prevent frost and wind damage
Habit Upright, branching with age
Leaf Semi-evergreen, grey-green, lance-shaped leaves, with some red shading, 10–17cm (4–7in) long; the silver reverse shown off in wind
Flower Orange-scarlet clusters of strap-like petals in late spring
Use As a late-spring-flowering specimen shrub for woodland or similar areas
Needs Propagate commercially by layering or from seed. No pruning required
Varieties *E. coccineum* the main form planted, orange-scarlet flowers • *E. c.* Lanceolatum Group lance-shaped foliage, good flower performance, may be the best choice where only one can be planted • *E. c.* Longifolium Group longer leaves, also worth planting

ENKIANTHUS
Ericaceae
REDVIEW ENKIANTHUS

▲ ❀ ❦ S spring–autumn
H 5 yrs 1.5m (5ft)
S 5 yrs 1m (3ft)
H 10 yrs 2.5m (8ft)
S 10 yrs 2m (6ft)
❄ -15°C (4°F)
Z 5–8

**ENKIANTHUS
CAMPANULATUS**

A plant for acid soil, where it produces interesting flowers and good autumn foliage colour. Although it is not small, it has a neat habit and, therefore, can be accommodated in the smaller garden. The flowers are not spectacular, but when they are seen close to, their subtle coloration is revealed.

Soil Acid and moisture-retentive soil, high in organic material; dislikes alkaline soil
Aspect Does best in light shade
Habit Upright when young, becoming branching and twiggy, then forming a rounded, spreading yet neat shrub at maturity
Leaf Deciduous, light green to grey-green, round to oval, leaves 2.5–4cm (1–1½in); excellent orange-red autumn colour
Flower Pretty sulphur yellow to bronze, small to medium, hanging, cup-shaped flowers borne in small clusters
Use Free-standing as a specimen solo or mass-planted for spring flowers and autumn foliage in a woodland or similar shady position where the right soil conditions can be achieved; useful for cutting
Needs Propagate by layering in spring. Requires no pruning
Varieties *E. campanulatus* ♀ the main species planted • *E. c.* f. *albiflorus* white flowers • *E. cernus* f. *rubens* ♀ deep red fringed flowers • *E. chinensis* large, yellow-red flowers with dark veins • *E. perulatus* ♀ hanging, urn-shaped white flowers

ERICA

Ericaceae
HEATHER, HEATH,
WINTER-FLOWERING
HEATHER

▲ ❀ ❦ SI all year E
H 5 yrs 50cm (20in)
S 5 yrs 75cm (30in)
H 10 yrs 50cm (20in)
S 10 yrs 75cm (30in)
❀ -15°C (4°F)
Z 5–10

**ERICA CARNEA
'MYRETOUN RUBY'**

Little need be said about this plant except to underline the importance of selecting the right type for your soil. *Erica carnea*, formerly *E. herbacea*, provides good ground cover.

Soil Neutral to acid soil; *E. carnea* tolerates some alkalinity
Aspect Does best in very light shade but tolerates full sun
Habit Upright, quickly becoming spreading and mat-forming
Leaf Evergreen, lance-shaped, leaves, light to dark purple-green or gold, 1cm (½in) long
Flower Small, bell-shaped flowers, ranging from white through pink to purple
Use In mass-plantings on banks or in large rock gardens; good for underplanting
Needs Propagate from cuttings in summer. Trim lightly after flowering
Varieties *E. carnea* 'Ann Sparkes' ♥ golden-yellow foliage, rose-pink flowers • *E. c.* 'Aurea' golden foliage, pink flowers • *E. c.* 'Myretoun Ruby' ♥ deep purple-pink flowers • *E. c.* 'Pink Spangles' ♥ rose-pink flowers • *E. c.* 'Ruby Glow' ruby pink flowers • *E. c.* 'Springwood Pink' spreading habit, pink flowers • *E. c.* 'Springwood White' ♥ spreading habit, white flowers • *E. c.* 'Vivellii' ♥ dark foliage, deep pink flowers • *E. c.* 'Westwood Yellow' ♥ yellow foliage, pink flowers • *E. × darleyensis* 'Arthur Johnson' ♥ deep purple-pink flowers • *E. × d.* 'Darley Dale' pale purple flowers • *E. × d.* 'Ghost Hills' ♥ rose-pink flowers • *E. × d.* 'Jack H. Brummage' golden foliage, pink flowers • *E. × d.* 'Silber-schmelze' ('Molten Silver') pure white flowers

ESCALLONIA

Escalloniaceae
ESCALLONIA

▲ ❀ ❦ SI summer E
H 5 yrs 60cm (2ft)
S 5 yrs 60cm (2ft)
H 10 yrs 1m (3ft)
S 10 yrs 4m (13ft)
❀ -15°C (4°F)
Z 4–10

**ESCALLONIA RUBRA
'CRIMSON SPIRE'**

This genus of evergreen or deciduous shrubs offers a wide range of varieties of flower colour and also of foliage size and colour, including some forms with golden foliage.

Soil Most, except extremely alkaline soil
Aspect Full sun to medium shade; good for maritime gardens
Habit Upright, becoming arching and branching with age
Leaf Light to dark green, oval leaves, 2.5–4cm (1–1½in) long, indented edges, glossy upper surfaces and grey undersides
Flower Bell-shaped flowers, single or in short racemes, in various shades of pink to pink-red or white in late spring to early summer; intermittent flowering later in year
Use Free standing or for large shrub borders; semi-formal hedge planted at distances of 75cm (30in); can be fan-trained
Needs Propagate from cuttings in summer. Remove one-third of oldest wood after flowering
Varieties *E.* 'Apple Blossom' ♥ apple blossom pink flowers • *E.* 'C.F. Ball' rich red flowers • *E.* 'Donard Beauty' rose-carmine flowers • *E.* 'Donard Brilliance' rose-red flowers • *E.* 'Donard Radiance' ♥ rich pink flowers • *E.* 'Donard Seedling' pink in bud opening to rose-tinted white flowers • *E.* 'Donard Star' deep rosy pink flowers • *E.* 'Edinensis' ♥ carmine-pink flowers • *E.* 'Gwendolyn Anley' flowers pink in bud, opening to paler pink • *E.* 'Iveyi' ♥ white flowers • *E. laevis* 'Gold Brian' golden foliage, pink flowers • *E.* 'Peach Blossom' ♥ clear pink flowers • *E. rubra* 'Crimson Spire' crimson flowers • *E. r.* var. *macrantha* scented, rose-carmine flowers

SHRUBS

EUCRYPHIA
Eucryphiaceae
BRUSH BUSH

▲ ❀ ❦ SI all year E
H 5 yrs 2m (6ft)
S 5 yrs 1m (3ft)
H 10 yrs 4m (13ft)
S 10 yrs 2m (6ft)
❄ -5°C (23°F) to -10°C (14°F)
Z 4–8

**EUCRYPHIA × NYMANSENSIS
'NYMANSAY'**

Aristocrats among shrubs and often reaching the proportions of trees, eucryphias will thrive only in the correct soil and light. However, if these are provided, this plant will reward the gardener with a magnificent display of flowers.

Soil Neutral to acid soil that is moist but not waterlogged and that is rich in organic material; *E. cordifolia* and *E.* × *nymansensis* will tolerate some alkalinity
Aspect Light shade or in woodland clearing
Habit Upright, becoming more branching with age
Leaf Evergreen or deciduous, oval leaves, 4–8cm (1½–3in) long, with glossy upper surfaces and grey undersides
Flower White, large, single, saucer-shaped flowers with pronounced stamens shown off against dark foliage
Use As a free-standing specimen shrub or small tree; can be fan-trained on a wall
Needs Propagate from cuttings in summer. No pruning required
Varieties *E. cordifolia* (ulmo) evergreen, heart-shaped leaves, white flowers • *E. glutinosa* ♀ deciduous, grey-green foliage, white flowers • *E.* × *intermedia* 'Rostrevor' ♀ pendulous branches, evergreen foliage, fragrant white flowers • *E. lucida* (leatherwood, pinkwood) dark grey-green evergreen foliage, fragrant, white, pendent flowers • *E. milliganii* small, dark grey-green evergreen leaves, white, cup-shaped flowers • *E.* × *nymansensis* 'Nymansay' ♀ dark green evergreen foliage, pure white flowers, the best and main variety planted

EUONYMUS
Celastraceae
EUONYMUS

▲ ❀ ❦ SI all year E some
H 5 yrs 0.6–2m (2–6ft)
S 5 yrs 1–2m (3–6ft)
H 10 yrs 0.6–4m (2–13ft)
S 10 yrs 2–4m (6–13ft)
❄ -25°C (-13°C)
Z 3–6

A very large group of plants with many different characteristics, ranging from the evergreens with their winter foliage to the deciduous forms with their ornamental spindle fruits.

Soil Prefers alkaline soil but tolerates all
Aspect Full sun to light shade; tolerates deeper shade
Habit Some low and spreading, others upright
Leaf Deciduous or evergreen, narrow, oval leaves, 2.5–9cm (1–3½in) long
Flower Inconspicuous green to green-yellow flowers in spring
Use As a specimen in mixed borders or as ground cover
Needs Propagate from cuttings in summer. No pruning required but can be reduced
Varieties <u>Deciduous</u>: *E. alatus* (winged spindle) ♀ scarlet autumn colour • *E. europeaus* 'Red Cascade' ♀ autumn colour, rosy red fruit • *E. planipes* (syn. *E. sachalinensis*) ♀ red and orange autumn colour, pink fruit <u>Evergreen</u>: *E. fortunei* 'Coloratus' green leaves, purple in winter • *E. f.* 'Emerald 'n' Gold' ♀ dark grey-green, gold-edged leaves • *E. f.* 'Silver Queen' ♀ creamy yellow young leaves, turning green with white margin • *E. f.* 'Sunshine' grey-green, gold-edged leaves • *E. f.* 'Variegatus' grey-green, white-margined leaves • *E. japonicus* 'Albomarginatus' dark green leaves with white outer margins, tender • *E. j.* 'Aureus' (syn. *E. j.* 'Aureopictus') dark green foliage with bold gold centre, tender • *E. j.* 'Macrophyllus' large, oval, green leaves, tender • *E. j.* 'Ovatus Aureus' ♀ (syn. *E.* 'Aureovariegatus') creamy yellow variegation, tender

**EUONYMUS FORTUNEI
'EMERALD 'N' GOLD'**

EXOCHORDA
Rosaceae
EXOCHORDA,
PEARLBUSH

▲ ❀ ❦ SI spring
H 5 yrs 1.5m (5ft)
S 5 yrs 1.8m (5ft 6in)
H 10 yrs 2m (6ft)
S 10 yrs 2.5m (8ft)
❄ -15°C (4°F)
Z 4–8

The elegant, arching branches are adorned with a bold display of white flowers towards the end of spring. The combination of habit and flowers makes this a spectacular shrub, and it is surprising that it is not more widely planted since it is also relatively undemanding.

Soil Does well on most soils; dislikes very dry conditions
Aspect Full sun to very light shade
Habit Upright when young, quickly arching to form an attractive, weeping shrub
Leaf Deciduous, grey-green, lance-shaped leaves, 4–8cm (1½–3in) long; good yellow autumn colour
Flower Masses of racemes of single, saucer-shaped, white flowers in spring
Use As a late-spring-flowering shrub worth a featured position; good in mixed and shrub borders; possible short-term use in a large container; with time can be trained as a short mop-headed standard tree; as an informal hedge planted at distances of 75cm (30in)
Needs Propagate from cuttings in summer. Pruning not required except at maturity to remove a few old flowering shoots after flowering
Varieties *E. giraldii* var. *wilsonii* stiff, upright habit of growth, largest flowered variety with each flower 5cm (2in) across • *E.* × *macrantha* 'The Bride' ♚ most floriferous variety, the main variety available and planted

EXOCHORDA × **MACRANTHA 'THE BRIDE'**

FATSIA
Araliaceae
JAPANESE ARALIA,
GLOSSY LEAVED PAPER
PLANT

▲ ❀ ❦ SI all year E
H 5 yrs 2m (6ft)
S 5 yrs 2m (6ft)
H 10 yrs 3m (10ft)
S 10 yrs 3m (10ft)
❄ -10°C (14°F)
Z 4–6

The fatsia's enormous leaves and ultimate size make it one of the most striking of plants for a shady part of the garden. The flowers, which are followed by fruits, are also large and striking. The overall appearance is oriental, but the fatsia is unique in that it can be grown outdoors as well as in without any harmful effects unless the winter is extremely severe.

Soil Does well on most types, but plants in rich, deep, moist soil produce the largest leaves
Aspect Best in deep to medium shade; dislikes full sun; suitable for maritime gardens
Habit Upright, forming a tall, rigid structure
Leaf Evergreen, dark to mid-green, hand-shaped leaves, 6–16cm (2½–6½in) wide and 23–50cm (9–20in) long, with a glossy upper surface and paler underside; there are variegated forms
Flower Silver-green clusters opening to milk white flowers in summer, followed by bunches of small, black fruits in autumn
Use As a free-standing evergreen for shady areas; as a wall shrub if carefully trained; good in large containers
Needs Propagate from cuttings taken in summer. No pruning required
Varieties *F. japonica* ♚ dark green leaves • *F. j.* 'Aurea' golden-yellow variegation, very tender • *F. j.* 'Variegata' ♚ white to creamy-white variegation to lobes and tips of foliage, tender

FATSIA JAPONICA

FORSYTHIA

Oleaceae

FORSYTHIA, GOLDEN BALL

❀ ❦ SI spring
H 5 yrs 2.5m (8ft)
S 5 yrs 1.5m (5ft)
H 10 yrs 3.5m (12ft)
S 10 yrs 2.5m (8ft)
❄ -15°C (4°F)
Z 5–9

FORSYTHIA × INTERMEDIA 'LYNWOOD'

One of the best-known spring-flowering shrubs, and although it might be thought to be too widely planted, it has a true role to play in brightening up the garden in spring.

Soil Does well on any soil
Aspect Full sun to medium shade
Habit Upright, arching and spreading with age, eventually forming a round-topped shrub
Leaf Deciduous, light to mid-green, oval to lance-shaped leaves, 4–6cm (1½–2½in) long, tooth-edged; autumn colour
Flower Profuse lemon-yellow to golden-yellow, pendent, bell-shaped flowers
Use As a free-standing shrub or in a mixed border; as an informal hedge planted at distances of 0.75–1m (30–36in); as a small tree on 1–2m (3–6ft) high stem; some climbing forms
Needs Propagate from cuttings in summer or winter. Remove some shoots after flowering
Varieties *F.* 'Arnold Dwarf' dwarf, yellow-green flowers • *F.* 'Beatrix Farrand' canary yellow, pendent flowers • *F. giraldiana* pale yellow flowers • *F. × intermedia* (border forsythia) golden-yellow flowers, fading to white-yellow • *F. × i.* 'Lynwood' 🏆 rich yellow flowers • *F. ovata* (Korean forsythia) dwarf, yellow to amber-yellow flowers • *F. o.* 'Tetragold' bell-shaped, golden-yellow flowers • *F. suspensa* (climbing forsythia) 🏆 light yellow flowers, best climbing form • *F. s.* f. *atrocaulis* pale lemon-yellow flowers • *F.* 'Tremonia' cut leaves, golden-yellow flowers • *F. viridissima* 'Bronxensis' very low growing, small lemon-yellow flowers

---

FOTHERGILLA

Hamamelidaceae

FOTHERGILLA

▲ ❀ ❦ SI spring and autumn SC
H 5 yrs 1m (3ft)
S 5 yrs 1m (3ft)
H 10 yrs 2m (6ft)
S 10 yrs 2m (6ft)
❄ -25°C (-13°C)
Z 5–9

FOTHERGILLA MAJOR

A shrub for acid soils only, but in the right conditions this is one of the most spectacular of foliage shrubs in the autumn. In the early spring there are delightful pale primrose to white flowers. The neat habit and unassuming nature are further reasons for growing this delightful shrub.

Soil Acid soil, high in organic material; dislikes any alkalinity
Aspect Light shade; dislikes full sun
Habit Very branching, forming a ball shape
Leaf Deciduous, grey-green, oval leaves, often with grey, glaucous undersides, 2.5–6cm (1–2½in) across; brilliant yellow, orange and red autumn colours without fail
Flower Clusters of fragrant white stamens forming small to medium, rounded inflorescence in mid- to late spring before leaves appear
Use As an early-spring-flowering shrub but planted mainly for its autumn colour; ideal for woodland planting either as a single specimen or in a group
Needs Propagate in spring by layering or from seed. No pruning required
Varieties *F. gardenii* (witch alder, dwarf fothergilla) low growing, good spring flowering and fine autumn colour • *F. major* (large fothergilla) 🏆 slower growing, round, very glaucous foliage, the main variety planted • *F. m.* Monticola Group (Alabama fothergilla) slower growing, good autumn colour, good spring flowers

FREMONTODEN-DRON
Sterculiaceae
FLANNEL BUSH,
CALIFORNIA BEAUTY

▲ ❀ ❦ SI summer E
H 5 yrs 3m (10ft)
S 5 yrs 3m (10ft)
H 10 yrs 5m (16ft)
S 10 yrs 5m (16ft)
❄ -10°C (14°F)
Z 3–5

FREMONTODENDRON 'CALIFORNIA GLORY'

One of the most eye-catching of summer-flowering shrubs and often reaching the proportions of a small tree, the fremont-odendron will grow freely in a number of sheltered locations but is possibly best planted near the protection of a wall. Do not underestimate its ultimate size and beware of the dust on flowers, foliage and stems, which can cause allergic reactions.

Soil Any; tolerates high alkalinity
Aspect Prefers full sun but tolerates very light shade
Habit Upright when young, becoming more spreading and eventually forming a tall, upright shrub or small tree; when grown as a free-standing shrub will require support until established
Leaf Evergreen, grey-green, heart-shaped, 3–7 lobed leaves, 5–10cm (2–4in) long, covered in dust that can cause irritation
Flower Large, to 6cm (2½in) across, saucer-shaped yellow calyx with golden-yellow stigma and stamens protruding from centre throughout summer
Use As a free-standing shrub or small tree in very mild areas; as a wall shrub in colder areas
Needs Propagate from cuttings in early spring or from seed. Cut back all spring-produced new growth in midsummer by 50 per cent to encourage branching and to keep the shape neat; this pruning does involve sacrificing some flowers
Varieties *F.* 'California Glory' ♀ larger than type species, lemon-yellow to yellow flowers, the main form planted • *F. californicum* golden-yellow flowers • *F. mexicanum* golden-yellow, more star-like flowers

FUCHSIA
Onagraceae
HARDY FUCHSIA

▲ ❀ ❦ SI summer–autumn
H 5 yrs 0.6–1m (2–3ft)
S 5 yrs 0.6–1m (2–3ft)
H 10 yrs 0.6–1.2m (2–4ft)
S 10 yrs 0.6–1.5m (2–5ft)
❄ -10°C (14°F)
Z 6–8

FUCHSIA 'MADAME CORNELISSEN'

This plant is loved for its summer and autumn flower displays, but hardiness can be a problem in cold areas.

Soil Any well-drained soil; tolerates both alkalinity and acidity
Aspect Prefers full sun but tolerates light shade
Habit Upright, becoming arching with age
Leaf Deciduous, oval, green leaves, 5–8cm (2–3in) long; some variegated or purple-tinged forms
Flower Hanging, blue, pink, white, purple, red or bi-coloured flowers in summer and autumn
Use As a free-standing, summer-flowering shrub; as an informal hedge planted at distances of 75cm (30in); good in containers
Needs Propagate from cuttings. Cut growth to ground level in spring
Varieties *F.* 'Alice Hoffman' small scarlet and white flowers • *F.* 'Chillerton Beauty' ♀ white shaded deep rose and violet flowers • *F.* 'Golden Treasure' golden foliage, small red and purple flowers • *F.* 'Lady Thumb' ♀ dwarf, red and white flowers • *F.* 'Madame Cornelissen' ♀ scarlet and white flowers • *F. magellanica* var. *gracilis* 'Variegata' scarlet and violet flowers • *F. m.* var. *molinae* (syn. *F. m.* 'Alba') white-tinged, soft pink flowers • *F. m.* 'Riccartonii' scarlet and violet flowers • *F. m.* 'Versicolor' ♀ scarlet and violet flowers • *F.* 'Margaret' ♀ large semi-double, scarlet and violet flowers • *F.* 'Mrs Popple' ♀ crimson-violet and crimson flowers • *F.* 'Tom Thumb' ♀ dwarf, scarlet and violet flowers

GARRYA
Garryaceae
SILK TASSEL,
TASSEL TREE

▲ ❀ ❦ SI winter E
H 5 yrs 2.5m (8ft)
S 5 yrs 1.5m (5ft)
H 10 yrs 3.5m (12ft)
S 10 yrs 2.5m (8ft)
❄ -10°C (14°F)
Z 6–8

GARRYA ELLIPTICA

Rightly one of the most popular winter-flowering shrubs, garryas can be grown either as free-standing feature plants or against a wall or fence. The long male catkins, which can be seen to perfection against the dark foliage, live up to their common name. Do not be concerned if a few leaves die in spring – this is nothing more than the natural changing of old to new.

Soil Prefers fertile, well-fed soil but does well on almost any
Aspect Full sun to medium shade; good in maritime gardens because tolerates salt-laden wind
Habit Upright, becoming branching and spreading with age
Leaf Evergreen, leathery, dark green, broadly ovate leaves, 4–8cm (1½–3in) long, with glossy upper surfaces and glaucous undersides
Flower Male plants have long, grey-green hanging catkins; female plants have insignificant flowers and catkins; only male plants are normally grown
Use As a free-standing, large specimen shrub or wall shrub against a high wall or fence
Needs Propagate from cuttings in summer. No pruning required but, if wished, can be reduced in size after flowering in spring. When planting against a wall, allow for the potential forward protrusion
Varieties *G. elliptica* the main form grown • *G. e.* 'James Roof' ♀ catkins twice the length and thicker than those of type species • *G. fremontii* (fever bush, skunk bush) more oval, twisted leaves, shorter catkins

GENISTA
**Leguminosae/
Papilionaceae**
BROOM, GORSE

▲ ❀ SI spring SC
H 5 yrs 0.3–3m (1–10ft)
S 5 yrs 0.6–2.5m (2–8ft)
H 10 yrs 0.3–4m (1–13ft)
S 10 yrs 1–3.5m (3–12ft)
❄ -10°C (14°F)
Z 6–10

GENISTA HISPANICA

A genus of plants that is closely related to peas and beans, and the spring flowers are the same shape. There is a wide range of forms, ranging from varieties that can be grown as carpeting plants to those that will attain the dimensions of trees.

Soil Most; tolerates both acid and alkaline soil but dislikes extreme waterlogging
Aspect Does best in full sun; dislikes any shade
Habit Carpet-, shrub- or tree-forming growth; tree-like forms bring architectural shape to the garden
Leaf Deciduous, grey-green, lance-shaped leaves, 1cm (½in) long, sparsely produced and insignificant
Flower Single, golden-yellow, pea-like flowers in spring
Use Best as single specimen plants or in a group
Needs Propagate from cuttings in summer. No pruning
Varieties *G. aetnensis* (Mount Etna broom) ♀ masses of single, golden-yellow flowers on graceful branches, quickly reaches tree proportions • *G. hispanica* (Spanish gorse) bush-forming, single, light yellow flowers, branches and shoots armed with spines • *G. lydia* ♀ carpet-forming, single, golden-yellow flowers entirely cover branches • *G. pilosa* very low carpet-forming, numerous yellow flowers • *G. p.* 'Vancouver Gold' carpet-forming, golden-yellow flowers • *G. tenera* 'Golden Shower' (syn. *G. cinerea* 'Golden Showers') ♀ graceful, arching branches to 3m (10ft), bright golden-yellow flowers, a gem • *G. tinctoria* 'Royal Gold' ♀ shrub-forming to 1m (3ft), single, golden-yellow flowers

GRISELINIA
Griseliniaceae
GRISELINIA

▲ ❀ ❦ SI all year E
H 5 yrs 1.5m (5ft)
S 5 yrs 1.5m (5ft)
H 10 yrs 2.5m (8ft)
S 10 yrs 2.5m (8ft)
❀ -5°C (23°F)
Z 3–5

**GRISELINIA LITTORALIS
'VARIEGATA'**

An ideal plant for maritime areas, griselinia is capable of producing a solid screen of foliage. Further inland, however, its hardiness is suspect. The variegated varieties are more tender, but if the right conditions can be provided, it is a worthy addition to the range of winter evergreens.

Soil Almost any but dislikes being waterlogged; may show signs of chlorosis on extremely alkaline soil; will withstand salt winds
Aspect Full sun to very light shade; in shadier areas the growth habit will be more open
Habit Upright, becoming branching with time; in the right conditions grows into a dense screen and in maritime areas can reach the dimensions of a small tree
Leaf Evergreen, bright green, slightly curled, broadly oval leaves, 2.5–8cm (1–3in)
Flower Inconspicuous; some plants carry all male flowers, others all female; does not normally fruit
Use As a free-standing shrub or in large shrub borders; as a fine evergreen hedge planted at distances of 1m (3ft)
Needs Propagate from cuttings in summer. No pruning required but can be cut to ground level if it becomes old and woody. Can be trimmed very hard
Varieties *G. littoralis* ♀ leathery, bright green leaves •
G. l. 'Dixon's Cream' leaves with creamy-white marks •
G. l. 'Variegata' white-variegated leaves

HALESIA
Styracaceae
SNOWDROP TREE,
SILVERBELL TREE

▲ ❀ ❦ SI summer
H 5 yrs 1.5m (5ft)
S 5 yrs 2m (6ft)
H 10 yrs 3m (10ft)
S 10 yrs 4m (13ft)
❀ -10°C (14°F)
Z 4–8

HALESIA MONITCOLA

The common names of this beautiful shrub describe it perfectly: the branches of mature plants are festooned by the hanging, bell-shaped flowers. Halesias will grow in a wide range of conditions, so it is worth considering introducing one into your own garden.

Soil Most types but prefers well-drained soil; may show signs of distress on very alkaline conditions but more from drying out than for other reasons
Aspect Full sun to light shade
Habit Upright when young, becoming branching and twiggy with age and forming a large, round-topped shrub
Leaf Deciduous, light grey-green, broadly oval leaves, 5–13cm (2–5in) long and 5cm (2in) wide; good yellow autumn colour
Flower Very attractive, green to white, nodding, bell-shaped flowers, borne in clusters of 3–5 along the underside of branches
Use As a free-standing flowering shrub, planted as a specimen to be seen to full effect
Needs Propagate by layering or from cuttings in summer. Requires no pruning
Varieties *H. carolina* (syn. *H. tetraptera*; Carolina silverbell) white, bell-shaped, nodding flowers grouped along branches. • *H. monticola* (mountain silverbell) larger flowers and fruit • *H. m.* var. *vestita* ♀ large-flowering form with flower clusters, sometimes pink-tinged, to 2.5–4cm (1–1½in) across

SHRUBS

HAMAMELIS
Hamamelidaceae
WITCH-HAZEL

▲ ❀ SI winter–autumn SC
H 5 yrs 1.5m (5ft)
S 5 yrs 2m (6ft)
H 10 yrs 3m (10ft)
S 10 yrs 4m (13ft)
❀ -25°C (-13°C)
Z 4–8

HAMAMELIS MOLLIS

Few other plants can brighten a dark winter's day quite as well as witch-hazel. Given the right conditions, it provides not only colour but also scent early in the year, and the long-lasting autumn colour is an added bonus.

Soil Neutral to acid; will not tolerate alkaline soil
Aspect Prefers light shade but will tolerate full sun
Habit Upright, becoming spreading and branching with age and may become a small tree
Leaf Deciduous, ovate leaves, 8–13cm (3–5in) long; good orange-yellow autumn colour
Flower Small strap-like petals, ranging from lemon-yellow through gold, brown and orange to dark red, depending on variety; most varieties are scented
Use As a specimen flowering shrub; ideal for woodland planting, singly or in a group; if space permits, plant *en masse* for a spectacular display
Needs Propagate commercially by grafting. No pruning
Varieties *H.* 'Brevipetala' bronze-yellow, scented flowers • *H.* × *intermedia* 'Diane' ♀ good autumn colour, slightly scented, rich copper-red flowers • *H.* × *i.* 'Jelena' slightly scented, bright copper-orange flowers • *H.* × *i.* 'Pallida' ♀ primrose-yellow flowers • *H.* × *i.* 'Ruby Glow' copper-red flowers • *H. japonica* 'Zuccariniana' (Japanese witch-hazel) small leaves, grey buds opening to scented, lemon-yellow flowers • *H. mollis* (Chinese witch-hazel) golden-yellow, very fragrant flowers, the best form • *H. virginiana* (common witch-hazel, Virginian witch-hazel) golden-yellow flowers

HEBE
Scrophulariaceae
VERONICA

▲ ❀ ❦ SI all year E
H 5 yrs 0.3–1m (1–3ft)
S 5 yrs 0.75–1m (30–36in)
H 10 yrs 0.5–1.2m (20–48in)
S 10 yrs 1–2m (3–6ft)
❀ -5°C (23°F)
Z 10–11

HEBE 'MIDSUMMER BEAUTY'

Originally from New Zealand, hebes have become permanent features of our gardens, and there is a wide range of varieties. The disease phytophera can be a problem, as can hardiness.

Soil Well-drained, light in texture, alkaline or acid
Aspect Prefers full sun but tolerates light shade
Habit Shrub, normally dome shaped
Leaf Evergreen leaves, light to dark purple-green or silver variegated, broad or narrow, round to oval or lance-shaped, 1–10cm (½–4in) long
Flower Dark red, blue, white or purple flowers borne in racemes, 2.5–15cm (1–6in) long, in summer and autumn
Use As a specimen shrub in shrub or mixed borders; as an informal hedged planted at distances of 50–75cm (20–30in)
Needs Propagate from cuttings in summer. Cut back hard to ground level every 3–4 years
Varieties *H.* 'Great Orme' ♀ light green foliage, pink flowers • *H.* 'Marjorie' mid-green foliage, pale violet flowers • *H.* 'Midsummer Beauty' ♀ mid- to dark green foliage, pale purple-blue flowers • *H.* 'Pewter Dome' ♀ grey-green foliage, white flowers • *H. pimeleoides* 'Quicksilver' ♀ silver-grey foliage, white flowers • *H. pinguifolia* 'Pagei' ♀ glaucous grey-green foliage, small white flowers • *H.* 'Purple Queen' purple-green to purple foliage, purple flowers • *H. rakaiensis* ♀ bright green foliage, white flowers • *H.* 'Red Edge' ♀ grey, red-edged foliage, white flowers • *H. salicifolia* light green leaves, light blue flowers • *H.* 'Simon Delaux' ♀ light to mid-green foliage, crimson flowers

HIBISCUS SYRIACUS
Malvaceae
TREE HOLLYHOCK, MAL-
LOW, GIANT MALLOW

▲ ❀ ❦ SI autumn
H 5 yrs 1m (3ft)
S 5 yrs 1m (3ft)
H 10 yrs 1.5m (5ft)
S 10 yrs 1.5m (5ft)
❄ -15°C (4°F)
Z 5–9

**HIBISCUS SYRIACUS
'BLUE BIRD'**

The colourful flowers are a reminder of holidays in hot countries, and although this is not the vibrant form found in really warm places, it does have much of the same charm. A slow-growing species, it does not mix well with other plants and is best planted as a specimen, but is otherwise quite easy going and may only occasionally be damaged by late frosts.

Soil Open, well-drained soil
Aspect Very light shade but tolerates full sun
Habit Slow growing into a tall, upright, globe-shaped shrub
Leaf Deciduous, light grey to mid-green, ovate laves, 4–6cm (1½–2½in) long, with toothed edges; some varieties have white-variegated leaves; yellow autumn colour
Flower Single, semi-double or double, large, trumpet-shaped flowers in colours ranging through white, pink, blue and red to combinations of these colours
Use As late-summer to early-autumn-flowering shrub for planting on its own to show off shape
Needs Propagate from cuttings in summer. No pruning
Varieties *H. s.* 'Blue Bird' ♀ deep blue flowers • *H. s.* 'Hamabo' ♀ pink flowers • *H. s.* 'Jeanne d'Arc' semi-double, white flowers • *H. s.* 'Meehanii' (syn. *H. s.* 'Variegatus') white-variegated leaves, lilac-mauve flowers • *H. s.* 'Red Heart' ♀ white flowers with red eye • *H. s.* 'Russian Violet' ♀ violet-pink flowers • *H. s.* 'Speciosus' double, white flowers with red centre • *H. s.* 'William R. Smith' white flowers • *H. s.* 'Woodbridge' ♀ pink-red flowers

HIPPOPHAE RHAMNOIDES ♀
Elaeagnaceae
SEA BUCKTHORN

❦ SI summer–autumn
H 5 yrs 2m (6ft)
S 5 yrs 2m (6ft)
H 10 yrs 4m (13ft)
S 10 yrs 4m (13ft)
❄ -15°C (4°F)
Z 3–7

HIPPOPHAE RHAMNOIDES

Its silver foliage and speed of growth make this a useful shrub when a large plant is needed. The orange fruits are pretty, but there is no certainty that they will be produced. The male and female flowers are borne on separate plants, and at present the sexes are not separated in commercial production so you can never be sure whether you have a male or a female plant.

Soil Prefers light, sandy soil but tolerates both alkaline and acid conditions; can become invasive on sandy soils
Aspect Full sun or very light shade
Habit Upright, becoming branching and spreading with age to form a tall, round-topped shrub; the stems are armed with sharp spines, which can cause injury
Leaf Deciduous, attractive, silver-grey to grey-green, lance-shaped leaves, 2.5–6cm (1–2½in) long
Flower Sulphur yellow, inconspicuous, male or female flowers, singly sexed on individual plants; female plants produce large, attractive clusters of orange fruits in late summer and autumn
Use As a silver-leaved shrub, singly or in a group; ideal as a windbreak in maritime areas
Needs Propagate from seed sown in spring. No pruning required but can be reduced in size by cutting back in spring
Varieties None of garden interest

HOHERIA
Malvaceae
LACE BARK

▲ ❀ ✌ SI summer
H 5 yrs 2m (6ft)
S 5 yrs 2m (6ft)
H 10 yrs 3.5m (12ft)
S 10 yrs 3.5m (12ft)
❄ -5°C (23°F)
Z 4–8

HOHERIA SEXSTYLOSA

A beautiful flowering shrub, which deserves to be much more widely planted in gardens where it can be protected from winter cold. The flowers are spectacular, and the plant itself is easy going, tolerating most soil types and requiring no pruning.

Soil Prefers deep, rich, acid to neutral, light soil; tolerates some alkalinity
Aspect Prefers light shade but tolerates full sun; requires some protection in winter
Habit Upright, becoming branching and spreading with age to form a tall, round-topped shrub
Leaf Deciduous, grey to grey-green, ovate leaves, 5–11cm (2–4½in) long, sometimes toothed and lobed; yellow autumn colour
Flower White, saucer-shaped flowers borne in bold clusters
Use As a tall, midsummer-flowering shrub; good fan-trained on a sunny wall
Needs Propagate from cuttings or by layering. No pruning required but over-sized branches may be cut back
Varieties *H. glabrata* ♀ white flowers • *H. lyallii* (syn. *Gaya lyallii*, *Plagianthus lyalli*) ♀ clusters of white flowers • *H. populnea* large clusters of pure white flowers • *H. p.* 'Foliis Purpureis' undersides of leaves plum-coloured, white flowers • *H. p.* 'Variegata' yellow-green leaves, ageing to white with deep green margins, white flowers • *H. sexstylosa* ♀ large, upright shrub or small tree, narrow mature leaves, pure white flowers

HYDRANGEA
Hydrangeaceae
HYDRANGEA

▲ ❀ ✌ SI summer–autumn
H 5 yrs 1m (3ft)
S 5 yrs 1m (3ft)
H 10 yrs 2m (6ft)
S 10 yrs 2m (6ft)
❄ -15°C (4°F)
Z 6–10

HYDRANGEA MACROPHYLLA 'MISS BELGIUM'

Little need be said about this well-known shrub other than to note its ultimate size and need for moisture.

Soil Deep, rich, moist soil; acid soils produce blue flowers
Aspect Light shade; dislikes both full sun and deep shade
Habit Upright but spreading with age to become dome shaped
Leaf Deciduous, light to mid-green, large oval leaves, 10–20cm (4–8in) long and 10–15cm (4–6in) wide
Flower Lacecap varieties have round central clusters of flowers, white through pink to blue, surrounded by ray florets; mop-headed (hortensia) varieties ball shaped
Use As a free-standing shrub, massed, singly or in groups
Needs Propagate from cuttings. No pruning required. Avoid cutting back hard as this stop the following year's flowering
Varieties Lacecap: *H. macrophylla* 'Lanarth White' ♀ central flowers blue, ray florets pure white • *H. m.* 'Mariesii' central flowers rosy pink to blue-pink on acid soil • *H. m.* 'Mariesii Perfecta' (syn. *H. m.* 'Blue Wave') pink flowers on alkaline soil, blue on acid soil • *H. m.* 'Sea Foam' blue central flowers surrounded by white florets • *H. m.* 'Tricolor' ♀ pale pink variegation to mid-green leaves
Mop-headed: *H. macrophylla* 'Altona' cherry pink or mid-blue flowers • *H. m.* 'Deutschland' pale pink or pink-blue flowers • *H. m.* 'Hamburg' pink-rose or purple-rose flowers • *H. m.* 'Harry's Red' red or deep red flowers • *H. m.* 'Madame Emile Mouillère' ♀ pure white or white flowers with some pink shading • *H. m.* 'Miss Belgium' red to rose-red flowers

HYPERICUM
Clusiaceae/Guttiferae
ROSE OF SHARON,
ST JOHN'S WORT

❀ ✿ SI summer
H 5 yrs 60cm (2ft)
S 5 yrs 60cm (2ft)
H 10 yrs 1m (3ft)
S 10 yrs 1m (3ft)
❅ -15°C (4°F)
Z 6–9

HYPERICUM 'HIDCOTE'

This enduringly popular garden plant is always bright and cheerful, and it has few rivals when it comes to creating a splash of colour.

Soil Does well on most soils
Aspect Prefers light shade but tolerates full sun
Habit Upright, branching at extremities; ground-cover types spread by underground shoots
Leaf Deciduous and semi-evergreen, oval leaves, 2.5–8cm (1–3in) long and 2.5cm (1in) wide, mid-green, glossy and sometimes shaded red
Flower Good-sized, yellow, cup-shaped flowers in summer
Use As free-standing specimens or mass-planted; in shrub borders; as ground cover
Needs Propagate from cuttings in summer. Prune back hard in spring
Varieties *H. calycinum* ground cover, large, golden-yellow flowers • *H.* 'Hidcote' ♀ golden-yellow flowers • *H. × moserianum* ♀ golden-yellow flowers with red shading, prominent red anthers • *H.* 'Rowallane' ♀ large, golden-yellow, bowl-shaped flowers <u>Fruiting forms</u>: *H. androsaemum* (tutsan) red fruit, turning black • *H. × inodorum* 'Elstead' (syn. *H. elatum* 'Elstead') variegated and golden foliage, long, salmon red fruit • *H. × i.* 'Summer Gold' lime green to pale yellow leaves ageing to gold • *H. × i.* 'Ysella' very soft lime green foliage • *H. × moserianum* 'Tricolor' striped gold foliage with red shading • *H. patulum* 'Variegatum' long, narrow leaves, streaked with white variegation

---

ILEX
Aquifoliaceae
HOLLY

▲ ✿ SI all year E
H 5 yrs 2m (6ft)
S 5 yrs 1.5m (5ft)
H 10 yrs 4m (13ft)
S 10 yrs 2.5m (8ft)
❅ -25°C (-13°F)
Z 7–9

**ILEX AQUIFOLIUM
'HANDSWORTH NEW SILVER'**

The berry-laden branches are a traditional part of our Christmas decorations, but remember that you will need both male and female plants if you are to have fruit.

Soil Does well on any soil
Aspect Full sun to medium shade
Habit Upright, forming a pyramidal shrub or small tree
Leaf Evergreen, ovate leaves, 5–10cm (2–4in) long and 5–8cm (2–3in) wide, with some spines at outer lobed edges, glossy, waxy upper surfaces, mainly green, some variegated
Flower Small clusters of insignificant white flowers; female plants produce the attractive berries
Use As a free-standing shrub or tree
Needs Propagate from cuttings in early summer. No pruning
Varieties *I. × altaclerensis* 'Golden King' ♀ female, green on bright gold leaves • *I. × a.* 'Lawsoniana' ♀ female, dark green leaves bright yellow leaves variegation • *I. aquifolium* 'Argentea Marginata Pendula' (Perry's weeping holly) female, slow-growing, weeping • *I. a.* 'Bacciflava (syn. *I. a.* 'Fructu Luteo') female, bright yellow fruit • *I. a.* 'Golden Milkboy' ♀ male, green leaves with large golden centre • *I. a.* 'Golden Queen ♀ (syn. *I. a.* 'Aurea Regina) male, very dark green leaves edged with yellow • *I. a.* 'Golden van Tol' female, less spiny, golden margins to leaves • *I. a.* 'Handsworth New Silver' ♀ female, creamy-white margins to leaves, orange-red fruit • *I. a.* 'J.C. van Tol' ♀ female, dark green foliage, almost spineless • *I. a.* 'Madame Briot' ♀ female, dark green leaves with yellow-gold margins

INDIGOFERA
**Leguminosae/
Papilionaceae**
INDIGO BUSH

▲ ❀ ❦ SI summer
H 5 yrs 1.2m (4ft)
S 5 yrs 1.5m (5ft)
H 10 yrs 1.8m (5ft 6in)
S 10 yrs 2.5m (8ft)
❋ -10°C (14°F)
Z 6–8

This charming shrub is best described as delicate, but only as far as the habit, foliage and flower are concerned, for it is easy going when it comes to its needs and cultivation. It can be used either as a free-standing shrub or planted against a wall.

Soil Does well on all soil conditions, especially dry areas by walls once it is established
Aspect Full sun to very light shade
Habit Long and arching, becoming twiggy and shrub-forming; can be fan-trained to good effect
Leaf Attractive, deciduous, grey-green, pinnate leaves, 5–10cm (2–4in) long, with 13–21 leaflets to 1cm (½in) long
Flower Racemes of purple-pink pea flowers
Use As a midsummer- to early-autumn-flowering shrub for dry sunny areas; good as a fan-trained wall shrub, especially in colder areas, where it will attain one-third more height and spread than if free-standing
Needs Propagate from cuttings in spring or early summer. If not destroyed by winter cold, reduce long arching stems by two-thirds or more in spring to encourage new growth; in mild areas leave to encourage a large free-standing shrub
Varieties *I. heterantha* (syn. *I. gerardiana*) ♥ purple-pink pea flowers • *I. potaninii* long racemes of pink flowers to 10–13cm (4–5in)

INDIGOFERA HETERANTHA

ITEA
Escalloniaceae
SWEETSPIRE

▲ ❀ ❦ SI all year E some
H 5 yrs 1.2m (4ft)
S 5 yrs 1.5m (5ft)
H 10 yrs 1.8m (5ft 6in)
S 10 yrs 2.5m (8ft)
❋ -5°C (23°F)
Z 6–8

Itea ilicifolia is a gem of a plant, and although it is a little tender, it is worth growing where the shelter of a wall can be provided. The hanging, long, yellow, catkin-like, summer racemes are pretty, if not spectacular. *I. virginiana* is not as flamboyant in appearance.

Soil Does well on almost any soil except very dry or wet
Aspect Prefers light shade but tolerates full sun to medium shade; leaves are easily damaged by severe wind chill
Habit *I. ilicifolia*: strong and upright when young, becoming weeping with age to form a round, drooping effect when free-standing or a cascading weeping shrub when grown against a wall or fence; *I. virginiana*: more bushy and shrub-forming
Leaf *I. ilicifolia*: evergreen, dark glossy green leaves with purple hue underlying base colour and silver undersides; *I. virginiana*: deciduous light green, some yellow autumn colour; both oval, 5–13cm (2–5in) long
Flower *I. ilicifolia*: white, green to green-white ageing to yellow-green, catkin-like racemes, to 40cm (16in) long; *I. virginiana*: shorter flowers
Use As a free-standing shrub in mild areas; as a wall shrub in colder areas
Needs Propagate from cuttings in summer. Normally requires no pruning
Varieties *I. ilicifolia* racemes of fragrant green to green-white flowers to 40cm (16in) long • *I. virginiana* light green leaves, round, upright, fragrant creamy-white racemes

ITEA ILICIFOLIA

JASMINUM
Oleaceae
JASMINE

▲ ❀ ❦ SI summer E some
H 5 yrs 1.5m (5ft)
S 5 yrs 1.5m (5ft)
H 10 yrs 2m (6ft)
S 10 yrs 2m (6ft)
✷ -15°C (4°F)
Z 7–10

JASMINUM HUMILE 'REVOLUTUM'

Jasmine is often thought of as a climbing plant, but some forms grow as shrubs. Although they are not spectacular in flower, they do have a certain charm, and given the space to grow and careful siting they can be used in an architectural role. Regular pruning is necessary, but they need little other attention.

Soil Any soil; often tolerates poor conditions
Aspect Tolerates a range of conditions from sun through to medium shade
Habit Upright or more lax in growth depending on variety
Leaf Deciduous or evergreen, bright green, 3-fingered leaves, to 2cm (¾in) long; some yellow autumn foliage colour
Flower Small, short, trumpet-shaped flowers in shades of yellow
Use As a free-standing shrub for either summer or winter flowers; *J. humile* 'Revolutum' and *J. nudiflorum* do well as wall shrubs
Needs Propagate from cuttings in summer. After flowering, remove one-third of shoots, choosing the oldest, cutting to ground level on mature established shrubs
Varieties *J. humile* 'Revolutum' ♀ evergreen, bright green leaves, ovate to round in groups of 5–7 leaflets, clusters of deep yellow flowers • *J. nudiflorum* (winter jasmine) ♀ long, leafless, dark green arching branches in winter, covered by bright yellow flowers, can be used as a wall shrub • *J. parkeri* dwarf, prostrate, spreading shrub, forming a low mound, tiny yellow flowers in summer

KALMIA LATIFOLIA
Ericaceae
CALICO BUSH, SPOON WOOD, MOUNTAIN LAUREL

▲ ❀ ❦ SI spring E
H 5 yrs 1.5m (5ft)
S 5 yrs 1.5m (5ft)
H 10 yrs 2m (6ft)
S 10 yrs 2m (6ft)
✷ -10°C (14°F)
Z 3–5

KALMIA LATIFOLIA

An aristocrat among shrubs, this kalmia has the most wonderful displays of flowers, and it should be given a position where it can be seen to best advantage. Like all rhododendron-type plants it requires an acid soil if it is to thrive and flower to the full. The degree of light and shade can also be important.

Soil Deep, moist, rich acid soil; dislikes alkalinity
Aspect Prefers full light but will tolerate full sun provided soil is adequately moist
Habit Upright when young, quickly becoming spreading and bushy with age; can eventually reach dimensions of a small tree
Leaf Evergreen, large, elliptical leaves, 10–15cm (4–6in) long and 4–5cm (1½–2in) wide, mid-green with purple veins
Flower Large clusters of attractive, saucer-shaped, bright pink to red flowers in spring; interesting when in bud
Use As a flowering shrub to grow with rhododendrons; good in large containers when a lime-free potting compost is used
Needs Propagate from commercial layers in summer. Requires no pruning, but old shrubs can be reduced in size
Varieties *K. latifolia* ♀ large clusters of pink flowers • *K. l.* 'Bullseye' white flowers • *K. l.* 'Clementine Churchill' deep red flowers • *K. l.* 'Elf' compact habit, white opening to pink flowers • *K. l.* f. *myrtifolia* smaller leaves, smaller pink flowers • *K. l.* 'Ostbo Red' ♀ red buds opening to dark pink flowers

SHRUBS

KERRIA
Rosaceae
JEW'S MALLOW,
SAILOR'S BUTTON

❀ SI winter–spring
H 5 yrs 1m (3ft)
S 5 yrs 1m (3ft)
H 10 yrs 1.2m (4ft)
S 10 yrs 1.2m (4ft)
❄ -25°C (-13°F)
Z 5–9

**KERRIA JAPONICA
'PLENIFLORA'**

This shrub has been grown for centuries. The flowers are well known, but the green winter stems should not be overlooked, and they can be encouraged to the full by the right pruning. Although it is sometimes regarded as invasive, planted in the right place its display can brighten a dull winter day.

Soil Any soil type and conditions
Aspect Full sun to medium shade
Habit Strong, upright and spreading; low-growing forms are bushy and round
Leaf Deciduous, bright green, elliptic leaves, 4–8cm (1½–3in) long; some silver and white variegated forms
Flower Single or double, buttercup-shaped flowers in shades of yellow in spring
Use As a spring-flowering shrub for a shrub border; for mass-planting on banks and difficult areas; for its winter green stems; can be grown against a wall to good effect
Needs Propagate from underground suckers or cuttings in winter or summer. Prune by cutting all shoots to ground level in mid- to late spring after flowering. On variegated forms only remove old and dying wood in early spring. Also cut hard down every third spring after flowering to rejuvenate
Varieties K. japonica green winter stems, single, yellow flowers in spring • K. j. 'Picta' (syn. K. j. 'Variegata') creamy-white variegated foliage, single yellow flowers • K. j. 'Pleniflora' (syn. K. j. 'Flore Pleno') ♀ double, golden-yellow flowers • K. j. 'Splendens' single, larger buttercup-yellow flowers

KOLKWITZIA
Caprifoliaceae
BEAUTY BUSH

▲ ❀ ❦ SI spring–autumn
H 5 yrs 1.5m (5ft)
S 5 yrs 1.5m (5ft)
H 10 yrs 2.5m (8ft)
S 10 yrs 2.5m (8ft)
❄ -15°C (4°F)
Z 4–9

KOLKWITZIA AMABILIS

The common name of this plant sums up its appearance when it is in full flower. The long, arching branches are covered with flowers from end to end. Often growing larger than anticipated, it needs room to develop its shape fully. The autumn foliage colour is a bonus.

Soil Any soil except very dry
Aspect Prefers full sun but tolerates light shade
Habit Strong and upright at first, becoming arched and spreading with age
Leaf Deciduous, ovate leaves, 2.5–4cm (1–1½in) long, light olive green to grey-green with red shading and silver undersides and slightly toothed edges; good autumn colour
Flower Pink, bell-shaped flowers borne in late spring or early summer in small, bold clusters along the branches of plants from 2 years old
Use As a medium sized to large shrub to stand on its own, forming an attractive symmetrical clump or for use in a large shrub border
Needs Propagate from cuttings in summer. Prune by removing one-third of shoots, choosing the oldest, by cutting to ground level after flowering
Varieties K. amabilis soft pink flowers with a yellow throat, the main variety to be grown • K. a. 'Pink Cloud' ♀ strong deeper pink flowers, may be less vigorous than type species

LAURUS
Lauraceae
BAY

▲ ❀ ❦ SI all year E
H 5 yrs 1.5m (5ft)
S 5 yrs 1m (3ft)
H 10 yrs 2.5m (8ft)
S 10 yrs 2m (6ft)
❅ -5°C (23°F)
Z 8–10

LAURUS NOBILIS

A large shrub or small tree, the leaves of which have been used as a herb since Roman times and possibly before. It is still grown for its culinary value, but it can also be planted for its ornamental foliage and flowers. Its hardiness can be suspect, and in cold gardens it may need some protection. It is possible to clip and train bushes to create geometric shapes.

Soil Tolerates most types of soil; use good quality potting compost when planting in containers
Aspect Full sun to light shade; tolerates moderate shade
Habit Upright, becoming branching and forming a natural pyramidal shape; can be grown in a number of topiary shapes, including mop-headed standards
Leaf Evergreen, dark green or yellow, oval leaves, 5–10cm (2–4in) long, with glossy upper surfaces and dull grey-green undersides; a golden-leaved variety is worth growing
Flower Yellow-green flowers in small tufts with very prominent stamens produced in summer
Use As a free-standing, large evergreen for mild locations; can be clipped to a pyramid ball or short pompon-top standard; does well in large containers; green-leaved form used in cooking
Needs Propagate from cuttings taken in summer. Can be clipped hard as required and will rejuvenate if reduced to ground level
Varieties *L. nobilis* ♀ dark green evergreen leaves • *L. n.* 'Aurea' ♀ golden-yellow evergreen leaves

LAVANDULA
Lamiaceae/Labiatae
LAVENDER

▲ ❀ ❦ SI summer SC E
H 5 yrs 50cm (20in)
S 5 yrs 60cm (2ft)
H 10 yrs 75cm (30in)
S 10 yrs 75cm (30in)
❅ -10°C (14°F)
Z 5–10

LAVANDULA ANGUSTIFOLIA 'HIDCOTE'

Scent, flowers, aromatic foliage and versatility – this plant has them all. For centuries used in cosmetic preparations, lavender has rightly gained a place in gardens of all sizes.

Soil Light and well-drained soil; dislikes waterlogging
Aspect Full sun; dislikes shade
Habit Limited branching, upright or spreading, surmounted by tall, flower-carrying stems
Leaf Evergreen, aromatic, narrowly lance-shaped, grey- to silver-green
Flower Upright, very sweetly scented spikes in shades of blue, pink or white
Use As low shrubs for edging in shrub borders, planted singly or in groups; dwarf varieties are useful for under-planting; as a hedge when planted at distances of 40cm (16in)
Needs Propagate from cuttings in summer. Prune by hard to medium trimming in spring as new growth starts. Remove dead flowers
Varieties *L. angustifolia* (syn. *L. officinalis*, *L. spica*; Old English lavender) ♀ mid-blue flowers • *L. a.* 'Alba' white flowers • *L. a.* 'Hidcote' ♀ violet-blue, very thick flowers • *L. a.* 'Loddon Pink' pale blue to pink-blue flowers • *L. a.* 'Munstead' lavender-blue flowers, use for hedging or under-planting • *L. a.* 'Nana Alba' white flowers, to 30cm (1ft) • *L. a.* 'Rosea' blue-pink to pink flowers • *L. a.* 'Twickel Purple' ♀ lavender-blue to purple flowers • *L. stoechas* (French lavender) ♀ scented dark purple flowers, tender • *L. s.* var. *albiflora* scented white flowers, tender

LAVATERA
Malvaceae
TREE MALLOW,
TREE LAVATERA

❀ ❦ SI summer–autumn
H 5 yrs 2.5m (8ft)
S 5 yrs 2m (6ft)
H 10 yrs 3m (10ft)
S 10 yrs 3m (10ft)
❋ -5°C (23°F)
Z 8–10

LAVATERA 'ROSEA'

These large, bold and very showy shrubs are available in a range of varieties and colours. They must be correctly pruned if they are to do well and be long lived, and they need careful positioning if they are not to overpower neighbouring plants.

Soil Light, moisture-retentive soil, both acid and alkaline
Aspect Full sun; tolerates very light shade
Habit Strong and upright, spreading with age
Leaf Deciduous, light green to grey-green, broad, hand-shaped, 5-lobed leaves, 8–10cm (3–4in) long and wide
Flower Numerous large, saucer-shaped pink to silver-pink, white and mauve flowers open for a day and are then replaced; main flowering in summer but intermittent flowers continue to appear until the first frost of winter
Use As a late-flowering summer shrub, either on its own or in a large shrub border
Needs Propagate from cuttings in winter or early summer. Cut all shoots produced in spring and summer to within 5cm (2in) in mid- to late spring to encourage new strong flowering shoots and to prevent the plant from dying out
Varieties *L.* 'Barnsley' ♀ silver-pink flowers, can revert to type species • *L.* 'Bredon Springs' mauve-flushed pink flowers • *L.* 'Bressingham Pink' pale pink flowers • *L.* 'Burgundy Wine' very dark pink flowers • *L.* 'Candy Floss' pale pink flowers • *L.* 'Kew Rose' bright pink flowers • *L.* 'Rosea' (syn. *L. arborea* 'Rosea') ♀ the main pink-flowering variety • *L. thuringiaca* 'Ice Cool' (syn. *L. t.* 'Peppermint') white flowers

---

LEUCOTHOE
Ericaceae
DROOPING LEUCOTHOE,
FETTERBUSH

▲ ❦ SI all year E
H 5 yrs 1m (3ft)
S 5 yrs 1m (3ft)
H 10 yrs 1.5m (5ft)
S 10 yrs 2m (6ft)
❋ -10°C (14°F)
Z 8–10

**LEUCOTHOE WALTERI
'RAINBOW'**

A useful evergreen plant with attractive foliage that has specific soil and environmental requirements if it is to thrive. It is useful all year round, but comes into its own in winter, when it is often planted in containers for decorative effect.

Soil Rich, deep, acid to neutral soil that is high in organic material; dislikes alkalinity
Aspect Does best in light shade; dislikes full sun
Habit Upright when young, quickly becoming arching; spreads by non-invasive underground shoots
Leaf Evergreen, leathery, broadly lance-shaped, purple-tinged green leaves, 5–10cm (2–4in) long, turning rich red or bronze-purple in autumn and winter
Flower Hanging racemes of small, off-white, pitcher-shaped flowers in summer
Use As a medium sized shrub for underplanting or ground cover; can be planted in its own right as a feature plant; good for short-term container planting
Needs Propagate from cuttings in summer. Cut back one-third of shoots, choosing the oldest wood, to ground level each spring on established plants to encourage growth of new, clean, attractive foliage
Varieties • *L.* 'Scarletta' dark red new foliage in spring turning dark green later • *L. walteri* (syn. *L. fontanesiana*) purple-tinged green leaves, white flowers • *L. w.* 'Rainbow' (syn. *L. w.* 'Multicolor') creamy yellow and pink variegated leaves, white flowers • *L. w.* 'Rollissonii' ♀ narrower leaves, good winter colour, white flowers

LEYCESTERIA FORMOSA
Caprifoliaceae
PHEASANT BERRY, HIM-
ALAYAN HONEYSUCKLE

▲ ❀ ✾ SI autumn–winter
H 5 yrs 2.5m (8ft)
S 3 yrs 2.5m (8ft)
H 10 yrs 2.5m (8ft)
S 10 yrs 3.5m (12ft)
❄ -10°C (14°F)
Z 8–10

LEYCESTERIA FORMOSA

An attractive shrub that offers flower, fruit and winter stem interest, the fruits also being of value to wildlife in winter. Given the right treatment, the winter stems can be really beautiful, and there is the added bonus that the shape of the plant and the flowers and fruits are improved.

Soil Almost any soil except very dry
Aspect Full sun to light shade
Habit Upright, spreading, open-topped shrub with attractive mid-green winter stems
Leaf Deciduous, pointed, broad, lance-shaped leaves, 5–18cm (2–7in) long, dark green to olive green with some red shading; some yellow autumn colour
Flower Heavy racemes of white flowers surmounted by long, pendent, purple-red bracts in late summer, followed by an abundance of attractive, round, deep purple, glossy fruit
Use As a flowering shrub on its own or in a large shrub border; good for mass-planting, especially for winter effect; combines well with water features
Needs Propagate from seed sown in spring; will self-seed but not invasively. Cut all shoots to within a few inches of ground level in early to mid-spring as winter stem display is no longer required. May attract wasps to the garden when in flower or fruit
Varieties *L. formosa* is the only species grown

LIGUSTRUM
Oleaceae
PRIVET

▲ ❀ ✾ SI spring–autumn
E some
H 5 yrs 0.5–3m (20in–10ft)
S 5 yrs 0.3–3m (1–10ft)
H 10 yrs 0.75–4m (30in–13ft)
S 10 yrs 0.5–4m (20in–13ft)
❄ -25°C (-13°F)
Z 4–9

**LIGUSTRUM OVALIFOLIUM
'ARGENTEUM'**

Often regarded as a rather mundane genus, *Ligustrum* actually contains many interesting forms. Undemanding and always reliable, several varieties are worthy of wider use.

Soil Most but will not thrive in extremely dry soil
Aspect Full sun to very deep shade
Habit Upright, vigorous, branching with age to form a round-topped, dome-shaped shrub
Leaf Deciduous to semi-evergreen, ovate, pointed leaves, 2.5–4cm (1–1½in) long, mid- to dark green, pale yellow and golden, with some variegated forms
Flower Short, upright panicles of whitish flowers with a musty scent are borne in midsummer
Use As a compact, semi-evergreen hedge planted at distances of 50cm (20in); can be used as a windbreak
Needs Propagate from cuttings in summer or winter. May be reduced to ground level and will rejuvenate
Varieties *L. ovalifolium* (California privet) green hedging privet • *L. o.* 'Argenteum' grey-green leaves with creamy-white margins • *L. o.* 'Aureum' (golden privet) ♀ rich golden-yellow leaves with green centres • *L. quihoui* ♀ grey to olive-green leaves, large panicles of white to creamy-white flowers • *L. sinense* (Chinese privet) mid-green leaves, panicles of white flowers • *L.* 'Vicaryi' (golden Vicary privet, golden privet) lime green leaves, ageing to golden-yellow in summer, creamy-white flowers on mature shrubs • *L. vulgare* (common privet, European privet) dark green, pointed leaves, short, wide-based racemes of off-white flowers

LONICERA
Caprifoliaceae
SHRUBBY
HONEYSUCKLE

✽ ❦ SI winter–summer SC
E some
H 5 yrs 0.4–3m (16in–10ft)
S 5 yrs 1.2–3m (4–10ft)
H 10 yrs 0.75–4m (30in–13ft)
S 10 yrs 2–4m (6–13ft)
✽ -25°C (-13°F)
Z 2–9

LONICERA × PURPUSII

Like their climbing cousins, these interesting shrubs carry the scent if not the size of flower. Although they are mostly deciduous, there are some useful ground-cover evergreens.

Soil Most but dislikes extremely alkaline soil
Aspect Full sun to light shade
Habit Upright, becoming branching with age
Leaf Deciduous or evergreen, bright green, grey to grey-green or dark green, oval leaves
Flower Small clusters of fragrant, yellow, lilac or pink flowers in winter or summer, followed by red fruit
Use As free-standing shrubs or in a mixed or shrub border
Needs Propagate from cuttings in summer. Cut back one-third of old flowering shoots to ground level after flowering
Varieties <u>Winter flowering</u>: *L. fragrantissima* (winter honeysuckle) small, scented, creamy-white flowers • *L.* × *purpusii* fragrant, white flowers • *L.* × 'Spring Purple' new foliage purple-green, fragrant, white flowers • *L. standishii* fragrant, white flowers, red fruit <u>Summer flowering</u>: *L. nitida* (poor man's box) evergreen, small, scented, sulphur yellow flowers, good for hedging at distances of 60cm (2ft) • *L. n.* 'Baggesen's Gold' ♀ evergreen, yellow foliage • *L. pileata* (privet honeysuckle) low growing, evergreen, small, scented, pale yellow flowers • *L. p.* 'Silver Beauty' low growing, evergreen, white-variegated leaves • *L. rupicola* var. *syringantha* (lilac-scented shrubby honeysuckle) tall growing small, fragrant, lilac-coloured flowers • *L. tatarica* 'Hack's Red' (tatarian honeysuckle) deep rose-pink flowers

LOTUS HIRSUTUS
Leguminosae/
Papilionaceae
HAIRY CANARY CLOVER

▲ ✽ ❦ SI all year E
H 5 yrs 60cm (2ft)
S 5 yrs 75cm (30in)
H 10 yrs 75cm (30in)
S 10 yrs 1m (3ft)
✽ -5°C (23°F)
Z 3–10

LOTUS HIRSUTUS

This plant, which used to be known as *Dorycnium hirsutum*, provides interest all year – the evergreen leaves are a silvery colour and the clover-like flowers are followed by mahogany-brown seedheads – and its gentle pendulous habit makes it ideal for planting in isolation or in groups. Although its hardiness is a little suspect, if it is carefully sited in a sunny spot it should survive all but the very coldest winters. Pruning is important if it is to grow to best effect.

Soil Most but shows distress on very alkaline, dry soil
Aspect Full sun to very light shade; does best in a warm, sunny corner that provides winter protection
Habit Upright, becoming arching and spreading
Leaf Small, attractive, evergreen, oval, silver-green leaves, borne in a ring at regular intervals up the wiry stems
Flower Small, pale pink to off-white, clover-like flowers, 5mm (¼in) long and wide, through late spring to autumn, followed by small clusters of mahogany-brown, torpedo-shaped fruit
Use As a specimen plant; in a shrub or mixed border; often used among paving
Needs Propagate from cuttings in summer. Often self-seeds invasively. Prune by cutting all previous year's shoots to ground level in mid- to late spring just before new growth starts
Varieties None of garden interest

MAGNOLIA
Magnoliaceae
MAGNOLIA

▲ ❀ ❦ SI spring–summer
SC E some
H 5 yrs 1–2m (3–6ft)
S 5 yrs 1–2m (3–6ft)
H 10 yrs 2–4m (6–13ft)
S 10 yrs 2–4m (6–13ft)
❄ -10°C (14°F)
Z 4–9

**MAGNOLIA ×
SOULANGEANA**

The genus offers a very wide range of interest, from the star-
or tulip-shaped blooms of the spring-flowering varieties to the
hanging cups of the summer-flowering forms.

Soil Neutral to acid soils; dislikes alkalinity
Aspect Prefers light shade; tolerates medium shade and sun
Habit Upright and spreading, forming a round shrub
Leaf Deciduous or evergreen, long oval leaves, from dark to
bright or light to grey-green
Flower Creamy-white, white, pale to deep pink or purple,
globe-, tulip-, saucer- or star-shaped blooms
Use As a free-standing feature or in a large shrub border
Needs Propagate by layering or summer cuttings. No pruning
Varieties Spring flowering: *M. liliiflora* 'Nigra' ♀ reflexed,
star-shaped flowers, deep purple outside, white-purple inside
• *M. × loebneri* 'Leonard Messel' ♀ fragrant, deep pink
flowers, opening lilac-pink • *M. × l.* 'Merrill' ♀ large,
fragrant, white, star-shaped flowers • *M. × soulangeana*
(saucer magnolia, tulip magnolia, Chinese magnolia) pink
flowers with purple bar • *M. × s.* 'Alba Superba' (syn. *M. ×
s.* 'Alba') large, scented, white, tulip-shaped flowers • *M. ×
s.* 'Lennei' ♀ goblet-shaped flowers, rose-purple on outside,
white-stained purple within • *M. stellata* (star magnolia) ♀
white, slightly scented, narrow, strap-like, star-shaped
flowers Summer flowering: *M. grandiflora* (large-flowered
magnolia) evergreen, large, creamy-white, fragrant flowers
• *M. sieboldii* (syn. *M. parviflora*) ♀ fragrant, white, cup-
shaped flowers with rose-pink to crimson central stamens

MAHONIA
Berberidaceae
OREGON GRAPE,
HOLLY GRAPE

▲ ❀ ❦ SI all year SC
some E
5 yrs 1–1.5m (3–5ft)
S 5 yrs 1–1.2m (3–4ft)
H 10 yrs 1–3m (3–10ft)
S 10 yrs 1–3m (3–10ft)
❄ -25°C (-13°F)
Z 4–8

**MAHONIA AQUIFOLIUM
'APOLLO'**

Two forms are of interest: one has candle-like flowers, the
other rosettes or racemes of often scented yellow flowers.

Soil Tolerates an extremely wide range of conditions but may
show distress on very dry or alkaline soil
Aspect Full sun to very light shade; becomes lax in deep
shade
Habit Upright or bushy, depending on variety; may not
branch unless correctly pruned
Leaf Large, evergreen, dark green, pinnate leaves with small
spines on ends and a reddish hue
Flower Upright yellow candles in late spring or long racemes
in late winter, some fragrant; may be followed by blue fruit
Use Free standing or in a large shrub border; single or mass-
planting; candle-flowering forms can be used as ground cover
Needs Propagate from summer cuttings. Terminal clusters of
foliage to be removed after flowering to encourage branching
Varieties *M. aquifolium* yellow flowers in upright candles •
M. a. 'Apollo' ♀ bold yellow flowers in upright candles •
M. a. 'Atropurpurea' purple-red to bronze-red foliage, yellow
flowers • *M. japonica* ♀ racemes of yellow to lemon-yellow,
fragrant flowers • *M. × media* 'Buckland' racemes of yellow
flowers, followed by blue-black fruit • *M. × m.* 'Charity' ♀
bright yellow racemes to 20–25cm (8–10in) long • *M. × m.*
'Lionel Fortescue' ♀ upright racemes of scented, yellow
flowers • *M. × m.* 'Winter Sun' ♀ upright racemes of
scented, yellow flowers • *M. × wagneri* 'Undulata' ♀ short,
stout candles of yellow flowers

MYRTUS
Myrtaceae
MYRTLE

▲ ❀ ❦ SI all year SC E
H 5 yrs 1m (3ft)
S 5 yrs 1m (3ft)
H 10 yrs 2m (6ft)
S 10 yrs 2m (6ft)
❄ -5°C (23°F)
Z 8–10

Once thought to carry the gift of fertility, myrtle has long been valued for its fragrant leaves. Easy going as far as its cultural requirements are concerned, it is, unfortunately, not reliably hardy in the coldest gardens.

Soil Does best on well-drained soil; tolerates both alkalinity and acidity
Aspect Full sun to mid-shade
Habit Upright, becoming branching and shrub-forming with age; after 20 years can achieve the proportions of a small tree
Leaf Evergreen, round to ovate leaves, 2.5–5cm (1–2in) long, dark green with a duller underside; a silver-variegated form is more tender; all forms have attractive winter bark
Flower Small, tufted white flowers appear in profusion in early summer
Use As a free-standing, evergreen shrub or, in colder gardens, as a wall shrub; can be grown in a container, when size will be limited; as a hedge planted at distances of 60cm (2ft)
Needs Propagate from cuttings in summer. No pruning required but can be cut back hard or trimmed
Varieties *M. apiculata* (syn. *M. luma*, *Luma apiculata*) tufted white flowers borne singly at each leaf axil cover the shrub in late summer, followed by edible red to black fruit • *M. communis* (common myrtle) ♀ white, round, tufted flowers, purple-black fruit • *M. c.* ssp. *tarentina* ♀ white tufted flowers, white berries • *M. c.* 'Variegata' creamy-white margins to leaves

MYRTUS COMMUNIS

OLEARIA
Asteraceae/Compositae
DAISY BUSH

▲ ❀ ❦ SI all year E
H 5 yrs 1m (3ft)
S 5 yrs 1m (3ft)
H 10 yrs 2m (6ft)
S 10 yrs 2m (6ft)
❄ -5°C (23°F)
Z 8–10

The olearia originated in New Zealand, but it has gained a rightful place in gardens in the northern hemisphere as few other shrubs offer as much in the way of flower and foliage. It has no particular soil requirements, which makes it versatile, but its hardiness is suspect in cold areas.

Soil Most; will tolerate moderately dry soils
Aspect Full sun; dislikes shade
Habit Upright, becoming branching and shrub-forming
Leaf Evergreen, sea green to grey-green leaves, normally ovate but with some variation of shape and size according to variety
Flower Clusters of daisy-like, white, creamy-white, pink or blue flowers in summer
Use As a free-standing shrub in medium sized to large shrub borders; as a wall shrub for a sheltered sunny aspect; good in containers; as a hedge planted at distances of 75cm (30in)
Needs Propagate from cuttings taken in summer. Remove one-third of old flowering wood after flowering to encourage rejuvenation. Can be trimmed if required
Varieties *O.* × *haastii* masses of fragrant white flowers • *O.* × *macrodonta* (New Zealand holly) ♀ clusters of white flowers • *O. nummariifolia* small, fragrant, white flowers • *O. phlogopappa* (syn. *O. gunniana*; Tasmanian daisy bush) panicles of white flowers • *O. p.* Splendens Group (syn. *O. stellulata* 'Splendens') blue, white or pink flowers • *O. p.* var. *subrepanda* (syn. *O. subrepanda*) white flowers • *O.* × *scilloniensis* masses of white flowers

OLEARIA × HAASTII

OSMANTHUS
Oleaceae
SWEET OLIVE,
CHINESE HOLLY

▲ ✿ SI all year SC E
H 5 yrs 1–2m (3–6ft)
S 5 yrs 1–2m (3–6ft)
H 10 yrs 1–3m (3–10ft)
S 10 yrs 1–3m (3–10ft)
❄ -10°C (14°F)
Z 8–10

**OSMANTHUS HETERO-
PHYLLUS 'VARIEGATUS'**

This useful late-winter- to early-spring-flowering shrub offers not only flowers but scent as well.

Soil Most but resents waterlogged or very dry conditions
Aspect Light, dappled shade but tolerates full sun
Habit Upright, becoming more branching with age
Leaf Evergreen, oval leaves, 1–4cm (½–1½in) long, with soft, holly-like points around edges
Flower White or cream, trumpet-shaped, scented flowers
Use As a free-standing shrub for medium sized to large shrub borders; as a hedge planted at distances of 60cm (2ft); in a container
Needs Propagate from cuttings in summer. No pruning required but may be trimmed
Varieties *O. armatus* white, sweetly scented flowers • *O.* × *burkwoodii* (syn. × *Osmarea burkwoodii*) ♀ white, very fragrant flowers • *O. delavayi* ♀ very sweetly scented white flowers • *O. heterophyllus* (syn. *O. ilicifolius*; holly osmanthus, false holly) small to medium dark green, holly-shaped leaves, white, scented, tubular flowers • *O. h.* 'Aureomarginatus' holly-like leaves with golden-yellow to deep yellow variegated margins, white flowers • *O. h.* 'Gulftide' ♀ leaves twisted and lobed with strong spines, white, scented flowers • *O. h.* 'Purpureus' holly-shaped, purple leaves, white, purple-tinged flowers • *O. h.* 'Rotundifolius' round, tooth-edged, leathery, dark green leaves, white, scented flowers • *O. h.* 'Variegatus' ♀ holly-like, grey-green leaves with creamy-white borders

---

PACHYSANDRA
Buxaceae
MOUNTAIN SPURGE

▲ ✿ ✾ SI all year E
H 5 yrs 20cm (8in)
S 5 yrs 1m (3ft)
H 10 yrs 30cm (1ft)
S 10 yrs 1.5m (5ft)
❄ -10°C (14°F)
Z 5–9

PACHYSANDRA TERMINALIS

Pachysandras are grown mostly for their foliage, and they are useful ground-covering plants for shady areas. They look especially well grown in association with rhododendrons and other acid-loving plants in a woodland setting.

Soil Acid to neutral soil that is moisture retentive and high in organic material
Aspect Does best in shade, although tolerates full sun as long as soil does not dry out
Habit A low-growing carpet, spreading by means of non-invasive suckers
Leaf Evergreen, glossy green, diamond-shaped leaves with toothed edges, 2.5–8cm (1–3in) long; a silver to white variegated form is worth planting although slower growing and requiring even more organic material in the soil to do well
Flower Spikes of green-white flowers, ageing to white, produced at terminals of previous year's shoots
Use As a low-growing carpeting shrub for acid soils; good for mass-planting; ideal for planting around rhododendrons and similar plants in woodland situations
Needs Propagate by division or from cuttings in early summer. If untidy or foliage is damaged, hard trimming in early spring will encourage a new leaf canopy
Varieties *P. terminalis* ♀ green-white flowers ageing to white • *P. t.* 'Variegata' ♀ white-edged leaves, white flowers

PAEONIA
Paeoniaceae
TREE PEONY

▲ ❀ ✔ SI summer
H 5 yrs 1.5m (5ft)
S 5 yrs 2m (6ft)
H 10 yrs 2.5m (8ft)
S 10 yrs 4m (13ft)
❋ -10°C (14°F)
Z 3–8

These slow-growing but long-lived shrubs are grown for their striking foliage and wonderful flowers, which look as if they have been created from exotically coloured tissue paper. They can be the stars of any garden and are surprisingly robust. Cultivars of *P. suffruticosa* are available but not widely.

Soil Most, only disliking very dry or wet conditions; added organic material helps root growth
Aspect Prefers full sun but tolerates light shade
Habit Irregular in shape, which often adds to the charm, except for *P. lutea* var. *ludlowii*, which is a round, spreading, large shrub; all are slow to mature
Leaf Deciduous, light green to mid-green, large, lobed and cut leaves, pinnate to 20–25cm (8–10in) across; *P. suffruticosa* has greyish-blue sheen; all have yellow autumn foliage colour
Flower Cup- or saucer-shaped flowers in colours from white, pink and red to yellow with bi-colours
Use As a free-standing specimen shrub or in medium sized to large shrub borders
Needs Propagate from seed. Nor pruning required except for *P. lutea* var. *ludlowii*, on which, 3–5 years after planting, remove one-third of oldest flowering shoots each year in early spring to encourage new growth
Varieties *P. delavayi* ♀ blood-red flowers with golden stamens • *P. lutea* var. *ludlowii* ♀ golden-yellow, saucer-shaped flowers • *P. suffruticosa* (Japanese tree peony) large, double, cup-shaped flowers in range of colours

PAEONIA DELAVAYI VAR. LUDLOWII

PEROVSKIA
Lamiaceae/Labiatae
RUSSIAN SAGE

❀ ✔ SI summer–autumn
H 5 yrs 75cm (30in)
S 5 yrs 1m (3ft)
H 10 yrs 75cm (30in)
S 10 yrs 1m (3ft)
❋ -10°C (14°F)
Z 7–10

As its common name suggests, this plant does indeed originate in Russia, but it does not look like a sage, although it is in the same plant family. Given a little support, its long, graceful, silver stems and leaves are of real value, and they are topped with delightful flower spikes.

Soil Well-drained, alkaline to acid soil but dislikes very dry conditions
Aspect Full sun; dislikes shade of any degree, becoming weak and straggly in growth
Habit Upright, spreading when in flower, when it always requires support
Leaf Deciduous, grey, aromatic, oval, deeply toothed leaves, 2.5–6cm (1–2½in) long, borne on silver-white, down-covered stems, which are attractive and worth retaining into winter
Flower Lavender-blue panicles of small flowers to 2.5–4cm (1–1⅛in) long in late summer to early autumn
Use As a grey-leaved shrub, massed on its own or for edging small to medium shrub borders; can be treated as a herbaceous plant for mixed borders; good in association with pink-flowering plants
Needs Propagate from cuttings in spring or summer. Reduce all shoots to ground level each spring to induce new, attractive silver shoots and leaves as well as the late-summer flowers
Varieties *P. atriplicifolia* ♀ lavender-blue flowers • *P. a.* 'Blue Spire' ♀ large panicles of lavender-blue flowers, the main variety now planted

PEROVSKIA ATRIPLICIFOLIA 'BLUE SPIRE'

PHILADELPHUS
Hydrangeaceae
MOCK ORANGE

▲ ❀ ❦ SI summer SC
H 5 yrs 0.6–3m (2–10ft)
S 5 yrs 1–2m (3–6ft)
H 10 yrs 1–4m (3–13ft)
S 10 yrs 1–3m (3–10ft)
❄ -10°C (14°F)
Z 5–9

PHILADELPHUS 'VIRGINAL'

The flowers that appear in midsummer have a wonderful fragrance, and some cultivars have the bonus of coloured foliage.

Soil Any
Aspect Full sun to medium shade
Habit Upright, round-topped shrub; may spread with age
Leaf Deciduous, oval, light to mid-green, tooth-edged leaves, 4–10cm (1½–4in) long; yellow autumn colour; some gold or variegated forms
Flower Double or single, creamy-white to pure white, often fragrant, flowers, 2cm (¾in) wide, some with purple markings
Use For the shrub or mixed border or mass-planting; as an informal hedge planted at distances of 1m (3ft)
Needs Propagate from cuttings in summer. Prune established plants after flowering by removing one-third of shoots, choosing the oldest, to near ground level
Varieties *P.* 'Beauclerk' ♀ single, scented, white flowers with pink centre • *P. coronarius* single, scented, white flowers • *P. c.* 'Aureus' ♀ golden foliage, single, scented, white flowers • *P. c.* 'Variegatus' ♀ grey-green leaves with creamy-white margins, single to semi-double, scented, white flowers • *P.* 'Manteau d'Hermine' ♀ low growing, double, scented white to creamy-white flowers • *P. microphyllus* low growing, single, very small, scented, white flowers • *P.* 'Silberregen' ('Silver Showers') double, scented, white flowers • *P.* 'Sybille' ♀ single, orange-scented, almost square, purple-stained white flowers • *P.* 'Virginal' ♀ double, very fragrant, white flowers

PHLOMIS
Lamiaceae/Labiatae
PHLOMIS

▲ ❀ ❦ SI all year E
H 5 yrs 1m (3ft)
S 5 yrs 1m (3ft)
H 10 yrs 1m (3ft)
S 10 yrs 1.2m (4ft)
❄ -10°C (14°F)
Z 7–10

PHLOMIS FRUTICOSA

The bright summer flower display appears against the evergreen silver foliage, which provides year-round interest, as does the shape of the shrub. The correct pruning helps to maintain the overall appearance, which can otherwise become rather ungainly.

Soil Will tolerate dry conditions, acid or alkaline, but dislikes waterlogging
Aspect Full sun; dislikes shade; may need protection in winter
Habit Upright when young, spreading with age
Leaf Evergreen, grey-green, downy, oval or lance-shaped leaves, 2.5–5cm (1–2in) long
Flower Interesting tubular, yellow or pink flowers borne in upright spikes or clusters throughout summer
Use As low to medium, grey foliage plant for shrub or mixed borders; ideal for single or mass-planting; as an informal hedge planted at distances of 75cm (30in)
Needs Propagate from cuttings in summer. Best foliage and flowers are borne on new shoots, so trim all shoots by cutting back by one-third in late spring to induce new growth
Varieties *P. chrysophylla* ♀ bushy habit, round, metallic blue, new leaves, against battleship grey, older ones, golden-yellow flowers • *P. fruticosa* (Jerusalem sage) ♀ upright habit when young spreading with age, oval, silver-grey leaves, bright yellow flowers, can be trained as a wall shrub • *P. italica* upright habit, lance-shaped leaves, pale lilac-pink flower spikes

PHORMIUM
Agavaceae/
Phormiaceae
FLAX LILY

▲ ❀ ❦ SI all year E
H 5 yrs 1m (3ft)
S 5 yrs 1m (3ft)
H 10 yrs 1.5m (5ft)
S 10 yrs 2m (6ft)
❄ -10°C (14°F)
Z 8–10

PHORMIUM 'DAZZLER'

There is some doubt as to whether this plant with its iris-like leaves should be regarded as a shrub or perennial. It is included with shrubs here because of its ability to retain its long, narrow, spear-like leaves throughout winter.

Soil Well-drained, open soil; dislikes waterlogging
Aspect Full sun; suitable for maritime and industrial areas because it tolerates high degrees of pollution
Habit Upright but spreading with age
Leaf Evergreen, upright, leathery, lance-shaped leaves, 2.5–2.8m (8–9ft) long and 10–13cm (4–5in) wide; available in a wide range of colour combinations
Flower Upright panicles of bronze-red flowers in summer are followed by strangely shaped, bird-like seedheads
Use As a feature plant; in large containers not less than 75cm (30in) across and 60cm (2ft) deep
Needs Propagate by division. No pruning required
Varieties *P.* 'Bronze Baby' bronze-purple foliage, fewer flowers • *P. cookianum* ssp. *hookeri* 'Cream Delight' ♀ olive-green leaves with creamy central band • *P. c.* ssp. *hookeri* 'Tricolor' ♀ green-striped leaves with white and red margins • *P.* 'Dazzler' red-brown leaves with carmine-red bands • *P.* 'Maori Sunrise' red-purple, rose-pink and bronze veining on leaves • *P. tenax* (New Zealand flax) ♀ grey to grey-green leaves with red veins • *P. t.* Purpureum Group ♀ bronze-purple leaves • *P. t.* 'Variegatum' ♀ green leaves with creamy-white margins and red veining • *P.* 'Yellow Wave' ♀ golden-yellow leaves with green edges

PHOTINIA
Rosaceae
CHRISTMAS BERRY

▲ ❀ ❦ SI all year E
H 5 yrs 1.5m (5ft)
S 5 yrs 2m (6ft)
H 10 yrs 2m (6ft)
S 10 yrs 3m (10ft)
❄ -15°C (4°F)
Z 3–8

**PHOTINIA × FRASERI
'RED ROBIN'**

This native to New Zealand tolerates a wide range of soil types. In recent times the genus *Stranvaesia* has been incorporated within the genus *Photinia*, but species in both groups have the new red foliage and flower displays that make them attractive all year round.

Soil Does well on most soils; dislikes extreme alkalinity
Aspect Full sun to light shade
Habit Upright and branching with age
Leaf Evergreen, large, oval to lance-shaped leaves, 10–20cm (4–8in) long and 4–9cm (1½–3½in) wide, often tooth-edged, dark glossy green when mature, young growth dark red or brilliant red (*Stranvaesia* forms less so)
Flower Clusters of coral-coloured buds opening to white; *Stransvaesia* forms have pale pink buds opening to white in summer
Use As a foliage shrub for large shrub borders; as an informal hedge planted at distances of 1m (3ft); fan-trained on walls
Needs Propagate from cuttings in summer. No pruning required but can be cut back moderately hard
Varieties *P. davidiana* (syn. *Stranvaesia davidiana*) flowers followed by red fruit • *P. d.* 'Fructu Luteo' (syn. *Stranvaesia davidiana* 'Fructu Luteo') yellow fruit • *P.* × *fraseri* 'Birmingham' dark coppery red to dark red new growth • *P.* ×*f.* 'Red Robin' ♀ new growth brilliant red, ageing to bronze • *P.* ×*f.* 'Rubens' (syn. *P. glabra* 'Rubens) slightly smaller and broader • *P. serratifolia* (syn. *P. serrulata*; Chinese hawthorn) coppery red foliage

PHYSOCARPUS OPULIFOLIUS
Rosaceae
NINEBARK

❀ ❦ SI summer
H 5 yrs 1.5m (5ft)
S 5 yrs 1.5m (5ft)
H 10 yrs 2.5m (8ft)
S 10 yrs 2.5m (8ft)
❉ -25°C (-13°F)
Z 5–9

PHYSOCARPUS OPULIFOLIUS 'DART'S GOLD'

This foliage plant looks at its best when it is planted where the golden-leaved forms can contrast with purples and reds. The purple-leaved form looks best with the opposite associations. It is ideal for the back of a shrub or mixed border, providing good contrast with the plants nearer the front, and its use as an informal hedge should not be overlooked.

Soil Most soils except very alkaline, where it may show signs of distress caused by drought
Aspect Very light, dappled shade; in full sun leaf scorch may be a problem in very hot weather
Habit Upright when young, spreading with age
Leaf Deciduous, clear yellow or golden-yellow or purple, 3-lobed leaves, 4–5cm (1½–2in) wide and long, with toothed edges
Flower Clusters of off-white flowers borne in early to midsummer
Use As a medium to tall foliage shrub; in large to medium shrub borders or for mass-planting
Needs Propagate from cuttings in summer or winter. Remove one-third of total number of shoots, choosing the oldest. Prune in early spring to encourage good coloured foliage
Varieties *P. opulifolius* 'Dart's Gold' ♀ more plentiful bright golden foliage, less susceptible to sun scorch • *P. o.* 'Diabolo' purple foliage • *P. o.* 'Luteus' soft yellow leaves

---

PIERIS
Ericaceae
PIERIS

▲ ❀ ❦ SI spring SC E
H 5 yrs 75cm (30in)
S 5 yrs 1m (3ft)
H 10 yrs 1.2m (4ft)
S 10 yrs 2m (6ft)
❉ -10°C (14°F)
Z 5–8

PIERIS JAPONICA 'FIRECREST'

These shrubs have both scented flowers and spring foliage to recommend them. They are not without problems, however, requiring acid soil and not being reliably hardy.

Soil Acid to neutral; dislikes alkalinity
Aspect Light to medium shade; dislikes full sun
Habit Upright, becoming spreading with age
Leaf Evergreen, broad, lance-shaped leaves, 3.5–7.5cm (1¼–3¼in) long, tooth-edged, red-orange ageing to bronze and finally light to mid-green; some white-variegated forms; very susceptible to spring frost
Flower Broad, pendent or upright panicles of pitcher-shaped, white or pink flowers in spring;prone to frost damage
Use In woodland gardens; can be grown in a large container with lime-free potting compost for several years
Needs Propagate from cuttings in summer or layers. No pruning required
Varieties *P.* 'Forest Flame' ♀ large, red new growth, changing from red through pink to white and finally green, large panicles of white flowers • *P. formosa* var. *forrestii* red young growth, panicles of white, slightly scented, flowers • *P. f.* var. *f.* 'Wakehurst' vivid red young foliage, hanging panicles of white flowers • *P. japonica* 'Firecrest' ♀ red new foliage, waxy, scented, white flowers • *P. j.* 'Pink Delight' ♀ bronze foliage in spring turns green, pink to white flowers • *P. j.* 'Scarlet O'Hara' new foliage red, creamy-white, red-speckled flowers • *P. j.* 'Variegata' grey-green leaves with white-pink variegation

PITTOSPORUM
Pittosporaceae
PITTOSPORUM

▲ ❀ ❦ SI all year SC E
H 5 yrs 1.5m (5ft)
S 5 yrs 1m (3ft)
H 10 yrs 3m (10ft)
S 10 yrs 2m (6ft)
❄ -5°C (23°F)
Z 7–10

**PITTOSPORUM TENUIFOLIUM
'SILVER QUEEN'**

This is a useful evergreen shrub for warm maritime areas, although its hardiness is more suspect inland. In cold areas, it can be planted in a large container for winter protection.

Soil Well-drained soil; use a good quality potting compost in containers
Aspect Full sun or very light shade
Habit Upright, becoming branching and twiggy with age to form an upright, pyramidal shrub
Leaf Evergreen, glossy, thick textured, oval to round leaves, 2.5–6cm (1–2½in) long, in shades of olive green, purple, silver or gold; some variegated forms
Flower Small, unusual chocolate-brown to purple, honey-scented flowers in summer
Use As free-standing shrub or in a medium to large shrub border; good in containers; a good hedge for mild gardens planted at distances of 1m (3ft)
Needs Propagate from cuttings in summer. No pruning required but can be trimmed quite harshly
Varieties *P.* 'Garnettii' ♀ white-variegated, pink-flushed leaves • *P. tenuifolium* ♀ grey-green, slightly twisted leaves • *P. t.* 'Irene Paterson' ♀ marbled, creamy-white foliage • *P. t.* 'James Stirling' small, silver-green, round or oval leaves • *P. t.* 'Purpureum' pale green leaves turn to deep bronze-purple • *P. t.* 'Silver Queen' ♀ narrow, ovate, pointed and tightly bunched leaves • *P. t.* 'Tresederi' amber leaves, mottled gold when young • *P. t.* 'Warnham Gold' ♀ yellow to yellow-green leaves, ageing to gold

PONCIRUS TRIFOLIATA
Rutaceae
JAPANESE BITTER ORANGE

▲ ❀ SI all year SC
H 5 yrs 1m (3ft)
S 5 yrs 1m (3ft)
H 10 yrs 2m (6ft)
S 10 yrs 2m (6ft)
❄ -10°C (14°F)
Z 7–10

PONCIRUS TRIFOLIATA

This unusual plant is unlike any other. The almost bare stems display scented, citrus-type, round, flat, white flowers, which are followed by green fruits that ripen to yellow. The overall shape is not uninteresting and the green stems provide winter colour. It is, in fact, not a member of the citrus family but is related to the herb rue.

Soil Well-drained, open, light soil; tolerates alkaline and acid conditions
Aspect Full sun to light shade; hardiness is suspect
Habit Branching, stout, green, angular stems form a ball-shaped shrub of architectural interest; good winter stem colour
Leaf Deciduous, bright green, sparse, broadly oval leaves, 2.5–6cm (1–2½in) long; yellow autumn colour
Flower White, orange-blossom type flowers, very sweetly orange-scented and 4–5cm (1½–2in) across, borne in good numbers in summer
Use As a free-standing specimen shrub for architectural shape and interesting flowers, fruit and winter stems
Needs Propagate from seed. No pruning required
Varieties None

POTENTILLA
Rosaceae
SHRUBBY CINQUEFOIL

❀ ❦ SI summer
H 5 yrs 75cm (30in)
S 5 yrs 75cm (30in)
H 10 yrs 1.2m (4ft)
S 10 yrs 1.2m (4ft)
❄ -25°C (-13°F)
Z 2–9

Versatile plants producing flowers throughout summer in a galaxy of colours on low, bushy, deciduous shrubs.

Soil Wide range of soils; distressed only by extremely dry, wet or very alkaline conditions
Aspect Prefers full sun but tolerates mid-shade
Habit Some varieties are upright and round-topped, others mound-forming or almost prostrate
Leaf Deciduous, light sage green to silver-green, cut, lobed, 3–7 leaflets, 1–2.5cm (½–1in) long
Flower White, primrose, yellow, pink, orange, red in summer
Use In a border as a single specimen or massed together; as an informal hedge planted at distances of 60cm (2ft)
Needs Propagate from cuttings in summer. Each spring take back one-third of shoots to ground level, choosing the oldest
Varieties *P. fruticosa* 'Abbotswood' ♛ mound-forming, grey-green foliage, white flowers • *P. f.* 'Daydawn' ♛ bushy, green foliage, peach-pink to cream flowers • *P. f.* 'Elizabeth' ♛ mound-forming, grey-green foliage, canary yellow flowers • *P. f.* 'Maanelys' ('Moonlight') ♛ low growing, grey-green foliage, primrose-yellow flowers • *P. f.* 'Primrose Beauty' ♛ bushy, grey foliage, primrose-yellow flowers • *P. f.* 'Princess' ('Blink') bushy, green foliage, rose-pink flowers • *P. f.* 'Red Ace' bushy, green foliage, red flowers • *P. f.* 'Royal Flush' bushy, green foliage, rose-pink flowers • *P. f.* 'Tangerine' ♛ bushy, green foliage, copper yellow to tangerine-orange-yellow flowers • *P. f.* 'Tilford Cream' ♛ bushy, grey-green foliage, creamy-white flowers

POTENTILLA FRUTICOSA 'ABBOTSWOOD'

PRUNUS
Rosaceae
SHRUBBY PRUNUS

▲ ❀ ❦ SI spring
H 5 yrs 1m (3ft)
S 5 yrs 75cm (30in)
H 10 yrs 1.5m (5ft)
S 10 yrs 1.2m (4ft)
❄ -15°C (4°F)
Z 4–9

The range of forms is sufficiently wide for there to be at least one that is suitable for every kind of garden, and looking forward to the spring blossom is one of the joys of gardening.

Soil Any except extremely alkaline soil
Aspect Full sun to light shade; dislikes deep shade
Habit Upright shrub with a slow to medium growth rate
Leaf Deciduous, grey-green or purple-red, lance- to oval-shaped leaves, 4–9cm (1½–3½in) long, with slightly tooth edges; some orange-yellow autumn colour
Flower Profuse, small, round, off-white, pink or peach-pink flowers
Use As a small individual shrub or small or medium sized shrub for a mixed border
Needs Propagate by grafting or budding. No pruning required, except for *P. triloba*
Varieties *P. × cistena* (purple-leaved sand cherry) ♛ purple-red foliage, white flowers on bare purple stems, can be used for hedging planted at distances of 60cm (2ft) • *P. glandulosa* (dwarf flowering almond) double, many-petalled, small pink or white flowers produced profusely along entire length of upright shoots • *P. tenella* (dwarf Russian almond) small, round, pink flowers, profusely produced on upright stems in early spring • *P. t.* 'Fire Hill' the best form • *P. triloba* (flowering almond) double, rosette-shaped, peach-pink flowers borne on entire length of bare stems in mid-spring, cut back one-third of old flowering shoots moderately hard after flowering to induce new flowering wood

PRUNUS TENELLA 'FIRE HILL'

PYRACANTHA
Rosaceae
FIRETHORN

▲ ❁ ❦ SI all year E
H 5 yrs 2m (6ft)
S 5 yrs 1.2m (4ft)
H 10 yrs 3.5m (12ft)
S 10 yrs 2m (6ft)
❋ -25°C (-13°F)
Z 3–7

PYRACANTHA 'MOHAVE'

Foliage, flowers, fruits and trainable growth all make this one of the most versatile of plants.

Soil Most, except extremely alkaline soils
Aspect Full sun to deep shade
Habit Upright, wide-topped shrub or a flat fan-shape for walls, some pendulous forms; in the right conditions can achieve the proportions of a small tree
Leaf Evergreen, glossy, light to mid-green leaves; some grey and variegated leaved varieties
Flower White flowers with a musty scent in early summer, followed by coloured fruit
Use For shrub borders; as a free-standing shrub; as an informal hedge planted at distances of 75cm (30in); fan-trained
Needs Propagate from cuttings in summer and from seed in spring. Trim or train as required
Varieties *P.* 'Alexander Pendula' long, weeping branches, coral-red fruit • *P. angustifolia* grey-green foliage, orange-yellow fruit • *P. atalantioides* (syn. *P. gibbsii*) scarlet fruit • *P. a.* 'Aurea' (syn. *P. gibbsii* 'Flava') yellow fruit • *P. coccinea* 'Red Cushion' red fruit • *P.* 'Golden Charmer' golden-yellow fruit • *P.* 'Harlequin' grey-green foliage with silver-white edges, small orange-red fruit • *P.* 'Mohave' orange-red fruit • *P.* 'Orange Charmer' deep orange fruit • *P.* 'Orange Glow' ♀ orange-red fruit • *P. rogersiana* 'Flava' ♀ yellow fruit • *P.* 'Shawnee' yellow to light orange fruit • *P.* 'Soleil d'Or' deep yellow fruit • *P.* 'Sparkler' white-variegated leaves, orange-red fruit

RHAMNUS ALATERNUS
Rhamnaceae
ITALIAN BUCKTHORN

❁ ❦ SI all year E
H 5 yrs 2m (6ft)
S 5 yrs 1m (3ft)
H 10 yrs 3.5m (12ft)
S 10 yrs 2m (6ft)
❋ -15°C (4°F)
Z 2–7

**RHAMNUS ALATERNUS
'ARGENTEOVARIEGATA'**

A useful evergreen shrub, some forms of which have attractive variegated leaves. It is not reliably hardy when planted in exposed gardens, but in the correct conditions it makes a fine feature plant.

Soil Most types; dislikes extremely wet or dry conditions
Aspect Medium shade to full sun
Habit Upright, becoming very branching with age and forming an upright pyramidal shape
Leaf Evergreen and boldly white-variegated, oval leaves, 2.5cm (1in) long; the variegated forms will revert to all-green shoots, which must be removed as soon as they are noticed
Flower Inconspicuous, small, pale cream flowers sometimes followed by red, ageing to black, fruit
Use As a large specimen shrub in mild areas and for fan-training on walls in colder areas; as a hedge in maritime gardens planted at distances of 30cm (1ft); will grow in a container for several years before needing to be planted out
Needs Propagate from cuttings in summer. No pruning required; best left free growing but can be trimmed if required to contain or if grown as a hedge
Varieties *R. alaternus* 'Argenteovariegata' ♀ attractive, upright, pyramidal habit, evergreen, grey-green leaves with irregular white to creamy-white margins, slightly tender, minimum winter temperature -5°C (23°F)

RHODODENDRON
Ericaceae
RHODODENDRON

▲ ❀ ❦ SI spring E
H 5 yrs 0.6–1.2m (2–4ft)
S 5 yrs 0.6–1.5m (2–5ft)
H 10 yrs 0.75–2m (30in–6ft)
S 10 yrs 1–2.5m (3–8ft)
❅ -15°C (4°F)
Z 3–7

**RHODODENDRON
'PINK PEARL'**

This well-known plant can be grown successfully in containers provided it is given a good lime-free compost.

Soil Neutral to acid soils; dislikes alkalinity or waterlogging
Aspect Prefers light shade but tolerates full sun
Habit Branching habit, forming a dome-shaped shrub
Leaf Evergreen or deciduous, round to oval, dark green
Flower Clusters of flowers in blue, pink, purple, red, yellow or white in spring
Use Dwarf forms associate well with heathers and dwarf conifers; on rock gardens; for massed or single planting
Needs Propagate from cuttings or by grafting in summer
Varieties Dwarf: _R._ Carmen Group bell-shaped, dark crimson flowers with pale pink throats • _R._ 'Elisabeth Hobbie' ♀ scarlet flowers • _R._ Humming Bird Group scarlet flowers • _R._ Moonstone Group rose-crimson buds opening to cream and pale primrose flowers • _R._ 'Pink Drift' grey-green aromatic foliage, lavender-rose flowers • _R._ 'Scarlet Wonder' ♀ ruby red flowers with frilly margins • _R._ Yellow Hammer Group ♀ bright yellow flowers in spring and autumn
Large hybrids: • _R._ 'Bagshot Ruby' ♀ ruby red flowers • _R._ 'Blue Peter' ♀ cobalt blue flowers • _R._ 'Britannia' ♀ scarlet-crimson flowers • _R._ 'Cynthia' ♀ rose-crimson flowers • _R._ 'Goldsworth Yellow', pink buds opening to primrose-yellow flowers with brown markings • _R._ 'Pink Pearl' lilac-pink flowers turning white with age • _R._ 'Purple Splendour' ♀ royal purple-blue flowers • _R._ 'Sappho' ♀ white flowers with purple spots

RIBES
Grossulariaceae
FLOWERING CURRANT

▲ ❀ ❦ SI spring SC E some
H 5 yrs 1.5m (5ft)
S 5 yrs 1m (3ft)
H 10 yrs 2m (6ft)
S 10 yrs 2m (6ft)
❅ -25°C (-13°F)
Z 3–6

**RIBES SANGUINEUM
'KING EDWARD VII'**

A spring-flowering shrub with a wider range of varieties than may be realized. It is almost a tradition to plant one of the pink-flowering varieties with a yellow-flowering forsythia.

Soil Most, showing signs of distress only on very dry soils
Aspect Full sun to light shade
Habit Strong and upright, branching with age to form a round-topped shrub
Leaf Deciduous or evergreen, light green, 3-lobed leaves, 4–5cm (1½–2in) long and wide; some gold-leaved forms
Flower Small, hanging clusters in shades of pink, yellow, green-yellow or white in early spring
Use As a spring-flowering shrub or in a mixed borders; for mass or solo planting
Needs Propagate from cuttings taken in summer or winter. After flowering, remove one-third of shoots to ground level, choosing the oldest; evergreen varieties need no pruning
Varieties _R._ × _gordonianum_ flowers bronze-red on outside with yellow inner shading • _R. laurifolium_ evergreen, green-white flowers in winter • _R. odoratum_ (buffalo currant, clove currant) yellow, clove-scented flowers, black berries • _R. sanguineum_ (winter currant) mid-pink flowers, black fruit • _R. s._ 'Atrorubens' blood-red flowers • _R. s._ 'Brocklebankii' ♀ golden-yellow foliage, pale pink flowers • _R. s._ 'King Edward VII' intense crimson flowers • _R. s._ 'Pulborough Scarlet' ♀ deep red flowers • _R. s._ 'Tydeman's White' ♀ white flowers

ROMNEYA COULTERI
Papaveraceae
CALIFORNIAN TREE POPPY

❀ ✓ SI summer SC
H 5 yrs 1m (3ft)
S 5 yrs 1m (3ft)
H 10 yrs 1m (3ft)
S 10 yrs 2m (6ft)
❋ -15°C (4°F)
Z 6–10

ROMNEYA COULTERI

Almost paper-like white flowers with bold yellow centres are borne above the silver foliage. In the right conditions it grows like a weed, but otherwise it struggles. However, it is worth persisting, because the flowers are among the great pleasures of summer. It is sometimes regarded as a perennial rather than a shrub because in many areas it dies down to ground level in winter.

Soil Moderately dry, light, open but moisture-retentive soil that is high in organic material will help plants to become established
Aspect Full sun; dislikes any degree of shade
Habit Upright stems may need a little support in exposed gardens; dies to ground level each winter in most areas
Leaf Deciduous, grey to grey-silver or green, oval and indented leaves, 3.5–8cm (1¼–3in) wide and long
Flower Fragrant, white, slightly waxy, paper-like flowers, with central golden-yellow stamens and 10–15cm (4–6in) across in summer
Use As a clump-forming plant producing attractive foliage and flowers throughout summer
Needs Propagate from root cuttings taken in spring. Best grown alone to allow root system to develop. Cut shoots that do not die back in winter to ground level in spring
Varieties *R. coulteri* ♀ the basic form and possibly the best • *R. c.* 'White Cloud' said to be stronger growing and to have larger flowers than the type species, although this is debatable

ROSMARINUS
Lamiaceae/Labiatae
ROSEMARY

▲ ❀ ✓ SI all year SC E
H 5 yrs 75cm (30in)
S 5 yrs 1m (3ft)
H 10 yrs 1.2m (4ft)
S 10 yrs 1.5m (5ft)
❋ -10°C (14°F)
Z 7–10

ROSMARINUS OFFICINALIS

Grown for centuries for its medicinal and culinary properties, today this herb is as widely planted for its aromatic foliage and pretty flowers as for its other qualities. It is also used for its architectural character in garden layouts.

Soil Light, open soil; liable to chlorosis on extreme alkalinity
Aspect Full sun but tolerates light shade
Habit Upright, becoming arching and spreading with age
Leaf Evergreen, narrow, lance-shaped leaves, 0.5–3.5cm (¼–1⅜in) long, grey with white underside; some gold-variegated aromatic forms
Flower Small flowers in various shades of blue or white are produced repeatedly in summer
Use In shrub or mixed borders or in herb gardens; as a low, informal hedge planted at distances of 60cm (2ft)
Needs Propagate from cuttings in spring. Each spring cut back one-third of shoots to ground level, choosing the oldest
Varieties *R. officinalis* (common rosemary) grey-green foliage, pale to mid-blue flowers • *R. o.* var. *albiflorus* white flowers • *R. o.* var. *angustissimus* (syn. *R. angustifolius*) very narrow foliage, deep blue flowers • *R. o.* var. *a.* 'Corsican Blue' narrow foliage, bright blue flowers • *R. o.* 'Aureus' (syn. *R. o.* 'Aureovariegatus') pale gold-splashed foliage, light blue flowers • *R. o.* 'Benenden Blue' bright blue flowers • *R. o.* Prostratus Group (syn. *R.* × *lavandulaceus*) prostrate, carpeting, blue flowers • *R. o.* 'Severn Sea' ♀ low growing, blue flowers • *R. o.* 'Tuscan Blue' bright blue flowers

RUBUS
Rosaceae
BRAMBLE

▲ ❀ ✿ SI all year SC some
E some
H 5 yrs 0.5–1m (20–36in)
S 5 yrs 0.5–1.5m (20in–5ft)
H 10 yrs 0.5–2m (20in–6ft)
S 10 yrs 2–2.5m (6–8ft)
❈ -25°C (-13°F)
Z 4–8

RUBUS COCKBURNIANUS

A large group of shrubs with very diverse features – from winter stems to summer flowers – and habit – from carpeting to large, upright shrubs.

Soil Most, except very dry
Aspect Tolerates full sun to very deep shade
Habit Upright, becoming spreading or ground covering
Leaf Evergreen or deciduous, trifoliate, silvery to dark green leaves, from 3.5–13cm (1¼–5in) long and wide; some varieties have lacerated leaves
Flower Single or double, white or pink to pinkish-purple flowers, borne singly or in clusters
Use Planted singly or grouped; as ground cover; for fruit
Needs Propagate from cuttings in spring or summer; some varieties from root suckers or by division. Each spring cut back to ground level one-third of shoots; remove all growth of white-stemmed forms to ground level in spring
Varieties <u>Flowering</u>: *R.* 'Benenden' (syn. *R.* Tridel 'Benenden') ♀ large, single, white flowers, 5cm (2in) across, in summer • *R. odoratus* (flowering raspberry, thimbleberry) large leaves, fragrant, purple-rose flowers • *R. phoenicolasius* (Japanese wineberry) pink flowers, orange-red, edible fruit • *R. spectabilis* (salmonberry) single, fragrant, bright magenta-rose flowers <u>Ground cover</u>: *R. tricolor* creeping form, white flowers, occasionally followed by fruit <u>White-stemmed</u>: *R. cockburnianus* ♀ strong, vivid white stems in winter • *R. thibetanus* (ghost bramble) ♀ purple-brown stems with white bloom, purple flowers, red fruit

---

SALIX
Salicaceae
WILLOW

❀ (catkins) ✿ SI winter–spring
H 5 yrs 0.6–4m (2–13ft)
S 5 yrs 1–1.5m (3–5ft)
H 10 yrs 1–5m (3–16ft)
S 10 yrs 1.5–2.5m (5–8ft)
❈ -25°C (-13°F)
Z 2–9

SALIX ALBA VAR. SERICEA

The display of catkins makes the willow one of the most popular spring plants.

Soil Any; good in wet areas
Aspect Sun to medium shade
Habit Upright or spreading
Leaf Deciduous, oval, purple-grey, grey-green or green leaves; some variegated forms
Flower Yellow, white or black catkins borne in spring
Use For rock gardens or water features
Needs Propagate from cuttings in winter. Cut back hard each spring
Varieties <u>Short and low-growing varieties</u>: *S. gracilistyla* 'Melanostachys' (syn. *S.* 'Kuro-me'; black catkin willow) black catkins • *S. hastata* 'Wehrhahnii' ♀ goblet-shaped habit, silver catkins • *S. helvetica* (Swiss willow) ♀ grey foliage, pale yellow catkins • *S. lanata* (woolly willow) ♀ silver-grey foliage, yellow-grey catkins • *S. repens* var. *argentea* ♀ grey-green foliage, silver-grey catkins <u>Medium height varieties</u>: *S. elaeagnos* (syn. *S. incana*; hoary willow) ♀ grey foliage • *S. exigua* (coyote willow) silver foliage • *S. irrorata* stems covered in bloom, red and black buds, yellow catkins <u>Tall-growing varieties</u>: *S. acutifolia* 'Blue Streak' ♀ black to purple stems covered in white bloom • *S. alba* var. *sericea* (syn. *S. a.* f. *argentea*) silver-grey leaves, greenish-yellow catkins • *S. a.* var. *vitellina* (golden willow) ♀ bright yellow shoots • *S. a.* var. *v.* 'Britzensis' (syn. *S. a.* 'Chermesina'; scarlet willow) bright orange stems

SHRUBS

SAMBUCUS
Caprifoliaceae
ELDER

▲ ❀ ♥ SI summer–autumn
H 5 yrs 3m (10ft)
S 5 yrs 2m (6ft)
H 10 yrs 4m (13ft)
S 10 yrs 3.5m (12ft)
❊ -10°C (14°F)
Z 5–9

SAMBUCUS RACEMOSA
'PLUMOSA AUREA'

To achieve the best results the pruning and soil requirements for the elder should be followed carefully. Although it produces flowers and fruit, these are normally sacrificed in favour of achieving a good foliage display.

Soil Any soil, as long as it is moist; tolerates wet conditions
Aspect Prefers very light shade but accepts full sun to medium shade
Habit Upright, spreading and forming a dome-shaped, tall shrub
Leaf Deciduous, large, pinnate leaves, green to grey-green, purple, white- or gold-variegated
Flower Convex clusters of tufted white flowers on unpruned shoots one year old or more are followed by red fruit
Use As a free-standing shrub or for mass-planting
Needs Propagate from seed or by layering or grafting. Prune all growth to ground level in early spring to encourage new growth and new, good coloured foliage
Varieties *S. canadensis* 'Maxima' leaves 40cm (16in) long, rose-purple, flowers 30cm (1ft) across. • *S. nigra* 'Albo-variegata' grey-green leaves with creamy-white margins • *S. n.* 'Aurea' (golden elder) ♀ yellow foliage, turning gold with age. • *S. n.* 'Guincho Purple' ♀ purple foliage and flower buds opening to white • *S. n.* f. *laciniata* (fern-leaved elder, parsley-leaved elder) ♀ green, fern-like foliage • *S. n.* 'Pulverulenta' green leaves striped and mottled white • *S. racemosa* 'Plumosa Aurea' (red-berried elder) divided golden foliage • *S. r.* 'Sutherland Gold' very finely cut, golden leaves

SANTOLINA
Asteraceae/Compositae
COTTON LAVENDER

▲ ❀ ♥ SI all year SC E
H 5 yrs 50cm (20in)
S 5 yrs 70cm (27in)
H 10 yrs 50cm (20in)
S 10 yrs 1m (3ft)
❊ -10°C (14°F)
Z 6–10

SANTOLINA
CHAMAECYPARISSUS

With the right pruning santolina is a very useful and versatile plant; left to its own devices, however, it can be a disaster. Although the forms with silver-grey leaves are the most widely planted, the green form is attractive.

Soil Well-drained and open; tolerates all soil types
Aspect Full sun to very light shade
Habit Low-spreading, bun-shaped shrub
Leaf Evergreen, aromatic, green or grey to silver-grey, very small, linear, finely divided leaves, 2.5–4cm (1–1½in) long
Flower Small round flowerheads, primrose- to lemon- to golden-yellow; remove flowers regularly to maintain good foliage colour
Use As a foliage shrub for edges of shrub borders, large rock gardens or among bedding plants; as an informal, low hedge planted at distances of 40cm (16in); good in large containers
Needs Propagate from cuttings in summer. Once signs of spring growth are seen, reduce almost to ground level
Varieties *S. chamaecyparissus* (syn. *S. incana*) ♀ low mound, silver foliage, bright yellow flowers • *S. c.* var. *nana* (syn. *S. c.* var. *corsica*) more compact form, grey-silver foliage, small lemon-yellow flowers • *S. pinnata* ssp. *neapolitana* ♀ more upright habit, very feathery divided leaves, bright lemon-yellow flowers • *S. p.* ssp. *n.* 'Sulphurea' grey-green foliage, pale primrose-yellow flowers • *S. rosmarinifolius* ssp. *rosmarinifolius* (syn. *S. virens*, *S. viridis*) low mound, green to bright green thread-like foliage, bright lemon-yellow flowers

SARCOCOCCA
Buxaceae
CHRISTMAS BOX,
SWEET BOX

▲ ❀ ✿ SI winter SC E
H 5 yrs 25cm (10in)
S 5 yrs 30cm (1ft)
H 10 yrs 1m (3ft)
S 10 yrs 40cm (16in)
❄ -15°C (4°F)
Z 5–10

SARCOCOCCA HOOKERIANA VAR. DIGYNA

Every winter, if it is planted in the right conditions, this low-growing shrub produces a multitude of small, highly scented flowers. There is the added bonus of black or red spherical fruits.

Soil Most, but dislikes poor soils; add organic material
Aspect Full sun to medium shade
Habit Upright to spreading; a slow growth rate; needs to be able to sucker but is not invasive
Leaf Evergreen, dark green or purple-green, narrow, oval leaves, 2.5–6cm (1–2½in) long, with shiny upper surfaces and duller undersides
Flower Small, white, very fragrant male flowers and insignificant female flowers are produced in the same cluster in winter
Use As a low-growing, winter-flowering, evergreen shrub for planting on its own, in mass groupings or at edge of shrub borders; as a low hedge if planted at distances of 30cm (1ft)
Needs Propagate from cuttings in summer. No pruning required
Varieties *S. confusa* ♀ dark, glossy green foliage, fragrant, white flowers, shiny black fruit • *S. hookeriana* var. *digyna* ♀ green-purple, narrow, lance-shaped leaves, scented pink-white flowers, black fruit • *S. h.* var. *humilis* deep green foliage, white male flowers with pink anthers, black fruit • *S. ruscifolia* dark green, leathery, thick, shiny, ovate leaves, red fruit

SKIMMIA
Rutaceae
SKIMMIA

▲ ❀ ✿ SI autumn–winter
SC some E
H 5 yrs 40cm (16in)
S 5 yrs 40cm (16in)
H 10 yrs 60cm (2ft)
S 10 yrs 60cm (2ft)
❄ -15°C (4°F)
Z 7–9

SKIMMIA JAPONICA (FEMALE PLANT)

A well-known plant that is not always as well grown as it might be to get the best results. The overriding need is an acid soil with a high degree of organic material. Although a few forms produce fruit without a pollinating variety present, most require separate male and female plants to bear fruit.

Soil Acid to neutral; dislikes any alkalinity and requires a high organic content
Aspect Full sun to medium shade
Habit Upright, spreading and branching with age
Leaf Large, evergreen, green, oval leaves, 8–11cm (3–4½in) long, with purple veins and silver backs
Flower Panicles 8–13cm (3–5in) tall, of fragrant, white flowers
Use As flowering and fruiting shrubs for woodland and shrub borders; in containers in lime-free potting compost
Needs Propagate from cuttings in summer, rooted suckers or seed. No pruning required
Varieties *S. japonica* (Japanese skimmia) raised from seed and therefore variable as to sex and habit • *S. j.* 'Fragrans' ♀ male, scented white flowers • *S. j.* 'Nymans' ♀ female, red fruit • *S. j.* Rogersii Group (syn. *S. rogersii*) female, red fruit, dwarf • *S. j.* 'Rubella' ♀ male, dark green foliage, deep red in bud, opening to white • *S. j.* 'Veitchii' (syn. *S. j.* 'Foremanii') female, white flowers, red fruit • *S. j.* 'Wakehurst White' (syn. *S. j.* 'Fructu Albo') female, white fruit • *S. laureola* female, dark green foliage, green-yellow, fragrant flowers, red fruit

SORBARIA
Rosaceae
TREE SPIRAEA

▲ ❀ ❦ SI summer
H 5 yrs 2m (6ft)
S 5 yrs 2m (6ft)
H 10 yrs 3m (10ft)
S 10 yrs 4m (13ft)
❄ -25°C (-13°F)
Z 2–8

SORBARIA KIRILOWII

A large shrub that needs room if it to achieve its full height and spread – indeed, it is the plant's bulk, which is needed to carry the plumes of summer flowers, that gives it some of its attraction. The foliage is large, too, and complements the flowers, particularly the dissected form.

Soil Prefers rich, deep soil, moist and well-drained, but tolerates a wide range of conditions
Aspect Full sun to light shade
Habit Tall, non-branching, thicket-forming
Leaf Deciduous, light green leaves with grey-silver undersides; yellow autumn colour
Flower Large, cream to white, terminal panicles, 20cm (8in) long or more, in summer
Use As individual shrubs, for mass-planting, or for the back of medium to large shrub borders
Needs Propagate from cuttings or division. Cut back one-third of the oldest stems each spring to ground level to keep the shrub rejuvenated
Varieties *S. kirilowii* (syn. *S. arborea*) the main variety planted, large green foliage, good autumn colour, large white flowers • *S. sorbifolia* light green foliage, narrow white flowers in erect panicles • *S. tomentosa* var. *angustifolia* (syn. *S. aitchisonii*) attractive glabrous, dissected leaves, large panicles of creamy-white flowers

SPARTIUM JUNCEUM
Leguminosae/
Papilionaceae
SPANISH BROOM,
WEAVER'S BROOM

▲ ❀ SI late spring–autumn
H 5 yrs 0.75–2m (30in–6ft)
S 5 yrs 1–1.5m (3–5ft)
H 10 yrs 1–3m (3–10ft)
S 10 yrs 1.5–2m (5–6ft)
❄ -15°C (4°F)
Z 6–10

SPARTIUM JUNCEUM

This member of the broom and pea family is often overlooked when planting schemes are being developed. Free flowering throughout summer, with some spring and autumn showing, and neat in habit when it is given space to develop its goblet formation of shoots, it is an attractive plant. The only problem is that if it is overplanted for the space available, controlling its size can be difficult as it can resent pruning.

Soil Most but dislikes very thin, chalky soils
Aspect Full sun
Habit Strong, upright or spreading, becoming branching and then woody with age
Leaf Deciduous, sparse, grey to silvery-grey or grey-green, lance-shaped leaves, 1–2cm (½–¾in) long and wide
Flower Yellow to golden-yellow pea-shaped flowers in profusion in spring and autumn
Use As a free-standing shrub or for large shrub borders; very good for mass-planting
Needs Propagate from cuttings taken in summer. No pruning required
Varieties None

SPIRAEA
Rosaceae
SPIRAEA

▲ ❀ ❦ SI spring–summer
H 5 yrs 40cm (16in)
S 5 yrs 50cm (20in)
H 10 yrs 60cm (2ft)
S 10 yrs 70cm (27in)
❄ -25°C (-13°C)
Z 4–10

SPIRAEA 'ARGUTA'

A very large group of deciduous or semi-evergreen plants offering interest over many weeks of spring and summer. Both flowers and foliage play a role in this display, and the range of sizes available adds to the uses to which they can be put.

Soil Most; dislikes only extremely alkaline or dry soils
Aspect Full sun to medium shade
Habit Normally upright, becoming branching with age
Leaves Oval, mainly light to dark green leaves, 2.5–8cm (1–3in) long, often tooth-edged; golden-leaved forms available
Flower Clusters of small white, pink or pink-red flowers in spring or summer
Use As flowering shrubs for individual planting, shrub borders or mass-planting
Needs Propagate from cuttings in summer
Varieties S. arcuata white flowers in spring • S. 'Arguta' (syn. S. × arguta 'Bridal Wreath') white flowers in spring • S. japonica 'Anthony Waterer' dark pink-red flowers • S. j. var. fortunei purple-green-red foliage, pink flowers • S. j. 'Golden Princess' small mounds, golden-yellow foliage, pink flowers • S. j. 'Goldflame' ♀ orange-apricot and gold foliage, pink-red flowers • S. j. 'Little Princess' dwarf, spreading, light green foliage, deep pink flowers • S. j. 'Shirobana' ♀ flowers pink or all white or pink and white in summer • S. nipponica 'Snowmound' ♀ white flowers in summer • S. thunbergii (Thunberg spiraea) ♀ grey-green flowers, white flowers in spring • S. × vanhouttei ♀ plum-coloured autumn foliage, white flowers

STACHYURUS
Stachyuraceae
STACHYURUS

▲ ❀ ❦ SI winter–spring
H 5 yrs 2m (6ft)
S 5 yrs 2m (6ft)
H 10 yrs 3m (10ft)
S 10 yrs 3m (10ft)
❄ -15°C (4°F)
Z 4–7

STACHYURUS PRAECOX

Hanging pendants of golden flowers adorn this statuesque shrub in late winter and early spring. The stems and foliage are of equal value, and they make this a valuable addition to any garden where its size can be used. Once thought to require an acid soil, it is now known to tolerate quite high degrees of alkalinity. There is one drawback: until it has grown to over 1m (3ft) high it is susceptible to spring frosts.

Soil Most, except waterlogged or very dry soils
Aspect Full sun to mid-shade
Habit Upright and arching when young, becoming more branching and forming a dome-shaped shrub; stems purple to dark brown in winter
Leaf Deciduous, dark green, large, elliptical, pointed leaves, 8–15cm (3–6in) long and 5–8cm (2–3in) wide and tinged purple with purple veining; some useful autumn colouring
Flower Numerous rigid and hanging racemes, 4–6cm (1½–2⅖in) long and consisting of over 20 yellow, cup-shaped flowers, borne along the length of branches
Use As a free-standing winter shrub or in large shrub borders
Needs Propagate by layering or from cuttings in summer. On established shrubs, 5 years old or more, remove one-third of oldest shoots to ground level following flowering to encourage rejuvenation
Varieties S. chinensis short flower racemes • S. c. 'Magpie' white margin variegation on leaves, yellow flowers, more tender • S. praecox ♀ racemes of pale yellow cup-shaped flowers

STAPHYLEA
Staphyleaceae
BLADDERNUT

▲ ❀ ❦ SI summer–autumn
SC
H 5 yrs 1.5m (5ft)
S 5 yrs 1m (3ft)
H 10 yrs 2.5m (8ft)
S 10 yrs 1.5m (5ft)
✳ -10°C (14°F)
Z 4–7

STAPHYLEA COLCHICA

A large shrub with interesting flowers, which are followed by unusual fruit capsules or pods, staphylea is planted not only for its fruit and flowers but for its quick rate of growth to form an architectural shape in the garden.

Soil Does best on neutral to acid fertile soil, but tolerates moderate alkalinity
Aspect Full sun or light shade
Habit Upright, fast growth rate when young, slowing with age; new shoots are green and have some winter interest
Leaf Deciduous, oval to oblong leaves, composed of 3–5 leaflets to 10cm (4in) long, dull grey-green upper surface and glossy undersides; good yellow autumn colour
Flower White or pink, fragrant, upright or hanging flower panicles over 13cm (5in) long, followed by translucent boulder-shaped fruits almost equal to the flowers in interest
Use As a single feature shrub or for a woodland garden; look good when planted as sentinels to mark a gate or drive
Needs Propagate from seed or by layering. No pruning required
Varieties *S. colchica* ♀ fragrant, white upright or hanging panicles • *S. holocarpa* flowers pink, opening to white • *S. h.* var. *rosea* flowers soft pink to pink borne in clusters • *S. pinnata* white flowers in thin, hanging panicles

STEPHANANDRA
Rosaceae
STEPHANANDRA

▲ ❀ ❦ SI all year
H 5 yrs 1.5m (5ft)
S 5 yrs 1.5m (5ft)
H 10 yrs 2m (6ft)
S 10 yrs 2m (6ft)
✳ -25°C (-13°F)
Z 5–8

STEPHANANDRA TANAKAE

Two quite different species in this genus are worthy of inclusion in the garden. *Stephandra tanakae* produces strong, bright mahogany stems in winter, which are among the finest of any plant if they are correctly pruned. *S. incisa* is much smaller with less winter interest, its beauty coming from its delicate, light green foliage, which turns pale orange in autumn.

Soil Does well on most soils, except very dry
Aspect Full sun to medium shade
Habit Upright when young, quickly becoming arching; attractive stems in winter
Leaf Deciduous, oval, 3–5 lobed leaves, to 13cm (5in) long; leaves of *S. incisa* are deeply toothed
Flower Racemes of green-white flowers in summer
Use <u>*S. incisa*</u>: as low front shrub for any size of shrub border; ideal for ground cover and bank stabilization when mass-planted; as an informal hedge when planted at distances of 40cm (16in); can be planted in containers not less than 60cm (2ft) in diameter and 40cm (16in) in depth in good quality potting compost. <u>*S. tanakae*</u>: as a free-standing single shrub or grouped for winter stem effect
Needs Propagate from cuttings in summer. Remove one-third of shoots, choosing the oldest, after flowering
Varieties *S. incisa* small panicles of green-white flowers • *S. i.* 'Crispa' more crinkled and cut leaves • *S. tanakae* deep mahogany-brown stems, green-white flowers

SYMPHORICARPOS
Caprifoliaceae
SNOWBERRY

☙ SI summer
H 5 yrs 1.5m (5ft)
S 5 yrs 1m (3ft)
H 10 yrs 2.5m (8ft)
S 10 yrs 2m (6ft)
❄ -25°C (-13°F)
Z 3–9

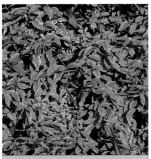

**SYMPHORICARPOS ORBICU-
LATUS 'FOLIIS VARIEGATIS'**

A plant for difficult soil or a harsh environment where little else will grow.

Soil Any
Aspect Full sun to deep shade; full sun for variegated forms
Habit Some forms are thicket-forming with suckering shoots, others simply shrub-forming
Leaf Deciduous, dull green, oval to round leaves, 1–5cm (½–2in) long, tinged with grey; some silver and gold variegated forms
Flower Inconspicuous, pink, bell-shaped flowers in summer are followed by limited numbers of purple fruit, mainly in hot summers
Use Suckering forms ideal for ground cover, bank retention and large-scale planting; good planted singly in medium to large shrub borders; some forms as informal hedging when planted at distances of 60cm (2ft)
Needs Propagate from cuttings in summer. In early spring remove one-third of shoots on established shrubs, choosing the oldest. Very old shrubs can be pruned back hard in spring and will rejuvenate
Varieties *S.* × *chenaultii* 'Hancock' bright green leaves , pink flowers, purple fruit • *S.* × *doorenbosii* pink-tinged fruit • *S.* × *d.* 'Magic Berry' rose-pink fruit • *S.* × *d.* 'Mother of Pearl' white, pink-flushed fruit • *S.* × *d.* 'White Hedge' white fruit • *S. orbiculatus* 'Albovariegatus' white-margined variegation • *S. o.* 'Foliis Variegatis' (syn. *S. o.* 'Variegatus') small, light grey-green foliage with yellow margins

---

SYRINGA
Oleaceae
LILAC

❀ ☙ SI spring SC
H 5 yrs 1.2 (4ft)
S 5 yrs 1m (3ft)
H 10 yrs 2.5m (8ft)
S 10 yrs 1.5m (5ft)
❄ -25°C (-13°F)
Z 3–7

**SYRINGA VULGARIS
'MADAME LEMOINE'**

The lilac has long been a favourite of gardeners. Its scented flowers conjure up thoughts of summer holidays.

Soil Most soils, but may show signs of chlorosis on severely alkaline types
Aspect Prefers full sun but tolerates medium shade
Habit Upright, conical or multi-stemmed tree after 15 years
Leaf Deciduous, dark green to mid-green, medium sized, oval leaves, 5–15cm (2–6in) long and 3.5–6cm (1¼–2½in) wide; yellow autumn colour
Flower Large single or double florets in fragrant panicles in blue, lilac, pink, red, purple, white or yellow; some bicolour
Use Free-standing, singly or in groups; ideal for mass or specialist planting, or as background for larger shrub borders
Needs Propagated by commercial budding or grafting. Requires very little pruning
Varieties <u>Single-flowered varieties</u>: *S. vulgaris* 'Congo' large panicles of rich, lilac-red flowers • *S. v.* 'Firmament' ♀ flowers mauve in bud, opening to clear lilac-blue • *S. v.* 'Primrose' pale primrose-yellow to yellow-white flowers • *S. v.* 'Sensation' large panicles of purple to purple-red, white-edged florets • *S. v.* 'Souvenir de Louis Spaeth' large, wine-red flowers <u>Double-flowered varieties</u>: *S. vulgaris* 'Charles Joly' ♀ dark red-purple flowers • *S. v.* 'Katherine Havemeyer' ♀ purple-lavender flowers turning to lilac-pink • *S. v.* 'Madame Lemoine' ♀ white flowers • *S. v.* 'Mrs Edward Harding' ♀ semi-double, purple-red fragrant flowers • *S. v.* 'Souvenir d'Alice Harding' white flowers

TAMARIX
Tamaricaceae
TAMARISK, SALT CEDAR

▲ ❀ ❦ SI spring–summer
H 5 yrs 1.5m (5ft)
S 5 yrs 1.5m (5ft)
H 10 yrs 2.5m (8ft)
S 10 yrs 2.5m (8ft)
❋ -10°C (14°F)
Z 2–10

TAMARIX RAMOSISSIMA

Delicate foliage and habit make this tall-growing shrub a worthwhile choice. Doing well in coastal locations, it is hardy inland, too. It can reach the proportions of a small tree in the right conditions.

Soil Prefers light, well-drained soil; dislikes any water-logging
Aspect Full sun or very light shade
Habit A spreading, delicately shaped shrub or small tree, medium to fast growth rate
Leaf Deciduous, light green or glaucous-blue, very small, oval, scale-like leaves
Flower Long, graceful, plume-like racemes in shades of pink borne at terminals of branches
Use As a single shrub or grouped; can be used for mid- to background planting for larger shrub borders; as an informal hedge or windy maritime areas planted at distances of 1m (3ft); can be clipped
Needs Propagate from cuttings in summer. Shrubs can be left unpruned; but cut back hard varieties that flower on current season's growth in early to mid-spring and varieties flowering on previous season's growth after flowering
Varieties *T. parviflora* (small-flowered tamarix) deep pink flowers • *T. ramosissima* (syn. *T. pentandra*; five-stamen tamarix) rose-pink flowers • *T. r.* 'Pink Cascade' racemes of pink flowers • *T. r.* 'Rubra' ♀ deep pink flowers, purple in bud • *T. tetandra* ♀ pink flowers in graceful racemes

---

VIBURNUM
Caprifoliaceae
VIBURNUM

▲ ❀ ❦ SI all year SC some
E some
H 5 yrs 1–2.5m (3–8ft)
S 5 yrs 1–2m (3–6ft)
H 10 yrs 1.5–3.5m (5–12ft)
S 10 yrs 1.5–3m (5–10ft)
❋ -15°C (4°F) to -25°C (-13°F)
Z 4–9

VIBURNUM PLICATUM 'GRANDIFLORUM'

A very diverse group of shrubs, deciduous or evergreen, offering interest from a range of forms all year long.

Soil Tolerates a wide range except waterlogged or dry soils
Aspect Light shade; tolerates full sun to medium shade
Habit Wide range, from upright, spreading to mound shaped
Leaf Deciduous or evergreen, green, oval leaves, 5–10cm (2–4in) long; good autumn colour
Flower Clusters of small, white, flowers in winter to summer, some are scented, some are with fruit
Use As foliage or fruiting shrubs, standing alone or grouped
Needs Propagate from cuttings in summer
Varieties *V. × bodnantense* 'Dawn' ♀ upright, large pink, scented flowers in winter • *V. × burkwoodii* (Burkwood viburnum) fragrant, pink-white flowers in spring • *V. × carlcephalum* ♀ fragrant flowers, white-pink in bud, in spring • *V. carlesii* 'Aurora' ♀ red flower buds, opening to fragrant, pink, tubular flowers • *V. davidii* ♀ evergreen male or female white flowers, blue fruit in autumn • *V. farreri* (syn. *V. fragrans*) ♀ upright, scented, pink-white flowers in winter • *V. opulus* 'Notcutt's Variety' ♀ white lacecap flowers, succulent red fruit in autumn • *V. plicatum* 'Grandiflorum' ♀ large, round to globular, sterile heads of white florets • *V. p.* 'Mariesii' ♀ white lacecap flowers on tiered branches in summer • *V. p.* 'Pink Beauty' ♀ white lacecap flowers ageing to pink in summer • *V. p.* 'Watanabe' compact, white lacecap flowers, orange-red fruit • *V. tinus* (*laurustinus*) evergreen, white flowers, pink in bud in winter

WEIGELA
Caprifoliaceae
WEIGELA

❀ ❦ SI summer
H 5 yrs 1.2m (4ft)
S 5 yrs 1.2m (4ft)
H 10 yrs 1.8m (5ft 6in)
S 10 yrs 1.8m (5ft 6in)
❀ -25°C (-13°C)
Z 5–9

WEIGELA 'BRISTOL RUBY'

A well-loved shrub, available in a wide range of flower and foliage colours. Weigela reacts well to pruning, which increases the size and profusion of the flowers and foliage.

Soil Any except very dry
Aspect Prefers full sun but tolerates light to medium shade
Habit Upright, becoming spreading with age
Leaf Deciduous, oval leaves, 4–13cm (1½–5in) long, in shades of green and purple, and gold- and silver-variegated
Flower Yellow, white, pink, purple and red, funnel-shaped flowers
Use As a free-standing shrub or as mid- to background planting in a shrub or mixed border
Needs Propagate from cuttings in summer. Each year, from 2 years after planting, remove one-third of shoots to ground level, choosing the oldest, after flowering
Varieties *W.* 'Boskoop Glory' salmon-pink • *W.* 'Briant Rubidor' yellow foliage, ruby red flowers • *W.* 'Bristol Ruby' ruby red flowers • *W.* 'Candida' (syn. *W.* 'Avalanche') white flowers • *W.* 'Eva Rathke' crimson-red flowers • *W. florida* f. *alba* leaves with creamy-white edges, pale pink flowers • *W. f.* 'Aureovariegata' yellow-variegated foliage, pink flowers • *W. f.* 'Foliis Purpureis' ♀ purple foliage and flowers • *W.* 'Looymansii Aurea' pale pink, golden foliage • *W.* 'Mont Blanc' ♀ fragrant white flowers • *W. middendorffiana* sulphur yellow flowers with dark orange markings • *W.* 'Newport Red' good, dark red flowers • *W.* 'Praecox Variegata' ♀ cream-white variegated foliage, scented, pink flowers

YUCCA
Agavaceae
YUCCA

▲ ❀ ❦ SI all year SC
some E
H 5 yrs 1m (3ft)
S 5 yrs 1m (3ft)
H 10 yrs 2m (6ft)
S 10 yrs 2m (6ft)
❀ -10°C (14°F)
Z 5–11

YUCCA FILAMENTOSA

The planting of a yucca gives any garden a warm, seaside atmosphere. Hardiness can be a little suspect in cold gardens, and flowering is sometimes shy unless it has been a hot, sunny summer. The varieties with variegated foliage are of especial interest, but all yuccas can be put to a wide range of architectural uses.

Soil Well-drained, acid or alkaline soils
Aspect Full sun; resents shade
Habit Upright, slow growing into a rigid framework of sparse shoots, each topped with a rosette of foliage
Leaf Evergreen, grey-green, silver- or gold-variegated, narrow, lance-shaped leaves, 15–50cm (6–20in) long; upright when young, spreading with age
Flower Large creamy-white flowers, 4–8cm (1½–3in) long, produced on upright conical panicles, 1–2m (3–6ft) high
Use Feature for tropical or Mediterranean effect; good in large containers
Needs Propagate from seed or division. No pruning required
Varieties *Y. filamentosa* main variety planted • *Y. f.* 'Bright Edge' yellow margined leaves • *Y. f.* 'Variegata' white edges to leaves • *Y. flaccida* 'Golden Sword' ♀ yellow-edged leaves • *Y. f.* 'Ivory' ♀ flowers creamy-white, stained green • *Y. gloriosa* (Spanish dagger) glaucous-green leaves, creamy-white flowers • *Y. recurvifolia* ♀ recurving glaucous leaves, creamy-white flowers • *Y. r.* 'Variegata' pale green foliage with a central band of yellow • *Y. whipplei* grey-green foliage, fragrant, green-white, purple-marked flowers

98

CLIMBERS

ACTINIDIA
Actinidiaceae
ACTINIDIA

▲ ❀ ✿ SI summer–autumn
SC some
H 5 yrs 1.5–3.7m (5–12ft)
S 5 yrs 1.5–3.7m (5–12ft)
H 10 yrs 4–6m (13–20ft)
S 10 yrs 4–6m (13–20ft)
❊ -10°C (14°F)
Z 7–10

ACTINIDIA KOLOMIKTA

In both its green and variegated forms, this is one of the most charming and interesting of climbers. Both forms need space, and *A. chinensis* can cover twice the area indicated. In most instances, both male and female plants must be grown if fruits – Chinese gooseberries or Kiwi fruit – are to be produced.

Soil Most, but needs deep and moist soil for best results
Aspect Full sun to very light shade
Habit Twining and twisting
Leaf Deciduous, pointed, oval leaves, to 13cm (5in) long, light green when young, ageing brown-green; *A. kolomikta* tips start white and age to pink; yellow autumn colour
Flower Fragrant, white, creamy-white or pale yellow flowers in summer; female forms of *A. deliciosa* produce edible fruit in late summer to autumn if a male plant is present
Use On walls and fences or through trees and large shrubs
Needs Propagate by seed or cuttings in summer. Pruning not normally required but can be contained
Varieties *A. arguta* green leaves, fragrant, white flowers with dark purple anthers borne in pairs • *A. deliciosa* (syn. *A. chinensis*; Chinese gooseberry, Kiwi fruit) fragrant creamy-white to pale yellow flowers • *A. d.* 'Blake' self-fertile form • *A. d.* 'Heywood' female form • *A. c.* 'Tomuri' male form • *A. kolomikta* ♀ pink-white new foliage on new shoots, fragrant, white flowers with yellow anthers

AKEBIA QUINATA
Lardizabalaceae
CHOCOLATE VINE

▲ ❀ ✿ SI summer–autumn
SC
H 5 yrs 2m (6ft)
S 5 yrs 2m (6ft)
H 10 yrs 5.5m (18ft)
S 10 yrs 5.5m (18ft)
❊ -15°C (4°F)
Z 4–10

AKEBIA QUINATA

This climber is usually grown for its attractive foliage and flower, but it also has curious, sausage-shaped fruit in autumn. Although it will grow against a wall, it is perhaps more rewarding to allow it to grow up and over a tree, so that it can be seen from below, against the light of the sky.

Soil Tolerates most; does well on alkaline soils; responds to high levels of organic material in the soil at planting time
Aspect Light shade to full sun but needs protection from strong, midday summer sun, which may scorch the leaves
Habit Loosely twining, wiry in nature
Leaf Deciduous to evergreen, light to mid-green, oblong to oval, 4–8cm (1½–3in) long; yellow autumn colour
Flower Male and female flowers borne on separate plants; male flowers fragrant, pale purple, borne in racemes 8–10cm (3–4in) long; female flowers chocolate purple, 2.5–3.5cm (1–1¼in) wide, in pairs; unusual sausage-shaped, grey-violet fruits can give off a pungent odour
Use For growing up through other shrubs or small trees or against walls or fences
Needs Propagate from cuttings in summer. Allow to grow free but every 5–6 years lightly trim in early spring with hedging shears
Varieties None of garden interest

AMPELOPSIS GLANDULOSA
Vitaceae
AMPELOPSIS

▲ ❀ ❦ SI summer–autumn
H 5 yrs 3m (10ft)
S 5 yrs 3m (10ft)
H 10 yrs 5m (16ft)
S 10 yrs 5m (16ft)
✳ -10°C (14°F)
Z 5–10

AMPELOPSIS GLANDULOSA VAR. BREVIPEDUNCULATA

For most of the year the green-leaved form of ampelopsis is a little mundane, but it comes into its own in autumn with leaf colour and pale blue bird's egg-like clusters of fruit. Although not a strongly growing plant, the variegated form is worth growing for its pink, white and green foliage display.

Soil Moderately alkaline to acid with a high content of organic material
Aspect Sheltered; prefers light shade but tolerates full sun if adequate moisture is available
Habit Not self-clinging; will twine around a support
Leaf Deciduous, hand-shaped leaves from 5–10cm (2–4in) long, with some lobed indentations on outer edges, mid-green above and with grey-green undersides; good orange-red autumn colour
Flower Small clusters of creamy-white flowers; in autumns following hot summers may produce small, round, clear blue fruits with black spots
Use Climber for sheltered walls and fences; *A. g.* var. *b.* 'Elegans' will require the protection of a greenhouse or conservatory in cold, exposed gardens
Needs Propagate from cuttings in summer. Prune all side shoots from last year to 2 buds of origin, except those for training
Varieties *A. glandulosa* var. *brevipendunculata* green foliage, sometimes autumn fruit • *B. g.* var. *b.* 'Elegans' white to pink variegated green, more indented leaves, creamy-white flowers, less vigorous than the green form

---

ARISTOLOCHIA MACROPHYLLA
Aristolochiaceae
DUTCHMAN'S PIPE, BIRTHWORT

▲ ❀ ❦ SI spring–summer
H 5 yrs 2m (6ft)
S 5 yrs 1.2m (5ft)
H 10 yrs 3m (10ft)
S 10 yrs 3m (10ft)
✳ -10°C (14°F)
Z 4–8

ARISTOLOCHIA MACROPHYLLA

The giant, heart-shaped leaves alone make this plant a must for a garden that has the space to accommodate it. The light green leaves are a perfect foil for the small but interesting pipe-shaped flowers from which it gets its common name.

Soil Moderately alkaline to acid, well-fed soil, high in organic material to allow for free expansion by the fleshy root system
Aspect Does best in very light shade but tolerates some shade and some sun; requires some shelter
Habit Twining, not self-supporting, with a medium to fast growth rate; does best when provided with horizontal wires approximately 50cm (18in) apart, so that growth will spread evenly over as wide an area as possible
Leaf Deciduous, large, light green, kidney- or heart-shaped, blunt or pointed leaves, 10–25cm (4–10in) long and wide, with downy undersides; some yellow autumn colour
Flower Yellow-green, pipe-shaped flowers, 2.5–4cm (1–1½in) long, with an 'open-mouth' effect at top, purple-brown around edges, appear in early summer
Use As a climber for sheltered walls, fences and pillars to show off flowers and foliage
Needs Propagate from cuttings in spring or early summer. Prune back shoots by 50 per cent in early spring before leaves show to encourage new, large foliage and flowers
Varieties None of garden interest

BERBERIDOPSIS CORALLINA
Flacourtiaceae
CORAL PLANT

▲ ❀ ✋ SI all year E
H 5 yrs 1.5m (5ft)
S 5 yrs 1m (3ft)
H 10 yrs 3m (10ft)
S10 yrs 2m (6ft)
❉ -5°C (23°F)
Z 7–10

BERBERIDOPSIS CORALLINA

There are only a small number of evergreen climbers, so this unusual plant is a worthy addition to the garden, not only for its foliage but for the waxy, red flowers in summer. Care has to be taken with preparing the soil and providing shade, but in the right conditions this is a striking plant.

Soil Neutral to acid; tolerates only limited alkalinity; incorporate large quantities of organic material in the soil to make sure that the plant becomes established
Aspect Very sheltered position required; does best in light shade although tolerates slightly more shade and some sun
Habit Sprawling and spreading and not self-clinging; needs support and tying in; moderate growth rate
Leaf Evergreen, glossy, mid-green, oblong leaves to 8cm (3in) long and 4cm (1½in) wide, with toothed edges; some orange-red shading in autumn as old leaves die
Flower Small, waxy, crimson, globe-shaped flowers hanging in short racemes in late spring to early summer
Use As a small climbing shrub for sheltered walls and fences; ideal in a woodland setting, climbing up tree trunks, provided there is adequate moisture
Needs Propagate by seed in spring or from cuttings in summer; can be layered in autumn to good effect. No pruning required
Varieties None

BILLARDIERA LONGIFLORA
Pittosporaceae
BILLARDIERA

▲ ❀ ✋ SI summer
H 5 yrs 1.5m (5ft)
S 5 yrs 1.5m (5ft)
H 10 yrs 3m (10ft)
S 10 yrs 3m (10ft)
❉ -5°C (23°F)†
Z 7–10

BILLARDIERA LONGIFLORA

A charming, small-flowered climber with a gentle habit of growth. Although it is not fully hardy, if a warm, sheltered wall is available it is worth the effort of searching for from a specialist nursery.

Soil Neutral to acid soil with a high organic content; tolerates small amount of alkalinity
Aspect Very sheltered position required; prefers light shade but may tolerate more shade or more sun
Habit Twining, not self-clinging, so needs support (such as wires) to climb on; slow to medium rate of growth
Leaf Evergreen, light green, hanging, narrow, lance-shaped leaves, 4.5cm (1¾in) long and 1cm (½in) wide
Flower Tubular flowers, yellow-green then turning purple, in summer, followed by interesting sausage-shaped fruits in late summer
Use For sheltered walls and fences or under the protection of a greenhouse or conservatory
Needs Propagate from cuttings in summer or seed sown in spring. Trim lightly in spring to remove any dead or winter-damaged shoots
Varieties None

†*in sheltered locations*

CAMPSIS
Bignoniaceae
TRUMPET CREEPER

▲ ❀ ❦ SI summer
H 5 yrs 3m (10ft)
S 5 yrs 3m (10ft)
H 10 yrs 6m (20ft)
S 10 yrs 6m (20ft)
❄ -15°C (4°F)
Z 6–10

**CAMPSIS × TAGLIABUANA
'MADAME GALEN'**

A large plant, which requires careful positioning and space if it is to produce the very large, trumpet flowers in any number. The plant must be in a warm, sunny spot so that the shoots that produce the flowers will ripen.

Soil Moderately alkaline to acid, deep, well-fed and well-drained soil, with a high organic content
Aspect Must be in full sun to ripen previous season's growth to encourage flowering; ideally grow on or along a very sunny wall
Habit Twining, with retaining tendrils; fast rate of growth; the shoots are an attractive yellow-brown in winter
Leaf Deciduous, light to mid-green, pinnate leaves, 20–30cm (8–12in) long, with toothed edges; good yellow autumn colour
Flower Clusters of orange-red, large, trumpet-shaped flowers 5–8cm (2–3in) long; main flowering at midsummer but intermittent flowers later; some varieties have red and yellow flowers
Use For sunny walls and fences or climbing through large, high-canopied trees where adequate sunshine is available
Needs Propagate from root-cuttings, self-rooted suckers or cuttings in winter or seed. Cut long, unwanted shoots hard back in autumn after leaf fall
Varieties *C. grandiflora* orange-red flowers • *C. radicans* orange-red flowers • *C. r.* f. *flava* (syn. *C. r.* 'Yellow Trumpet') good, bold yellow flowers • *C.* × *tagliabuana* 'Madame Galen' ♀ large, salmon red flowers, the most spectacular form

---

CELASTRUS ORBICULATUS
Celastraceae
CLIMBING BITTER-SWEET, STAFF VINE

▲ ❀ ❦ SI autumn
H 5 yrs 3m (10ft)
S 5 yrs 3m (10ft)
H 10 yrs 6m (20ft)
S 10 yrs 6m (20ft)
❄ -15°C (4°F)
Z 5–9

CELASTRUS ORBICULATUS

This is a monster of a climber, rambling many metres before flowering and developing its cascades of orange-yellow fruits. For the rest of the year the foliage is tidy but not especially interesting and the flowers are not spectacular. However, if there is room for it to grow to its full potential it is worth the space and the effort.

Soil Most, alkaline and acid, but dislikes dry conditions because it requires a lot of moisture to set seed
Aspect Full sun to medium shade
Habit Twisting and twining but not self-clinging; very vigorous
Leaf Deciduous, light to mid-green, pointed oval leaves, to 13cm (5in) long; good yellow autumn colour
Flower Small, rather insignificant, green flowers in summer in clusters of up to 4
Use For growing over large buildings, through large established trees and shrubs; needs space to do well
Needs Propagate from seed or by layering in spring and summer. Pruning not normally practical as it covers an extremely large area but can be reduced in size after fruiting if necessary
Varieties *C. orbiculatus* Hermaphrodite Group ♀ this is the form normally sold in nurseries and seen fruiting in gardens

CLIMBERS

CLEMATIS
Ranunculaceae
SPECIES CLEMATIS

▲ ❀ ❦ SI spring–summer–
autumn
H 2 yrs 3m (10ft)
S 2 yrs 3m (10ft)
❄ -10°C (14°F)
Z 5–8

These gems among climbers can offer flowers for every season.

Soil Most that have adequate moisture
Aspect All but most exposed; roots should be shaded
Habit Twining leaf stalks act as tendrils; medium growth rate
Leaf Deciduous or evergreen, green, oval to lance-shaped
leaves, 8–13cm (3–5in) long
Flower Wide range of colours and shapes
Use On walls, fences, pillars, trellis, pergolas; through trees
Needs Propagate from internodal cuttings in summer.
Prune early-flowering, *alpina* and *macropetala* forms after
flowering; prune late-flowering forms in early spring
Varieties *C.* 'Abundance' (*viticella*) light red to purple
flowers in summer, prune hard in spring • *C. alpina* ♀
nodding, violet-purple, pink or white flowers in spring, prune
hard after flowering • *C. armandii* evergreen, white, saucer-
shaped flowers to 5cm (2in) across in late winter, normally
needs no pruning, pale pink forms available • *C. cirrhosa*
var. *balearica* ♀ evergreen, cream flowers in winter, trim
lightly after flowering • *C. florida* 'Sieboldii' creamy, green-
striped flowers with purple stamens in summer • *C. macro-*
petala nodding, blue or pink flowers in spring, prune hard
after flowering • *C. montana* pink or white flowers in spring
after 5 years, cut hard back • *C. rehderiana* ♀ fragrant,
creamy-white, bell-shaped flowers in summer, trim lightly in
spring • *C. tangutica* yellow flowers in autumn, prune hard
in spring • *C. viticella* double and single flowers in a range of
colours in summer, leave unpruned or prune hard in spring

CLEMATIS ALPINA 'RUBY'

CLEMATIS
Ranunculaceae
LARGE-FLOWERED
CLEMATIS

▲ ❀ ❦ SI summer
H 2 yrs 3.5m (12ft)
S 2 yrs 3.5m (12ft)
❄ -15°C (4°F)
Z 5–8

Cultivars in every possible colour, combined with the size of
the flowers, provide almost unbelievable displays in summer.

Soil All except for extremely alkaline soils
Aspect All except exposed positions; full sun to light shade
with the roots covered
Habit Twining; medium to fast growth rate
Leaf Mid-green to grey-green leaves, formed from 3–5 lance-
to oval-shaped leaflets, each to 10cm (4in) long; leaf stalks act
as tendrils to help support the plant
Flower Between 4 and 8 oval sepals make up a flat, plate-
shaped flower, 8–20cm (3–8in) across, in early to late summer
Use For walls, fences, trellis or walkways or as ground cover
Needs Propagate from internodal cuttings in summer.
Pruning: (group 1) reduce by one-third the previous season's
shoots in spring; (group 2) remove all last season's growth to
30cm (1ft) of origin in spring
Varieties Group 1: *C.* 'Bees' Jubilee' ♀ deep pink flowers
with rose-pink bar • *C.* 'H.F. Young' ♀ Wedgwood-blue
flowers with cream anthers • *C.* 'Lasurstern' ♀ pale mauve
flowers with creamy-white anthers • *C.* 'Miss Bateman' ♀
creamy-white flowers with chocolate-coloured anthers •
C. 'Mrs Cholmondeley' ♀ lavender-blue flowers with brown
anthers • *C.* 'Niobe' ♀ velvety textured, deep ruby red flowers
with yellow anthers • *C.* 'The President' ♀ blue-purple
flowers with paler stripe and red-purple anthers Group 2: *C.*
'Comtesse de Bouchaud' ♀ mauve-pink flowers with yellow
anthers • *C.* 'Jackmannii Superba' larger, dark purple flowers

**CLEMATIS 'COMTESSE DE
BOUCHAUD'**

CLEMATIS
Ranunculaceae
DOUBLE-FLOWERED
CLEMATIS

▲ ❀ ❦ SI summer
H 2 yrs 2.2m (7ft)
S 2 yrs 2.2m (7ft)
❄ -10°C (14°F)
Z 5–8

**CLEMATIS
'VYVYAN PENNELL'**

Of all the clematis that are available, this group perhaps offers the most fascination and interest.

Soil Tolerates all soil conditions if there is adequate moisture
Aspect Full sun to light shade, prefers full sun; dislikes extremely exposed situations
Habit Twining, with additional support provided by leaf tendrils; medium to fast growth rate
Leaf Deciduous, mid- to grey-green, single, oval or sometimes 3–5 lance-shaped or oval leaflets, each to 10cm (4in) long, make up a single pinnate leaf; leaf stalks act as tendrils for support
Flower Semi-double or double, with numerous sepals in a wide range of colours and flowering times
Use For fences, walls or pillars; rambling through shrubs and up small trees
Needs Propagate from internodal cuttings in summer. Thin by one-third the growth made in the previous season in late winter or early spring on well-established plants; do not reduce in length because this reduces the production of double flowers
Varieties *C.* 'Beauty of Worcester' rich, deep mauve-blue flowers with creamy-white anthers • *C.* 'Duchess of Edinburgh' not as large growing as most, very double, green flowers ageing to white, very interesting as well as attractive • *C.* 'Vyvyan Pennell' ♀ the 'queen' of clematis, deep violet-blue, red-tinged flowers, a second crop of single flowers in late summer

COBAEA SCANDENS
Cobaeaceae
CLIMBING CATHEDRAL
BELLS

▲ ❀ ❦ SI summer
H 1 yr 4.5m (15ft)
S 1 yr 4.5m (15ft)
❄ 0°C (32°F)
Z 7–9

COBAEA SCANDENS

This generally annually sown and grown climber is being increasingly grown for its large, bell-shaped, late summer flowers. One of the main problems is that it does not have time to become sufficiently mature to flower before it is killed by winter frost. However, it is worth taking the risk, because the flowers are magnificent. One solution is to grow it in a large container so that it can be given cover in areas where it will not overwinter in the garden; the flowers will appear earlier in the following year.

Soil Any average, moisture-retentive soil; requires good quality compost when grown in a container
Aspect Sheltered summer planting area in full sun; dislikes shade
Habit Self-clinging by twining and tendrils, but needs something to cling to
Leaf Deciduous, grey-green, purple-hued, pinnate leaves with 3 pairs of leaflets, to 10cm (4in) long and 5cm (2in) wide
Flower Large, bell-shaped flowers to 5–8cm (2–3in) long, with green inner colouring towards base and violet-purple outside; there is an all-white form
Use As an annual climber for walls and fences to cascade through shrubs; as a greenhouse or conservatory climber
Needs Propagate from seed in spring. No pruning required
Varieties *C. scandens* ♀ the type species • *C. s.* var. *alba* ♀ pure white form

ECCREMOCARPUS
Bignoniaceae
CHILEAN GLORY FLOWER

❀ ❦ SI summer E
H 1 yr 2m (6ft)
S1 yr 2m (6ft)
❄ -5°C (23°F)
Z 7–9

ECCREMOCARPUS RUBER

This useful climbing plant is grown mainly as an annual, although in sheltered, warm gardens it may become a perennial. There is never much structure to its growth, and it scrambles through and over other plants. The bright flowers appear throughout the summer and often into early autumn.

Soil Most, but must be well drained
Aspect Full sun to light shade; must be very sheltered if overwintering is attempted
Habit Rambling, not self-clinging; medium to fast rate of growth; often grown as an annually sown plant
Leaf Evergreen (in sheltered, warm gardens), attractive, light green, pinnate leaves, 4cm (1½in) long
Flower Racemes of narrow, tubular, deep orange-red flowers, to 3cm (1¼in) long, are followed by large seedpods which carry the seed that can be sown in the following spring to produce new plants; varieties with yellow and deep pink flowers also available
Use As an annual climber for sunny walls and fences; rambling over shrubs; can be allowed to spread over the soil as summer ground cover
Needs Propagate from seed annually; normally killed during winter
Varieties *E. ruber* orange-red flowers • *E. scaber* f. *aureus* yellow-orange flowers • *E. s.* f. *coccineus* orange-red flowers • *E. s.* f. *roseus* deep pink flowers

---

FALLOPIA BALDSCHUANICA 🏆
Polygonaceae
MILE-A-MINUTE VINE, RUSSIAN VINE

▲ ❀ ❦ SI summer–autumn
H 5 yrs 6m (20ft)
S 5 yrs 6m (20ft)
H 10 yrs 12.2m (40ft)
S 10 yrs 12.2m (40ft)
❄ -18°C (0°F)
Z 4–8

FALLOPIA BALDSCHUANICA

In the right place, this plant, which used to be known as *Polygonum baldschuanica*, is a quick-growing, wide-ranging climber. In the wrong place it is a menace, spreading at an amazing rate. It will cover high fences and even whole buildings or scramble through trees to show off its large sprays of flowers and autumn colours to the full.

Soil Any, but dislikes extremely dry soils when first planted
Aspect Full sun to medium shade, including very exposed sites; flowers best in sunny positions
Habit Loosely twining and very fast growing; can make 4.6m (15ft) of growth in one season
Leaf Light green, ageing to yellow-green, oval-shaped leaves, to 5cm (2in) long and 2.5cm (1in) wide; good autumn yellow and bronze colour
Flower Small, white flowers in panicles, 25–45cm (10–18in) long and 8cm (3in) wide, in late summer and early autumn; seedheads have limited attraction
Use As fast-growing climber for walls, fences and through trees or large shrubs; ideal for covering an ugly building
Needs Propagate from seed in spring or cuttings in summer. No pruning required but often needs containing within an allotted area
Varieties None of garden interest

× FATSHEDERA LIZEI
Araliaceae
ARALIA IVY

▲ ✿ ✾ SI all year E
H 5 yrs 2m (6ft)
S 5 yrs 2m (6ft)
H 10 yrs 4m (13ft)
S 10 yrs 4m (13ft)
❄ -10°C (14°F)
Z 8–10

× **FATSHEDERA LIZEI**

This sprawling evergreen is a cross between an ivy and fatsia, and it deserves to be more widely grown. Given room, it can be used to good effect to cover large areas as a climber or as ground cover. Hardiness can be a problem in exposed gardens, but even if damaged in winter, it normally recovers quickly the following spring.

Soil Most, but prefers moisture-retentive soil with high organic content
Aspect Does well in deep shade; tolerates medium to light shade; dislikes full sun; requires some protection in exposed sites
Habit Rambling; a fast rate of growth as climber or ground cover
Leaf Evergreen, dark green, large, leathery, hand-shaped leaves, 10–25cm (4–10in) wide, with shiny upper surfaces, duller undersides; some variegated forms
Flower Clusters of round, green flowers borne almost year round; followed by black fruits
Use As a spreading, rambling evergreen for shady walls and fences; can also be fan-trained on walls
Needs Propagate from cuttings in summer. No pruning required, although very old shoots can be removed or the overall area covered can be reduced
Varieties × *Fatshedera lizei* ♀ all-green foliage • × *F. l.* 'Aurea' gold-splashed, dark green leaves • × *F. l.* 'Variegata' grey-green leaves with creamy-white margins

HEDERA
Araliaceae
IVY

▲ ✿ ✾ SI all year E
H 5 yrs 1–3.5m (3–12ft)
S 5 yrs 0.6m–1.5m (2–5ft)
H 10 yrs 1.5–5m (5–16ft)
S 10 yrs 1.2–5m (4–16ft)
❄ -15°C (4°F)
Z 4–10

HEDERA COLCHICA
'SULPHUR HEART'

Often wrongly thought of as mundane, but whenever an evergreen climber is required for a cold, dark position, ivy comes into its own. It is also useful in other situations.

Soil Does well on all soil types but resents very dry conditions until established
Aspect Full sun to deep shade; suitable for all but the most exposed positions
Habit Self-clinging and spreading
Leaf Evergreen, 3- to 5-lobed, ivy- or diamond-shaped leaves, from light to dark glossy green, yellow or variegated
Flower Small, ball-shaped clusters of light to dark green flowers in winter, followed by black fruit
Use For covering all types of construction
Needs Propagate from cuttings in summer
Varieties *H. canariensis* 'Gloire de Marengo' (syn. *H. c.* 'Variegata') oval, leathery, dark green leaves with silvery reverse and creamy-white margins • *H. colchica* 'Dentata' ♀ oval, leathery, dark, matt green leaves • *H. c.* 'Dentata Variegata' ♀ mid-green leaves with yellow-cream variegation • *H. c.* 'Sulphur Heart' (syn. *H. c.* 'Paddy's Pride') ♀ central yellow splash on pale to mid-green leaves • *H. helix* 'Glacier' ♀ silver-grey-green leaves with silvery white edges • *H. h.* 'Goldchild' ♀ gold-edged leaves • *H. h.* 'Goldheart' (syn. *H. h.* 'Jubilee') 3- or 5-pointed, dark green, yellow-splashed leaves • *H. h.* 'Sagittifolia' triangular leaves with purple or silver veining • *H. h.* 'Sagittifolia Variegata' cream- and green-variegated leaves

HUMULUS LUPULUS
Cannabaceae
HOP

▲ ❀ ❦ SI spring–autumn
H 5 yrs 3.5m (12ft)
S 5 yrs 3.5m (12ft)
H 10 yrs 6m (20ft)
S 10 yrs 6m (20ft)
❋ -10°C (14°F)
Z 3–10

**HUMULUS LUPULUS
'AUREUS'**

Beer is usually the first thing that comes to mind when we see this fast-growing ornamental climber, and the hop fruits themselves are attractive and add to the display. The fact that it dies down to ground level in winter is an advantage rather than a handicap for it means that old leaves are replaced by bright new foliage each spring. Although the golden form is the most widely grown, the green type is interesting, particularly when in fruit.

Soil Does well on acid, neutral and moderately alkaline soils
Aspect Full sun to very light shade; does well in all but the most exposed positions
Habit Twining and self-supporting but needs something to cling to; very fast growing, and once established reaches its ultimate size in one spring
Leaf Deciduous, mid-green, trifoliate leaves, 13cm (5in) wide and 15cm (6in) long; main form planted yellow to gold leaves; green form has some yellow autumn colour
Flower Male, green-yellow, leaf-like flowers in small panicles; female flowers in spikes
Use As a fast-growing perennial; for growing over walls, buildings, trees and up poles
Needs Propagate by division in spring. All top growth should be removed to within 23cm (9in) of the ground in autumn; remove remaining 23cm (9in) to ground level the following spring
Varieties *Humulus lupulus* green foliage • *H. l.* 'Aureus' ♥ golden-yellow foliage

IPOMOEA HEDERACEA
Convolvulaceae
MORNING GLORY

▲ ❀ ❦ SI summer
H 1 yr 3.5m (12ft)
S 1 yr 3.5m (12ft)
❋ not winter hardy
Z 7–9

IPOMOEA HEDERACEA

Few other plants offer such intensely blue flowers as this. It has to be replanted each year, but the display of summer flowers is a wonderful reward for the extra work. Ipomoeas look particularly good when grown in association with plants with golden foliage.

Soil Tolerates all soil conditions; if grown in a container requires good quality compost and regular watering
Aspect Does best in full sun; requires protection from wind and heavy rain
Habit Twining and self-supporting; fast rate of growth
Leaf Broad, light to mid-green, oval to heart-shaped leaves, to 13cm (5in) long and 2.5cm (1in) wide
Flower Intense blue, trumpet-shaped flowers, with reflexed mouth and white central eye; forms available with flowers in shades of pale pink to purple-pink, but blue flowers are the most pleasing
Use As an annual climber for walls and fences, rambling over large shrubs or conifers
Needs Propagate from seed in early spring under protection or purchase ready-grown young plants in early summer. No pruning required as it is killed by frosts in autumn
Varieties *I. hederacea* is the only form available; often sold in its mixed form, so try to find all-blue selection

JASMINUM
Oleaceae
JASMINE

▲ ❀ ❦ SI summer–winter
SC some E some
H 5 yrs 1.5–3.5m (5–12ft)
S 5 yrs 1.5–3.5m (5–12ft)
H 10 yrs 3–7.3m (10–24ft)
S 10 yrs 3–7.3m (10–24ft)
❋ -5°C (23°F) to -15°C (4°F)
Z 7–10

JASMINUM × STEPHANENSE

The fragrance is usually given as the reason for growing jasmine, but even those varieties that are not scented should be grown for their flowers. The genus includes both summer- and winter-flowering forms.

Soil Most, as long as it is moist
Aspect Full sun to medium shade; can withstand being in an exposed position, except *J. officinale*, which requires more shelter and a position in full sun to very light shade
Habit Partially twining; medium rate of growth
Leaf Deciduous to semi-evergreen, pinnate, grey-green to dark green leaves
Flower Flowers with 5 petals, to 1cm (½in) across and long, in a range of colours; some fragrant
Use As a climber for walls, fences, pillars and pergolas
Needs Propagate from cuttings in summer. Remove one-third of old flowering shoots to ground level in early spring
Varieties *J. beesianum* red flowers in summer • *J. nudiflorum* (winter jasmine) ♀ butter-yellow flowers carried at leaf joints from early winter to early spring in mild weather • *J. officinale* ♀ white-scented flowers in summer, strong growing • *J. o.* 'Aureum' gold-variegated leaves, white, very fragrant flowers • *J. o.* 'Variegatum' white-variegated leaves, scented, white-tinged pink flowers in summer • *J. polyanthum* ♀ small reflexed petals, white on inside and rosy white on outside, borne in panicles, very fragrant, needs protection • *J. × stephanense* pale pink flowers in summer

---

LAPAGERIA ROSEA
Philesiaceae/Liliaceae
CHILEAN BELLFLOWER

▲ ❀ ❦ SI summer–autumn
E
H 5 yrs 2.2m (7ft)
S 5 yrs 2.2m (7ft)
H 10 yrs 4.4m (14ft)
S 10 yrs 4.4m (14ft)
❋ 0°C (32°F)
Z 7–9

LAPAGERIA ROSEA

Sadly, this beautiful climbing plant is not hardy in any but the warmest of gardens. Thankfully, it is a good conservatory specimen, growing freely in a large container, so even gardeners without a frost-free garden can grow it.

Soil Add additional sharp sand and peat to provide moisture-retentive, well-drained soil; use a large container for growing indoors with a good quality compost
Aspect Light shade; dislikes full sun; requires very sheltered site or to be grown in a conservatory or greenhouse
Habit Loosely twining; not self-clinging or supporting; medium rate of growth
Leaf Evergreen, broad, oval, pointed, leathery, grey-green leaves, to 8cm (3in) long
Flower Large, pendent, fleshy, bell-shaped flowers, 8cm (3in) long, in white, pink or dark pink to red according to variety
Use As a climbing plant for very sheltered gardens or for use in conservatories and greenhouses
Needs Propagate from seed or cuttings in summer. Pruning not normally required but can be cut back if necessary in early spring and will regenerate
Varieties *L. rosea* ♀ pale pink flowers • *L. r.* var. *albiflora* pure white flowers • *L. r.* 'Nash Court ♀ dark pink to red flowers

LATHYRUS
**Leguminosae/
Papilionaceae**
EVERLASTING PEA

▲ ❀ ❦ SI summer SC
H 1 yr 2–3m (6–10ft)
S 1 yr 1.5–2m (5–6ft)
❅ -10°C (14°F)
Z 3–10

**LATHYRUS LATIFOLIUS
'WHITE PEARL'**

This close relative of the sweet pea has gained a place in gardens for its summer flowers. Its planting position must be chosen with care so that it can scramble freely where it wants. It is a large plant which requires space and room to show itself off to the maximum.

Soil Tolerates both alkaline and acid conditions; requires moisture-retentive soil and a high degree of organic material
Aspect Full sun to light shade
Habit Rambling, clinging and quick growing. Attractive angular, grey-green stems
Leaf Deciduous, grey-green, elliptic leaves, 4–5cm (1½–2in) long, in pairs with tendrils
Flower Back shield with two wings either side and two forward-facing petals, forming typical sweet pea flower, 4cm (1½in) wide and deep, in a range of colours, followed by silver-grey, down-covered seedpods
Use Walls, fences, pillars but at its best when rambling and scrambling through large shrubs
Needs Propagate from seed or by division of root-clumps in spring. Dies down in winter to regenerate the following year
Varieties *L. grandiflorus* pink-purple and red flowers • *L. latifolius* ♀ pink flowers • *L. l.* 'Albus' pure white flowers • *L. l.* 'Red Pearl' light red flowers • *L. l.* 'Rosa Perle' ('Pink Pearl') pale pink flowers • *L. l.* 'White Pearl' ('Weisse Perle') ♀ white flowers • *L. rotundifolius* purple-pink to red flowers

LATHYRUS
ODORATUS
**Leguminosae/
Papilionaceae**
ANNUAL SWEET PEA

▲ ❀ ❦ SI summer SC
H 1 yr 2.7m (9ft)
S 1 yr 1m (3ft)
❅ not winter hardy
Z 7–9

LATHYRUS ODORATUS

No other plant has a scent to compare with that of the annual sweet pea, and the range of soft pastel colours of the flowers adds to the pleasure.

Soil Deep, well-prepared soil, both alkaline and acid, containing organic material
Aspect Full sun to light shade; protect from wind and rain
Habit Loosely twining; fast rate of growth
Leaf Deciduous, grey-green, oval leaves, normally in pairs
Flower Two wings either side of a large back shield, to 4cm 1½in) wide and deep, in a range of colours; highly fragrant
Use To cover walls, fences, pillars or pergolas or grow through large shrubs or over prepared supports
Needs Propagate from seed or purchase ready-grown young plants
Varieties *L. odoratus* Spencer Hybrids 'Aerospace' white flowers • 'Air Warden' cerise-scarlet flowers • 'Beaujolais' burgundy-red flowers • 'Blue Danube' deep blue flowers • 'Carlotta' carmine flowers with white blotch • 'Cream Beauty' cream flowers with frilled edges • 'Dorothy Sutton' rose-pink on cream flowers • 'Elizabeth Taylor' mauve flowers • 'Garden Party' red, orange-tinged flowers • 'Larkspur' blue to lavender flowers • 'Lemington' lavender flowers • 'Mrs R. Bolton' almond-blossom pink flowers • 'Royal Flush' salmon-pink on cream flowers • 'Royal Wedding' white flowers • 'Swan Lake' white flowers • 'Welcome' scarlet flowers • 'Winston Churchill' crimson flowers

LONICERA
Caprifoliaceae
HONEYSUCKLE

▲ ❀ ❦ SI spring–summer
SC some E some
H 5 yrs 1.5–4.5m (5–15ft)
S 5 yrs 2–3.5m (6–12ft)
H 10 yrs 2.5–9m (8–30ft)
S 10 yrs 1.5–6m (5–20ft)
❅ -15°C (4°F) to -10°C (14°F)
Z 6–9

**LONICERA PERICLYMENUM
'SEROTINA'**

This has been a favourite garden plant for years for its scented flowers and attractive climbing habit. There are many varieties, not all with scent.

Soil Most, but must be moisture-retentive
Aspect Does best in light shade but tolerates full sun; will grow in all but the most exposed positions
Habit Loosely twining; slow to fast growth rate
Leaf Deciduous or evergreen, bright green, grey to grey-green, dark green, oval leaves
Flower Tubular florets or clusters of funnel-shaped trumpets, scented in a range of colours; red fruits
Use For walls, fences, trellis, large shrubs and trees
Needs Propagate by cuttings in summer. Every 4 years thin out shoots in spring
Varieties *L. × americana* (syn. *L. × italica)* yellow flowers with purple shading • *L. × brownii* 'Dropmore Scarlet' bright scarlet flowers • *L. caprifolium* (Italian woodbine) ♀ trumpet-shaped, yellow-white florets with pink tinge • *L. etrusca* 'Superba' creamy-yellow flowers turning orange • *L. japonica* 'Aureoreticulata' (golden variegated Japanese honeysuckle) gold-variegated foliage, fragrant, bright yellow flowers • *L. j.* 'Halliana' ♀ evergreen, white flowers, sometimes tinged purple, ageing to yellow • *L. periclymenum* 'Belgica' ♀ scented, deep purple-red flowers fading to yellow-red • *L. p.* 'Serotina' ♀ scented, red-purple flowers creamy-white • *L. × tellmanniana* ♀ orange-yellow flowers • *L. tragophylla* ♀ strong growing, large yellow flowers

---

PARTHENOCISSUS
Vitaceae
VIRGINIA CREEPER, BOSTON IVY

▲ ❀ ❦ SI autumn
H 5 yrs 1.5–2.5m (5–8ft)
S 5 yrs 1.5–2.5m (5–8ft)
H 10 yrs 3–5m (10–16ft)
S 10 yrs 3–5m (10–16ft)
❅ -18°C (0°F)
Z 3–10

**PARTHENOCISSUS
TRICUSPIDATA**

Parthenocissus is one of the fastest growing climbing plants. It is self-clinging, and the fact that it will grow against exposed walls makes it even more useful. Before planting, inspect the brickwork because it can cause damage.

Soil Most soils provided they are moisture-retentive
Aspect Full sun to light shade
Habit Self-clinging, fast growing
Leaf Mid- to dark green, hand-shaped leaves, to 10cm (4in) long and 15cm (6in) wide, oval and toothed; autumn colour
Flower Insignificant, green to green-yellow flowers in clusters; in very hot summers followed by small, blue-black fruits
Use For large walls and fences; through trees or large hedges
Needs Propagate from cuttings in summer. Requires no pruning but can be shortened by up to 60cm (2ft) close to windows and doors or cut to ground level, when will rejuvenate over next 2–3 years
Varieties *P. henryana* (syn. *Vitis henryana)* ♀ young foliage dark green with silver-white veining, vivid orange-scarlet autumn colour • *P. quinquefolia* (syn. Vitis *quinquefolia)* ♀ dull to mid-green foliage, ageing to grey-brown • *P. tricuspidata* ♀ crimson autumn colour • *P. t.* 'Beverley Brook' purple foliage, orange-scarlet autumn colour • *P. t.* 'Green Spring' small, green leaves, good autumn colour • *P. t.* 'Veitchii' (syn. *Ampelopsis tricuspidata* 'Veitchii', *Vitis inconstans* 'Purpurea') mid- to dark green, turning vivid crimson and scarlet in autumn

PASSIFLORA
Passifloraceae
PASSION FLOWER

▲ ❀ ❦ SI summer–autumn
SC
H 5 yrs 2.4m (8ft)
S 5 yrs 2.4m (8ft)
H 10 yrs 4.9m (16ft)
S 10 yrs 4.9m (16ft)
❄ -5°C (23°F)
Z 5–10

Not always easy to grow, when it is given the warmth of a sunny wall the passion flower will produce not only its beautiful flowers but also fruit. There are other varieties than those listed below, but their hardiness is very suspect.

Soil Any, but dislikes extremely alkaline and dry soils
Aspect Full sun to very light shade; requires sheltered, warm position
Habit Twining and climbing; very fast growth rate
Leaf Deciduous (in all but the warmest garden), mid-green, hand-shaped with 5- to 7-lobed leaflets, each oblong to lance-shaped and 10–18cm (4–7in) long and 5cm (2in) wide
Flower Fragrant flowers, borne singly, to 10cm (4in) wide, sepals and petals white or pink-white, central area 5cm (2in) across with spiky blue filaments, white in centre, purple at base; followed by egg-shaped yellow fruits in autumn
Use For walls or fences, to cover archways or pillars and to grow over pergolas
Needs Propagate from seed or cuttings in summer. Can be cut to within 1m (3ft) of ground level every 5–6 years in spring and will quickly rejuvenate
Varieties *P. caerulea* ♀ white or pink-white flowers •
P. c. 'Constance Elliott' ♀ white flowers with spiky, pale blue filaments, slight fragrance

PASSIFLORA CAERULEA

PILEOSTEGIA VIBURNOIDES ♀
Hydrangeaceae
CLIMBING VIBURNUM

▲ ❀ ❦ SI all year E
H 5 yrs 1m (3ft)
S 5 yrs 1m (3ft)
H 10 yrs 1.8m (6ft)
S 10 yrs 1.8m (6ft)
❄ -10°C (14°F)
Z 5–10

Pileostegia is slow to grow but spectacular when it does. The evergreen foliage can be damaged by cold winds, so it needs a sheltered corner to do well, and the roots respond to high levels of organic material in the soil at planting time. Given time, it is one of the finest of evergreen climbing plants.

Soil Does well on all soil types as long as plenty of organic material is provided at planting time
Aspect Full sun to light shade; does well in all positions but dislikes extreme degrees of wind chill and draught, which will damage the evergreen foliage
Habit Slow to mature; requires support to climb to any height. Snow can break the shoots, so should be removed as soon as possible
Leaf Evergreen, leathery, narrow oblong or lance-shaped leaves, 6–15cm (2½–6in) long, dark green above with pitted-silver undersides
Flower Many small flowers, creamy-white in bud, opening to white with prominent stamens, carried in panicles to 10–15cm (4–6in) long in summer
Use For covering large walls and fences where it can be fan-trained
Needs Propagate from cuttings in summer or self-produced layers. Pruning not normally required
Varieties None

PILEOSTEGIA VIBURNOIDES

RHODOCHITON ATROSANGUINEUS

♛

Scrophulariaceae
PURPLE BELLS

▲ ❀ ❦ SI summer
H 2 yrs 1.2m (4ft)
S 2 yrs 1.2m (4ft)
❄ 0°C (32°F)
Z 5–10

RHODOCHITON ATROSANGUINEUS

This tender climbing plant is normally grown as an annual, and seeds are sown each spring. It can be regarded as perennial only in very sheltered gardens or if grown in a conservatory. It is attractive as a general climber, but when it is planted in a hanging basket it is a spectacular sight from late spring until the first frosts of winter.

Soil Moderately alkaline to acid; if grown in a container use good quality compost
Aspect Does best in full sun but tolerates light shade; requires a very sheltered, warm, sunny, frost-free position
Habit Rambling and partially twining; medium rate of growth
Leaf Attractive mid-green, narrowly pointed leaves with purple hue around veins, some small teeth and light downy covering
Flower Attractive blood-red to dark blood-red, ageing to purple-red, pendent, bell-shaped, 5-petalled flowers arranged along stems throughout summer and early autumn
Use As a low climber for very warm sunny positions; as a greenhouse or conservatory climber; can be grown in containers, including hanging baskets, to good effect
Needs Propagate from seed sown in spring. Pruning not usually required. Tie to support
Varieties None

RUBUS
Rosaceae
FRUITING BRAMBLE

▲ ❀ ❦ SI summer–autumn
D
H 1 yr 2.4m (8ft)
S 1 yr 2.4m (8ft)
❄ -18°C (0°F)
Z 4–8

RUBUS FRUTICOSUS 'HIMALAYAN GIANT'

The genus *Rubus* includes a wide range of plants and you should plant named cultivars for the best fruit. Thorns can make cultivation difficult.

Soil All soils
Aspect Full sun to medium shade to ripen fruit
Habit Arching, strong, roots at the tips of the shoots; grows into clump
Leaf Deciduous, semi-evergreen or evergreen, light to dark green, 3- to 5-lobed leaves, 10cm (4in) long with a silver reverse
Flower White or pink, saucer-shaped flowers, 2cm (¾in) across
Use Fan-trained against walls and fences; supported in the garden
Needs Propagate by layering in summer; cut to ground in spring of first year, cut all canes to ground after fruiting thereafter
Varieties *R. fruticosus* 'Bedford Giant' large fruit with good flavour • *R. f.* 'Himalayan Giant' large fruit, • *R. f.* 'Loch Ness' ♛ good fruit • *R. f.* 'Oregon Thornless' (cut-leaved bramble) good, medium sized fruit, semi-evergreen

SCHISANDRA RUBRIFLORA
Schisandraceae
SCHISANDRA

▲ ❀ ❦ SI spring–summer
H 5 yrs 1.5m (5ft)
S 5 yrs 1.5m (5ft)
H 10 yrs 3m (10ft)
S 10 yrs 3m (10ft)
❊ -10°C (14°F)
Z 7–10

Fascinating red flowers peep out from the mid-green leaves of this interesting plant, and in winter the glossy brown stems are attractive. It is not fast to mature and may take several years to reach its full display potential.

Soil Does well on moderately alkaline and acid soils as long as adequate moisture is available; dislikes dry conditions, which quickly damage the foliage
Aspect Tolerates all but the most exposed positions
Habit Moderately twining; slow to medium growth rate; neat and undemanding habit
Leaf Deciduous, mid-green, oval to lance-shaped leaves, 13cm (5½in) long and 5cm (2in) wide; good yellow autumn colour
Flower Pendulous, deep crimson flowers, borne singly at leaf joints, hanging on stalks in small bunches in late spring to early summer
Use For walls, fences, poles and pergolas
Needs Propagate from seed in spring or cuttings in summer. Pruning not normally required, but can be reduced in size in early spring if necessary
Varieties None

SCHISANDRA RUBRIFLORA

SCHIZOPHRAGMA
Hydrangeaceae
SCHIZOPHRAGMA

▲ ❀ ❦ SI summer–autumn
H 5 yrs 1.5m (5ft)
S 5 yrs 1.5m (5ft)
H 10 yrs 3m (10ft)
S 10 yrs 3m (10ft)
❊ -15°C (4°F)
Z 6–9

A spectacular plant when it is fully grown, the schizophragma needs both time and space if it is to achieve any real height. The flowers start to be of interest in midsummer, when they are green. They then turn white and finally brown for winter. The leaf is also pleasant, as are the bare shiny brown stems in winter. If you are prepared to wait 5–10 years, this is one of the finest of the large climbers.

Soil Any, but dislikes extreme alkalinity and dryness
Aspect Does best in full sun but tolerates very light shade; will withstand all but the severest weather
Habit Branching and slow growing; best fan- or flat-trained on a large wall or fence
Leaf Deciduous, green, broad, oval-shaped leaves, to 7.5–13cm (3–5in) long, with toothed edges; yellow-brown autumn colours
Flower Small, yellow-white flowers, ringed by large (4cm/1½in) long, white or pink bracts carried in large spear-shaped clusters in late summer to midwinter; ageing to yellow-brown
Use For large walls and fences or to grow up short-trunked large trees
Needs Propagate from commercial cuttings in summer. Pruning not normally required but cut back in spring if necessary
Varieties S. hydrangeoides (Japanese hydrangea vine) yellow-white flowers • S. h. 'Roseum' pale pink bracts • S. integrifolium ♀ larger leaves and flowerheads

SCHIZOPHRAGMA HYDRANGEOIDES

SOLANUM
Solanaceae
SOLANUM

▲ ❀ ❦ SI summer SC some
E (semi)
H 5 yrs 3m (10ft)
S 5 yrs 3m (10ft)
H 10 yrs 4m (13ft)
S 10 yrs 4m (13ft)
❄ -10°C (14°F)
Z 7–10

**SOLANUM CRISPUM
'GLASNEVIN'**

This is a large genus of herbs, shrubs and trees as well as some climbing species, which are sometimes known as climbing potato vines. Among these is *Solanum crispum*, a plant whose overall size, in terms not only of height and spread but of forward projection, is often underestimated. The remainder of the group are less demanding of space, but all produce a fine display of summer flowers.

Soil Most, except very dry soils; dislikes high alkalinity
Aspect Full sun to light shade in a sheltered position
Habit Upright, becoming branching; medium to fast growth rate
Leaf Deciduous to semi-evergreen, narrow, oval leaves, dark green above, paler beneath
Flower Star-shaped flowers, with 5 pale-blue, violet-blue or white, fleshy petals surmounted by a central, bright yellow bunch of anthers, each flower 2.5cm (1in) across and borne in clusters in summer; some forms scented
Use Free-standing or climbing on large walls and fences
Needs Propagate from cuttings in summer. Remove one-third of oldest growth to ground level in spring once established for more than 3 years
Varieties *S. crispum* 'Autumnale' very large, free-standing plant, pale blue flowers • *S. c.* 'Glasnevin' ♀ larger flowers of slightly darker blue • *S. dulcamara* 'Variegatum' variegated white foliage, purple-blue flowers, poisonous red fruits • *S. jasminoides* scented, blue-purple flowers • *S. j.* 'Album' ♀ white flowers, less hardy and needs protection in winter

SOLLYA HETEROPHYLLA
Pittospraceae
AUSTRALIAN BLUEBELL,
BLUEBELL CREEPER

▲ ❀ ❦ SI summer–autumn
SC E
H 2 yrs 2m (6ft)
S 2 yrs 2m (6ft)
H 5 yrs 2.7m (9ft)
S 5 yrs 2.7m (9ft)
❄ -5°C (23°F)† Z 7–9

SOLLYA HETEROPHYLLA

The intense blue flowers of this Australian plant, which used to be classified as *Sollya fusiformis*, are very appealing, but unfortunately, it is not hardy can be grown only in the most sheltered and warmest of gardens. Luckily, it responds to the conditions provided by a conservatory or greenhouse.

Soil High in organic material because resents drying out; if grown in a container use good quality compost
Aspect Sheltered, semi-shade but tolerates full sun; requires winter protection
Habit Twining and self-supporting; medium to fast growth rate
Leaf Evergreen, oval to lance-shaped, pointed leaves, to 6cm (2½in) long and 2cm (¾in) wide, light, bright green ageing to dark green
Flower Pendent clusters of 4–12 deep blue flowers, each approximately 1cm (½in) across and consisting of 5 small, pointed petals, borne through summer and early autumn
Use As self-clinging climber for very sheltered walls and fences or in a greenhouse or conservatory; can be grown in a large container
Needs Propagate from cuttings in early summer. Pruning not normally required but can be reduced in size if necessary
Varieties None

†*in very sheltered areas only*

TRACHELOSPERMUM
Apocynaceae
TRACHELOSPERMUM

▲ ❀ ❦ SI summer SC E
H 5 yrs 1–1.5m (3–5ft)
S 5 yrs 1–1.5m (3–5ft)
H 10 yrs 2–3m (6–10ft)
S 10 yrs 2–3m (6–10ft)
❄ -10°C (14°F)
Z 3–8

**TRACHELOSPERMUM
JASMINOIDES**

Few climbers can compete with trachelospermum when it comes to scent, and this, combined with the white, star-shaped flowers and dark green foliage, make the climber almost perfect. The major problem is that it is a tender plant, which needs the protection of a warm, sunny corner or to be grown in a conservatory or greenhouse to keep the worst of the cold weather away. The variegated form, with creamy-white edges to the leaves and scented flowers, is more tender and needs protection in all but the most sheltered of gardens.

Soil Moderately alkaline to acid; dislikes extremely dry conditions
Aspect Full sun to very light shade in a sheltered position
Habit Upright, becoming spreading with age; slow to medium growth rate
Leaf Evergreen, oval to lance shaped, grey-green to dark green leaves, to 11cm (4½in) long; variegated forms have irregular white marginal variegation turning pink in winter
Flower Fragrant, creamy-white to white, 5-petalled flowers borne in clusters or terminal racemes to 10cm (4in) long
Use On sheltered walls, fences and pillars; in a conservatory or large greenhouse; all forms grow in large containers
Needs Propagate from cuttings in summer. Pruning not normally required
Varieties *T. asiaticum* ♀ open clusters of small creamy-white flowers • *T. jasminoides* ♀ racemes of white flowers • *T. j.* 'Variegatum' ♀ variegated form, less hardy, to two-thirds average height and spread

TROPAEOLUM
Tropaeolaceae
NASTURTIUM

▲ ❀ ❦ SI summer
H 1 yr 1.2–2m (4–6ft)
S 1 yr 1.2m (4ft)
❄ -10°C (14°F)
Z 7–9

TROPAEOLUM SPECIOSUM

This group includes both perennial and hardy annual forms of plants that offer bright colourful flower displays. Some of the perennial forms can be tender and require winter protection. Half-hardy varieties may sow themselves in the second and subsequent years or they can be sown each spring.

Soil Most, but perennial varieties require well-prepared soil
Aspect Flowers in full sun to light shade
Habit Trailing and intertwining but not truly self-clinging
Leaf Deciduous, hand-shaped, lightly lobed, light to mid-green leaves, 4cm (1½in) long
Flower Red to red and yellow in summer
Use Growing over large shrubs or on supports against walls
Needs Propagate from root rhizomes or from seed
Varieties Perennial varieties: *T. pentaphyllum* small yellow flowers • *T. speciosum* ♀ red-orange, 5-petalled flowers • *T. tuberosum* attractive red-yellow flowers, needs protection • *T. t.* 'Ken Aslet' ♀ orange flowers, needs protection Half-hardy varieties: *T. majus* 'Alaska Mixed' white-splashed leaves, mixed flower colours • *T. m.* 'Climbing Mixed' mixed flower colours • *T. m.* 'Double Gleam Mixed' double, mixed flower colours • *T. m.* 'Empress of India' dark foliage, crimson-scarlet flowers • *T. m.* 'Fiery Festival' scented, deep scarlet flowers • *T. m.* 'Golden Gleam' semi-double, yellow flowers • *T. m.* 'Jewel Mixed' semi-double flowers in very bright, mixed colours • *T. m.* 'Orange Gleam' semi-double, orange-red flowers • *T. m.* 'Peach Melba' light yellow flowers with scarlet blotches

VITIS
Vitaceae
VINE

▲ ❀ ❦ SI autumn
H 5 yrs 3m (10ft)
S 5 yrs 3m (10ft)
H 10 yrs 4.5–6m (15–20ft)
S 10 yrs 4.5–6m (15–20ft)
❊ -15°C (4°F)
Z 3–11

VITIS 'BRANT'

With its leaf colour and potential for fruit, some large enough to be edible, the vine is one of the stars of the autumn, although it needs space and a sunny position to perform to its best. Pruning is important, as is the choice of variety.

Soil All, but requires adequate moisture and root run
Aspect Light shade to full sun
Habit Clinging tendrils, partially self-supporting; vigorous
Leaf Deciduous, light green, 5-fingered, maple-shaped leaves, to 30cm (1ft) across; brilliant autumn colours
Flower Small, creamy-green clusters in summer; green-yellow or ageing to black fruit, often with blue bloom, in autumn
Use Fast-growing climber to cover walls, fences or wires; over large shrubs or trees
Needs Propagate from cuttings in spring. Can be left to ramble or treated as a fruiting vine by cutting back all previous season's shoots close to the main stems in spring
Varieties <u>Ornamental varieties</u>: *Vitis* 'Brant' good autumn colour, small, edible, purple-blue fruits • *V. coignetiae* (crimson glory vine) heart-shaped foliage, brilliant crimson and scarlet autumn colour • *V. vinifera* 'Purpurea' ❦ leaves with downy, claret-red upper surface, purple-blue undersides, good purple autumn colour <u>Fruiting varieties</u>: *V. vinifera* 'Cascade' ('Seibel 13053') white-yellow, wine • *V. v.* 'Léon Millot' white-yellow, wine • *V. v.* 'Schiava Grossa' ('Black Hamburgh') black skin, wine or dessert • *V. v.* 'Strawberry Grape' white-yellow, dessert

---

WISTERIA
Leguminosae/
Papilionaceae
WISTERIA

▲ ❀ ❦ SI spring SC some
H 5 yrs 5.5m (18ft)
S 5 yrs 5.5m (18ft)
H 10 yrs 11m (36ft)
S 10 yrs 11m (36ft)
❊ -10°C (14°F)
Z 5–9

WISTERIA SINENSIS

Few other climbers offer such a wonderful display, and spring would not be spring without the blue flowers, although white and pink varieties are available. Pruning is important.

Soil All types but must have adequate root run
Aspect Sheltered position; must be in sun to flower well
Habit Twisting and twining; fast growing
Leaf Deciduous, light green, pinnate leaves, 30–45cm (12–18in); yellow autumn colour
Flower Racemes of pea-like flowers, 15–23cm (6–9in) long, in a range of colours in spring; long grey-green seedpods
Use On sunny walls, fences and pergolas; through trees
Needs Propagate by commercial grafting. Important: cut back in winter all current season's shoots to 5cm (2in) of origin once framework is in place
Varieties *W. floribunda* blue racemes to 60cm (2ft) • *W. f.* 'Alba' (syn. *W. multijuga* 'Alba') ❦ white racemes 30cm (1ft) • *W. f.* 'Kuchi-beni' (syn. *W. f.* 'Peaches and Cream') rose-pink flowers, opening to white • *W. f.* 'Purple Patches' (syn. *W. f.* 'Murasaki-naga') violet-purple flowers • *W. f.* 'Rosea' (*W. f.* 'Pink Ice') rose-pink flowers • *W. f.* 'Snow Showers' (syn. *W. f.* 'Shiro-nagi') pure white flowers • *W. × formosa* 'Issai' ('Domino') lilac-blue flowers • *W. ×f.* 'Kokkuryu' ('Black Dragon') double, dark purple flowers • *W. sinensis* ❦ traditional blue form • *W. s.* 'Alba' ('Shiro-capital') ❦ white flowers • *W. s.* 'Caroline' deep blue, scented flowers • *W. venusta* mid-blue, waxy flowers • *W. v.* var. *violacea* deep blue, waxy flowers • *W. v.* 'White Silk' white, waxy flowers

ROSA
Rosaceae
HYBRID TEA BUSH
ROSE, SINGLE-
FLOWERED ROSE

▲ ❀ ❦ SI summer SC some
H 2 yrs 75cm (30in)
S 2 yrs 75cm (30in)
❀ -10°C (14°F)
Z 6–10

ROSA 'ERNEST H. MORSE'

These are the elite among roses. The shape and colours of the flowers, the fact that many are fragrant and their neat habit have led to their being planted in almost every garden.

Soil Most, except very dry or wet
Aspect Prefers full sun but tolerates very light shade
Habit Upright, sometimes spreading with age
Leaf Deciduous, typical mid- to dark green rose leaves
Flower Goblet-shaped, sometimes scented flowers in summer
Use For solo or mass-planting
Needs Propagate by commercial budding. Prune by reducing in spring all previous season's growth by as much as 95 per cent, cutting the weakest hardest
Varieties *R.* 'Alec's Red' very fragrant, deep, bright crimson flowers • *R.* 'Apricot Silk' apricot flowers • *R.* 'Blessings' ♀ coral-pink flowers • *R.* 'Duke of Windsor' bright vermilion-orange flowers • *R.* 'Ernest H. Morse' fragrant, pure turkey-red flowers • *R.* 'Grandpa Dickson' deep lemon-yellow flowers • *R.* 'King's Ransom' large blooms of rich, deep gold flowers • *R.* 'Mischief' coral-salmon flowers with carmine shading • *R.* 'Mister Lincoln' deep crimson flowers • *R.* 'Pascali' pure white flowers • *R.* 'Peace' ♀ vigorous, yellow-edged, pink flowers • *R.* 'Piccadilly' scarlet flowers with yellow reverse • *R.* 'Pink Favorite' fragrant, deep rose-pink flowers • *R.* 'Silver Jubilee' ♀ fragrant, apricot and pink flowers • *R.* 'Super Sun' deep yellow flowers • *R.* 'Wendy Cussons' fragrant, deep carmine-pink flowers • *R.* 'Whisky Mac' fragrant, rich amber-apricot flowers

ROSA
Rosaceae
FLORIBUNDA ROSE,
CLUSTER ROSE

▲ ❀ ❦ SI summer SC some
H 2 yrs 75cm (30in)
S 2 yrs 75cm (30in)
❀ -10°C (14°F)
Z 6–10

ROSA 'ICEBERG'

For sheer intensity of flowering, few plants can compare with these roses. The range of varieties and colours is seemingly endless, as are the possible planting combinations.

Soil Tolerates all except extremely alkaline soil
Aspect Full sun to medium shade
Habit Bushy
Leaf Deciduous, dark green to mid-green, typical rose leaves
Flower Single, double or semi-double flowers, in a wide range of colours in summer
Use For solo or mass-planting in rose or mixed borders; good cut flowers
Needs Propagate by commercial budding. Prune in spring by reducing all previous season's growth by as much as 70 per cent, cutting weaker shoots the hardest
Varieties *R.* 'Anne Cocker' mid- to deep pink flowers • *R.* 'Arthur Bell' ♀ bright gold flowers, some scent • *R.* 'Chanelle' double, palest pink flowers • *R.* 'City of Belfast' bright red flowers • *R.* 'City of Leeds' deep pink flowers with paler outsides of petals • *R.* 'Dearest' clear, soft rosy-salmon flowers • *R.* 'Evelyn Fison' ('Irish Wonder') scarlet flowers • *R.* 'Frensham' scarlet flowers • *R.* 'Iceberg' ('Schneewittchen') pure white flowers • *R.* 'Lilli Marlene' single, clear red flowers • *R.* 'Rosemary Rose' purplish-cerise-pink flowers • *R.* 'Southampton' ♀ pale apricot flowers • *R.* 'The Queen Elizabeth' ♀ tall growing, dawn pink flowers • *R.* 'Tip Top' double, shell pink flowers • *R.* 'Trumpeter' ♀ scented, bright red flowers • *R.* 'Woburn Abbey' tangerine flowers

ROSA
Rosaceae
CLIMBING ROSE, PILLAR ROSE

❀ ❦ SI summer SC
H 2 yrs 2.7m (9ft)
S 2 yrs 2.7m (9ft)
❄ -15°C (4°F)
Z 6–10

ROSA 'MAIGOLD'

Climbing roses are the mainstay of flowering summer climbers, offering almost every conceivable flower colour, together with the possibility of scent.

Soil Does well on all but extremely alkaline soil
Aspect Full sun to medium shade
Habit Basically upright and branching; medium to fast growth rate
Leaf Deciduous, dark green leaves; some varieties with purple hue or purple backing
Flower Single or semi-double, strongly scented, flowers in clusters in many colours
Use For walls, fences, pillars, pergolas, buildings and trellis
Needs Propagate by commercial budding. Little pruning needed; dead-head and remove old or dead wood in autumn
Varieties *R.* 'Casino' scented, double, yellow flowers • *R.* 'Compassion' ♀ apricot to copper flowers with yellow and pink highlights • *R.* 'Danse du Feu' brick red flowers • *R.* 'Dreaming Spires' scented, bright golden-yellow flowers • *R.* 'Galway Bay' scented, dark red flowers • *R.* 'Golden Showers' ♀ deep golden-yellow flowers ageing to cream • *R.* 'Handel' ♀ semi-double, scented, white flowers with pink-red markings • *R.* 'Maigold' ♀ semi-double, copper-yellow flowers • *R.* 'Masquerade' semi-double, yellow flowers, ageing to pink, finally red • *R.* 'Parade' ♀ scented, deep pink flowers • *R.* 'Pink Perpétué' double, fragrant, deep pink flowers • *R.* 'Swan Lake' double, white flowers with pale pink shading • *R.* 'White Cockade' ♀ double, white flowers

ROSA
Rosaceae
RAMBLING ROSE

❀ ❦ SI summer SC
H 2 yrs 4.5m (15ft)
S 2 yrs 4.5m (15ft)
❄ -15°C (4°F)
Z 6–10

ROSA 'EXCELSA'

Their free-flowing habit allows these roses to grow over fences and buildings and through trees and large shrubs. Although most flower only once, they are worth planting.

Soil Alkaline and acid; in extremely alkaline soils may show signs of chlorosis
Aspect Does best in full sun to light shade; some tolerate shade
Habit Rambling and branching; fast to medium growth rate
Leaf Pinnate, light to mid-green leaves, of 5–7 round leaflets
Flower Single or semi-double flowers, borne in clusters, in a range of colours from white, yellow, pink, red to mauve; most single but some varieties repeat flowering
Use For fences, walls, pergolas, archways and through trees
Needs Propagate by budding. Before planting reduce the top growth to 0.6–1m (2–3ft) and remove any weak shoots
Varieties *R.* 'Albéric Barbier' ♀ double, fragrant, creamy-white flowers • *R.* 'Albertine' ♀ fragrant, copper-orange flowers, opening pink with gold shading • *R.* 'American Pillar' single, pink flowers with central white eye • *R.* 'Dorothy Perkins' clusters of double, clear pink flowers • *R.* 'Emily Gray' fragrant, large golden-yellow flowers • *R.* 'Excelsa' double, light crimson flowers in large trusses • *R.* 'François Juranville' ♀ double, mid-pink flowers • *R.* 'Mermaid' ♀ single, large golden-yellow flowers • *R.* 'Paul's Scarlet Climber' double, scarlet flowers borne in clusters • *R.* 'Sander's White Rambler' ♀ pure white, rosette-shaped flowers in cascading clusters

ROSA
Rosaceae
MINIATURE ROSE

▲ ❀ ❦ SI summer SC some
H 2 yrs 30cm (1ft)
S 2 yrs 30cm (1ft)
❄ -10°C (14°F)
Z 6–10

ROSA **'COLIBRE'**

True gems of the rose world, these dainty plants have many uses, from the rock garden to containers. Many mimic their larger hybrid tea and floribunda rose counterparts, but be sure to buy only plants that have been grown by commercial budding for outdoor growing. Those grown as house plants may not have the same vigour as the budded stock.

Soil All except extremely alkaline soil
Aspect Full sun to medium shade
Habit Bushy
Leaf Deciduous, small, dark to mid-green, typical rose leaves
Flower Single, double or semi-double flowers in wide range of colours in summer
Use For solo planting or in groups in rose or rock gardens; for spot planting or containers
Needs Propagate by commercial budding. Prune established plants in spring by removing one-third of the shoots, choosing the oldest and cutting as close as possible to ground level
Varieties *R.* 'Baby Masquerade' white, pink-flushed flowers • *R.* 'Baby Sunrise' double, golden-yellow flowers • *R.* 'Bianco' dwarf floribunda, pure white flowers • *R.* 'Colibre' larger, semi-double, golden, pink-edged flowers • *R.* 'Hot Line' semi-double, red flowers • *R.* 'Peek A Boo' semi-double, pale golden flowers • *R.* 'Pink Sunblaze' semi-double, deep pink flowers • *R.* 'Swany' 🏆 semi-double, white flowers • *R.* 'The Fairy' 🏆 dwarf polyantha, double, very pale pink flowers • *R.* 'White Angel' white flowers with pink-tinged edges

---

ROSA
Rosaceae
PATIO ROSE

▲ ❀ ❦ SI summer SC some
H 2 yrs 40cm (15in)
S 2 yrs 40cm (15in)
❄ -10°C (14°F)
Z 6–10

ROSA **'ANGELA RIPPON'**

In terms of height, these useful roses fit between the miniatures and the floribundas, from which they are largely derived. The group name, patio roses, is rather misleading, because they can be used in many more places than the patio.

Soil Most, except extremely alkaline soils
Aspect Full sun to medium shade
Habit Very bushy and compact; quick to establish
Leaf Deciduous, typical mid- to dark green rose leaves; disease resistant
Flower Bold clusters of semi-double or double flowers in a wide range of colours, some scented, in summer
Use Solo or in groups; good for mass-planting; will tolerate being grown in large containers for a short period
Needs Propagate by commercial budding. Prune by reducing previous season's growth in spring by 50 per cent or more if wished to achieve good regeneration of flowering shoots
Varieties *R.* 'Angela Rippon' double, rose-salmon pink flowers • *R.* 'Benson and Hedges Special' double, yellow flowers • 'Bright Smile' semi-double, scented, yellow flowers • *R.* 'Chelsea Pensioner' double, dark red flowers • *R.* 'Gentle Touch' 🏆 double, scented, pale salmon pink flowers • *R.* 'Penelope Keith' double, old gold flowers • *R.* 'Regensberg' double, deep pink flowers • *R.* 'Sweet Dream' 🏆 double, peach-apricot flowers • *R.* 'Sweet Magic' 🏆 double, apricot-orange and yellow flowers

ROSA
Rosaceae
GROUND-COVER ROSE

▲ ❀ ❦ SI summer–autumn
SC some
H 2 yrs 60cm (30in)
S 2 yrs 2m (6ft)
❊ -10°C (14°F)
Z 6–10

ROSA 'NOZOMI'

Finding ground cover that will both suppress weeds and provide interest and colour is a challenge faced by most gardeners at some time. Ground-covering roses, assuming the site is well dug and perennial weeds are removed before planting, can meet this need. They also look attractive when their trailing action is allowed to cascade over walls and banks.

Soil All soils but may show some signs of chlorosis on extremely alkaline soils
Aspect Full sun to medium shade
Habit Creeping and spreading
Leaf Small, green, rose leaves; some yellow autumn colour
Flower Double or single, flat flowers in a range of colours, some scented, throughout summer and early autumn
Use For ground cover and to stabilize and cover banks; attractive when grown to cascade down walls
Needs Propagate by commercial budding. Prune in spring by removing one-third of the shoots, choosing the oldest
Varieties *R.* 'Flower Carpet' ♀ large, double, deep pink flowers • *R.* × *jacksonii* 'Max Graff' very vigorous, covering to 4m (13ft) in spread, large, single pink flowers with white centres • *R.* × *j.* 'Red Max Graff' red form of above • *R.* 'Nozomi' ♀ small, single, pale pink-white flowers • *R.* 'Red Blanket' ♀ large, semi-double, scarlet flowers, ageing to white at the base, borne in large clusters • *R.* 'Snow Carpet' ♀ compact habit, small, double, creamy-white flowers

See also the County Series Roses (page 120)

ROSA
Rosaceae
OLD ENGLISH SHRUB ROSE

▲ ❀ ❦ S summer SC some
H 2 yrs 1.2m (4ft)
S 2 yrs 1.2m (4ft)
❊ -10°C (14°F)
Z 6–10

ROSA 'GRAHAM THOMAS'

Rightly among some of the best-loved modern roses, all the cultivars were developed by one grower, who wanted to bridge the gap between the floribundas and the shrub roses.

Soil All except extremely alkaline soil
Aspect Full sun to medium shade
Habit Bushy; some upright
Leaf Deciduous, large, dark green, typical rose leaves
Flower Single, double or semi-double flowers in a wide range of colours
Use For mass-planting; solo or in small groups
Needs Propagate by commercial budding. Prune in spring, on bushes established for more than 3 years, by cutting back one-third of the oldest shoots to ground level
Varieties *R.* 'Chaucer' strongly scented, rose-pink flowers • *R.* 'Dove' pale apricot flowers • *R.* 'Graham Thomas' ♀ tea-scented, pale yellow flowers • *R.* 'Heritage' repeat flowering, lemon-scented, shell pink flowers • *R.* 'Mary Rose' vigorous, scented, mid- to pale pink flowers • *R.* 'Othello' scented, scarlet flowers, purple with age • *R.* 'Prospero' scented, crimson flowers, purple with age • *R.* 'Red Coat' single, bright red flowers with yellow centre • *R.* 'Scintillation' single, scented, pale pink flowers • *R.* 'The Knight' cerise-pink flowers • *R.* 'The Reeve' spreading and arching habit, scented, mid-pink flowers • *R.* 'The Squire' scented, scarlet flowers • *R.* 'The Wife of Bath' scented, pale pink flowers • *R.* 'Warwick Castle' scented, bright pink flowers • *R.* 'Wenlock' scented, bright pink flowers

ROSA
Rosaceae
COUNTY SERIES SHRUB
ROSE

▲ ❀ ❦ SI summer–autumn
H 2 yrs 1m (3ft)
S 2 yrs 1m (3ft)
❄ -10°C (14°F)
Z 6–10

Rarely in gardening does a new group of plants appear that merits any excitement, but this group of roses is the exception. The high, bushy, contained habit and colour range are delightful, and all are disease resistant.

Soil Most, except very dry or wet
Aspect Full sun to light shade
Habit Bushy and compact; the height of these roses is often underestimated
Leaf Typical mid-green rose leaves
Flower Small to medium flowers, mostly single, some semi-doubles, in large clusters in a wide range of colours throughout summer and into early autumn
Use Mass-planting of a single variety for effect; solo or in small groups as spot plants in mixed borders; for ground cover or in large containers
Needs Propagate by commercial budding. Prune by removing one-third of the shoots to as close as ground level as possible, choosing the oldest shoots first; prune the second spring after planting and annually thereafter
Varieties *R.* 'Avon' semi-double, off-white flowers • *R.* 'Essex' single, reddish-pink flowers • *R.* 'Hampshire' single, scarlet flowers with white centres • *R.* 'Kent' semi-double, white flowers • *R.* 'Surrey' ♀ double, rose-pink flowers

ROSA 'SURREY'

ROSA
Rosaceae
STANDARD HYBRID TEA,
STANDARD FLORIBUNDA
ROSE

▲ ❀ ❦ SI summer SC some
H 2 yrs 1.2m (4ft)
S 2 yrs 75cm (30in)
❄ -10°C (14°F)
Z 6–10

These sentinels of the rose world have long been favourites. Almost any variety can be grown as a standard, but those listed below are possibly the most reliable.

Soil All except extremely alkaline soil
Aspect Full sun to medium shade
Habit Upright, becoming spreading on stems
Leaf Deciduous, dark to mid-green, typical rose leaves
Flower Single, double or semi-double flowers in a range of colours, some scented, in summer
Use For feature planting in rose borders or in rows
Needs Propagate from commercial budding. Prune as hybrid tea or floribunda roses. Staking is important in order to prevent serious wind damage
Varieties <u>Standard floribunda</u>: *R.* 'Allgold' rich golden-yellow flowers • *R.* 'Chinatown' ♀ fragrant, clear yellow flowers • *R.* 'Dearest' soft rosy-salmon flowers • *R.* 'Glenfid-dich' yellow-tinted amber flowers • *R.* 'Iceberg' white flowers • *R.* 'Joyfulness' pure apricot flowers • *R.* 'The Queen Elizabeth' dawn pink flowers • *R.* 'Woburn Abbey' vivid tangerine flowers <u>Standard hybrid tea</u>: *R.* 'Alec's Red' deep, bright crimson flowers • *R.* 'Apricot Silk' apricot flowers • *R.* 'Duke of Windsor' bright vermilion-orange flowers • *R.* 'Ernest H. Morse' scented, pure turkey-red flowers • *R.* 'Fragrant Cloud' scented, coral-red flowers • *R.* 'King's Ransom' large, deep gold flowers • *R.* 'Mischief' coral-salmon flowers with carmine shading • *R.* 'Pascali' white flowers • *R.* 'Super Star' scented, orange-vermilion flowers

ROSA 'KING'S RANSOM'

ROSA
Rosaceae
WEEPING STANDARD
ROSE

▲ ❀ ❦ SI summer SC
H 2 yrs 2.2m (7ft)
S 2 yrs 1m (3ft)
❄ -10°C (14°F)
Z 6–10

ROSA 'DOROTHY PERKINS'

Used as a feature plant, weeping standard roses give climbing and rambling roses a new dimension of elegance. Their tall, weeping formation is an ideal centrepoint for formal and semi-formal plantings of many kinds. They need a little more care and cost more than regular varieties, but are well worth it.

Soil All except extremely alkaline soil
Aspect Full sun to medium shade
Habit Pendulous to weeping from the top of a straight, main, single rose stem
Leaf Deciduous, dark green to mid-green, typical rose leaves
Flower Single, double or semi-double flowers, in wide range of colours, in summer
Use As specimens in semi-formal or formal gardens for their habit and summer flowers
Needs Propagate from commercial budding at the top of a tall rose stem
Varieties *R.* 'Albertine' coppery buds opening to soft pink flowers • *R.* 'Dorothy Perkins' small, double, pink flowers • *R.* 'Emily Gray' double, golden-yellow flowers • *R.* 'Excelsa' small, double, crimson flowers • *R.* 'Golden Showers' semi-double, fragrant, daffodil-yellow flowers, perpetual flowering • *R.* 'Paul's Scarlet Climber' vigorous, double, vivid scarlet flowers in large trusses • *R.* 'Pink Perpétué' double, fragrant, deep pink flowers • *R.* 'Sander's White Rambler' small, single, pure white flowers • *R.* 'Sparkling Scarlet' double, striking red flowers • *R. xanthina* 'Canary Bird' single, lemon-yellow flowers, spring-flowering

ROSA
Rosaceae
STANDARD SHRUB ROSE

▲ ❀ ❦ SI summer SC some
H 2 yrs 1.2m (4ft)
S 2 yrs 75cm (30in)
❄ -10°C (14°F)
Z 6–10

ROSA XANTHINA
'CANARY BIRD'

Like statuary, standard roses can add height and interest to an otherwise flat or low planting. The range of shrub roses that is available as standards is very wide, but some named cultivars may need ordering from a specialist grower. Many shrub rose varieties in addition to those few that are listed here may be found grown and available as standards and are worth planting.

Soil All except extremely alkaline soil
Aspect Full sun to medium shade
Habit Bushy, strong upright stem; shorter, half-standard varieties are obtainable
Leaf Deciduous, dark to mid-green, typical rose leaves
Flower Single, double or semi-double flowers, in wide range of colours
Use As feature plants to add height and interest
Needs Propagate from commercial budding. Prune by removing one-third of the shoots, choosing the oldest, to their point of origin in spring and shorten remainder by about 25 per cent of their overall length
Varieties *R.* 'Ballerina' pink flowers with white eye • *R.* County Series (*see page 120*) • *R.* 'Nozomi' pale pink-white flowers • *R.* 'Snow Carpet' white flowers • *R.* 'The Fairy' pink flowers • *R. xanthina* 'Canary Bird' vigorous, single, yellow flowers • *R.* × f. *hugonis* primrose-yellow flowers

ROSA
Rosaceae
**SPRING-FLOWERING
SPECIES ROSE**

▲ ❀ ❦ SI spring
H 2 yrs *see below*
S 2 yrs *see below*
❊ -15°C (4°F)
Z 6–10

These generally large, elegant plants need space to mature
and to show off their massed displays of flowers. It could be
argued that as they only flower once in spring and offer no
interesting fruit or autumn colours they should not be
planted. That would be a mistake, however, for when they
are in flower, the display rivals that of any other plant.

Soil Most
Aspect Sun to light shade
Habit Upright when young, soon becoming spreading and
very bushy; armed with thorns; some grow as climbers
Leaf Typical rose leaves, normally small and dark green
Flower Small double or single flowers, produced *en masse* in
a range of colours in spring
Use As large specimen plants solo or in groups; can be fan-
trained on a large wall; will climb on walls and through trees
Needs Propagate by seed or commercial budding. No
pruning required
Varieties *R. banksiae* 'Lutea' (Banksian rose, Banksia rose)
♡ less hardy climber, double, yellow flowers, to 7 × 7m
(23 × 23ft) • *R.* 'Cantabrigiensis' purple new stems, primrose-
yellow flowers, to 2.5 × 2.5m (8 × 8ft) • *R. ecae* low growing,
mahogany coloured stems, bright gold flowers, to 1.2 × 1.2m
(4 × 4ft) • *R. e.* 'Helen Knight' climber, mahogany new
stems, single, bright gold flowers, to 3 × 3m (10 × 10ft) •
R. xanthina 'Canary Bird' ♡ large shrub, bright golden-
yellow flowers, to 3 × 3m (10 × 10ft) • *R.* × f. *hugonis*
golden-yellow flowers, to 3 × 3m (10 × 10ft)

ROSA 'CANTABRIGIENSIS'

ROSA
Rosaceae
**SUMMER-FLOWERING
SPECIES ROSE**

▲ ❀ ❦ SI summer–autumn
SC some
H 2 yrs *see below*
S 2 yrs *see below*
❊ -10°C (14°F)
Z 6–10

Many of these are of garden merit for their flowers, fruit,
stems and, sometimes, foliage.

Soil Most
Aspect Sun to light shade
Habit Bushy and upright when young, spreading with age; a
few with winter attraction in the form of hips
Leaf Small, sometimes silver-grey; autumn colour
Flower Small, pink or white flowers in cluster; some bear
red, purple or orange fruit
Use As specimen plants solo or in groups
Needs Propagate from seed. No pruning required
Species *R. californica* pink flowers, very thorny, to 2.5 ×
2.5m (8 × 8ft) • *R. fedtschenkoana* grey foliage, white flowers,
to 2 × 2m (6 × 6ft) • *R. foetida* single, yellow flowers in early
summer, to 1.2 × 1.2m (4 × 4ft) • *R. f.* 'Bicolor' single, orange-
copper flowers, to 1.2 × 1.2m (4 × 4ft) • *R. glauca* (syn. *R.
rubrifolia*) purple foliage and winter stems, purple flowers
with white eye, followed by red fruits, to 1.5 × 1.5m (5 × 5ft)
• *R. nitida* orange-scarlet autumn colour, single, bright pink
flowers, very thorny, to 60 × 60cm (2 × 2ft) • *R. sericea* ssp.
omeiensis f. *pteracantha* white flowers, red fruit, new shoots
with large, scarlet thorns ageing to black, finally brown and
retained in this form, to 4 × 4m (13 × 13ft) • *R. willmottiae*
fern-like greyish leaves and grey young shoots, purplish-pink
flowers, very thorny, to 2.7 × 2.7m (9 × 9ft) • *R.* 'Wolley-
Dod' (syn. *R. pomifera* 'Duplex') semi-double, pink flowers,
followed by round purple fruits, to 2 × 2m (6 × 6ft)

ROSA FOETIDA 'BICOLOR'

ROSA
Rosaceae
SPECIES CLIMBING
MUSK ROSE, HIMALAYAN
MUSK ROSE

▲ ❀ ❦ SI summer SC some
H 5 yrs *see below*
S 5 yrs *see below*
❋ -10°C (14°F)
Z 6–10

These giants – in the wrong place, the thugs – of the garden world will climb many metres over buildings and through trees. Where space allows and when they are in flower, however, the cascade of flower colour is a spectacular sight.

Soil Most
Aspect Full sun to very light shade
Habit Ranging, spreading shoots, growing to 10m (32ft) in one spring; armed with sharp, fish-hook-like thorns
Leaf Pinnate, light to mid-green leaves, 13–17cm (5–7in) long and formed of 5–7 leaflets, often with a grey sheen; some yellow autumn colour
Flower Single, semi-double or double, white flowers with yellow stamens, some scented, borne in bunches in summer
Use To grow over large buildings and through trees
Needs Propagate by commercial budding. Prune to contain if you dare
Varieties *R. brunonii* pale green foliage, large clusters of white flowers with yellow anthers early in summer, small, red hips, to 8 × 8m (26 × 26ft) • *R. filipes* 'Kiftsgate' ♀ small, white flowers in clusters in midsummer, small, red fruits, minimum dimensions 12 × 12m (39 × 39ft) • *R. longicuspis* glossy green foliage, single, white flowers, to 6 × 6m (20 × 20ft) • *R.* 'Paul's Himalayan Musk' ♀ semi-double, scented, pinkish-white flowers early in summer, to 6 × 6m (20 × 20ft) • *R.* 'Rambling Rector' ♀ semi-double, white flowers, small fruits, to 6 × 6m (20 × 20ft) • *R.* 'Wedding Day' scented, pale buff to white flowers, to 8 × 8m (26 × 26ft)

**ROSA 'PAUL'S
HIMALAYAN MUSK'**

ROSA
Rosaceae
OLD FASHIONED
HYBRID SHRUB ROSE

▲ ❀ ❦ SI summer SC some
H 2 yrs *see below*
S 2 yrs *see below*
❋ -10°C (14°F)
Z 6–10

The roses in this group carry all the good points of their parents and very few, if any, of the bad characteristics. Their height can easily be controlled by pruning, and they are available in a wonderful range of colours. Most have now been in cultivation for some time and have proved their worth.

Soil Most, except extremely alkaline soils
Aspect Full sun to medium shade
Habit Bushy
Leaf Deciduous, dark to mid-green, pinnate, leaves, 13–17cm (5–7in) long, made up of 5, oval to round leaflets
Flower Double or semi-double flowers in colours from pink, white and purple to red
Use For solo or mass-planting as specimens or as part of a rose or mixed planting; many good as informal hedges if planted at distances of 1m (3ft)
Needs Propagate by commercial budding. Prune by cutting back one-third of shoots, choosing the oldest, to ground level in spring on roses established for more than 3 years
Varieties *R.* 'Frau Karl Druschki' large, white flowers, buds often pink-tinged, to 2m (6ft) • *R.* 'Mrs John Laing' double, soft pink flowers, to 1.2m (4ft) • *R.* 'Paul Neyron' highly scented, pink and deeper pink flowers, to 2m (6ft) • *R.* 'Reine des Violettes' sweetly scented flowers open carmine then shaded violet, to 2m (6ft) • *R.* 'Vick's Caprice' very double, pink and white striped flowers, to 1.8m (5ft 6in)

**ROSA 'FRAU
KARL DRUSCHKI'**

ROSA
Rosaceae
MODERN HYBRID
SHRUB ROSE

▲ ❀ ❦ SI summer SC some
H 2 yrs *see below*
S 2 yrs *see below*
❋ -10°C (14°F)
Z 6–10

This group of relatively new varieties has all the versatility in colour and height and in some cases scent as the older forms. Most have been in cultivation for several years and have proved their worth.

Soil Most, except extremely alkaline soils
Aspect Full sun to medium shade
Habit Bushy
Leaf Deciduous, dark to mid-green, pinnate leaves, 13–17cm (5–7in) long, made up of 5 oval to round leaflets
Flower Double or semi-double flowers in colours from pink, white and purple to red
Use As specimen plants when solo or mass-planted; as part of a rose or mixed planting; many good as informal hedges if planted at distances of 1m (3ft)
Needs Propagate by commercial budding. Prune by cutting back one-third of shoots, choosing the oldest, to ground level in spring on roses established more than 3 years
Varieties *R.* 'Cerise Bouquet' large growing, double, cerise-pink flowers, to 3 × 3m (10 × 10ft) • *R.* 'Golden Wings' large, single, pale yellow flowers in profusion, to 2 × 2m (6 × 6ft) • *R.* 'Marguerite Hilling' ♀ double, scented, strong pink flowers, to 1.5 × 1.5m (5 × 5ft) • *R.* 'Nevada' ♀ semi-double, scented, large, cream flowers, to 2 × 2m (6 × 6ft) • *R.* 'Scharlachglut' ('Scarlet Fire') single, bold red flowers on arching branches, to 2 × 2m (6 × 6ft)

ROSA 'NEVADA'

ROSA
Rosaceae
ALBA ROSE

▲ ❀ ❦ SI summer SC some
H 2 yrs *see below*
S 2 yrs *see below*
❋ -10°C (14°F)
Z 6–10

In its original form, *Rosa alba* was almost the first rose to be grown by gardeners many centuries ago, and it is still top of the list of those to chose from. The simple charm of the flowers makes it among one of the most beautiful of roses.

Soil Most, except very alkaline soils
Aspect Full sun to light shade
Habit Bushy, upright, becoming spreading; medium to fast growth rate; may need support in exposed gardens
Leaf Deciduous, green, sometimes grey, pinnate leaves, 13–18cm (5–7in) long, composed of 5–7 leaflets
Flower Single, semi-double or double flowers, some scented, in wide range of colours in summer
Use As specimen plants, solo or in groups; in rose or mixed plantings; can be fan-trained on walls and fences
Needs Propagate from commercial budding. Prune by removing one-third of the shoots to ground level in spring, choosing the oldest on roses established for more than 3 years
Varieties *R.* × *alba* 'Maxima' (Jacobite rose, great double white rose, Cheshire rose) flat, double, white flowers, to 2 × 2m (6 × 6ft) • *R.* 'Belle Amour' semi-double, fragrant, salmon pink flowers, to 2 × 2m (6 × 6ft) • *R.* 'Céleste' ('Celestial') semi-double, soft pink flowers, to 2.2 × 2.2m (7 × 7ft) • *R.* 'Félicité Parmentier' ♀ scented, soft pink, reflexed petals forming a double flower, to 1.5 × 1.5m (5 × 5ft) • *R.* 'Maiden's Blush' double, sweet-scented, blush pink flowers, to 3.5 × 3.5m (7 × 7ft) • *R.* 'Madame Plantier' double, small, white flowers borne in clusters, to 2 × 2m (6 × 6ft)

ROSA 'MAIDEN'S BLUSH'

ROSA
Rosaceae
BOURBON ROSE

▲ ❀ ❦ SI summer SC some
H 2 yrs *see below*
S 2 yrs *see below*
❄ -10°C (14°F)
Z 6–10

ROSA 'MADAME ISAAC PEREIRE'

Old fashioned, yes, but still one of the best groups of roses. Steeped in the history of Europe and a must for the modern garden. The flowers are good, and even though the foliage can be prone to disease, they should be more widely planted.

Soil Most, except very alkaline soils
Aspect Full sun to light shade
Habit Bushy, upright when young, becoming spreading with age; medium to fast growth rate
Leaf Deciduous, pinnate leaves, 13–17cm (5–7in) long, made up of 5–7 leaflets, green, often with a grey-green sheen; some yellow autumn colours
Flower Single, semi-double or double flowers, some scented, in wide range of colours in summer
Use As specimen plants; in borders; can be fan-trained
Needs Propagate by commercial budding. Prune in spring by removing one-third of shoots, choosing the oldest, to ground level on roses established for more than 3 years
Varieties *R.* 'Adam Messerich' deep pink flowers, to 2m × 2m (6 × 6ft) • *R.* 'Boule de Neige' very fragrant, creamy-white flowers with pink edges, to 1.2 × 1.2m (4 × 4ft) • *R.* 'Louise Odier' double, fragrant, deep flesh-pink flowers, to 1.5 × 1.5m (5 × 5ft) • *R.* 'Madame Isaac Pereire' large, purple-crimson, rosette-shaped flowers, to 2.5 × 2.5m (8 × 8ft) • *R.* 'Madame Pierre Oger' scented, pale silver-pink, cup-shaped flowers, to 2 × 2m (6 × 6ft) • *R.* 'Reine Victoria' ('La Reine Victoria') warm rose pink, cup-shaped flowers, to 2m (6ft) × 1m (3ft)

ROSA
Rosaceae
CENTIFOLIA ROSE

▲ ❀ ❦ SI summer SC
H 2 yrs *see below*
S 2 yrs *see below*
❄ -10°C (14°F)
Z 6–10

ROSA 'FANTIN-LATOUR'

The beauty of this very old group of roses is all most impossible to describe. Grown for centuries, it still has a major role to play in the development of new forms.

Soil Most, except very alkaline soils
Aspect Full sun to light shade
Habit Bushy, upright when young, spreading with age
Leaf Deciduous, pinnate, dark to mid-green leaves, 13–17cm (5–7in) long and made up of 5 ovate to round leaflets
Flower Single, double or semi-double, scented flowers, in wide range of colours in summer
Needs Propagate from commercial budding. Prune in spring, by cutting back one-third of shoots to ground level, choosing the oldest on roses established for more than 3 years
Varieties *R.* × *centifolia* (Provence rose, cabbage rose, Holland rose) double, richly scented, clear pink flowers, to 1.5 × 1.5m (5 × 5ft) • *R.* × *c.* 'Cristata' ('Chapeau de Napoleon') double, clear pink flowers, to 1.2 × 1.2m (4 × 4ft) • *R.* × *c.* 'Parvifolia' dwarf, upright habit, deep cerise pink flowers, to 1 × 1m (3 × 3ft) • *R.* 'De Meaux' small, dainty, light pink flowers, to 75 × 75cm (30 × 30in) • *R.* 'Fantin-Latour' ♀ flat, pink flowers, to 1.2 × 1.2 (4 × 4ft) • *R.* 'Petite de Hollande' double, white flowers, to 1.2 × 1.2m (4 × 4ft) • *R.* 'Tour de Malakoff' large magenta-purple flowers, to 2 × 2m (6 × 6ft), needs support • *R.* 'Unique Blanche' ('White Provence') thin pure white scented flowers, 1.5 × 1.5m (5 × 5ft) • *R.* 'Variegata' rounded, pink, variegated flowers, to 2 × 2m (6 × 6ft)

ROSA
Roseaceae
CHINA ROSE

▲ ❀ ❦ SI summer SC
H 2 yrs *see below*
S 2 yrs *see below*
❄ -10°C (14°F)
Z 6–10

ROSA 'CLIMBING CECILE BRUNNER'

It has been said that no garden is complete without a China rose. The range of sizes and colours makes it easy to find a candidate to use in just about any situation.

Soil Most, except extremely alkaline soils
Aspect Full sun to medium shade
Habit Bushy, with a range of different habits; on the whole the framework of branches is one of its attractions
Leaf Deciduous, dark to mid-green, pinnate leaves, 13–17cm (5–7in) long and made up of 5 ovate to round leaflets
Flower Single, double or semi-double, scented, in a range of colours, borne in summer
Use As a specimen plant, solo or in groups; in mixed or rose borders; for large walls and fences, pergolas and trellis as a fan-trained climber
Needs Propagate by commercial budding. Pruning not normally required
Varieties *R.* 'Bloomfield Abundance' large sprays of mid-pink flowers, to 2 × 2m (6 × 6ft) • *R.* 'Climbing Cecile Brünner' ♀ perfect miniature flowers, mother-of-pearl pink, in large sprays, to 7.5 × 6m (25 × 20ft), prune as rambling rose • *R.* × *odorata* 'Mutabilis' flowers opening yellow, turning pink, finally crimson, to 2.5 × 2.5m (8 × 8ft) • *R.* × *o.* 'Pallida' ('Old Blush China') silvery pink flowers, flushed crimson, to 1 × 1m (3 × 3ft) • *R.* × *o.* 'Viridiflora' (green rose, monstrosa) scaly green petals, later tinged with red, to 1 × 1m (3 × 3ft)

ROSA
Rosaceae
DAMASK ROSE

▲ ❀ ❦ SI summer SC
H 2 yrs *see below*
S 2 yrs *see below*
❄ -10°C (14°F)
Z 6–10

ROSA 'LANEI'

The damask rose, *Rosa* × *damascena*, has been grown since the fourteenth century and should still be included in new rose plantings of any size. The foliage perfectly sets off the flowers.

Soil All except extremely alkaline
Aspect Full sun to medium shade
Habit Bushy, upright when young, spreading with age
Leaf Deciduous, dark to mid-green, pinnate leaves, 13–17cm (5–7in) long and made up of 5 ovate to round leaflets
Flower Double or semi-double, scented flowers in a wide range of colours in summer
Use As feature plants solo or in groups; in rose or mixed plantings; can be fan-trained for walls and fences
Needs Propagate from commercial budding. Prune in spring by removing one-third of shoots to ground level, choosing the oldest, on roses established for more than 3 years
Varieties *R.* 'Blush Damask' strongly scented, pale pink flowers with deeper pink centre, to 1.2 × 1.2m (4 × 4ft) • *R.* 'Celsiana' semi-double, fragrant, pink flowers, to 1.5 × 1.5m (5 × 5ft) • *R.* × *d.* 'Versicolor' (York and Lancaster rose) white flowers blotched with pink, to 2 × 2m (6 × 6ft) • *R.* 'Ispahan' ♀ semi-double, bright pink flowers, to 2 × 2m (6 × 6ft) • *R.* 'Lanei' pink to deep pink flowers, to 1.5 × 1.5m (5 × 5ft), thorny • *R.* 'Leda' (painted damask) white flowers suffused with pink, to 1 × 1m (3 × 3ft) • *R.* 'Madame Hardy' ♀ double white flowers with green eye, to 2 × 2m (6 × 6ft) • *R.* 'Nuits de Young' small, dark crimson flowers, to 1.5 × 1.5m (5 × 5ft)

ROSA
Rosaceae
GALLICA ROSE

▲ ❀ ✿ SI summer SC
H 2 yrs *see below*
S 2 yrs *see below*
✻ -15°C (4°F)
Z 6–10

**ROSA GALLICA
'VERSICOLOR'**

Almost as long as roses have been cultivated, this group has been a favourite with gardeners.

Soil All except extremely alkaline
Aspect Full sun to medium shade
Habit Bushy; upright when young, spreading with age
Leaf Deciduous, dark to mid-green pinnate leaves, 13–17cm (5–7in) long made up of 5 ovate to round leaflets
Flower Double or semi-double in a wide range of colours
Use As specimen plants, solo or in groups
Needs Propagate from commercial budding. Prune in spring by removing one-third of shoots to ground level, choosing the oldest growth on roses established for more than 3 years
Varieties *R.* 'Belle de Crécy' fragrant, bright pink flowers fading to pale violet, to 1.2m (4ft) high • *R.* 'Camaïeux' fragrant, pink flowers, splashed with white, some crimson shading, to 1.2 × 1.2m (6 × 6ft) • *R.* 'Charles de Mills' fragrant, velvety crimson flowers, to 1.5m (5ft) • *R.* 'Complicata' single, scented, pink flowers, to 2 × 2m. (6 × 6ft) • *R.* 'Duchesse de Montebello' well-scented, blush-pink flowers, to 1.5m (5ft) • *R. gallica* var. *officinalis* (apothecary's rose) fragrant, deep pink flowers, to 1.2 × 1.2 (4 × 4ft) • *R. g.* 'Versicolor' (rosa mundi) light crimson flowers, striped pink and white, to 2m (6ft) • *R.* 'Robert le Diable' sweetly scented flowers in mixture of purple, grey, cerise and scarlet, to 1.2m (4ft) • *R.* 'Tuscany Superb' double, dark purple-crimson flowers, to 1.5m (5ft) • *R.* 'Violacea' blackish-crimson flowers, ageing to violet with golden centre, to 2m (6ft)

ROSA
Rosaceae
ROSA EGLANTERIA,
SWEET BRIAR

▲ ❀ ✿ SI summer–autumn
SC leaf
H 2 yrs *see below*
S 2 yrs *see below*
✻ -15°C (4°F)
Z 6–10

ROSA 'FRITZ NOBIS'

An interesting group of roses that is suitable for natural and semi-wild planting. The roses not only have small, attractive flowers but also pleasantly aromatic foliage, which is mainly evident in the evenings or when the leaves are crushed.

Soil Most
Aspect Full sun to light shade
Habit Bushy; medium to fast growth rate
Leaf Light to mid-green, pinnate leaves, 13–17cm (5–7in) long and made up of 5–7 leaflets; sweetly aromatic
Flower Single or semi-double flowers, in a wide range of colours, including pink, white, purple and red
Use In large shrub borders; naturalized in a wild garden
Needs Propagate by commercial budding or from seed. Prune in spring by removing one-third of shoots to ground level, choosing the oldest on established roses
Varieties *R.* 'Anne of Geierstein' single, light crimson flowers, to 2m (6ft) • *R. eglanteria* (syn. *R. rubiginosa*) ♀ the basic form, rose-pink flowers in summer, to 2.5m (8ft) • *R.* 'Flora McIvor' single, white flowers • *R.* 'Fritz Nobis' ♀ single, white-salmon pink flowers, to 2m (6ft) • *R.* 'Greenmantle' single, rosy-red flowers with white eye and yellow stamens, to 1.2m (4ft) • *R.* 'Hebe's Lip' double, cream flowers, to 1.2m (4ft) • *R.* 'Lady Penzance' apple-scented foliage, single, apple pink-yellow flowers, to 2.5m (8ft) • *R.* 'Lord Penzance' single, copper-yellow flowers, to 2.5m (8ft) • *R.* 'Meg Merrilees' single, bright crimson flowers, to 2m (6ft) • *R.* 'Stanwell Perpetual' double, pale pink flowers, to 1.5m (5ft)

ROSA
Rosaceae
MUSK ROSE

▲ ❀ ♈ SI summer–autumn
SC some
H 2 yrs *see below*
S 2 yrs *see below*
❄ -10°C (14°F)
Z 6–10

ROSA 'PENELOPE'

The roses descended from *Rosa moschata* are equal to the modern floribunda roses in their display.

Soil All soils
Aspect Full sun to medium shade
Habit Bushy
Leaf Deciduous, light green to mid-green, typical rose leaves
Flower Semi-double or double, scented, flowers, each to 2.5cm (1in) across, normally carried in clusters, in a wide range of colours, in summer to autumn
Use As specimen plants, solo or massed in borders; as an informal hedge if planted at distances of 1m (3ft)
Needs Propagate by commercial budding. Prune in spring by shortening all previous year's shoots by at least 50 per cent; removing more will reduce ultimate height if required
Varieties *R.* 'Buff Beauty' ♀ double, fragrant, apricot-yellow to buff-yellow flowers in large trusses, to 2.2 × 2.2m (7 × 7ft) • *R.* 'Cornelia' ♀ double, fragrant, apricot flowers with pink shading, to 2.2 × 2.2m (7 × 7ft) • *R.* 'Felicia' ♀ one of the best roses, double, fragrant, silver-pink flowers fading to salmon pink, to 2 × 2m (6 × 6ft) • *R.* 'Félicité et Perpétué' ♀ double, fragrant, creamy-white flowers, to 4.5 × 4.5m (15 × 15ft) • *R.* 'Moonlight' single, lemon to white flowers, to 2.2 × 2.2m (7 × 7ft) • *R.* 'Penelope' ♀ semi-double, scented, creamy-pink flowers, to 2.2 × 2.2m (7 × 7ft) • *R.* 'Prosperity' double, strongly scented, creamy-white flowers, to 2.2 × 2.2m (7 × 7ft) • *R.* 'Thisbe' semi-double, scented, buff-yellow flowers, 2 × 2m (6 × 6ft)

ROSA
Rosaceae
HIP ROSE

▲ ❀ ♈ SI summer–autumn
H 2 yrs *see below*
S 2 yrs *see below*
❄ -15 (4°F)
Z 6–10

ROSA MOYESII

These large plants with their attractive flowers really come into their own in autumn, when the bold displays of bottle-shaped fruits are seen. Give these roses space in which to show off the hips to best effect.

Soil Most
Aspect Full sun to light shade
Habit Bushy; upright when young, spreading with age
Leaf Deciduous, light to mid-green leaves, 13–17cm (5–7in) long made up of 5–7 leaflets
Flower Single or semi-double flowers in a range of colours; followed by large, attractive orange or red bottle-shaped fruits
Use For specimen planting alone or for the back of a large shrub border, solo or in groups; fan-trained shrubs for walls and fences
Needs Propagate by commercial budding. Prune in spring by removing one-third of shoots to ground level, choosing the oldest, on roses established for more than 3 years
Varieties *R.* 'Eddie's Jewel' deep red flowers, large hips, to 3 × 3m (10 × 10ft) • *R.* 'Geranium' ♀ bright red flowers , good orange-red hips, to 2.7 × 2.7m (9 × 9ft) • *R. moyesii* dark coppery-red flowers, good hips, to 2m (6ft) • *R. soulieana* 'Crep' dainty climber, flowers yellow in bud fading to white, orange red, oval fruit 1cm (1/2in) long, to 4m (13ft) • *R. sweginzowii* small, single, pink flowers, orange-red, hips, to 3 × 3m (10 × 10ft) • *R. webbiana* single, pink flowers, large orange hips, to 3 × 3m (10 × 10ft)

ROSA
Rosaceae
RUGOSA ROSE

▲ ❀ ❦ SI summer–autumn
SC some
H 2 yrs *see below*
S5 yrs *see below*
❄ -14°C (4°F)
Z 6–10

ROSA 'ROSERAIE DE L'HAY'

Flowers, foliage and fruit combine with a strong constitution to make this group of roses among the most accommodating of plants in those gardens with plenty of space.

Soil All except extremely alkaline
Aspect Full sun to medium shade
Habit Bushy
Leaf Light green, pinnate leaves, 13–17cm (5–7in) long and made up of 5–7 leaflets
Flower Single, semi-double or double flowers, in a wide range of colours; many followed with large red hips in autumn
Use As specimen or spot plants in borders; solo or in large groups; as an informal hedge planted at distances of 1m (3ft)
Needs Propagate by commercial budding. Each spring thin out about 25 per cent of the oldest shoots on established plants
Varieties *R.* 'Agnes' double, scented, creamy-lemon flowers, to 2m (6ft) • *R.* 'Blanche Double de Coubert' ♀ semi-double, fragrant white flowers, to 2m (6ft) • *R.* 'Fru Dagmar Hastrup' single, pale pink flowers, to 2m (6ft) • *R.* 'Mrs Anthony Waterer', semi-double, bright red flowers, to 1.5m (5ft) • *R.* 'Pink Grootendorst' ♀ semi-double, mid- to dark pink flowers, to 1.5m (5ft)• *R.* 'Roseraie de l'Haÿ' single, vermilion-pink flowers, to 2m (6ft) • *R. rugosa* 'Alba' ♀ single, white flowers with yellow anthers, shiny orange-red hips, to 2m (6ft) • *R.* 'Sarah van Fleet', double, mid-pink flowers, to 2m (6ft) tall • *R.* 'Schneezwerg ('Snow Dwarf') ♀ single, white flowers, to 2.5m (8ft)

ROSA
Rosaceae
BURNET ROSE, SCOTCH ROSE

▲ ❀ ❦ SI spring–autumn
SC some
H 2 yrs *see below*
S 2 yrs *see below*
❄ -10°C (14°F)
Z 6–10

ROSA 'FRUHLINGSGOLD'

A very useful group of roses, closely related to the parent, *Rosa pimpinellifolia*, but with large flowers, often as much as 10cm (4in) across and looking rather like large fried eggs. The plants themselves are sturdy and upright, making them ideal for gardens where there is room to grow them.

Soil Most
Aspect Full sun to light shade
Habit Upright; fast to mature
Leaf Light to mid-green, pinnate leaves, 13–17cm (5–7in) long and made up of 5–7 leaflets; some yellow autumn colour
Flower Single, semi-double or double, often large, flowers in a wide range of colours; some with repeat summer flowering; some followed by tomato-shaped purple fruit
Use Solo or in groups; as specimens; in rose or mixed plantings
Needs Propagate by commercial budding. Prune in spring by removing one-third of the shoots to ground level, choosing the oldest first; prune only well-established plants
Varieties *R. pimpinellifolia* (syn. *R. spinosissima*) 'Früh-lingsanfang' ('Spring Opening') single, pale yellow flowers in spring, to 2.7 × 2.7m (9 × 9ft) • *R.* 'Frühlingsgold' ('Spring Gold') ♀ the best yellow form, semi-double, fragrant flowers looking like large fried eggs in spring, tomato-shaped fruits, to 2.2 × 2.2m (7 × 7ft) • *R.* 'Frühlingsmorgen' ('Spring Morning') soft yellow flowers with strong pink shading, large with a second, less numerous, crop, purple tomato-shaped fruits, to 2.2 × 2.2m (7 × 7ft)

ACANTHUS
Acanthaceae
BEAR'S BREECHES

▲ ❀ ❦ SI summer E (semi)
H 1–2 yrs 0.9–1.2m (3–4ft)
S 0.9–1.2m (3–4ft)
❄ -10°C (14°F)
Z 7–10

For thousands of years the architectural merits of this plant have been recognized not only in gardening but in building, and many a classical column is decorated by a crown of acanthus leaves. Whether it will be evergreen in your garden will depend on your geographical location – the milder the garden, the greater the likelihood.

Soil Moderately alkaline to acid soil; must be deep and moisture retentive
Aspect Full sun to light shade
Habit Upright foliage gradually spreads outwards to show off the upright flower spikes
Leaf Deciduous to evergreen, depending on geographical location; glossy dark green, oval leaves, to 60cm (2ft) long and 25–30cm (10–12in) wide; some varieties deeply lobed, others indented
Flower Tri-coloured green, white and purple, lipped, tubular flowers borne on upright spikes, 45–60cm (18–24in) long
Use Solo or in groups; ideal for the back of mixed borders; display for its overall shape; good cut flower or dried for winter use
Needs Propagate by division or seed. Rarely requires division. If evergreen, remove old leaves as required
Varieties *A. hungaricus* (syn. *A. longifolius*) purple flowers • *A. mollis* white, pink or mauve flowers • *A. m.* Latifolius Group, broad leaves, 60cm (2ft) high, white flowers • *A. spinosus* ♀ possibly the most attractive form, very indented leaves and strong spikes of flowers

ACANTHUS SPINOSUS

ACHILLEA
Asteraceae/Compositae
MILFOIL, YARROW

❀ ❦ SI summer
H 1–2 yrs 0.6–1.2m (2–4ft)
S 0.6–1m (2–3ft)
❄ -10°C (14°F)
Z 3–10

For boldness of summer flowering, few perennial plants can compete with this very robust plant. In its wild form it was once used as a medicinal herb for both animals and humans.

Soil All soil types except very wet
Aspect Best in full sun; hardy
Habit Sturdy, upright clumps
Leaf Deciduous, fern-like, mid-green leaves, 10cm (4in) long and 8cm (3in) wide
Flower Very small, daisy-like flowers formed into many individual bold, flat clusters, each 8–15cm (3–6in) across; many varieties ranging in flower colour from white, yellow, gold to various shades of pink
Use As a solo plant or in groups; ideal for a mixed border of other perennials or with shrubs; useful as a cut flower, both fresh or dried
Needs May require staking. To propagate or every 5 years, for continued good performance, in spring dig up established root clumps, divide and replant divisions
Varieties *A.* 'Coronation Gold' ♀ medium height, golden-yellow flowers • *A. filipendulina* 'Cloth of Gold' tall, golden-yellow flowers • *A. f.* 'Gold Plate' ♀ tall, bright yellow flowers • *A.* 'Lachsschönheit' ('Salmon Beauty') medium height, salmon-pink flowers • *A. millefolium* 'Cerise Queen' medium height, deep pink flowers • *A.* 'Moonshine' ♀ medium height, pale yellow flowers • *A. ptarmica* The Pearl Group short, white flowers

ACHILLEA 'MOONSHINE'

AGAPANTHUS
Alliaceae/Liliaceae
AFRICAN LILY

▲ ✿ ✾ SI summer E (semi)
H 1–2 yrs 0.6–1m (2–3ft)
S 45–60cm (18–24in)
✶ -5°C (23°F)
Z 8–10

AGAPANTHUS HEADBOURNE HYBRIDS

Elegant, exotic and statuesque aptly describe this beautiful plant, whose botanical name translates as 'love flower'. It is native to South Africa, which rightly suggests that it should be planted in a sheltered position or in containers, an environment it relishes. The blue forms are well known, but the white-flowering varieties are also worthy of note.

Soil Moderately alkaline to acid soil, high in organic material and well fed
Aspect Full sun to light shade; sheltered and south- or west-facing for best results
Habit Leaves and flower spikes upright when young, arching with age
Leaf Semi-evergreen, glossy dark green, narrow, lance-shaped leaves, 25–40cm (10–16in) long
Flower Many funnel-shaped flowers make up a ball-shaped flowerhead, to 10cm (4in) across, in shades of blue or white in late summer
Use As a feature plant using both flower and foliage; ideal as a solo plant or planted in rows to mark a path or drive; breathtaking in a group; ideal for containers
Needs Containers planted with established plants can be damaged by root pressure. Propagate in spring by division of the root clump
Varieties *A.* 'Blue Moon' short, pale blue flowers •
A. campanulatus var. *albidus* medium height, white flower •
A. c. 'Isis' tall, dark blue flowers • *A.* Headbourne Hybrids tall, deep blue reliable, most reliable

ALCHEMILLA
Rosaceae
LADY'S MANTLE

✿ ✾ SI summer
Alpines: H 1–2 yrs 15–25cm (6–10in)
S 30–40cm (12–16in)
Perennials: H 1–2 yrs 30–40cm (12–16in)
S 60cm (2ft)
✶ -10°C (14°F)
Z 3–9

ALCHEMILLA MOLLIS

A well-known, interesting and versatile plant, which can be used in numerous ways in the garden. It is found in both alpine and perennial forms and is very hardy.

Soil Any except very dry
Aspect Any except very hot, where it may wilt; tolerates light to medium shade as long as soil is moist
Habit Tidy clump-forming in spring, becoming straggly later
Leaf Attractive, deciduous, light green, fan-shaped leaves, 10cm (4in) wide and long, covered with grey hairs
Flower Very small, starry flowers in irregular clusters to 15cm (6in) long and 3–5cm (1–2in) wide in early summer; yellow to pale green, becoming brown with age
Use Solo or in groups; ideal edging plant for borders and paths; works well in association with water; good in containers; flowers and foliage can be dried for flower arranging
Needs Every 5 years or to propagate, divide the root clump in late winter or early spring and replant. Straggly plants can be cut back to within 5cm (2in) of ground level and will produce a new canopy of foliage
Varieties Alpine varieties: *A. alpina* low growing and carpet-forming, below 15cm (6in) • *A. conjuncta* leaves more dissected and with a silver sheen, to 23cm (9in) •
A. erythropoda ♀ blue-green foliage, to 15cm (6in)
Perennial varieties: *A. mollis* (lady's mantle) ♀ the main perennial variety

ALSTROEMERIA
Alstroemeriaceae/ Liliaceae
PERUVIAN LILY, LILY OF THE INCAS

❀ ❦ SI summer
H 1–2 yrs 1m (3ft)
S 0.6–1m (2–3ft)
❄ -5°C (23°F)
Z 7–10

ALSTROEMERIA LIGTU HYBRIDS

This aristocrat among plants has gained a rightful place as a flowering plant in our gardens. However, it is not without its problems. Many new forms that were created for raising in heated greenhouses to supply the cut-flower market are now being offered for garden use, but take care when you buy, for not all, if any, of these, are hardy.

Soil Moderately alkaline to acid; dislikes wet, clay soils
Aspect Full sun; sheltered position
Habit Upright; always needs support
Leaf Deciduous, lance-shaped, grey-green leaves, to 10–13cm (4–5in) long and 2–2.5cm (¾–1in) wide
Flower Petals in 2 sets of 3 in a triangular arrangement from mid- to late summer; front petals face downwards, back petals upwards to form a flower 5cm (2in) wide and in shades of yellow, pink and orange
Use As long-term planting normally *en masse*; will tolerate being in a container for no more than 2 years; an ideal cut flower, lasting a long time in water
Needs If roots are disturbed or damaged by a fork the plant may bleed and die. Propagate by removing the root tubers before growth starts in spring. The tubers are grown on in pots for a year to establish fully. In ideal conditions may need controlling to keep in bounds
Varieties *A. aurea* (syn. *A. aurantiaca*) deep yellow flowers • *A. a.* 'Dover Orange' bright orange flowers • *A. a.* 'Orange King' deep orange flowers • *A. ligtu* Hybrids flowers in pastel shades of white, pink and lilac

ANAPHALIS
Asteraceae/Compositae
PEARLY EVERLASTING

▲ ground cover ❀ ❦ SI spring–summer–autumn
H 1 yr 30–45cm (12–18in)
S 38cm (15in)
❄ -10°C (14°F)
Z 3–9

ANAPHALIS TRIPLINERVIS

Given the right conditions and space, this plant has potential for a wide range of use. The silver foliage looks bright and clean, and, as the common name suggests, its flowers last a very long time, even when cut. It is a delightful foil for pink flowers, especially roses.

Soil Well-drained but moisture-retentive soil; needs to be well fed
Aspect Full sun to very light shade
Habit Spreading and loose carpet-forming
Leaf Deciduous, silver to silver-grey, narrowly oval leaves, 6–10cm (2½–4in) long and 2–2.5cm (¾–1in) wide
Flower Bold clusters of round, white, fluffy flowerheads to 5cm (2in) through summer and autumn, retained into winter as attractive grey to brown seedheads
Use Good for ground cover, edging borders such as rose beds. Can be used in summer containers and hanging baskets. Will cascade down low walls.
Needs Propagate by division in spring, needs correct soil and aspect. Should be cut to ground level every spring
Varieties *A. margaritacea* good strong-growing form • *A. m.* var. *yedoensis* ♀ taller growing, larger leaves and flowers • *A. triplinervis* ♀ the basic form, very worthy of planting • *A. t.* 'Sommerschnee' ('Summer Snow') ♀ more compact, very silver foliage, early white flowers

ANEMONE
Ranunculaceae
JAPANESE ANEMONE,
WINDFLOWER

❀ ❦ SI autumn
H 1–2 yrs 0.45–1.2m
(18in–4ft)
S 45–60cm (18–24in)
❄ -10°C (14°F)
Z 6–10

**ANEMONE HUPEHENSIS
'SEPTEMBER CHARM'**

One of the treasures of autumn-flowering plants and never failing to produce a bold display of flowers in shades of pink and white, these hybrid anemones are elegant in habit and tolerant of a wide range of conditions.

Soil Most, but does best in moist conditions
Aspect Full sun to medium shade
Habit Upright and normally self-supporting
Leaf Deciduous, glossy green, oval, trifoliate leaves, 8–13cm (3–5in) long and 8–9cm (3–3½in) wide, with dull undersides
Flower Clusters of single, semi-double or double flowers in white and shades of pink to red, 5–6cm (2–2½) across
Use Attractive when naturalized under trees; good for planting singly or in groups in mixed borders to add autumn interest; self-seeding but not invasive
Needs Propagate in spring by lifting and dividing established clumps. May need supporting in windy spots. Feed in late spring for best flowers
Varieties *A. hupehensis* 'Hadspen Abundance' ♀ single, deep pink to red flowers • *A. h.* var. *japonica* 'Bressingham Glow' semi-double, rosy red flowers • *A. h.* var. *j.* 'Prinz Heinrich' ♀ single, red to deep pink flowers • *A. h.* 'September Charm' ♀ single, soft pink flowers • *A.* × *hybrida* 'Honorine Jobert' ♀ single, white flowers • *A.* × *h.* 'Königin Charlotte' ('Queen Charlotte') single, pink flowers • *A.* × *h.* 'Luise Uhink' semi-double, white flowers • *A.* × *h.* 'Margarete' semi-double to double, deep pink flowers • *A.* × *h.* 'Whirlwind' ('Wirbelwind') semi-double, white flowers

ANTHEMIS TINCTORIA
Asteraceae/Compositae
DYER'S CAMOMILE,
YELLOW CAMOMILE

❀ SI summer
H 1–2 yrs 60–75cm (24–30in)
S 60–75cm (24–30in)
❄ -10°C (14°F)
Z 3–10

**ANTHEMIS TINCTORIA
'E.C. BUXTON'**

This relation of the daisy can be relied on to brighten any garden, and it will produce large clusters of flowers every summer. It is native to Europe and is a generally robust and hardy plant.

Soil Most, but prefers well-drained soil
Aspect Full sun to light shade; may need protection from summer winds to prevent damage to plants and flowers
Habit Upright at first; spreading when in flower
Leaf Deciduous, bright green, oval leaves, deeply indented and lace-like; pleasantly aromatic
Flower Single daisy-like flowers, to 5cm (2in) across, in large clusters in shades of yellow, lemon and cream in summer
Use A star planted in small groups in a mixed border; spectacular when planted in large numbers; will grow in large containers to good effect; good as a cut flower and for flower arranging
Needs May require support in windy gardens. Remove first crop of flowers to encourage more later. Propagate from cuttings taken from the first new shoots in spring
Varieties *A. tinctoria* yellow flowers • *A. t.* 'Alba' white flowers • *A. t.* 'E.C. Buxton' refreshing lemon-yellow flowers • *A. t.* 'Grallach Gold' golden-yellow flowers • *A. t.* 'Kelwayi' good yellow flowers • *A. t.* 'Wargrave' cream-yellow flowers

PERENNIALS

AQUILEGIA
Ranunculaceae
COLUMBINE, GRANNY'S
BONNET

❀ ❦ SI late spring–early
summer
H 1–2 yrs 60–90cm (2–3ft)
S 60–90cm (2–3ft)
❅ -10°C (14°F)
Z 3–10

AQUILEGIA VULGARIS

A true cottage-garden plant, aquilegias have attractive
flowers and foliage. They appear in spring as if by magic not
only where they are expected but as self-sown seedlings.

Soil Most, except very wet or dry soils
Aspect Light shade for best results; will tolerate slightly
more or less shade
Habit Upright; dies down in midsummer
Leaf Deciduous, mid- to dark green, trifoliate leaves,
6–10cm (2½–4in) long and 9–10cm (3½–4in) wide
Flower Bi-coloured, 5 diamond-shaped petals surround a
central cup; a wide range of colours, including shades of
blue, pink, red, yellow and white
Use In mixed borders or solo or *en masse*; ideal for
naturalizing, especially in orchards
Needs Can be grown for larger flowers as a biennial by
sowing seeds in summer, replanting in autumn for flowering
the following spring and summer. May need support in windy
gardens
Varieties *A. alpina* flowers in shades of blue, to 30–45cm
(12–18in) high • *A.* McKana Hybrids long flower spurs of
mixed colours • *A.* Mrs Scott-Elliot Hybrids flowers with
very long spurs in a wide range of mixed colours •
A. vulgaris the basic form, flowers in a wide range of colours
• *A. v.* 'Nivea' ('Munstead White') ♀ pure white flowers •
A. v. 'Nora Barlow' ♀ attractive, short-spurred, red and
white flowers • *A. v.* 'Red Star' crimson flowers

ARTEMISIA
Asteraceae/Compositae
WORMWOOD, SAGE
BRUSH, MUGWORT

❦ SI all year SC foliage E
H 1–2 yrs 90cm (3ft)
S 90cm (3ft)
❅ -5°C (23°F)
Z 4–10

ARTEMISIA 'POWIS CASTLE'

The foliage of this plant is its main attraction. Some varieties
have a herbal use, but all are grown mainly for their silver-
grey, fern-like, aromatic foliage. Although it is classed as a
perennial, many forms grow into small shrubs.

Soil Moderately alkaline to acid, well-drained yet water-
retentive soil
Aspect Does best in full sun but will tolerate very light shade
Habit Upright when young, spreading and bushy with age
Leaf Evergreen, silver-grey, often hairy leaves, 8cm (3in)
long and wide, dissected or with narrow indentations; often
pleasantly aromatic; some yellow autumn colour
Flower Inconspicuous grey to green buds opening to form
clusters of small, pale green or sulphur yellow flowers in
summer
Use For mixed borders in groups or singly; good as a foil for
other colours, including pinks and blues; ideal for large
containers; as a low informal hedge
Needs For best foliage effect on all forms remove all last
season's shoots to within 5cm (2in) of origin each spring.
Taller varieties may require staking
Varieties *A. abrotanum* (southernwood) ♀ upright, grey-
green, very aromatic foliage, ideal for low hedging •
A. absinthium 'Lambrook Silver' ♀ very good silver foliage
• *A. arborescens* woody habit, dissected, silver foliage •
A. 'Powis Castle' ♀ mound-forming, finely dissected silver
foliage • *A. stelleriana* carpet-forming, broad, indented,
silver-white foliage, to 30cm (1ft) high

ARUM ITALICUM ssp. ITALICUM 'MARMORATUM' ♔
Araceae
VARIEGATED ITALIAN ARUM

❦ SI spring (foliage), autumn (fruit)
H 1–2 yrs 30cm (1ft)
S 45cm (18in)
✳ -10°C (14°F)   Z 7–10

ARUM ITALICUM ssp. ITALICUM 'MARMORATUM'

The leaves of this interesting plant, which used to be known as *Arum italicum* 'Pictum', appear in early spring; they die down, leaving the flowering and fruiting spike. Bright red, poisonous fruits follow in autumn. Its relative, *A. italicum* (cuckoo pint or lords and ladies), is regarded as a weed, although its green leaves have some ornamental value in the garden.

Soil Moderately alkaline to acid soil, moist and high in organic material as in the native woodland environment
Aspect Full sun to light shade
Habit Upright, then spreading in late spring
Leaf Glossy, dark green, spear-shaped leaves, 30–40cm (12–16in) long and 8–10cm (3–4in) wide, with attractive white veining
Flower Green to cream protective spathe surrounding green to pale yellow flower
Use As an individual display of foliage, singly or in a group; ideal planted in association with daffodils, particularly the early spring species daffodils; can be used to good effect in flower arrangements
Needs Apart from a moist, rich soil, it has no special requirements
Varieties None of garden interest

ARUNCUS
Rosaceae
GOAT'S BEARD

❁ ❦ SI summer
H 1–2 yrs 0.9–1.2m (3–4ft)
S 0.9–1.2m (3–4ft)
✳ -15°C (4°F)
Z 3–9

ARUNCUS DIOICUS

Handsome, elegant and bold, this long-lived, summer-flowering perennial has tall fronds of foliage topped by large plumes of flowers, making it a very useful plant for the larger garden. Smaller growing varieties exist, and these are suitable for any size of garden.

Soil Moist soil, high in organic material
Aspect Full sun to light shade
Habit Upright at first, becoming more spreading when in flower
Leaf Mid- to light green, pinnate leaves, 10–15cm (4–6in) long and 5–10cm (2–4in) wide; yellow autumn colour
Flower Pyramid-shaped clusters of creamy-white, opening to pure white flowers, to 30cm (1ft) long, in midsummer
Use As background planting for mixed borders; ideal solo or in large groups; attractive near a water feature
Needs Moist soil essential for success. Taller growing varieties may need support
Varieties *A. aethusifolius* graceful habit, cream flowers (often sold wrongly as the more attractive *A. dioicus*) • *A. dioicus* (syn. *A. plumosus*, *A. sylvestris*) ♔ cream to white flowers, elegant and possibly the best of the taller growing varieties • *A. d.* 'Glasnevin' white flower plumes, to 60 × 60cm (2 × 2ft) • *A. d.* 'Kneiffii' attractive, very finely cut, deep green leaves, white flowers, to 45 × 45cm (18 × 18in), a must for all gardens, can be grown in containers to good effect

ASTER
Asteraceae/Compositae
MICHAELMAS DAISY

✱ SI late summer–autumn
H 1–2 yrs 0.6–1.2m (2–4ft)
S 0.45–1m (18in–3ft)
✱ -15°C (4°F)
Z 4–10

ASTER NOVAE-ANGLIAE

Asters form a very large group of perennial plants, providing late summer and autumn interest.

Soil Any, but dislikes very dry or wet soil
Aspect Full sun to light shade
Habit Upright but may be more spreading when in flower
Leaf Mid- to dark green, lance-shaped leaves, 10–13cm (3–5in) long and 1–2cm (½–¾in) wide
Flower Single, semi-double or double, daisy-like flowers in mixed colours
Use Ideal for a mixed border; dwarf varieties can be used to edge paths and drives; good as a cut flower
Needs Taller varieties may require support. Some varieties may suffer from mildew
Varieties <u>Tall growing</u>: *A. novi-belgii* 'Chequers' violet-purple flowers, to 60cm (2ft) • *A. n.-b.* 'Marie Ballard' double, light blue flowers, to 90cm (3ft) • *A. n.-b.* 'White Ladies' single, white flowers, to 1.2m (4ft) • *A. n.-b.* 'Winston S. Churchill' single, ruby red flowers, to 75cm (30in) <u>Low growing</u>: *A. novi-belgii* 'Audrey' single, blue flowers, to 25–45cm (10–18in) • *A. n.-b.* 'Dandy' single, red-purple flowers, to 25–45cm (10–18in) • *A. n.-b.* 'Lady in Blue' semi-double, blue flowers, to 25–45cm (10–18in) • *A. n.-b.* 'Snowsprite' single, pure white flowers, to 25–45cm (10–18in) <u>Other types of value</u>: *A. amellus* varieties in a wide range of colours, to 60cm (2ft) • *A. × frikartii* 'Mönch' ♀ light blue flowers, to 75cm (30in) • *A. novae-angliae* (New England aster) vigorous, upright habit, to 75cm (30in)

ASTILBE
Saxifragaceae
ASTILBE

✱ ❦ SI summer
H 1–2 yrs 75–90cm (30–36in)
S 30–45cm (12–18in)
✱ -5°C (23°F)
Z 4–8

ASTILBE 'BRESSINGHAM BEAUTY'

When it is planted in association with water, this is one of the finest of summer-flowering plants. The wide range of flower colours and heights makes it an ideal garden plant, but one that responds well only if given the right growing conditions.

Soil Moderately alkaline to acid soil that must be continuously moist and high in organic material
Aspect Full sun to light shade
Habit Upright
Leaf Light to mid-green, dissected leaves, 13–15cm (5–6in) long and 8–10cm (3–4in) wide; some autumn colour
Flower Feathery plumes, 23–30cm (9–12in) long, in colours ranging from white to pink, salmon-pink, red and purple
Use Planted in association with a water feature, either singly or in a group; can be grown in a large container for a year before planting out but will require regular watering
Needs A moist soil. Leave all growth in place in winter to protect plant from cold, cutting back to ground level in mid-spring. Apply a 5–8cm (2–3in) layer of organic material in autumn each year to protect roots and help development
Varieties *Astilbe* 'Bressingham Beauty' (× arendsii) rich pink flowers • *A.* 'Düsseldorf' *(japonica* hybrid) cerise-pink flowers • *A.* 'Fanal' (× arendsii) deep red flowers • *A.* 'Federsee' (× arendsii) rosy red flowers • *A.* 'Irrlicht' (× arendsii) white flowers • *A.* 'Sprite' (simplicifolia hybrid) ♀ bronze foliage, pink flowers, to 30–45cm (12–18in) • *A.* 'Straussenfeder' ('Ostrich Plume'; *thunbergii* hybrid) coral-pink flowers

ASTRANTIA MAJOR
Apiaceae/Umbelliferae
GREATER MASTERWORT

❀ ❦ SI late spring–early
summer
H 1–2 yrs 60–90cm (2–3ft)
S 60cm (2ft)
❄ -10°C (14°F)
Z 4–9

A very interesting flowering perennial, with an unusually
shaped flower, that is worthy of consideration in any planting
scheme. It is also very popular with flower arrangers.

Soil Moderately alkaline to acid; dislikes heavy clay but
requires moisture
Aspect Full sun to light shade
Habit Dome-shaped at first, becoming more open as it
flowers
Leaf Hand-shaped, light green leaves, 10–13cm (4–5in) long
and 8–10cm (3–4in) wide; some yellow autumn colour
Flower Domed clusters of tiny white flowers, surrounded by
white, petal-like bracts, in late spring and early summer;
some varieties have purple-pink bracts
Use Ideal for mixed borders or for mass-planting; can be
grown in containers in the short term; good flowers for
picking and arranging
Needs Dislikes drought and needs regular watering. Can be
cut to ground level directly after flowering and will form a
new set of foliage and, in wet summers, a late autumn crop of
flowers
Varieties *A. major* the type species, creamy-white flowers •
A. m. 'Hadspen Blood' deep purple flowers • *A. m.* ssp.
involucrata 'Shaggy' (syn. *A. m.* ssp. *i.* 'Margery Fish') ♥
longer, purple-pink petals, giving a 'shaggy' appearance to
flowers • *A. m.* var. *rosea* shaded pink flowers • *A. m.* var.
rubra wine-red flowers • *A. m.* 'Sunningdale Variegated'
(syn. *A. m.* 'Variegata') ♥ large, white-variegated leaves

ASTRANTIA MAJOR

BERGENIA
Saxifragaceae
ELEPHANT'S EAR

❀ ❦ SI winter–spring E
H 1–2 yrs 30cm (1ft)
S 45–60cm (18–24in)
❄ -15°C (4°F)
Z 6–10

Both the winter and early spring foliage and flowers are
welcome when little else may be flowering in the garden.

Soil All; dislikes very dry soil, in which it will grow but the
leaves and flowers will be smaller
Aspect Full sun to deep shade; flowering may be reduced in
very deep shade
Habit Spreading by self-rooting
Leaf Evergreen, glossy, mid-green, rounded leaves, 15–30cm
(6–12in) across; turn bronze or purple-red in autumn and
winter
Flower Bell-shaped clusters, 13–15cm (5–6in) wide, on
upright stems in spring; flowers white, salmon, pink-red or
purple depending on variety
Use As ground cover for difficult areas; plant singly or in
groups for interest
Needs Remove dead leaves as they show. If wished, dig up
and replant every 7–10 years
Varieties *B.* 'Abendglut' ('Evening Glow') purple leaves in
winter, rosy-red flowers • *B.* Ballawley Hybrids mid-green
leaves, bright rose-red flowers • *B. cordifolia* dark green,
heart-shaped leaves, drooping, rose-pink flowers • *B. c.*
'Purpurea' ♥ good purple foliage almost year round,
pink flowers • *B. crassifolia* green foliage turning purple
in winter, large, open, pink flowers • *B.* 'Silberlicht'
('Silverlight') ♥ mid-green leaves, large clusters of white to
purple flowers • *B.* 'Sunningdale' green leaves, purple in
winter, red flowers

BERGENIA 'SILBERLICHT'

CALTHA
Ranunculaceae
MARSH MARIGOLD,
KING CUP, MEADOW
BRIGHT

▲ ❀ SI Spring D
H 1–2 yrs 30cm (1ft)
S 45–60cm (18–24in)
❄ -10°C (14°F)
Z 4–10

**CALTHA PALUSTRIS VAR.
RADICANS 'FLORE PLENO'**

Wherever there is water there should be a planting of marsh marigold to brighten the early days of spring. Its ability to tolerate planting right on the water's edge with its roots continuously standing in water makes it possible to contrive an arrangement in which the bright yellow or white flowers are reflected, to give double the enjoyment. It is not much to look at in summer, but often puts on a second, autumn show of flowers.

Soil Moderately alkaline to acid, moist to wet soils with a high organic content
Aspect Full sun to light shade
Habit Spreading and bushy
Leaf Shiny, dark green, heart-shaped leaves, 4–5cm (1½–2in) long and 4–6cm (1½–2½in) wide
Flower Golden-yellow or white, saucer-shaped, 5-petalled flowers; some double forms; profuse flowers in spring with some repeat flowering in autumn
Use Always by water as marginal planting or in damp bog gardens; rarely does well in other areas
Needs Its need for moisture and a soil high in organic material cannot be overemphasized
Varieties *C. palustris* ♀ dark green foliage, single, golden-yellow flowers • *C. p.* var. *alba* single, white flowers over a long period • *C. p.* var. *palustris* 'Plena' double, very showy, yellow flowers • *C. p.* var. *radicans* 'Flore Pleno' ♀ very double, very bold, yellow flowers

CAMPANULA
Campanulaceae
BELLFLOWER

❀ SI summer
H 1–2 yrs 0.5–1.4m
(20–54in)
S 0.5–1.2m (20–48in)
❄ -10°C (14°F)
Z 3–10

**CAMPANULA GLOMERATA
'SUPERBA'**

This large genus includes a variety of spring- and summer-flowering annuals, perennials and alpines. The hardy, tall-growing perennials described here have an upright, stately habit, which brings distinction to any planting scheme.

Soil Alkaline to acid, well-drained and well-fed soil
Aspect Full sun to light shade
Habit Upright
Leaf Light green, pointed oval leaves, 2.5–4cm (1–1½in) long and wide
Flower Bell-shaped flowers, 2.5–4cm (1–1½in) wide, in shades of blue, purple, pink or white
Use For mixed borders or background planting; for cutting
Needs May require staking in windy gardens. Propagate by division
Varieties *C. glomerata* deep blue to purple flowers, to 60cm (2ft) • *C. g.* var. *alba* pure white flowers, to 60cm (2ft) • *C. g.* 'Superba' ♀ larger blue to purple flowers, to 75cm (30in) • *C. lactiflora* pale to mid-blue flowers • *C. l.* 'Loddon Anna' ♀ pale pink flowers, to 1.2–1.4m (48–54in) • *C. l.* 'Prichards's Variety' ♀ violet-blue flowers, to 1.2–1.4m (48–54in) • *C. latifolia* lavender-blue flowers, to 1–1.2m (3–4ft) • *C. latiloba* lavender-blue flowers, to 0.75–1m (30–36in) • *C. l.* var. *alba* ♀ pure white flowers, to 0.75–1m (30–36in) • *C. l.* 'Hidcote Amethyst' ♀ lilac-pink flowers, to 0.75–1m (30–36in) • *C. persicifolia* lilac-blue flowers, to 0.75–1m (30–36in) • *C. p.* var. *alba* pure white flowers, to 0.75–1m (30–36in)

CENTRANTHUS RUBER
Valerianaceae
RED VALERIAN,
JUPITER'S BEARD

✿ ꝺ SI summer
H 1–2 yrs 45–90cm (18–36in)
S 45–60cm (18–24in)
✹ -10°C (14°F)
Z 4–10

CENTRANTHUS RUBER

This native of Europe can be found growing in the most unlikely places, including inhospitable-looking walls and derelict areas. It is, perhaps, not always regarded as a garden plant, but, given a sunny spot, it can be a treasure, often self-seeding to further underline its presence.

Soil Most, but prefers alkaline soil; adapts as well to poor, dry soils as to good, moderately wet soils
Aspect Full sun; dislikes shade; good in maritime gardens
Habit Upright when young, becoming attractively straggly when in flower
Leaf Attractive, blue-grey, glaucous, shield-shaped leaves, 8–10cm (3–4in) long and to 2.5cm (1in) wide
Flower Small, dark wine-red, mid-pink or white, star-shaped flowers produced in loose spikes to 20cm (8in) long throughout summer and often into autumn
Use Allow to naturalize throughout the garden; encourage to grow on walls; can be spectacular if planted *en masse* as a single colour
Needs Should be allowed to set seed at will, only controlled where needed. Can be cut hard back after first main flowering to regrow and flower. Propagate from seed
Varieties *C. ruber* deep pink flowers • *C. r.* var. *albus* pure white flowers, more glaucous foliage • *C. r.* var. *atrococcineus* deep red flowers • *C. r.* var. *coccineus* red flowers

COREOPSIS
Asteraceae/Compositae
ORNAMENTAL TICKSEED

✿ ꝺ SI summer–autumn
H 1–2 yrs 60cm (2ft)
S 60cm (2ft)
✹ -5°C (23°F)
Z 3–10

COREOPSIS VERTICILLATA

This is such a delicate-looking plant that it often gives the impression that it might fail, but in fact it is one of the most reliable of perennial plants. Grown in gardens for over a hundred years, it deserves to be much better known and more widely planted.

Soil Most, but dislikes poorly drained areas where root damage in winter may kill it
Aspect Full sun to very light shade
Habit Clump-forming and spreading just a little with age
Leaf Deciduous, pale to mid-green, finely dissected, pleasantly aromatic leaves
Flower Daisy-like flowers, to 4cm (1½in) wide, in profusion in late summer to autumn
Use Ideal for mixed borders; plant in 3s or 5s for best effects because spectacular when mass-planted; can be grown in containers to good effect; some value as a short-lived cut flower
Needs In windy gardens may need support. Propagate by division in early spring
Varieties *C.* 'Goldfink' yellow flowers, to 30cm (1ft) • *C. grandiflora* 'Badengold' buttercup-yellow flowers, may be short lived • *C. g.* 'Mayfield Giant' large, yellow flowers • *C.* 'Sunburst' rich golden-yellow flowers • *C. verticillata* the main form, rich golden-yellow flowers • *C. v.* 'Grandiflora' (syn. *C.* 'Golden Showers') golden-yellow flowers • *C. v.* 'Moonbeam' pale yellow flowers

PERENNIALS

CORYDALIS
Papaveraceae
FUMITORY

❀ ✿ SI spring–summer
H 1–2 yrs 30–40cm (12–16in)
S 40–45cm (16–18in)
❊ -5°C (23°F)
Z 4–10

CORYDALIS FLEXUOSA
'CHINA BLUE'

These charming, delicate plants seed themselves at random through the garden but rarely invasively so. The sap is an irritant, so take care both when you are planting it and when you are cutting the flowers or foliage.

Soil Most, but must be well drained
Aspect Full sun to light shade; normally hardy
Habit Forms loose clumps
Leaf Deciduous, mid-green, very dissected leaves; start to die down in mid- to late summer
Flower Moderately long tubular flowers, with lips at lower ends, in shades of yellow or blue, borne in clusters above the foliage in late spring with repeat flowering in late summer and autumn
Use As a spot plant, grown or self-sown where required; may naturalize itself in walls between bricks or paving on paths and steps; can be grown in containers outdoors to good effect
Needs Apart from well-drained soil has few other needs. Propagate by division or seed. Leave seedheads on established plants to ripen and self-seed
Varieties *C. cava* (syn. *C. bulbosa*) ♥ mauve flowers, best in shade • *C. flexuosa* very pale blue flowers • *C. f.* 'China Blue' china blue flowers, a gem • *C. f.* 'Père David' mid-blue flowers • *C. lutea* flowers in shades of yellow, repeat flowering in autumn • *C. ochroleuca* white flowers, seeds freely • *C. solida* ♥ mauve to blue flowers

CRAMBE
Brassicaceae/Cruciferae
CRAMBE

▲ ❀ ✿ SI summer–autumn
C. cordifolia: H 1–2 yrs 2–
2.5m (6–8ft) S 2–2.5m (6–8ft)
❊ -10°C (14°F)
C. maritima: H 1–2 yrs
75cm (30in) S 1m (3ft)
❊ -5°C (23°F)
Z 6–9

CRAMBE CORDIFOLIA

Crambe cordifolia is one of the tallest perennial plants found growing in temperate regions. The delicate tracery of the giant flowerhead contrasts wonderfully with the large leaves. *Crambe maritima* (sea kale) is also of interest, if not as spectacular, and it requires more specialist growing conditions. Its leaves are edible.

Soil Alkaline to moderately acid; *C. cordifolia*: deep and well-drained soil for root penetration and to prevent root rotting; *C. maritima*: very sandy soil to mimic a seashore habitat
Aspect Full sun; hardy in well-drained soil
Habit *C. cordifolia*: upright, becoming wide and spreading when in flower; *C. maritima*: short and squat
Leaf *C. cordifolia*: dark green, heart-shaped leaves, 30–90cm (1–3ft) long and wide; *C. maritima*: metallic blue, curled leaves, 25cm (10in) long and 10cm (4in) wide
Flower *C. cordifolia*: small white flowers on a network of branches forming inflorescence to 1.2m (4ft) high and wide in summer, normally taking a year to settle before flowering; *C. maritima*: thick clusters of white flowers, 20cm (8in) high, in summer
Use *C. cordifolia*: a focal point in a mixed border or solo in the garden; *C. maritima*: as a vegetable or for its blue foliage
Needs *C. cordifolia* may require support. Propagate by root cuttings
Varieties None of garden interest

CROCOSMIA
Iridaceae
MONTBRETIA

▲ ❀ ☙ SI late summer–
autumn
H 1–2 yrs 1m (3ft)
S 60cm (2ft)
❄ -15°C (4°F)
Z 4–8

CROCOSMIA MASONIORUM

If your garden needs a tall, graceful yet bright plant, this could be the plant for you. Although it is listed here under perennials, it is a corm, but it can be purchased in both forms for planting in the garden.

Soil Well-drained, moderately alkaline to acid
Aspect Full sun; very hardy
Habit Upright and clump-forming
Leaf Mid-green, sword-shaped leaves, 1m (3ft) long and 3–5 cm (1¼–2in) wide
Flower Tubular flowers, to 2.5cm (1in) long, from orange to red, in short, branched spikes in late summer
Use As a background plant for mixed borders; spectacular when mass-planted; works well when planted in association with water, although the roots must not be waterlogged
Needs In windy gardens may require support. Best lifted every 7–10 years and split, not only to propagate but to maintain growing vigour
Varieties *C.* 'Carmin Brilliant' (× *crocosmiiflora*) bright red flowers with yellow throat, to 60cm (2ft) • *C.* 'Emberglow' burnt orange-red flowers, vigorous • *C.* 'Emily McKenzie' (× *crocosmiiflora*) dark orange flowers, to 60cm (2ft) • *C.* 'Firebird' orange-flame flowers • *C.* 'Golden Fleece' golden-yellow flowers • *C.* 'Jackanapes' (× *crocosmiiflora*) red and yellow bicolour flowers, to 60cm (2ft) • *C.* 'Lucifer' ♀ flame red flowers • *C. masoniorum* ♀ bright red-orange flowers • *C.* 'Solfaterre' (× *crocosmiiflora*) ♀ apricot yellow flowers, tender • *C.* 'Vulcan' dark orange-red flowers

---

DARMERA
Saxifragaceae
UMBRELLA PLANT

▲ ❀ ☙ SI spring–autumn
H 1–2 yrs 90cm (3ft)
S 1.2m (4ft)
❄ -10°C (14°F)
Z 6–9

DARMERA PELTATA

A large, bold foliage plant, formerly classified in the genus *Peltiphyllum*, that is suitable only for those areas where the soil is constantly moist. Although the individual plants size is as shown, they spread by underground roots and require space to perform well. If you have the right conditions, you will find few other plants with such attractive leaves. The strange growth habit of flowering before the leaves emerge adds to the attraction.

Soil Moderately alkaline to acid; must be deep and moist, almost waterlogged, for best results
Aspect Light to full shade; tolerates full sun as long as the soil is reliably moist
Habit Forms large clumps, spreading by underground shoots
Leaf Deciduous, light to mid-green, glossy, parasol-like leaves, 25–45cm (10–18in) long and wide, heavily veined and with indented edges, borne at the top of leaf shoots; reliable yellow to bronze autumn colour over a long period
Flower Pink, dome-shaped clusters of flowers, 8–15cm (3–6in) across, on strong, stout, upright stems, 38–60cm (15–24in) tall; flowers in early spring, before the foliage emerges
Use As a feature plant where space allows; close to water features, such as a pond, stream or lake
Needs Propagate by division in early spring
Varieties *D. peltata* (syn. *Peltiphyllum peltata*) ♀ pale pink flowers with dark stigma to each • *D. p.* 'Nana' lower growing form, to 30cm (1ft)

DELPHINIUM
Ranunculaceae
DELPHINIUM GARDEN
HYBRIDS

❀ SI late summer
H 1–2 yrs 0.6–1.2m (2–4ft)
S 0.6–1m (2–3ft)
❄ -10°C (14°F)
Z 3–10

**DELPHINIUM KING ARTHUR
GROUP**

Always a stately plant with which to adorn our gardens, even
though it needs a little more work than most if it is to achieve
its full potential. This entry deals mainly with the garden
hybrids, which are grown for their tall flower spikes. The
Blue Fountains Group and *Belladonna* Group hybrids are
more graceful both in flower and growth.

Soil Moderately alkaline to moderately acid soil that is well
drained and high in organic material
Aspect Full sun to light shade; require a sheltered site for
best results
Habit Upright
Leaf Mid- to grey-green, palm-shaped, to 25cm (10in) long
Flower Florets, 3cm (1in) long and in colours ranging from
pink, white, shades of blue to purple, with some bicolour
varieties, clothe a flower spike often in excess of 1m (3ft) long
Use As background planting for mixed borders; spectacular
when mass-planted; very good cut flower
Needs Garden hybrids require support. Protect from slugs
and snails. Propagate by cuttings in late spring
Varieties *D. Belladonna* Group more open flowers in shades
of blue, to 0.75–1.2m (30–48in) tall • *D.* Black Knight Group
deep blue flowers • *D.* Blue Fountains Group lighter growth
structure, smaller flowers in shades of blue, to 60–75cm
(24–30in) • *D.* 'Blue Jay' mid-blue flowers with white eye •
D. King Arthur Group blue flowers • *D.* Pacific Hybrids
good range of mixed colours • *D.* × *ruysii* 'Pink Sensation'
(syn. *D. Belladonna* Group 'Pink Sensation') pink flowers

DICENTRA
Papaveraceae
BLEEDING HEART,
DUTCHMAN'S
BREECHES, LADY'S
LOCKET

❀ ❦ SI spring
H 1–2 yrs 38–45cm (15–20in)
S 45cm (18in)
❄ -10°C (14°F)
Z 3–9

DICENTRA SPECTABILIS

A most attractive, largely spring-flowering plant that in wet
summers may give a lesser display in late summer. The
flowers are charming, but in wet summers the foliage can
become unattractive before most other garden plants.

Soil Moderately alkaline to acid; dislikes very wet or dry
conditions
Aspect Full sun to light shade; normally hardy
Habit Clump-forming and slightly spreading; growth is
rather fragile
Leaf Deciduous, fleshy, dissected, light grey-green leaves
with red veining, 17–23cm (7–9in) long; some varieties more
glaucous
Flower Heart-shaped flowers, 1cm (½in) long, in colours
from red, purple and mauve to white
Use In mixed borders; attractive by water but dislikes very
wet soil; good in containers; for small areas of ground cover
Needs The right soil type is important. Propagate by
division in spring
Varieties *D.* 'Adrian Bloom' very grey foliage, carmine-red
flowers • *D.* 'Bountiful' dark purple crimson flowers •
D. eximia light purple-pink to soft pink flowers • *D. e.* 'Alba'
pure white flowers • *D. formosa* pink-mauve flowers •
D. f. var. *alba* white flowers • *D.* 'Luxuriant' ♀ bright red
flowers • *D.* 'Pearl Drops' mother-of-pearl pink flowers •
D. spectabilis ♀ grey foliage, rose-red flowers with white
droplet • *D. s.* 'Alba' ♀ green foliage, pure white flowers •
D. 'Stuart Boothman' ♀ carmine-red flowers

DICTAMNUS
Rutaceae
GAS PLANT, BURNING BUSH, DITTANY

▲ ❀ ❦ SI summer
H 1–2 yrs 45–75cm (18–30in)
S 45–60cm (18–24in)
❄ -5°C (23°F)
Z 2–9

A novelty, yes, but a beautiful one. The common names derive from the fact that, as the seed is ripening, you can set fire to the volatile gas without harming the plant. If you try this, take care that you do not harm yourself or anyone else. The flowers are, in any case, attractive in their own right. It is not always easy to find the plant in garden centres and nurseries, and it is difficult to establish once you have found it, but it is worth the effort.

Soil Moderately alkaline to acid; must contain high levels of organic material to retain moisture and allow for easy development and penetration of the fleshy root system
Aspect Full sun
Habit Upright
Leaf Glossy, dark green, pinnate leaves, 5–8cm (2–3in) long and formed of 7–13 oval leaflets
Flower Star-shaped, flowers, with 5 reflexed petals and long, protruding white stamens, forming upright spikes, 25cm (10in) long, in white, pale mauve through pale pink to rosy-red; as the seeds ripen they give off a flammable gas
Use As a novelty; for mid- or background planting in mixed borders; good planted *en masse*
Needs Well-prepared soil with added organic material. Protect from slugs and snails. Support in windy gardens
Varieties *D. albus* ♀ white or light mauve flowers with purple streaks • *D. a.* var. *purpureus* ♀ (syn. *D. fraxinella*) flowers with pale pink stripes and mauve reverse to petals

DICTAMNUS ALBUS VAR. PURPUREUS

DIERAMA
Iridaceae
ANGEL'S FISHING RODS, VENUS FISHING RODS, WAND FLOWER

▲ ❀ ❦ SI summer
H 1–2 yrs 1.2m (4ft)
S 1m (3ft)
❄ -10°C (14°F)
Z 4–9

A gem among plants, admired for the beautiful graceful habit of its long, waving flower spikes, so well described by its common names. In the right position, it is a delight to behold.

Soil Most, moisture-retentive but not waterlogged soils; provide room for its corms to develop by adding organic material at planting time
Aspect Full sun to very light shade
Habit Graceful and upright but spreading
Leaf Deciduous, grey-green, thin, lance-shaped leaves, to 75cm (30in) long and 1cm (½ in) wide
Flower Numerous bells in short clusters, hanging from slender flower shoots in late summer; colours range from shades of purple through pink
Use As a solo specimen plant; in mixed borders in bold group; ideal for planting in association with water; important to site carefully for best effect
Needs Propagate by seed or division of corms in spring. Really needs division to do well
Varieties *D. dracomontanum* (syn. *D. pumilum*) satin-rose flowers, to 60cm (2ft) • *D. pulcherrimum* flower in varying shades of purple • *D. p.* 'Blackbird' violet-mauve flowers • *D. p.* 'Jay' mid-pink flowers • *D. p.* 'Oberon' carmine-pink flowers, to 75cm (30in) • *D. p.* 'Puck' pale rose flowers, to 75cm (30in) • *D. p.* 'Windhover' lilac-rose flowers

DIERAMA PULCHERRIMUM

DODECATHEON
Primulaceae
SHOOTING STAR,
AMERICAN COWSLIP

❀ ❦ SI spring–early summer
H 1–2 yrs 45–60cm (18–24in)
S 30–60cm (12–18in)
❋ -5°C (23°F)
Z 4–9

DODECATHEON MEDIA

One of the most beautiful of garden plants, Dodecatheon is, unfortunately, also one of the most demanding in terms of planting and soil conditions. Its need for continuous moisture without waterlogging makes it difficult to position satisfactorily so that it becomes established and is able to show off its delicate flowers.

Soil Acid to moderately alkaline and high in organic material; because dodecatheons require a constant supply of moisture that is just below the root system but not swamping it for any length of time, it may be worth studying the intended planting site for a year or so to ensure that it is appropriate
Aspect Light shade for preference; may tolerate full sun
Habit Base foliage forms a rosette; flowers upright at first, splaying out attractively as they open to form an inverted cone shape
Leaf Attractive, dark glossy green, oval leaves, to 20cm (8in) long and 5cm (2in) wide
Flower Short clusters of small, cyclamen-shaped, pink or white flowers, resembling shooting stars
Use Best planted in association with a water feature
Needs The soil and moisture requirements are critical for success. Not always readily available from nurseries and garden centres
Varieties *D. media* ♀ pink flowers, the main variety available and planted • *D. m.* f. *album* ♀ pale green foliage, white flowers

DORONICUM
Asteraceae/Compositae
LEOPARD'S BANE

❀ ❦ SI spring
H 1–2 yrs 45–60cm (18–24in)
S 53–60cm (21–24in)
❋ -10°C (14°F)
Z 4–9

**DORONICUM
'FRUHLINGSPRACHT'**

Every spring this beautiful plant appears almost overnight as if from nothing, and it is a joy to behold. The mass of yellow daisy flowers brightens the garden and heralds the start of spring. Even the leaves are bright green, adding to the overall fresh effect.

Soil Most, except very dry
Aspect Full sun to light shade; although will tolerate high levels of shade if moisture is present, habit may be more open
Habit Clump-forming; may spread more open when in flower
Leaf Deciduous, mid-green, oval to heart-shaped leaves with notched edges, 9–10cm (3½–4in) long and 2.5–4cm (1–1½in) wide
Flower Numerous, small, golden-yellow, strap-like petals form a daisy-shaped flower; some double forms but normally single
Use For mass-planting or in small groups; solo planting or in mixed borders
Needs Apart from disliking drought and dry soils, it has few other needs. Propagate by division in spring. The fact that it dies down in midsummer could cause gaps in a planting display
Varieties *D.* × *excelsum* 'Harpur Crewe' yellow flowers • *D.* 'Frühlingspracht' ('Spring Beauty') very full, double, yellow flowers • *D.* 'Miss Mason' ♀ yellow flowers, possibly the best garden hybrid • *D. orientale* (syn. *D. caucasicum*) golden-yellow flowers • *D. o.* 'Magnificum' large yellow flowers

ECHINOPS
Asteracae/Compositae
GLOBE THISTLE

▲ ❀ ❦ SI summer–autumn
H 1–2 yrs 0.9–1.2m (3–4ft)
S 60–75cm (24–30in)
❋ -10°C (14°F)
Z 3–10

A giant among perennial plants and one that never fails to attract attention. The ball-shaped flowers, held like giant lollipops, are shown off by the interesting foliage.

Soil Deep, moderately alkaline to acid; dislikes waterlogging or extreme dryness
Aspect Full sun to light shade; normally hardy except in cold, wet and long winters
Habit Upright, spreading when in flower
Leaf Dark green or grey, thistle-like leaves, 23–30 (9–12in) long and 10–20cm (4–8in) wide, with silver underside; some forms have spines
Flower Ball-shaped, pale to deep blue, mauve-blue or white-grey flowers borne at the top of long, upright stems
Use As a specimen plant, standing alone or as background for mixed plantings
Needs Deep, well-prepared soil to allow free root run is important. May require support in windy gardens. Can be dried for flower arranging. Propagate by division or seed in spring
Varieties *E. bannaticus* 'Blue Globe' grey-green foliage, large, deep blue flowers • *E. b.* 'Taplow Blue' (syn. *E. humilis* 'Taplow Blue') ♀ grey foliage, deep blue flowers • *E.* 'Nivalis' very grey, spiny leaves, white to grey flowers, to 1.8m (5ft 6in) • *E. ritro* ♀ green leaves with grey reverse, mid-blue to mauve-blue flowers • *E. r.* 'Veitch's Blue' deep blue flowers • *E. sphaerocephalus* green leaves on green stems, grey flowerheads, very large plant, to 1.8m (5ft 6in)

ECHINOPS RITRO

EPIMEDIUM
Berberidaceae
BISHOP'S HAT, BISHOP'S MITRE, BARRENWORT

❀ ❦ SI all year E
H 1–2 yrs 25–30cm (10–12in)
S 45–60cm (18–24in)
❋ -15°C (4°F)
Z 5–9

This is an excellent plant for ground cover, the pretty, bell-shaped flowers being held above heart-shaped leaves.

Soil Most but does best in moist soil
Aspect Full sun to moderate shade
Habit Spreading ground cover
Leaf Evergreen leaves, 3–9 heart-shaped leaflets, to 6cm (2½in) long, on thin wiry stems; colours change seasonally
Flower Saucer-shaped flowers, to 2.5cm (1in) across, borne in open clusters in colours from white to yellow, pink and rose
Use Ground cover suitable for wide range of planting conditions; edging borders and pathways; in containers
Needs Cut away all foliage in early spring to show off flowers to best effect. Propagate by division in spring
Varieties *E. grandiflorum* ♀ attractive foliage, crimson-pink flowers • *E. g.* 'Nanum' ♀ dwarf form • *E. g.* 'Rose Queen' ♀ smaller leaves, large, deep pink flowers • *E. g.* 'White Queen' ♀ good foliage, white flowers • *E. × perralchicum* ♀ taller, large leaves, yellow flowers • *E. × p.* 'Frohnleiten' green foliage mottled red-bronze, yellow flowers • *E. perralderianum* light green leave, indented edges, coral-red to brown tint in late winter, bright yellow flowers • *E. pinnatum* ssp. *colchicum* ♀ good foliage, yellow flowers • *E. × rubrum* ♀ shorter, young foliage bronze-red turning light, rose-pink flowers • *E. × versicolor* 'Sulphureum' ♀ bronze foliage in spring, green in summer, turning bronze again in winter, sulphur yellow flowers • *E. × youngianum* 'Niveum' ♀ good foliage, white flowers

EPIMEDIUM × VERSICOLOR 'SULPHUREUM'

ERIGERON
Asteraceae/Compositae
FLEABANE

❀ SI summer–autumn
H 1–2 yrs 45–60cm (18–24in)
S 38cm (15in)
❄ -10°C (14°F)
Z 4–10

A gem of a summer- and autumn-flowering plant that seems, to have been largely forgotten by gardeners. Its low, clump-forming habit allows it to be used at the front of borders without outgrowing its allocated space. All the named forms were once listed as *Erigeron speciosus*, but today they should be seen and listed as hybrids in their own right.

Soil Most, except very dry
Aspect Full sun to very light shade
Habit Clump-forming
Leaf Deciduous, olive green to grey-green, lance-shaped leaves, to 10cm (4in) long
Flower Single or double, daisy-shaped flowers, 4–5cm (1½–2in) across, in pink, mauve, blue or purple with bright yellow centres, in summer
Use Ideal for the front of a mixed border; spectacular when planted *en masse*; can be grown in containers; good as short-stemmed cut flowers
Needs Lift and divide every 5 years. Propagate and divide in spring
Varieties *E.* 'Amity' single, lilac-pink flowers • *E.* 'Charity' single, clear pink flowers • *E.* 'Dignity' single, violet-blue flowers • *E.* 'Dimity' low growing, single, pink flowers • *E.* 'Dunkelste Aller' ('Darkest of All') single, deep violet-blue flowers • *E.* 'Foersters Liebling' ♀ double, pink flowers • *E.* 'Gaiety' single, pink flowers • *E. karvinskianus* (syn. *E. mucronatus*) ♀ low growing, single, pale pink flowers • *E.* 'Prosperity' semi-double, light blue flowers

ERIGERON 'DIGNITY'

ERYNGIUM
Apiaceae/Umbelliferae
SEA HOLLY

▲ ❀ ❦ SI summer–autumn
E (semi)
H 1–2 yrs 60–75cm (24–30in)
S 45cm (18in)
❄ -5°C (23°F)
Z 4–10

A perennial plant, providing interesting foliage and intriguing flowerheads. If you have the space, this is a worthwhile addition to any planting scheme.

Soil Moderately alkaline to acid, sandy and well drained with a high organic content
Aspect Full sun to light shade
Habit Upright plant with branching flowering shoots
Leaf Greyish-green, oval, deeply lobed, leaves, 5–10cm (2–4in) long, spiny and indented; depending on location and winter may remain as an evergreen
Flower Small, steely-blue, teasel-like flower with a cone ringed by spiked narrow bracts, often white
Use Singly or in mixed plantings where the height can be used to full advantage. Flowers can be dried
Needs Space is important. Propagate from seed in spring. Use self-sown plants
Varieties *E. alpinum* ♀ green foliage, very large, bright blue flowers • *E. amethystinum* green foliage, small, dark blue flowers, to 1m (3ft) • *E. bourgatii* foliage with good white veins, blue-green flowers • *E. giganteum* (Miss Willmott's ghost) ♀ grey foliage, blue-white flowers, propagates by self-seeding as a biennial, to 3–4m (10–13ft) • *E. × oliverianum* ♀ blue flowers, variable in colour and size • *E. planum* marbled coloured foliage, small, light to mid-blue flowers • *E. × tripartitum* ♀ more open, loose, graceful habit, steely blue flowers • *E. varifolium* round leaves, marbled in colour, may remain as evergreen, blue to grey flowers

ERYNGIUM × TRIPARTITUM

ERYSIMUM
Brassicaceae/Cruciferae
PERENNIAL WALL-
FLOWER

▲ ✿ ❦ SI almost all year
H 1–2 yrs 60cm (2ft)
S 60cm (2ft)
✳ -5°C (23°F)
Z 3–10

If an almost perpetual flowering plant is required, this relative of the wallflower, formerly in the genus *Cheiranthus*, under which name it is still sometimes found, stands out from the pack. It is an almost shrub-like plant, and the goblet shape is an added bonus.

Soil Most well-drained soils
Aspect Prefers full sun but tolerates very light shade
Habit Neat goblet shape or bushy habit
Leaf Evergreen, dark green with purple-grey sheen, narrow, lance-shaped leaves, to 8cm (3in) long
Flower Typical wallflower blooms in a range of colours
Use Best planted as a solo specimen in the garden or in a container; can be grouped in small numbers for use in mixed borders; ideal for larger rock gardens and often sold as an alpine plant
Needs Small when purchased and needs time to make a mark. Propagate from cuttings in early to midsummer
Varieties *E.* 'Bowles' Mauve' ♀ purple-grey leaves, mauve-purple flowers • *E.* 'Bredon' ♀ mustard yellow flowers • *E.* 'Butterscotch' pale cream-yellow flowers • *E. cheiri* 'Harpur Crewe' ♀ double yellow flowers • *E.* 'Constant Cheer' ♀ violet-mauve flowers with amber markings, very free flowering almost year round • *E.* 'Jacob's Jacket' multicoloured, amber, yellow and brown flowers • *E.* 'Moonlight' pale to lemon-yellow flowers, to 15cm (6in) • *E.* 'Orange Flame' very striking, orange-red flowers

ERYSIMUM 'BOWLES' MAUVE'

EUPHORBIA
Euphorbiaceae
SPURGE

▲ ✿ ❦ SI spring E some
H 1–2 yrs 30–90cm (18–36in)
S 30–90cm (18–36in)
✳ -5°C (23°F)
Z 3–10

A large group of plants, all of which are worthy of garden space. Beware: the sap can burn your skin.

Soil Moderately alkaline to acid, well-drained soil
Aspect Full sun to light shade
Habit Depends on variety
Leaf Lance-shaped leaves, 30–45cm (12–18in) long and 10–15cm (4–6in) wide
Flower Greenish-yellow or orange-red, bell-shaped flowers on short stalks rising from oval shields, borne in clusters in spring and early summer
Use Specimen plants solo or groups; useful in mixed borders; can be grown in containers in the short term
Needs Needs support. Propagate from seed or by division
Varieties *E. amygdaloides* 'Purpurea' (syn. *E. a.* 'Rubra') deciduous, purple leaves, purple flowers, to 45cm (18in) • *E. a.* var. *robbiae* ♀ evergreen, dark green foliage, light yellow-green flowers, ideal in shade as ground cover, to 45cm (18in) • *E. characias* ♀ evergreen, grey-blue foliage, greenish-yellow flowers, to 1m (3ft), cut to ground level in spring every fourth year • *E. c.* ssp. *wulfenii* ♀ larger, brighter flower-heads, treat as type species • *E. dulcis* 'Chameleon' deciduous, green to purple leaves, purple flowers, to 45cm (18in) • *E. griffithii* 'Fireglow' deciduous, purple, grey and green foliage, bright orange-red flowers in spring, to 75cm (30in) • *E. myrsinites* ♀ evergreen, grey foliage, pale green flowers, 30cm (1ft), spreading • *E. polychroma* (syn. *E. epithymoides*) ♀ deciduous, grey-green foliage, yellow flowers, to 45cm (18in)

EUPHORBIA CHARACIAS ssp. *WULFENII*

PERENNIALS

FILIPENDULA
Rosaceae
MEADOWSWEET,
DROPWORT

▲ ❀ ❦ SI late spring–early
summer
H 1–2 yrs 60–90cm (2–3ft)
S 60–90cm (2–3ft)
❋ -15°C (4°F)
Z 3–9

FILIPENDULA RUBRA

Although this plant is almost a weed – and the type species,
Filipendula ulmaria, grows wild in wet meadows – cultivated
forms can be used to delightful effect in the garden.

Soil Moderately alkaline to acid, moist and well fed
Aspect Light shade to full sun
Habit Upright, spreading when in flower
Leaf Deciduous, mid-green, some bright yellow, deeply
indented and pinnate leaves, 25–38cm (10–15in) wide and
long; some autumn colour
Flower Small creamy-white, pale pink or deep pink flowers,
borne in spreading plumes in late spring to summer; followed
by attractive brown seedheads
Use Ideal near a water feature; mass-planted or solo; will
grow in borders if soil is continuously moist; low-growing
forms can be used for ground cover
Needs Moist soil is imperative. Tall-growing varieties may
require support. Propagate by division
Varieties *F. palmata* hand-shaped leaves, light pink flowers,
to 1.2m (4ft) • *F. p.* 'Alba' white flowers • *F. p.* 'Rosea'
deeper pink flowers • *F. purpurea* (syn. *Spiraea palmata*)
♀ small, cerise-crimson, flat-headed flowers, to 1.2m (4ft) •
F. rubra very strong growing, large leaves, pink flowers, to
2.5m (8ft), needs moisture • *F. r.* 'Venusta' ♀ large, good
pink flowers • *F. ulmaria* 'Aurea' golden foliage, creamy-
white flowers, to 45cm (18in) • *F. u.* 'Variegata' white-
splashed leaves, white flowers • *F. v.* 'Multiplex' (syn.
F. hexapetala 'Flore Pleno') double, white flowers

GERANIUM
Geraniaceae
HARDY GERANIUM,
CRANESBILL

❀ ❦ SI summer
H 1–2 yrs 30–38cm (12–15in)
S 45–60cm (18–24in)
❋ -15°C (4°F)
Z 3–9

**GERANIUM SYLVATICUM
'ALBUM'**

Versatile, reliable and trouble-free – and with so many
varieties to choose from, every gardener is sure to find a
geranium to meet any need in the garden.

Soil Most; dislikes very wet or dry
Aspect Full sun to light shade
Habit Clump-forming, becoming more open with age
Leaf Deciduous, hand-shaped leaves with mid-green upper
surface, duller underside, 5–5.5cm (2–2¼) long and to 7cm
(2¾in) across; autumn colour
Flower Small clusters of pink or white, saucer-shaped
flowers, 2–3cm (¾–1⅛in) across, in summer and autumn;
some repeat flowering
Use For mass-planting and ground cover; for the front of
mixed borders; edging paths; short term in containers
Needs After the first flush of flower, cut all growth to within
3cm (1in) of ground level; plants will regrow, producing new
foliage. Propagate by division. Divide every 3–5 years
Varieties *G.* 'Buxton Blue' spreading habit, blue flowers
with white eye • *G. cinereum* 'Ballerina' ♀ low-growing
alpine, silvery-pink flowers • *G. endressii* ♀ pink flowers •
G. 'Johnson's Blue' ♀ mid-blue flowers • *G. macrorrhizum*
grey flowers, good ground cover • *G. m.* 'Album' ♀ white
flowers • *G. m.* 'Variegatum' white-splashed variegation on
leaves, pink flowers • *G.* × *oxonianum* 'A.T. Johnson' ♀
large pink flowers • *G.* × *o.* 'Wargrave Pink' ♀ salmon-pink
flowers • *G. renardii* ♀ semi-evergreen leaves, white, maroon-
veined flowers • *G. sylvaticum* 'Album' ♀ white flowers

GEUM
Rosaceae
AVENS

❀ SI summer E (some semi)
H 1–2 yrs 25–60cm (10–24in)
S 38–45cm (15–18in)
❄ -10°C (14°F)
Z 4–10

These gems brighten gardens throughout summer, and often have an autumn bonus of late flowers. They are evergreen or semi-evergreen, depending on geographical location.

Soil Moderately alkaline to acid and moist
Aspect Full sun to very light shade
Habit Clump-forming; spreading when in flower
Leaf Evergreen to semi-evergreen, mid- to light green, hairy, 3-lobed leaves, 5–6cm (2–2⅜in) long and wide
Flower Round petals form single, semi-double or double flowers, 2.5cm (1in) across, in open clusters above the foliage in white and shades of yellow, orange or red in summer
Use As a solo plant or in groups; for mass-planting; at the front of mixed borders; for short-term use in containers
Needs Divide every 3–5 years. Propagate from seed or by division
Varieties G. 'Borisii' semi-evergreen, semi-double orange flowers, to 30cm (1ft) • G. 'Coppertone' neat habit, single, deep orange flowers, to 25cm (10in) • G. 'Dolly North' double, orange flowers, to 45cm (18in) • G. 'Fire Opal' ♛ double, red-orange-flame flowers, to 60cm (2ft) • G. 'Georgenburg' single, coppery yellow flowers, to 25cm (10in) • G. 'Lady Stratheden' ♛ double, yellow flowers, to 60cm (2ft), propagate from seed • G. 'Lionel Cox' shrimp red flowers, to 30cm (1ft) • G. 'Mrs J. Bradshaw' ♛ double, brick red flowers, to 60cm (2ft), propagate from seed • G. r. 'Leonard's Variety' single, bell-shaped, creamy-pink, coppery flowers, flushed with orange, to 45cm (18in) tall

GEUM 'LADY STRATHEDEN'

GYPSOPHILA
Caryophyllaceae
GYPSOPHILA

▲ ❀ SI summer
H 1–2 yrs 60–90cm (2–3ft)
S 45–90cm (18–36in)
❄ -10°C (14°F)
Z 3–10

The airy lightness and dainty flowers of gypsophila add to its overall charm. It looks particularly delightful when it is planted in association with grey and silver plants. Make sure it has sufficient space, for even the alpine types spread.

Soil Prefers alkaline, well-drained, deep and light-textured soil but tolerates acid
Aspect Full sun
Habit Clump-forming, spreading with age
Leaf Attractive, deciduous, greyish-green, lance-shaped leaves, 5–8cm (2–3in) long
Flower Small, round flowers, in white to shades of pink, borne in spreading panicles and forming a domed canopy
Use For front of mixed borders, as edging or cascading over walls; for short-term use in containers; as a cut flower
Needs A free, deep root run is very important. Can be slow to establish. Taller varieties may require support. Propagate from cuttings in summer; some forms by commercial grafting
Varieties G. paniculata (baby's breath) the basic form, white flowers • G. p. 'Bristol Fairy' ♛ double, white flowers • G. p. 'Compacta Plena' double, white flowers, to 40cm (16in) • G. p. 'Flamingo' double, pale pink flowers • G. p. 'Schneeflocke' ('Snowflake') pure white flowers • G. repens ♛ alpine type, pale pink flowers, to 20cm (8in) • G. r. var. alba pure white flowers • G. r. 'Dorothy Teacher' ♛ mid-pink flowers • G. r. 'Rosa Schönheit' ('Pink Beauty) deep pink flowers • G. r. 'Rosea' pink flowers • G. 'Rosenschleier' ('Veil of Roses', 'Rosy Veil') double, pale pink flowers

GYPSOPHILA PANICULATA

PERENNIALS

HELENIUM
Asteraceae/Compositae
SNEEZEWEED

✤ SI late summer–autumn
H 1–2 yrs 0.6–1.2m (2–4ft)
S 60cm (2ft)
✳ -15°C (4°F)
Z 3–10

HELENIUM 'BRUNO'

This bold perennial deserves to be better known. The flowers, borne from late summer to autumn, are unaffected by rain and long lasting. Cut blooms last some time in water.

Soil Most, as long as the soil is deeply prepared and well fed
Aspect Full sun to light shade
Habit Upright
Leaf Deciduous, mid-green, lance-shaped leaves, 8–13cm (3–5in) long and 1cm (½in) wide
Flower Single, daisy-shaped flowers, 5–6cm (2–2½in) across, in yellow, gold, orange or red and some multicoloured forms; the darker central raised dome adds to flowers' attraction
Use For background or midway planting in mixed borders; spectacular planted *en masse*; good as cut flowers
Needs May need support in windy gardens. Lift and divide every 4–5 years. Propagate by division in spring
Varieties *H.* 'Bruno' mahogany red flowers, to 1.2m (4ft) • *H.* 'Butterpat' pure yellow flowers • *H.* 'Chipperfield Orange' orange-red flowers • *H.* 'Coppelia' copper-orange flowers • *H.* 'Crimson Beauty' brown-red flowers, to 60cm (2ft) • *H.* 'Goldlackzwerg' ('Mahogany') gold with brown and red • *H. hoopesii* large, leathery, grey-green leaves, golden-yellow flowers, to 75cm (30in) • *H.* 'Kupfersprudel' ('Copper Spray') large, coppery-red flowers • *H.* 'Moerheim Beauty' bronze-red flowers • *H.* 'Pumilum Magnificum' dark lemon-yellow flowers, to 45cm (18in) • *H.* 'Waldtraut' tawny orange flowers, strong growing • *H.* 'Wyndley' orange-yellow flowers, streaked reddish-brown, to 60cm (2ft)

HELIANTHUS
Asteraceae/Compositae
PERENNIAL SUNFLOWER

▲ ✤ SC SI late summer–
early autumn
H 1–2 yrs 0.6–2m (2–6ft)
S 0.6–1m (2–3ft)
✳ -15°C (4°F)
Z 4–10

HELIANTHUS SALICIFOLIUS

This close relative of the giant sunflower has a bright display like its larger relative. Tolerating the worst of both soil and climate conditions, this is the ideal starter plant for a new garden where a quick yet controllable effect is required.

Soil Most; has no particular requirements
Aspect Full sun to very light shade
Habit Upright, spreading when in flower
Leaf Deciduous, mid-green, rough-textured, oval leaves 10–15cm (4–6in) long and 3–8cm (1–3in) wide
Flower Single, semi-double or double, daisy-shaped, yellow flowers with black or brown central eye borne at the ends of wiry, multi-stemmed flowering shoots in late summer to early autumn
Use For the back of mixed borders, singly or in groups; planted *en masse* as a feature; a good cut flower
Needs Propagate by division or from seed in spring. In very windy gardens may require support. Dig up and divide every 5 years for best display
Varieties *H.* 'Capenoch Star' ♀ very old garden variety, single to semi-double, pale yellow flowers with black centre, to 75cm. (60in) • *H.* 'Lemon Queen' single to semi-double, lemon-yellow flowers with dark centre, to 75cm (30in) • *H.* 'Loddon Gold' ♀ very vivid, double, yellow flowers with black centres, to 75cm (30in) • *H.* 'Monarch' ♀ semi-double, very large, deep yellow flowers, to 1.5m (60in) • *H. salicifolius* (syn. *H. orgyalis*) single, bright yellow flowers with dark brown centres and reflexed petals, to 2m (6ft)

HELLEBORUS
Ranunculaceae
HELLEBORE

▲ ✿ ☙ SI all year SC E
H 1–2 yrs 30cm (1ft)
S 38cm (15in)
❋ -10°C (14°F)
Z 4–10

HELLEBORUS NIGER

A large group of plants with many species and named varieties, the hellebores offer interest through flowers in spring and attractive foliage throughout the year.

Soil Alkaline to acid but dislikes extremely wet or dry conditions and requires soil high in organic material
Aspect Full sun to full shade
Habit Upright, becoming spreading
Leaf Evergreen or semi-evergreen, dark green, oval leaflets form hand-shaped leaves, 15–23cm (6–9in) long and wide
Flower Saucer-shaped flowers, 6cm (2½in) across, in a wide range of colours
Use Best planted in isolation or *en masse* for good effect; in containers for a limited period
Needs Propagate by division or from seed in spring; often self-seeds; remove brown or black leaves as they die
Varieties *H. argutifolius* (syn. *H. corsicus*; Corsican hellebore) ♀ evergreen, yellow-green flowers in early spring • *H. foetidus* (stinking hellebore) finely divided leaves, green-edged, maroon flowers • *H. f.* Wester Flisk Group green flowers, purple flower stems • *H. niger* (Christmas rose) ♀ semi-evergreen, dark green leaves, white flowers • *H. n.* 'Potter's Wheel' very large, white flowers • *H. orientalis* (Lenten rose) large, hanging flowers in shades of pink, purple or white, buy when in flower to obtain required colour • *H. orientalis* ssp. *abchasicus* Early Purple Group (syn. *H. atrorubens*; oriental hellebore) purple, pink or white flowers in early to mid-spring • *H.* × *sternii* unusual pink-green flowers

HEMEROCALLIS
**Liliaceae/
Hemerocallidaceae**
DAY LILY

▲ ✿ ☙ SI summer SC
H 1–2 yrs 38–75cm (15–30in)
S 30–45cm (12–18in)
❋ -10°C (14°F)
Z 4–10

HEMEROCALLIS 'BONANZA'

This free-flowering perennial has much to offer. The foliage looks clean and fresh, and the bright display of flowers is found in a very wide range of colours.

Soil Alkaline to acid, well-drained, high in organic content
Aspect Prefers light shade but will grow in full sun
Habit Upright in spring, spreading in summer
Leaf Deciduous to semi-evergreen, light to mid-green, strap-shaped, 45–60cm (18–24in) long and 2–3cm (¾–1¼in) wide
Flower Trumpet-shaped flowers, 10–15cm (4–6in) across, in colours ranging from white to yellow, pink, red and orange, with some bicoloured forms; each lasts for a day
Use Ideal for mixed borders, planted singly or in groups; works well in association with water; a good, large cut flower
Needs Propagate by division in spring. Divide every 7 years
Varieties *H.* 'Bonanza' orange flowers with maroon centres • *H.* 'Burning Daylight' ♀ scented, glowing orange flowers • *H.* 'Cartwheels' ♀ golden-yellow flowers ♀ • *H.* 'Catherine Woodbery' pale lavender-pink flowers with lime green throat • *H. fulva* brownish-red flowers with darker centre • *H.* 'Golden Chimes' ♀ deep yellow flowers • *H.* 'Hyperion' scented, canary yellow flowers • *H. lilioasphodelus* (syn. *H. flava*) ♀ smaller, scented, yellow flowers • *H.* 'Marion Vaughn' ♀ clear lemon flowers • *H.* 'Neyron Rose' ♀ light red flowers • *H.* 'Pink Charm' pink flowers • *H.* 'Pink Damask' ♀ strong pink flowers • *H.* 'Stafford' deep red flowers with orange-yellow throat • *H.* 'Stella de Oro' ♀ fragrant, golden flowers with green throat

HEUCHERA
Saxifragaceae
CORAL BELLS, ALUM
ROOT

▲ ❀ ♉ SI summer E
H 1–2 yrs 0.45–1m (18–36in)
S 0.38–1m (15–36in)
❁ -10°C (14°F)
Z 3–10

This genus offers diversity in flowers and foliage. There are forms with flowers in pinks, reds with orange-brown, white and even green. The foliage ranges from green to purple, and even to white-splashed green as if covered with snow.

Soil Prefers acid, well-fed and well-drained soil; tolerates moderate alkalinity
Aspect Full sun or partial shade
Habit Clump-forming
Leaf Evergreen, glossy, mid-green, rounded leaves, 5-lobed and 6–8cm (2½–3in) across, with silver sheen on reverse; other forms purple or white-splashed green
Flower Tall spikes covered in very small flowers in shades of pink, red, orange-yellow, white and green in summer
Use For the front of a mixed border; ideal for edging; in containers; foliage and flowers good for flower arranging
Needs Propagate by division in spring.
Varieties *H.* Bressingham Hybrids flowers in shades of pink and red, to 60cm (2ft) • *H. cylindrica* 'Greenfinch' creamy-white flowers, to 1m (3ft) • *H.* 'Firebird' deep red flowers, to 60cm (2ft) • *H.* 'Leuchtkäfer' ('Firefly') green leaves, good red flowers, to 60cm (2ft) • *H. micrantha* var. *diversifolia* 'Palace Purple' (purple-leaved coral flower) ♀ deep purple foliage ageing to dark purple-green, orange-yellow flowers, to 75cm (30in) • *H.* 'Red Spangles' ♀ green leaves, red flowers, to 30cm (1ft) • *H.* 'Scintillation' ♀ dark pink flowers tipped with red, to 6cm (2ft) • *H.* 'Snow Storm' green foliage splashed with white, 40cm (16in)

HEUCHERA MICRANTHA VAR.
DIVERSIFOLIA 'PALACE PURPLE'

HOSTA
Hostaceae/Liliaceae
PLANTAIN LILY

▲ ❀ ♉ SI spring–summer
H 1–2 yrs 60–90cm (2–3ft)
S 60–90cm (2–3ft)
❁ -10°C (14°F)
Z 3–9

For a long time the hosta was the gardener's favourite foliage plant, and the flowers were regarded as nothing more than a bonus. The foliage is still the main reason for planting hosta, but many new varieties have attractive flowers.

Soil Alkaline to acid, moist and high in organic content
Aspect Prefers light shade but tolerates full sun
Habit Leafy clumps
Leaf Deciduous, oval or shield-shaped in all shades of green
Flower White, pale blue to mauve, tubular, bell-shaped
Use In association with water; in moist mixed borders; a good container plant; for flower arranging
Needs Propagate by splitting in spring. Protect from slugs and snails; split every 4 years
Varieties *H.* 'August Moon' large, pale gold, crinkled leaves, white to pale blue flowers • *H.* 'Blue Angel' (*sieboldiana* group) ♀ blue foliage, white flowers • *H. fortunei* var. *albopicta* (syn. *H.* 'Aureomaculata') golden-yellow variegated leaves • *H.* 'Frances Williams' (syn. *H.* 'Eldorado') ♀ grey-blue, yellow-edged leaves • *H.* 'Halcyon' (Tardiana Group) ♀ narrow, steel blue leaves • *H.* 'Honeybells' ♀ bright green foliage, scented, deep mauve flowers • *H.* 'Royal Standard' ♀ bright green leaves, scented, white flowers • *H. sieboldiana* var. *elegans* ♀ bold, clear blue, very large leaves • *H. undulata* var. *albomarginata* (syn. 'Thomas Hogg') green-blue, cream-edged leaves, mauve flowers • *H. undulata* var. *undulata* (syn. *H.* 'Argentea Variegata') white-green leaves

HOSTA SIEBOLDIANA
VAR. ELEGANS

HOUTTUYNIA
Saururaceae
HOUTTUYNIA

▲ ♥ SI spring–summer–
autumn SC E
H 1–2 yrs 60cm (2ft)
S 75cm (30in)
❋ -10°C (14°F)
Z 4–10

**HOUTTUYNIA CORDATA
'CHAMELEON'**

Although the other varieties are of interest, the cultivar
Houttuynia cordata 'Chameleon' is the star of the genus. Its
multicoloured foliage is very eye-catching when it is grown in
the right conditions. All the varieties are marginal, water-
loving perennials, but if they are grown in containers, when
extra care is required with watering, they can perform well.

Soil Must be constantly moist; if it is not, serious if not
terminal damage will result
Aspect Full sun to light shade
Habit Loose, clump-forming, spreading by underground
shoots; may become invasive in ideal conditions
Leaf Deciduous, oval leaves, dark purple-green, variegated
with white and pink; other forms have regular multicoloured
patterns, including shades of red, orange and yellow
Flower Single or double, waxy, white, multi-petalled flowers
borne singly above the foliage in summer and autumn
Use As a marginal water plant, as ground cover in other
continuously moist areas; can be grown in containers
Needs Propagate by division in spring or from cuttings in
early summer. Every 6 years, separate into small clumps,
prepare soil by digging and replant
Varieties *H. cordata* dark green leaves, turning dark
purple-red in autumn, white flowers • *H. c.* 'Chameleon'
(syn. *H. c.* 'Tricolor') multicoloured foliage, single white
flowers • *H. c.* 'Flore Pleno' dark green to purple foliage,
double, white flowers • *H. c.* Variegata Group variegated
leaves, single, white flowers

INCARVILLEA
Bignoniaceae
GARDEN GLOXINIA,
TRUMPET FLOWER

▲ ❀ ♥ SI spring–summer
H 1–2 yrs 45cm (18in)
S 45cm (18in)
❋ -10°C (14°F)
Z 4–10

INCARVILLEA DELAVAYI

Provided that you prepare the soil properly and do not
succumb to the temptation of buying the plants that are sold
in polythene packs hung up in garden centres in spring, this
beautiful plant can be a joy to grow. The common names
perfectly describe the flowers that are so well contrasted with
the dark green foliage.

Soil Alkaline to acid, well-drained soil with a high organic
content
Aspect Full sun
Habit Clump-forming from a tuberous root system
Leaf Deciduous, large, dark green leaves, 23–45cm (9–18in)
long and 8–15cm (3–6in) wide, deeply lobed at regular
intervals along the length
Flower Purple, pink or white, 4-petalled trumpets, 5–6cm
(2–2½in) long and 5cm (2in) wide, borne in small groups at
the top of upright stems in late spring and early summer
Use Best planted in isolation, either singly or in groups; as
part of a mixed border with care; can be grown in containers
in the short term; can be used as a house plant for a short
period when in flower
Needs Propagate by removing the small tuberous roots in
spring and establishing in pots before planting in final
growing position. Try always to purchase plants growing in
pots rather than roots packed in peat inside a plastic bag
Varieties *I. delavayi* purple-pink, trumpet-like flowers •
I. d. var. *alba* light green leaves, white flowers, not easy to
find • *I. d.* 'Bees' Pink' rose-pink flowers, not easy to find

IRIS
Iridaceae
IRIS, FLAG

▲ ❀ ❦ SI spring or summer
H 1–2 yrs 75cm (30in)
S 40cm (16in)
❋ -15°C (4°F)
Z 3–10

**IRIS GERMANICA
'DANCER'S VEIL'**

The iris is, rightly, one of the best loved of plants. With so many types and forms to choose from, the list below can offer only a taste of the colours and interest available.

Soil Most; *I. pseudocorus, I. laevigata, I. pallida* and *I. siberica* benefit from a moist soil; *I. germanica, I. foetidissima* and *I. unguicularis* prefer well-drained soil
Aspect Full sun to very light shade
Habit Upright
Leaf Deciduous, lance-shaped, thin, pointed and upright leaves, 75cm (30in) tall and 2.5cm (1in) wide
Flower In the form of 3 tubular florets, made up from 6 petals, each lipped, in either one colour or multicoloured; flowers, to 4cm (10in) wide, borne in groups at the tops of upright stems
Use Almost endless, including as specimen plantings, in mixed borders, near water features and in containers
Needs Propagate by division. May require support when in flower
Species *I. foetidissima* (stinking iris) lilac-green summer flowers, orange-red fruits • *I. germanica* (bearded iris) ♀ flowers in a wide range of colours in summer • *I. laevigata* (smooth iris) ♀ flowers in shades of blue or white in summer • *I. pallida* (pale iris) flowers in shades of blue or white in summer • *I. pseudacorus* (flag iris) ♀ yellow flowers in spring • *I. sibirica* (Siberian iris) ♀ flowers in blues, white or purples in spring • *I. unguicularis* (syn. *I. stylosa*; winter iris, Algerian iris) ♀ blue or white flowers

---

KNIPHOFIA
Liliaceae/
Asphodelaceae
RED HOT POKER

▲ ❀ ❦ SI summer–autumn
E
H 1–2 yrs 1–1.2m (3–4ft)
S 1m (3ft)
❋ -15°C (4°F)
Z 4–10

**KNIPHOFIA 'ROYAL
STANDARD'**

Among the stars of the late summer and early autumn garden, kniphofias are valued not only for their flowers but for their overall stature.

Soil Alkaline or acid, well-drained soil
Aspect Full sun to light shade
Habit Upright, spreading when in flower
Leaf Evergreen, light to mid-green, strap-shaped leaves, 45–60cm (18–24in) long and 2.5–4cm (1–1½in) wide
Flower Candle-shaped spikes in red, orange-red, yellow, cream, green or white at the top of strong stems; flowers can be mono- or bicoloured
Use Planted singly or for the back of mixed borders; ideal as features; in containers for a limited period; as cut flowers
Needs Propagate by division or from seed in spring
Varieties *K.* 'Bees' Sunset' ♀ orange-yellow flowers, to 1m (3ft) • *K.* 'Bressingham Beacon' bright red flowers, to 45cm (18in) • *K.* 'Bressingham Comet' red flowers, to 45cm (18in) • *K.* 'Brimstone' ♀ yellow flowers in autumn, to 75cm (30in) • *K.* 'Candlelight' lemon-yellow flowers, to 75cm (30in) • *K.* 'Goldelse' small yellow flowers, to 60cm (2ft) • *K.* 'Green Jade' green flowers, to 1m (3ft) • *K.* 'Little Maid' ♀ pale green buds, white flowers, to 60cm (2ft) • *K.* 'Maid of Orleans' primrose-yellow buds, white flowers, to 1m (3ft) • *K.* 'Mount Etna' (syn. *K.* 'The Rocket') bright red flowers, to 1m (3ft) • *K.* 'Royal Standard' ♀ scarlet buds, deep gold flowers, to 1m (3ft) • *K.* 'Samuel's Sensation' ♀ bright scarlet flowers, some yellow, to 1.5m (5ft)

LAMIUM
Labiatae
FLOWERING DEAD
NETTLE

✿ ❦ SI all year E (semi)
H 1–2 yrs 20–30cm (8–12in)
S 0.6–1m (2–3ft)
❋ -15°C (4°F)
Z 3–10

**LAMIUM MACULATUM
'AUREUM'**

Lamium used to be the Cinderella of plants, but since the introduction of new varieties it has taken its place as a ground-cover plant. It is increasingly used in containers, and it can now be seen in both summer and winter displays.

Soil Alkaline to acid, moist and well fed
Aspect Full sun to deep shade; does best in light shade
Habit Spreading, rooting as it grows
Leaf Semi-evergreen to evergreen, white-splashed green leaves, 4–8cm (1½–3in) long and 2.5–4cm (1–1½in) wide; some forms all gold or purple
Flower Tubular, 2-lipped flowers, 2.5cm (1in) long, in white, pink or purple, borne in clusters
Use As ground cover; for the front of mixed borders; planted singly or in groups of all sizes; will tumble over walls
Needs Propagate by division or from cuttings in spring. Cut all previous season's growth hard back in spring
Varieties *L. galeobdolon* green, white-variegated leaves, yellow flowers, vigorous • *L. g.* 'Hermann's Pride' deep green, pointed and indented leaves with bold white veins, yellow flowers • *L. maculatum* dark green, purple- and white-variegated leaves, purple flowers • *L. m.* var. *album* green leaves with white variegation, pure white flowers • *L. m.* 'Aureum' golden foliage, pink flowers • *L. m.* 'Beacon Silver' silver-white foliage, pink flowers • *L. m.* 'Chequers' white- and pink-marbled foliage, purple at times, pink flowers • *L. m.* 'White Nancy' ♀ green, white-variegated foliage, white flowers

LEUCANTHEMUM
Asteraceae/Compositae
LEUCANTHEMUM

▲ ✿ ❦ SI summer–autumn
H 1–2 yrs 0.4–1m (16–36in)
S 0.45–1m (18–36in)
❋ -15°C (4°F)
Z 4–10

**LEUCANTHEMUM ×
SUPERBUM 'ESTHER READ'**

A traditional garden plant, formerly classified in the genus *Chrysanthemum*, that is still worthy of planting. Almost indestructible and always producing an array of daisy flowers in late summer. New varieties have been added recently, offering a range of sizes to suit any garden.

Soil All; no particular preferences
Aspect From full sun to shade; in extreme shade can grow larger than expected, becoming loose and open in habit
Habit Upright, spreading when in flower; newer varieties dwarf and compact
Leaf Deciduous, dark green, oval leaves, with even, deep indentations along the edges, showing off the flowers perfectly
Flower Large, single or double, white daisies, to 8cm (3in) across, borne at the ends of strong flower shoots, most with a proud central darker eye
Use For planting in mixed borders or as single plantings in groups or solo; can use dwarf varieties in large containers to good effect; perfect cut flower, lasting a long time in water
Needs Propagate by division in spring. Lift and divide every 5 years in spring
Varieties *L.* × *superbum* 'Esther Read' (shasta daisy) double, white flowers, to 75cm (30in) • *L.* × *s.* 'Shaggy' very frilled, reflexed, white petals, to 75cm (30in) • *L.* × *s.* 'Snowcap' single white flowers, to 40cm (16in), good in containers • *L.* × *s.* 'T.E. Killin' ♀ single white flowers with fringed petals, to 75cm (30in) • *L.* × *s.* 'Wirral Supreme' ♀ semi-double, white flowers with green centre, to 1m (3ft)

LIATRIS
Asteraceae/Compositae
BLAZING STAR, GAY
FEATHER, BUTTON
SNAKE ROOT

▲ ❀ ❦ SI late summer
H 1–2 yrs 60cm (2ft)
S 60cm (2ft)
❅ -15°C (4°F)
Z 3–10

This plant is one of the most popular among flower arrangers,
but it has far wider uses than as a cut flower. In the garden it
bridges the gap between the spring- and autumn-flowering
varieties, and has the advantages of being easy to grow and
long lived. The varieties used in the cut-flower trade, with
their very long flower spikes, tend not to perform well in the
garden, but those listed below are very reliable.

Soil Most, except very wet or dry
Aspect Full sun to very light shade
Habit Clump-forming and upright
Leaf Deciduous, glossy, dark green, strap-like, pointed
leaves, 8cm (3in) long, along entire length of flower stem
Flower Spikes of fluffy purple, pink or white flowers, to
20cm (8in) long, opening from the top downwards over a long
period
Use For the front of mixed borders, singly or in groups;
make a bold show when planted *en masse*; can be used in
containers; a good cut flower, lasting a long time if cut just as
opening
Needs Propagate by division in spring. Lift and divide
established clumps every 5 years in spring. Remove dead
flowerheads as required. Buy pot-grown plants rather than
pre-packaged ones
Varieties *L. spicata* pink to purple flowers • *L. s.* 'Alba'
pure white flowers on long spikes • *L. s.* 'Floristan Weiss'
('Floristan White') white flowers • *L. s.* 'Kobold' ('Goblin')
bold mauve-pink flowers

LIATRIS SPICATA

LIGULARIA
Asteraceae/Compositae
LEOPARD PLANT

▲ ❀ ❦ SI summer
H 1–2 yrs 0.9–1.5m (3–5ft)
S 0.6–1.2m (2–4ft)
❅ -15°C (4°F)
Z 4–10

A very handsome group of plants which go well with the
water features that can provide them with the constant
supply of water they require.

Soil Moderately alkaline to acid, moist and well fed
Aspect Light to mid-shade
Habit Upright at first, spreading when in flower
Leaf Deciduous, grey-green or purple, heart-shaped leaves,
15–30cm (6–12in) long and wide; *L.* 'The Rocket' has spade-
shaped leaves, dark green and deeply indented
Flower Strap-like petals, in shades of yellow and orange,
around a central dome form a daisy-shaped flower to 15cm
(6in) across. *L.* 'The Rocket' has 30cm (1ft) long, deep yellow
to orange spikes of flowers
Use Ideal in association with water; for mixed borders as
long as the soil is moist; spectacular when mass-planted; good
plants for large bog gardens
Needs Propagate by division in spring. May require support
in windy gardens
Varieties *L. dentata* 'Desdemona' (syn. *L. clivorum*
'Desdemona') ♀ attractive, heart-shaped, new purple
foliage, golden-yellow flowers • *L. d.* 'Othello' purple-veined
foliage, orange-yellow flowers • *L.* 'Gregynog Gold' ♀
golden-yellow flowers, tall and strong growing • *L. × hessei*
yellow flowers, very strong growing • *L. hodgsonii* large
yellow flowers, very bold effect • *L.* 'The Rocket' (syn.
L. stenocephala 'The Rocket') orange-yellow flowers in
spikes on black stems, suffers worst from lack of moisture

**LIGULARIA DENTATA
'DESDEMONA'**

LINUM
Linaceae
FLOWERING FLAX

❀ 𝔙 SI summer
H 1–2 yrs 45cm (18in)
S 75cm (30in)
❄ -10°C (14°F)
Z 4–10

LINUM NARBONENSE

This genus contains a wide range of annual and perennial shrubs and herbs, and perhaps the best known is the plant that produces the flax used in the manufacture of ropes and clothes. All the members are worthy of space in the garden, but they need careful siting to be seen at their best.

Soil Alkaline or acid, well drained but moisture retentive
Aspect Full sun
Habit Spreading, forming loose clumps
Leaf Deciduous
Flower Saucer-shaped, blue, or yellow or white flowers borne in wide-spreading flowerheads in summer
Use In isolation as a feature, singly or in groups; for the front of mixed borders; in large containers for a limited period; smaller varieties can be planted on rock gardens
Needs Propagate by seed in spring. Can self-seed in some locations but not invasive. Side growths can be divided
Varieties *L. arboreum* ♥ shrubby habit, bright yellow flowers, to 20cm (8in) tall • *L. flavum* spreading habit, yellow flowers, to 40cm (16in) • *L.* 'Gemmell's Hybrid' ♥ compact habit, yellow flowers, may be tender • *L. hirsutum* hairy stems, blue flowers • *L. monogynum* white flowers, 30cm (1ft), tender • *L. narbonense* mid-blue flowers, to 60cm (2ft), a lovely plant • *L. n.* 'Heavenly Blue' ♥ pale blue flowers • *L. n.* 'Six Hills' good blue flowers • *L. n.* 'June Perfield' blue flowers , not easy to find but worth trying • *L. perenne* (perennial flax) grey-blue foliage, blue flowers, to 30cm (1ft) • *L. p.* var. *album* white flowers, a charming form

LIRIOPE
Liliaceae/
Convallariaceae
LILYTURF

▲ ❀ 𝔙 SI late summer–
autumn E
H 1–2 yrs 30–38cm (12–15in)
S 30–38cm (12–15in)
❄ -15°C (4°F)
Z 4–10

LIRIOPE MUSCARI

Liriope tends to resemble a bold clump of dark grass, and for a long time it was overlooked as a useful garden plant. Now its display of late flowers is finding greater favour. The purple-flowering form is widely available, but the interesting white form may not be so easily found. It needs to be carefully positioned because of its somewhat rigid habit and the soil conditions it requires.

Soil Moderately alkaline to acid; prefers moisture-retentive light sand or sandy loam
Aspect Full sun; does best in light shade
Habit Tufted and clump-forming, with upright foliage and flowers; planted for overall shape and flowers
Leaf Evergreen, dark green, strap-shaped leaves, 30cm (1ft) long or more and 5mm (¼in) wide
Flower Tiny, purple, bell-shaped flowers in spikes rising from central foliage tufts
Use As edging; as ground cover; for front of mixed borders in clumps; for short-term use in containers; can be used for flower arranging; plant in association with dwarf, late-flowering Michaelmas daisies (asters)
Needs Propagate by division in spring. Remove dead leaves as required. Lift and separate before replanting every 7 years. Remove dead flowers when finished
Varieties *L. muscari* ♥ very dark green foliage, purple flower spikes • *L. m.* 'Monroe White' (syn. *L. m.* 'Alba') white flowers in late summer to autumn • *L. m.* 'Variegata' white-variegated leaves, smaller, purple flowers

LOBELIA
Campanulaceae
CARDINAL FLOWER, INDIAN PINK

▲ ❀ ❦ SI late summer
H 1–2 yrs 1m (3ft)
S 40cm (16in)
❊ -10°C (14°F)
Z 2–10

LOBELIA 'QUEEN VICTORIA'

Lobelia cardinalis is the flowering sensation of the late summer flower garden. Sadly, however, without moisture in the soil and some protection from the worst of the weather it will fail.

Soil Acid or alkaline soil, moist but not waterlogged and high in organic material
Aspect Full sun to very light shade
Habit Upright
Leaf Deciduous, dark green or dark olive green with a purple-red hue, lance-shaped leaves, 8–13cm (3–5in) long and 2–3cm (¾–1⅛in) wide, carried at regular intervals on upright purple or green stems
Flower Red, brown or white flowers, 2cm (⅜in) across, formed of 3 oval petals surmounted by 2 strap-like, upward-pointing petals
Use Ideal for planting in association with water features, including bog gardens, or as a tall summer flowering bedding plant for the garden or a container
Needs Propagate by seed or division in spring. May require support. Can be short lived but worthy of replanting
Varieties *L. cardinalis* ♀ scarlet flowers, the hardiest form among the reds • *L. c.* 'Alba' green foliage, white flowers, tender • *L.* 'Cherry Ripe' cherry red leaves and flowers, tender • *L.* 'Dark Crusader' blood-red foliage and flowers • *L.* × *gerardii* 'Vedrariensis' dark foliage, crimson flowers • *L.* 'Queen Victoria' ♀ deep red foliage and flowers, can be tender • *L. tupa* dark green leaves, brown-red flowers

LUPINUS
Leguminosae/ Papilionaceae
LUPIN

▲ ❀ ❦ SI summer
H 1–2 yrs 1.2m (4ft)
S 0.6–1m (2–3ft)
❊ -10°C (14°F)
Z 4–9

LUPINUS 'THE GOVERNOR'

This garden favourite from the past is as popular today as it ever was. The Russell Hybrids are still the best choice, whether they are planted in groups of individual colours or in mixed groups. Only severe drought seems to upset them – otherwise they seem to grow for ever.

Soil Neutral to acid; alkaline soils may be too dry
Aspect Full sun to very light shade
Habit Upright, spreading when in flower
Leaf Deciduous, mid- to dark green, lance-shaped leaflets, 8–10cm (3–4in) long
Flower Wide colour range, in shades of white, red, pinks and yellow, mono- and bicoloured, pea-shaped on spikes, 45–60cm (18–24in) tall and 8cm (3in) wide
Use Ideal for the back of mixed borders, both singly or in groups; can be planted in large groups to good effect; a lupin walk is a breath-taking sight
Needs Propagate by division or from seed in spring. May require support. Protect from slugs and snails
Varieties *L.* 'Chandelier' flowers in shades of yellow and white • *L.* 'Lulu' flowers in mixed colours, to 45cm (18in) • *L.* 'My Castle' flowers in shades of dark red • *L.* 'Noble Maiden' flowers in shades of ivory and white • *L.* Russell Hybrids a mixture of every other colour in the lupin range • *L.* 'The Chatelaine' bold pink and white flowers • *L.* 'The Governor' marine blue flowers with white variegations • *L.* 'The Page' flowers in striking shades of carmine red

LYCHNIS
Caryophyllaceae
CAMPION, CATCHFLY

❀ ❦ SI summer
H 1–2 yrs 45–60cm (18–24in)
S 30–45cm (12–18in)
✳ -10°C (14°F)
Z 3–10

LYCHNIS CORONARIA

Although its early growth looks feeble, when the lychnis comes into flower it offers an almost unbelievable range of colours, set off in some varieties by grey foliage.

Soil Alkaline or acid, well-drained and well-fed soil
Aspect Full sun
Habit Upright but branching
Leaf Deciduous, grey or grey-green, oval to lance-shaped leaves, 8–9cm (3–4in) long and to 2cm (¾in) wide
Flower Flat, circular flowers, in white, orange, pink or purple-red, to 4cm (1½in) wide, borne in open clusters
Use In the foreground of mixed borders, planted singly or in large groups; spectacular when mono-planted in isolation
Needs Propagate by division or from seed in spring. May self-seed but not invasively. May require support in windy gardens as it often has a weak root system. Often dies down prematurely in late summer
Varieties *L. × arkwrightii* bronze to purple foliage, scarlet flowers, tender, to 60cm (2ft) tall • *L. chalcedonica* ♀ clear red flowers, to 1m (3ft) • *L. c.* var. *albiflora* white flowers • *L. c.* 'Flore Pleno' double, red flowers • *L. c.* 'Rosea' pink flowers • *L. coronaria* silver-grey leaves, purple-red flowers, to 75cm (30in) • *L. c.* Alba Group ♀ grey foliage, white flowers • *L. flos-jovis* grey felt-like foliage, red-purple flowers, to 40cm (16in) • *L. f.-j.* 'Hort's Variety' rose-pink flowers • *L. viscaria* cerise-pink flowers, to 30cm (1ft) • *L. v.* var. *alba* white flowers • *L. v.* 'Splendens Plena' ♀ double, carmine-rose flowers

LYSIMACHIA
Primulaceae
CREEPING JENNY,
LOOSESTRIFE

❀ ❦ SI summer E (creeping types)
H 1–2 yrs 5cm–1m (2–36in)
S 0.6–1m (2–3ft)
✳ -10°C (14°F)
Z 3–10

LYSIMACHIA PUNCTATA

Few other genera include plants with such different characteristics as *Lysimachia* – from creeping alpine carpets to upright, metre-high clump-formers. The foliage ranges from green to golden, but the flowers are unmistakable.

Soil Most types; moist, rich for best results; dislikes dry soil
Aspect Full sun to light shade
Habit Creeping and carpet-forming, or upright and clump-forming
Leaf Deciduous (perennial), evergreen (alpine), glossy, light green or gold, round to oval leaves, to 2.5cm (1in) long and wide
Flower Bright golden-yellow, cup-shaped flowers, 1.5cm (¾in) across; other forms with small, grey-white flowers; borne in leaf joints along creeping or upright stems
Use <u>Creeping varieties</u>: for ground cover and containers, including hanging baskets <u>Upright forms</u>: for back or middle of mixed borders; ideal for naturalizing, especially near a water feature
Needs Propagate by division in spring. Creeping type roots as it grows
Varieties *L. clethroides* ♀ green leaves, grey-white small flowers on upright stems, late flowering, to 1m (3ft) • *L. nummularia* creeping alpine, light green leaves, golden-yellow flowers, to 5cm (2in) tall • *L. n.* 'Aurea' ♀ creeping alpine, golden leaves and flowers • *L. punctata* (yellow loosestrife) green leaves, yellow flowers on upright stems, to 1m (3ft), can be invasive in the wrong place

MACLEAYA
Papaveraceae
PLUME POPPY

▲ ❀ ❦ SI late summer
H 1–2 yrs 2–3m (6–10ft)
S 1m (3ft)
❄ -10°C (14°F)
Z 4–10

MACLEAYA CORDATA

Very tall and sometimes invasive, but if you have the space, this is one of the most elegant of plants. Both the flowers and the foliage are delightful, and because it flowers in late summer, it seems to pick up the colours of the setting sun in its flowers. All varieties are of value, with the height perhaps being the deciding factor.

Soil Alkaline to acid, moist, deep and rich
Aspect Full sun to very light shade
Habit Upright stems from spreading clump and underground stems; may be invasive in ideal conditions
Leaf Handsome, deciduous, mid-green, hand-shaped, lobed leaves, 5–25cm (6–10in) long and wide, with grey and purple sheen and white undersides
Flower Petal-less, buff to yellow flowers borne in clusters, forming large upright open panicles, to 30cm (1ft)
Use At the back of large, mixed borders, planted singly or in groups; spectacular as a specimen planting in its own right; can be used as a cut flower
Needs Propagate by division
Varieties *M. cordata* (syn. *Bocconia cordata*) ♀ very tall, to 3m (10ft), needs careful placing • *M. c.* 'Flamingo' ivory-white flowers with white shading, to 1.2m (4ft) • *M. microcarpa* (syn. *Bocconia microcarpa*) 'Kelway's Coral Plume' ♀ buff-flesh to coral-yellow flowers, to 1.4–1.8m (52–66in)

MECONOPSIS
Papaveraceae
ASIATIC POPPY

▲ ❀ ❦ SI late spring–summer
H 2 yrs 0.6–1.2m (2–4ft)
S 38cm (15in)
❄ -10°C (14°F)
Z 5–10

**MECONOPSIS
BETONICIFOLIA**

In both its blue and orange forms this beautiful perennial plant cannot fail to please. However, it is important to provide the correct soil and moisture levels. Winter hardiness is also a problem in cold exposed gardens or bad winters.

Soil Moderately alkaline to acid; must be deep and rich, with a high leaf-mould content
Aspect Prefers light shade but tolerates full sun
Habit Clump-forming, with central upright flower spike
Leaf Deciduous, green to grey-green, lance-shaped leaves, 10–15cm (4–6in) long and 4cm (1½in) wide, covered with fine hairs
Flower Saucer-shaped, azure blue flowers with yellow centres, fading to pale blue, 5–6cm (2–2½in) across
Use Best planted in isolation or as a feature in a large group; good in association with water
Needs Propagate in spring by seed sown under protection or by division of the root clump. Protect root clump in winter
Varieties *M. betonicifolia* (syn. *M. baileyi*; blue poppy) ♀ azure blue flowers with yellow centres • *M. b.* var. *alba* white flowers • *M. cambrica* (Welsh poppy) pale orange flowers, short growing, self-seeds itself but not invasively, to 45cm (18in) • *M. grandis* ♀ very large, deep blue flowers to 13cm (5in) across, to 1.2m (4ft) • *M. × sheldonii* ♀ short growing, deep or pale blue flowers, to 1.2m (4ft) • *M. × s.* 'Slieve Donard' ♀ rich blue flowers with pointed petals, to 1m (3ft)

MIMULUS
Scrophulariaceae
MONKEY FLOWER

❀ ❦ SI summer
H 1–2 yrs 30cm (1ft)
S 45cm (18in)
❄ -5°C (23°F)
Z 4–9

**MIMULUS
'HIGHLAND YELLOW'**

Given the right conditions, mimulus provides one of the brightest of flowering displays. It is not reliably hardy in cold winters. The varieties listed below are fairly reliable, but many of the other forms will survive only with protection.

Soil Most; moist but not waterlogged and high in organic matter
Aspect Full sun to very light shade; not always fully hardy
Habit Clump-forming and spreading with age
Leaf Deciduous, dark to mid-green, pointed, oval leaves, 4–6cm (1½–2½in) long and wide, with indented edges; produced in pairs
Flower Tubular, 2-lipped flowers with 5 petal lobes, 4–5cm (1½–2in) long, in white, yellow, pink or red; some bicoloured
Use Ideal in association with a water feature; good in containers, including hanging baskets, must be regularly watered; for the front of mixed borders where adequate moisture is available
Needs Propagate from seed in spring or cuttings in early summer. Remove dead flowers throughout summer. Trim off dead growth in autumn to prevent rotting. Requires winter protection by covering the root clump with some form of organic material
Varieties *M. cupreus* 'Whitecroft Scarlet' ♀ scarlet flowers • *M.* 'Highland Orange' bright orange flowers • *M.* 'Highland Pink' bold pink flowers • *M.* 'Highland Red' ♀ deep red flowers • *M.* 'Highland Yellow' bright yellow flowers • *M.* 'Wisley Red' good red flowers

---

MONARDA
Lamiaceae/Labiatae
BERGAMOT, BEE BALM,
OSWEGO TEA

▲ ❀ SI summer SC foliage
H 1–2 yrs 1m (3ft)
S 0.6–1m (2–3ft)
❄ -15°C (4°F)
Z 4–10

**MONARDA
'CAMBRIDGE SCARLET'**

This plant has adorned our gardens for centuries, being valued both for its flowers and for its herbal properties. It is still grown, though largely for its flowers. Its upright, easy-going habit makes it a work-free plant – all that is required is to clear away the dead growth in winter to make way for the next year's display.

Soil Most types; does best in a moist soil and resents drought
Aspect Full sun to light shade
Habit Upright, strong shoots forming a clump
Leaf Deciduous, mid- to dark green, aromatic, oval to lance-shaped leaves, 5–10cm (2–4in) long and 1–4cm (½–1½in) wide
Flower Tubular, 2-lipped flowers, 3cm (1¼in) long, borne in dense terminal clusters in white, pink, red, purple, violet or blue
Use Ideal for the middle or back of mixed borders, planted singly or in groups; can be planted *en masse* to good effect; a good cut flower
Needs Propagate by root clump division in spring. Protect from slugs and snails in spring
Varieties *M.* 'Adam' cerise flowers • *M.* 'Beauty of Cobham' ♀ pale pink flowers • *M.* 'Cambridge Scarlet' ♀ crimson flowers • *M.* 'Croftway Pink' ♀ best deep pink form • *M.* 'Mahogany' Indian red flowers • *M.* 'Prärieglut' ('Prairie Glow') reddish-purple flowers • *M.* 'Prärienacht' ('Prairie Night') violet-purple flowers • *M.* 'Schneewittchen' ('Snow White'; 'Snow Maiden') pure white flowers

NEPETA
Lamiaceae/Labiatae
CATMINT, CATNIP

❀ ❦ SI summer–autumn SC
foliage E (semi)
H 0.3–1m (1–3ft)
S 45cm–1m (18–36in)
❊ -15°C (4°F)
Z 3–10

NEPETA × FAASENII

A favourite with gardeners, this a bold flowering plant with attractive foliage. As the common names suggest, most cats love it as a summer day-time sun-lounger. It has a wide range of uses in the garden, and its only drawback is that towards the end of summer it can become a little straggly.

Soil Alkaline or acid, moist and well-fed soil
Aspect Full sun to light shade
Habit Spreading, can be untidy towards autumn
Leaf Aromatic, deciduous, grey-green, indented, oval leaves, 6–8cm (2½–3in) long and 1–2cm (½–¾in) wide
Flower Small, blue, 2-lipped flowers, borne in panicles 8–13cm (3–5in) long; in profusion from spring to late autumn
Use Ideal as summer ground cover; good for edging borders, paths and drives; for the front of mixed borders, planted singly or in groups; good *en masse*; can be used in containers, including hanging baskets
Needs Propagate by division in early spring or from cuttings in early summer
Varieties *N. × faassenii* purple-blue flowers, larger form to 60cm (2ft) • *N. × f.* 'Blue Dwarf' to 30cm (1ft) • *N. govaniana* upright habit, light yellow foliage, to 1m (3ft) • *N. nervosa* bright blue flowers, sometimes yellow, to 60cm (2ft) • *N. racemosa* 'Snowflake' white flowers, to 45cm (18in) • *N.* 'Six Hills Giant' (syn. *N. gigantica*) 1 × 1m (3 × 3ft) • *N. sibirica* 'Souvenir d'André Chaudron' (syn. *N.* 'Blue Beauty') dwarf, compact habit, larger leaves, deep blue flowers, to 45cm (18in)

OENOTHERA
Onagraceae
EVENING PRIMROSE

▲ ❀ SI summer
H 1–2 yrs 15–75cm (6–30in)
S 45–60cm (18–24in)
❊ -10°C (14°F)
Z 4–10

**OENOTHERA FRUTICOSA
'YELLOW RIVER'**

The genus is known for its bright, profuse, if short-lived flowers, which close their flowers just before dusk to open again the next day. Some forms are upright, others spreading, but they are all at their best in late summer, making them useful additions to a perennial planting.

Soil Alkaline to acid, well-drained, light and open soil; dislikes waterlogging
Aspect Full sun to very light shade
Habit Some upright, others spreading
Leaf Deciduous, light green, lance-shaped leaves, 4–10cm (1½–4in) long and 1.2cm (½in) wide
Flower Yellow, fragrant, heart-shaped petals form wide, funnel-shaped flowers, 8cm (3in) across, borne in clusters and opening one or two at a time with the flowers closing just before dusk; some varieties with attractive red calyx
Use Solo or in groups in mixed borders; spectacular when mass-planted; good in containers
Needs Propagate by seed or division in spring
Varieties *O. fruticosa* 'Fyrverkeri' ('Fireworks') ♥ bright red buds, opening to yellow flowers with red calyx, to 60cm (2ft) • *O. f.* ssp. *glauca* ♥ blue-grey foliage, yellow flowers, to 75cm (30in) • *O. f.* 'Lady Brookborough' very large yellow flowers • *O. f.* 'Yellow River' bright yellow flowers, to 60cm (2ft) • *O. macrocarpa* (syn. *O. missouriensis*) ♥ the true evening primrose, spreading habit, large, bold yellow flowers, 60 × 75cm (24 × 30in) • *O. odorata* red stems and buds, pale yellow flowers ageing to coral

PAEONIA
Paeoniaceae
PEONY

▲ ✤ ❦ SI summer SC
H 1–2 yrs 0.75–1m (30–36in)
S 0.6–1m (2–3ft)
✱ -10°C (14°F)
Z 4–10

PAEONIA MLOKOSEWITSCHII

This elegant, almost regal plant has been planted by kings and emperors almost since gardening began. The range of cultivars has decreased, but modern commercial propagation methods are reinstating many worthy species and varieties.

Soil Moderately alkaline to acid, open, light, well drained and well fed
Aspect Full sun to light shade
Habit Upright in spring, spreading when in flower
Leaf Deciduous, dark green, divided leaves, 20–25cm (8–10in) long and 13–17cm (5–7in) wide, formed from 3 hand-shaped leaflets; leaves have grey sheen and red hue; leaf stalks may be red
Flower Large, round, double or single flowers, in white, pink or yellow, borne at the ends of shoots in summer
Use Spectacular when planted *en masse* to edge a path or drive where space allows; suitable for mixed borders
Needs Propagate by division of tubers or from seed in spring
Varieties *P. lactiflora* 'Bowl of Beauty' ♀ single flowers with pink outer petals, bold cream stamens • *P. l.* 'Duchess de Nemours' ♀ double, white flowers • *P. l.* 'Félix Crousse' ♀ double, deep pink flowers • *P. l.* 'Festiva Maxima' ♀ double, white flowers with crimson blotch • *P. l.* 'Globe of Light' large, double, pink flowers • *P. l.* 'Lady Alexandra Duff' ♀ semi-double, pink flowers • *P. l.* 'Monsieur Jules Elie' ♀ double, silvery rose-pink flowers • *P. l.* 'President Franklin D. Roosevelt' • *P. l.* 'Sarah Bernhardt' ♀ pale pink flowers • *P. mlokosewitschii* ♀ single, yellow flowers

PAPAVER ORIENTALE
Papaveraceae
ORIENTAL POPPY

▲ ✤ ❦ SI summer
H 1–2 yrs 75–90cm (30–36in)
S 75–90cm (30–36in)
✱ -10°C (14°F)
Z 4–10

PAPAVER ORIENTALE GOLIATH GROUP

When they are in full bloom, the flowers look almost unreal and are always the centre of attention. They give the impression of being fragile, but in the right conditions they are very long lived.

Soil Alkaline or acid
Aspect Full sun to light shade
Habit Upright at first, spreading when in flower; clump-forming
Leaf Deciduous, light to mid-green with grey sheen, hairy, dissected, lance-shaped leaves, 15–30cm (6–12in) long and 8–10cm (3–4in) wide
Flower Rounded or fringed petals form cup-shaped flower around a dark central cone; flowers 8–13cm (3–5in) across in a wide range of colours, mono- or multicoloured
Use Spectacular when mass-planted; good in association with other plants; can be grown in large containers
Needs Propagate from seed or by division in spring. Add organic compost before and after the plants are established
Varieties *P. orientale* 'Allegro' bright glowing red flowers • *P. o.* 'Beauty of Livermere' ♀ bright red flowers • *P. o.* 'Black and White' ♀ white flowers with central black blotches • *P. o.* 'Curlilocks' orange-red flowers with dark centre and fringed petal edges • *P. o.* Goliath Group crimson-scarlet flowers • *P. o.* 'Indian Chief' maroon flowers • *P. o.* 'Marcus Perry' red flowers • *P. o.* 'Mrs Perry' ♀ salmon-pink flowers • *P. o.* 'Perry's White' white flowers • *P. o.* 'Türkenlouis' ('Turkish Delight') ♀ purple-pink flowers

PENSTEMON
Scrophulariaceae
BEARD TONGUE

❀ ❦ SI summer–autumn
E (semi)
H 1–2 yrs 45–60cm (18–24in)
S 38cm (15in)
❋ -10°C (14°F)
Z 4–10

PENSTEMON 'FIREBIRD'

Although the hardiness of many varieties over very hard winters is doubtful, the range of sizes and flower colour seems endless, as new varieties are added to those available.

Soil Moderately alkaline to acid, well drained and well fed with a high organic content
Aspect Full sun to light shade
Habit Upright, becoming more spreading when in flower
Leaf Attractive, semi-evergreen, glossy, mid- to deep green, lance-shaped leaves, to 10cm (4in) long and 1.2cm (½in) wide
Flower Funnel-shaped, foxglove-like flowers, 5cm (2in) long, on tall, upright spikes, each to 45cm (10in) long, in a wide range of attractive colours
Use In mixed borders, singly or in large groups; can be grown in a large container for a few years before planting out
Needs Propagate by cuttings in early summer. For good growth it is important to prune all growth to within 5cm (2in) of soil level in mid- to late spring
Varieties *P.* 'Apple Blossom' ♀ apple blossom pink flowers • *P. barbatus* deep red flowers, very hardy • *P.* 'Blackbird' deep purple flowers • *P.* 'Burgundy' burgundy red flowers • *P.* 'Evelyn' ♀ rose-pink flowers • *P.* 'Firebird' bright red flowers • *P.* 'Garnet' red flowers, one of the hardiest varieties • *P.* 'Hewell Pink Bedder' pink with white throat • *P.* 'Hidcote Pink' ♀ pink • *P.* 'King George V' flowers with white throat and red outer • *P.* 'Schoenholzeri' ('Firebird') bright red flowers • *P.* 'Sour Grapes' purple-mauve flowers • *P.* 'White Bedder' ♀ pure white flowers

---

PERSICARIA
Polygonaceae
KNOTWEED

▲ ❀ ❦ SI summer–autumn
E (semi)
H 20–30cm (8–12in)
S 60cm (2ft)
❋ -10°C (14°F)
Z 3–9

**PERSICARIA AFFINIS
'DARJEELING RED'**

Formerly in the genus *Polygonum*, this is one of autumn's flowering stars, producing a mass of flowers over a long period, supported with attractive foliage, which in turn has its own late-autumn appeal. It is low carpet-forming in habit, which makes it suitable for use in many parts of the garden.

Soil Alkaline to acid; resents dry conditions
Aspect Full sun to light shade; prefers light shade
Habit Clump-forming and spreading
Leaf Evergreen or deciduous, dark green, lance-shaped leaves, 5–10cm (2–4in) long and 1cm (½in) wide, carried on strong, ground-hugging shoots and with a red hue in autumn; good deep orange-red autumn colour held well into winter
Flower Tiny, bell-shaped flowers, in dense, erect spikes, 10cm (4in) or more tall; flowers start as pink or white in bud, ageing to dark pink or red; attractive winter seedheads
Use Good ground cover for cultivated soil; mixes well in borders, particularly when planted at the front; to edge paths and planted beds; good in containers
Needs Propagate by division in spring or from cuttings in summer. Remove dead flowerheads. Plants can die out in centre
Varieties *P. affinis* (syn. *Polygonum affine*) 'Darjeeling Red' ♀ deep pink buds opening to red • *P. a.* (syn. *Polygonum affine*) 'Dimity' pure pink buds opening to deep red • *P. a.* (syn. *Polygonum affine*) 'Donald Lowndes' ♀ red buds opening to pink • *P. a.* 'Superba' (syn. *Polygonum affine* 'Superbum') ♀ white buds opening to deep red

PHLOX
PANICULATA
Polemoniaceae
BORDER PHLOX

▲ ❀ ❦ SI summer SC
H 0.9–1.2m (3–4ft)
S 45–60cm (18–24in)
❄ -15°C (4°F)
Z 3–9

PHLOX PANICULATA 'BRIGADIER'

A worthy garden favourite, phlox has adorned our gardens for decades. The range of flower colours is wide, as is the use to which the plants can be put. It is not particularly fussy about soil type, which adds to its charm.

Soil Moderately alkaline to acid, deep, moist and well fed
Aspect Full sun to light shade
Habit Upright
Leaf Deciduous, glossy, dark green, oval leaves, 8–10cm (3–4in) long and 1–2cm (½–¾in) wide
Flower Large clusters of tubular-based, primrose-shaped flowers, 2–2.5cm (¾–1in) across, borne at the tops of the tall stems in shades of pink, orange, scarlet, red and white
Use Ideal for the mixed border, blending well with other colours and plants; spectacular planted *en masse* or singly
Needs Propagate by division in early spring. Inherent virus can shorten the life-span of a plant. Will require support
Varieties *P. paniculata* 'Blue Ice' ♀ pink to blue flowers • *P. p.* 'Brigadier' ♀ reddish-pink flowers • *P. p.* 'Bright Eyes' ♀ pale pink flowers with central cerise eye • *P. p.* 'Fujiyama' ♀ white flowers • *P. p.* 'Harlequin' white-variegated foliage, light purple flowers • *P. p.* 'Mother of Pearl' ♀ soft pink flowers • *P. p.* 'Norah Leigh' white-variegated leaves, pink flowers • *P. p.* 'Prince of Orange' ♀ orange flowers • *P. p.* 'Prospero' ♀ pale lilac flowers • *P. p.* 'Sandringham' mid-pink flowers • *P. p.* 'Skylight' pale purple flowers • *P. p.* 'Starfire' very deep red flowers • *P. p.* 'White Admiral' ♀ white flowers

PHYGELIUS
Scrophulariaceae
CAPE FIGWORT

▲ ❀ ❦ SI late summer–autumn E (semi)
H 1–2 yrs 1–1.2m (3–4ft)
S 1–1.2m (3–4ft)
❄ -10°C (14°F)
Z 4–10

PHYGELIUS CAPENSIS VAR. COCCINEUS

Until recently the only variety grown in gardens was *P. capensis* var. *coccineus*, with its orange-red flowers, but there are now many relatively new varieties to choose from, including some yellow forms. All are worthy of garden space because few other plants flower for so long in the late summer and into autumn.

Soil Most, but must be moist
Aspect Full sun to light shade
Habit Upright at first, becoming spreading when in flower
Leaf Semi-evergreen, dark or light green, narrow, lance-shaped leaves, to 8cm (3in) long
Flower Long tubular flowers borne in clusters in late summer and into autumn; each tube to 8cm (3in) long; flowers in a range of colours
Use Ideal as a specimen plant or in mixed borders; singly or in groups; spectacular when planted *en masse*; good near a water feature; can be grown in large containers for a short period before planting out in garden
Needs Propagate by summer cuttings. May require support. Hardiness may be suspect in some gardens
Varieties *P. aequalis* dark foliage, coral-red flowers • *P. a.* 'Yellow Trumpet' bushy habit, light green foliage, long yellow flower tubes, a good form • *P. capensis* var. *coccineus* woody habit, dark green foliage, orange-scarlet flowers, will climb • *P.* × *rectus* 'African Queen' orange-red flowers • *P.* × *r.* 'Salmon Leap' mid-green foliage, salmon-pink flowers

PHYSALIS ALKEKENGI
Solanaceae
CHINESE LANTERN

❀ ❦ SI autumn fruit
H 30–60cm (1–2ft)
S 45–75cm (18–30in)
❋ -10°C (14°F)
Z 3–10

PHYSALIS ALKEKENGI VAR. FRANCHETII

Once this plant fruits it seems that autumn has begun in earnest. The flowers are inconspicuous, and physalis is planted for the decorative, lantern-like fruits. In the ideal position, it can become invasive but it should nevertheless be planted.

Soil Moderately alkaline to acid, well fed and well drained
Aspect Light shade to full sun
Habit Clump-forming, spreading by underground shoots and roots
Leaf Deciduous, light green, tapering, oval leaves, 5–8cm (2–3in) long; good yellow autumn colour; shed when fruits ripen
Flower In summer bell-shaped, somewhat inconspicuous, small flowers are borne in leaf axes, white to cream in colour. The main attraction are the large, 5cm (2in) long, lantern-shaped, bright orange-red fruits which follow
Use Grown for its autumn fruit and therefore best grown as a specimen plant in isolation; in a very large border can be used in the foreground to good effect
Needs Propagate by removing sections of root with part of old stem in early spring. Often looks weak in constitution when bought from a nursery or garden centre
Varieties *P. alkekengi* var. *franchetii* main plant to produce the interesting and colourful red-orange lanterns • *P. a.* var. *f.* 'Gigantea' taller growing, large orange-red lanterns, more invasive • *P. a.* var. *f.* 'Variegata' limited yellow to cream variegation, smaller orange-red lanterns

---

PHYSOSTEGIA
Lamiaceae/Labiatae
FALSE DRAGONHEAD

❀ SI late summer
H 0.45–1.2m (18–48in)
S 38cm (15in)
❋ -10°C (14°F)
Z 3–10

PHYSOSTEGIA VIRGINIANA 'VIVID'

Few other perennial plants offer the density of flower of physostegia. Each flower stands erect, making a uniform carpet of flower, and planted alongside other late-summer-flowering plants they not only make a contrast in flower colour but in shape and texture.

Soil Alkaline to acid; may show signs of distress in very dry conditions
Aspect Prefers light shade but tolerates full sun
Habit Low growing, neat and carpet-forming
Leaf Deciduous, light to mid-green, lance-shaped leaves, 8–10cm (3–4in) long and 1–2cm (½–¾in) wide, with toothed edges
Flower Stiff, angular, upright spikes of tubular flowers, to 15–23cm (6–9in) tall, rose-pink, white or purple in late summer; sometimes repeated in mid-autumn
Use Ideal for the front of mixed borders; good planted in groups or singly; can be used to edge a path or walkway; good ground cover when planted in weed-free soil; can be used in containers for summer flower display; flowers will cut for flower arranging
Needs Propagate by division in late spring. Dig up and divide every 4–5 years. Irrigate in drought conditions
Varieties *P. virginiana* 'Alba' white flowers • *P. v.* 'Crown of Snow' pure white flowers • *P. v.* ssp. *speciosa* 'Bouquet Rose' lilac-pink flowers • *P. v.* ssp. *s.* 'Variegata' white-variegated leaves, pink flowers • *P. v.* 'Summer Snow' ♀ white flowers • *P. v.* 'Vivid' ♀ dark rose-pink flowers

PLATYCODON
Campanulaceae
BALLOON FLOWER

❀ SI early summer
H 38–60cm (15–24in)
S 30–38cm (12–15in)
❄ -10°C (14°F)
Z 4–10

The common name of this interesting and attractive plant describes it perfectly. Each flower starts as a balloon before it opens into a large, bell-shaped flower. The plants can be just a little susceptible to winter cold, requiring extra protection in the lee of a sunny wall.

Soil Alkaline to acid, well-fed soil; good drainage is important, as is a good quantity of organic material in the soil
Aspect Best in full sun to very light shade
Habit Neat clump-forming; upright, wiry flower shoots
Leaf Deciduous, mid-green with grey sheen, oval to lance-shaped, toothed leaves, 4–8cm (1½–3in) long
Flower Balloon-shaped flower buds, formed of 5 petals, nodding and expanding into a large, bell-shape flower, 5–8cm (2–3in) across, in blue, pink or white, mainly in early summer, with intermittent flowers later
Use Best grown in isolation as specimen plants; ideal for containers, including hanging baskets; can be grown as a rockery plant on larger features; will grow well in a conservatory
Needs Propagate from seed in spring. It may be possible to divide them in spring. Will require winter protection in exposed areas
Varieties *P. grandiflorus* ♥ deep blue, velvety flowers • *P. g.* var. *albus* pure white flowers • *P. g.* var. *mariesii* ♥ mid-blue flowers, low growing • *P. g.* 'Perlmutterschale' ('Mother of Pearl') single, pale pink flowers

PLATYCODON GRANDI-FLORUS VAR. MARIESII

POLEMONIUM
Polemoniaceae
JACOB'S LADDER

▲ ❀ ❦ SI spring
H 1–2 yrs 45–90cm (18–36in)
S 30–60cm (1–2ft)
❄ -10°C (14°F)
Z 3–10

In early spring this plant grows just like a ladder, trying, it seems, to reach the sun as quickly as possible. Foliage, habit and flowers all add to the overall effect.

Soil Alkaline to acid; dislikes drying out and waterlogging
Aspect Light shade to full sun
Habit Upright columns of foliage and flower
Leaf Deciduous or semi-evergreen, light to bright green or cream-variegated, lance-shaped to oval leaflets, 8cm (3in) long, form feather-shaped leaves
Flower Small flowers formed of 5 round, pointed petals in early spring; individual or small clusters of flowers borne near top of leaf stalks in spring
Use Ideal for naturalizing in woodland or similar areas; in mixed borders with other spring flowers; will grow for a year or so in a container
Needs Propagate by division in spring; self-seeding
Varieties *P. caeruleum* light to mid-blue flowers, to 75cm (30in) • *P. c.* 'Brise d'Anjou' cream-margined leaves, pale blue flowers, to 60cm (2ft) • *P. carneum* 'Pink Dawn' pink flowers, to 25cm (10in) • *P. foliosissimum* pale blue flowers, to 1m (3ft) • *P. f.* 'Album' pure white flowers, to 75cm (30in) • *P.* 'Lambrook Mauve' (syn. *P. reptans* 'Lambrook Manor') ♥ mauve-blue flowers, to 75cm (30in) • *P. reptans* 'Blue Pearl' good blue flowers, to 25cm (10in) • *P. r.* 'Dawn Flight' white flowers, to 75cm (30in) • *P. r.* 'Pink Beauty' purple-pink with lavender flowers, to 30cm (1ft) • *P.* 'Sapphire' sky blue flowers, to 30cm (1ft)

POLEMONIUM FOLIOSISSIMUM

POLYGONATUM
Liliaceae/
Convallariaceae
SOLOMON'S SEAL

▲ ❀ ❦ SI spring
H 60–90cm (2–3ft)
S 60–75cm (24–30in)
❄ -10°C (14°F)
Z 4–10

**POLYGONATUM
MULTIFLORUM**

Interesting as well as beautiful, this plant appears each spring as if by magic to display its flowers. Almost as soon as it has finished flowering, it disappears again. The arrangement of its flowers is almost unique among other plants, and it is at its best in a woodland environment.

Soil Moderately alkaline to acid, deep, rich and high in organic material
Aspect Deep shade to full sun; prefers mid-shade
Habit Clump-forming, spreading to form new clumps by underground shoots
Leaf Deciduous, mid-green, oval to lance-shaped leaves, 45–60cm (18–24in) long and 8–15cm (3–6in) wide, regularly arranged along arching stem; white cream-edged variegated form available
Flower White, green-tipped, narrow, tubular, bell-shaped flowers, hanging on long stalks from the underside of long, curving stems; *P. odoratum* has slightly scented flowers
Use In a woodland or similarly shaded environment; can be grown in large containers as long as they are well watered
Needs Propagate by division of root clumps in autumn or early spring
Varieties *P. biflorum* (syn. *P. giganteum*, *P. commutatum*, *P. canaliculatum*) to 1.5m (5ft) • *P. falcatum* upright habit, to 20cm (8in) • *P. multiflorum* the true form of Solomon's Seal and as the general description • *P. odoratum* slightly scented, to 30cm (1ft) • *P. o.* 'Variegatum' white to cream margins around edges of leaves

POTENTILLA
Rosaceae
POTENTILLA

❀ ❦ SI summer
H 30–45cm (12–18in)
S 30–45cm (12–18in)
❄ -15°C (4°F)
Z 3–10

**POTENTILLA 'GIBSON'S
SCARLET'**

Perennial potentillas offer just as much interest in the garden as their shrubby relatives. Although not particularly compact in habit, they do provide colour throughout summer.

Soil Alkaline to acid; resents very dry conditions
Aspect Full sun to very light shade
Habit Clump-forming and spreading; sometimes ungainly
Leaf Deciduous, light to mid-green, hand-shaped leaves, 5–8cm (2–3in) long and wide, with hairy undersides and notched edges
Flower Single or double flowers, to 2.5cm (1in) across, made up of 5 or more heart-shaped petals in a range of colours
Use At the front or mid-ground of mixed borders; good in large groups or singly
Needs Propagate by division in spring. Lift and divide every 4–5 years. Some may require support of short twigs
Varieties *P. aurea* low growing, single, yellow flowers • *P.* 'Etna' single, maroon flowers • *P.* 'Flamenco' single, red flowers • *P.* 'Gibson's Scarlet' ♀ single, scarlet flowers • *P.* 'Gloire de Nancy' double, orange-brown flowers • *P.* 'Helen Jane', single, clear pink flowers • *P.* 'Monsieur Rouillard' double, mahogany-coloured flowers • *P. nepalensis* 'Miss Willmott' ♀ single, cherry-pink flowers • *P. n.* 'Roxana' single, vivid orange flowers • *P. recta* var. *pallida* ♀ single, pale yellow flowers • *P.* × *tonguei* single, light orange flowers with crimson central blotch • *P.* 'William Rollison' ♀ double, orange-red flowers with yellow reverse • *P.* 'Yellow Queen' double, bright yellow flowers with red eye

PRIMULA
Primulaceae
PRIMULA

▲ ❀ ❦ SI spring E (semi)
H 1–2 yrs 60–75cm (24–30in)
S 45–75cm (18–30in)
❊ -10°C (14°F)
Z 3–9

PRIMULA JAPONICA

The elegant flower spikes of candelabra primulas are a joy to see each spring, but if they are to give of their best, they need the right conditions.

Soil Acid or alkaline; continuously moist but not waterlogged and high in organic material
Aspect Full sun with very light shade
Habit Clump-forming
Leaf Semi-evergreen to deciduous, mid- to dark green, oval, deeply veined leaves, to 25cm (10in) long and 8cm (3in) wide; the extent to which they are evergreen depends on the coldness of the winter
Flower Pendent, small, bell-shaped flowers in a range of colours, arranged on regular rings of flowers, opening from the bottom up
Use Best grown in association with a water feature, such as a pool or stream
Needs Propagate by seed or division in spring; may self-seed
Varieties *P. denticulata* (drumstick primula) ♀ flowers in balls at the top of flowering shoots • *P. d.* var. *alba* white flowers • *P. d.* ruby red form • *P. florindae* ♀ yellow candelabra flowers • *P. japonica* shades of pink to red candelabra flowers • *P. j.* 'Miller's Crimson' crimson candelabra flowers • *P. j.* 'Postford White' white candelabra flowers • *P. vulgaris* (primrose) pale yellow flowers • *P.* 'Wanda' a primrose type, dark purple green leaves, deep purple flowers

PULMONARIA
Boraginaceae
LUNGWORT

❀ ❦ SI late winter–early spring E (semi)
H 1–2 yrs 30cm (1ft)
S 45cm (18in)
❊ -15°C (4°F)
Z 3–10

**PULMONARIA
ANGUSTIFOLIA**

At one time the blotches and marking on the leaves of this plant were thought to represent human lungs, and it was felt that they must be of some benefit in the treatment of lung ailments – hence both the botanical and common names.

Soil Moderately alkaline to acid; does best on soil with high organic content
Aspect Full sun to shade; very good in woodland positions
Habit Clump-forming with spreading ability
Leaf Deciduous, grey-green, oval leaves, 15–20cm (6–8in) long and 5–8cm (2–3in) wide, spotted or splashed with grey-white and covered with soft hairs; degree of marking varies
Flower Bell-shaped flowers, in clusters of 10–25, open at varying speeds; in white, pink, red or blue; the coloured calyx adds to the display
Use Ground cover *en masse* or solo; for the front of mixed borders, in particular those with spring interest
Needs Propagate by division at any time
Varieties *P. angustifolia* ♀ narrow green leaves, limited markings, deep blue flowers • *P. a.* ssp. *azurea* even deeper blue flowers • *P. a.* 'Munstead Blue' some leaf markings, pale to mid-blue flowers • *P. longifolia* very long, boldly marked leaves, blue flowers • *P. officinalis* 'Sissinghurst White' ♀ boldly marked leaves, white flowers • *P. rubra* 'Barfield Pink' velvety leaves, limited markings, pink flowers • *P. r.* 'Bowles Red' deep pink to red flowers • *P. saccharata* evergreen, boldly marked leaves, pink to blue flowers from pink buds and purple calyx • *P. s.* 'Alba' white flowers

PULSATILLA VULGARIS
Ranunculaceae
PASQUE FLOWER

▲ ❀ ❦ SI spring
H 1–2 yrs 30cm (1ft)
S 30–38cm (12–15in)
❄ -10°C (14°F)
Z 4–9

This beautiful plant appears in spring to display its lovely flowers, interesting foliage and distinctive seedheads. It should not be mixed with other species if its full charm is to be appreciated. The range of colours is worth exploring, and new cultivars are being introduced all the time.

Soil Acid to alkaline, well drained
Aspect Full sun to very light shade
Habit Clump-forming
Leaf Deciduous, beautiful light green to grey-green, finely cut and feathery leaves, 10–20cm (4–8in) long and 4–5cm (1½–2in) wide; leaves, stems and flowers emerge from clusters of silky, silvery hairs
Flower Open, bell-shaped flowers, 5–8cm (2–3in) wide, on nodding stems in early spring; mauve to purple-pink and white with pronounced yellow stamens and black stigma; followed in late spring to early summer by silvery, wispy seedheads
Use As a specimen, planted singly or in groups; for use in large rock gardens or other isolated areas where it can be admired to the full; can be grown in large containers to good effect; often used for flower arranging
Needs Propagate from seed or by division in spring; often self-seeds, when interesting colour variations may develop
Varieties *P. vulgaris* ♀ mauve flowers • *P. v.* var. *alba* ♀ pure white flowers • *P. v.* var. *rubra* wine-red flowers

PULSATILLA VULGARIS

RHEUM
Polygonaceae
ORNAMENTAL RHUBARB

▲ ❀ ❦ SI spring–autumn
H 1–2 yrs 1.5–2.4m (5–8ft)
S 2m (6ft)
❄ -15°C (4°F)
Z 4–10

Impressive and majestic in both foliage and flowers, rheums need constant moisture to maintain their vigour, and they also need adequate space. If you can meet both these requirements, there are few other plants that can compare with the overall appearance of an established rheum.

Soil Moderately alkaline to acid, well fed and moist at all times but not waterlogged
Aspect Full sun to light shade
Habit Clump-forming; upright but quickly spreading
Leaf Deciduous, mid- to dark green, palmate leaves, with purple hue and 5 broad, pointed fingers, 30–75cm (12–30in) long and wide, indented along the edges, with pronounced purple or red veins and silver-grey undersides
Flower Reddish, plume-like flowers, carried in bold, pointed clusters on upright, stout spikes from summer to early autumn; they turn brown to provide late autumn and early winter interest
Use In association with water features; for anywhere in the garden as long as the soil is moist; good in groups or planted singly; can give the effect of being naturalized
Needs Propagate by division of root clumps in early spring
Varieties *R.* 'Ace of Hearts' light green foliage, bright red flowers • *R. alexandrae* leaves and plant smaller than other forms, cream bracts hide red flowers • *R. palmatum* ♀ dark green, slightly purple leaves, red flowers • *R. p.* 'Atropurpureum' purple foliage, red flowers • *R. p.* 'Atrosanguineum' red-purple foliage, red flowers

RHEUM PALMATUM 'ATROPURPUREUM'

RODGERSIA
Saxifragaceae
RODGERSIA

▲ ❀ ❦ SI spring–summer
H 0.9–1.2m (3–4ft)
S 90cm (3ft)
❄ -15°C (4°F)
Z 4–10

Wherever a bold foliage display is required and a moist soil and space are available, this plant is worth considering. The foliage is not its only merit, as the flowers are attractive, too. It is the ideal plant to position near a stream or pool.

Soil Moderately alkaline to acid, deep, moist and high in organic content
Aspect Full sun to full shade; prefers light shade
Habit Clump-forming; new foliage upright, spreading towards autumn
Leaf Deciduous, bronze-green, pinnate leaves, 30–45cm (12–18in) long and 30–38cm (12–15in) wide, deeply veined and ageing to dark green; good orange-yellow autumn colour
Flower Very small creamy-white or pink flowers borne in broad spikes, 23–38cm (9–15in), tall in early summer
Use Best near a water feature or in bog garden planting for full effect; if soil is sufficiently moist can be used as a specimen plant
Needs Propagate by division in spring
Varieties *R. aesculifolia* ♀ creamy-white to pale pink flowers • *R. pinnata* creamy-pink flowers • *R. p.* 'Alba' white flowers • *R. p.* 'Elegans' flowers in shades of cream, one of the tallest • *R. p.* 'Superba' ♀ bold pink flowers • *R. podophylla* ♀ indented and lobed leaves, loose white flowers • *R. sambucifolia* creamy-white flowers • *R. tabularis* round leaves, white to cream flowers

RODGERSIA TABULARIS

RUDBECKIA
Asteraceae/Compositae
CONEFLOWER

▲ ❀ ❦ SI autumn
H 60–90cm (2–3ft)
S 45–60cm (18–24in)
❄ -10°C (14°F)
Z 3–10

There is nothing that can brighten an autumn day as well as rudbeckia. Each of the bright golden, daisy-shaped flowers has a dramatic central black eye. When you are buying, be careful that you do not obtain *R. hirta*, which is grown as an annual. Although it is an excellent form for summer bedding, it does not overwinter.

Soil Alkaline to acid, well drained and well fed; dislikes drought conditions
Aspect Full sun to light shade; prefers full sun
Habit Clump-forming; upright, spreading when in flower
Leaf Deciduous, light green, pointed, oval leaves, 6–13cm (2½–5in) long and 2.5cm (1in) or more wide
Flower Yellow to gold, strap-shaped petals surround a black centre to form daisy-like flowers, 6cm (2½in) across, borne in clusters at the top of wiry flower stalks; some forms have double flowers
Use Ideal for mid- or background planting in a mixed border; spectacular when mass-planted; a good cut flower, keeping well in water
Needs Propagate by division or from seed in spring. Lift and divide every 4 years. Will require support
Varieties *R. fulgida* var. *deamii* (black-eyed Susan) single, golden-yellow flowers with black central eye • *R. f.* var. *speciosa* single, golden-yellow flowers • *R. f.* var. *sullivantii* 'Goldsturm' ♀ single, golden-yellow flowers • *R.* 'Herbstsonne' ('Autumn Sun') single, yellow flowers, very tall • *R. subtomentosa* grey foliage, single, yellow flowers

RUDBECKIA FULGIDA VAR. SULLIVANTII 'GOLDSTURM'

SALVIA
Lamiaceae/Labiatae
SALVIA

▲ ❀ ❦ SI summer–autumn
E (semi)
H 60–90cm (2–3ft)
S 38–45cm (15–18in)
❄ -10°C (14°F)
Z 4–9

SALVIA × SYLVESTRIS 'MAINACHT'

These beautiful flowering plants really come into their own in autumn. Although they are mostly good tempered and easy to grow, many are not hardy. Those listed below are the best of the blue-flowered varieties.

Soil Alkaline to acid; dislikes extremely dry conditions
Aspect Full sun to very light shade
Habit Upright and clump-forming
Leaf Deciduous, dark grey-green, rough-textured, pointed, oval leaves, 4.5–8cm (1¾–3in) long and 1–2cm (½–¾in) wide
Flower Small, tubular, 2-lipped flowers, in shades of purple, blue and pink, form narrow spikes to 20cm (8in) long
Use Planted in groups or singly in the mixed border; good for edging paths and drives; can be grown in containers; a useful cut flower
Needs Propagate by division in spring or from cuttings in summer
Varieties *S. nemorosa* 'Lubecca' good dark blue flowers, to 60cm (2ft) • *S. n.* 'Ostfriesland' ('East Friesland') violet-purple flower spikes, to 60cm (2ft) • *S. × superba* ♀ blue flowers in profusion, to 45cm (18in) • *S. × sylvestris* 'Indigo' indigo to violet-blue flowers, to 45cm (18in) • *S. × s.* 'Lye End' lavender-blue, candelabra-shaped flower spikes, to 1.5m (5ft) • *S. × s.* 'Mainacht' ('May Night') deep indigo flowers, to 60cm (2ft) • *S. × s.* 'Rose Queen' rose-pink flowers • *S. uliginosa* ♀ long-ranging shoots carry bright blue flowers over a long period in late summer and autumn, hardiness is suspect in exposed gardens

SCABIOSA
Dipsaceae
SCABIOUS

❀ ❦ SI late summer–autumn)
H 60cm (2ft)
S 38–45cm (15–18in)
❄ -10°C (14°F)
Z 3–10

SCABIOSA BANATICA 'BUTTERFLY BLUE'

This widely grown plant tolerates a wide range of soil types, including very alkaline soil, on which its wild relative is found. Although bluish-mauve is the most usual colour, look out for forms with red, pink or white flowers.

Soil Alkaline to acid, well drained and open, with added organic matter; add a handful of garden lime to very acid soils each spring to keep soil alkaline
Aspect Prefers full sun but will tolerate light shade
Habit Clump-forming
Leaf Deciduous, bright green, divided leaves, 8–13cm (3–5in) long and 4–7cm (1½–2½in) wide, sparsely presented at base of flower stems
Flower Numerous oval, frilled petals, surrounding a central domed cushion, form semi-double flowers, 6cm (2½in) across, in shades of blue, red, pink and white and carried on tall, wiry stems in late summer to early autumn; some of the newer cultivars flower in early to midsummer
Use Possibly most showy when planted in isolation but can be used in the foreground of mixed borders; can be grown in containers; a good cut flower
Needs Propagate by division in spring
Varieties *S. banatica* 'Butterfly Blue' mid-blue flowers over long period • *S. caucasica* 'Clive Greaves' ♀ light blue flowers, one of the best • *S. c.* 'Miss Willmott' ♀ pure white flowers • *S. c.* 'Moerheim Blue' deep blue flowers • *S. c.* 'Moonstone' pale blue flowers • *S.* 'Pink Mist' pink flowers, free flowering over long period

SEDUM
Crassulaceae
SEDUM

▲ ❀ ❦ SI summer–autumn
H 1–2 yrs 15–75cm (6–30in)
S 0.6–1m (2–3ft)
❄ -10°C (14°F)
Z 4–10

SEDUM SPECTABILE

A gem of an autumn plant, with both foliage and flowers to admire and either growing upright or spreading according to the variety chosen.

Soil Most, if well drained
Aspect Prefers full sun; will tolerate light shade
Habit Upright or spreading, depending on form
Leaf Deciduous, oval, smooth-textured, leaves, thick and succulent-like, and silver to silver-grey, some with purple hue
Flower Small or large, upward-facing corymbs in shades of pink or red in autumn
Use Spreading types for underplanting and ground cover; upright types for mixed or solo planting; can be grown in containers; good as cut flowers
Needs Propagate by leaf cuttings in spring; remove entire leaf and insert base into potting compost
Varieties S. 'Ruby Glow' ♀ spreading, purple-grey leaves, medium sized, wine-red flowers, to 15cm (6in) • S. spectabile (syn. Hylotelephium spectabile; ice plant) ♀ upright, large corymbs of pale pink flowers, to 60cm (2ft) • S. s. 'Brilliant' ♀ upright, large, deep pink to red flowers, to 75cm (30in) • S. s. 'Meteor' upright, very large, deep red flowers, to 75cm (30in) • S. s. 'Variegatum' upright, variegated leaves, large, pink flowers • S. telephium (syn. Hylotelephium telephium; live-forever) upright, larger, grey, indented leaves, large pink flowers, to 75cm (30in) • S. t. ssp. maximum 'Atropurpureum' ♀ large, deep pink to red flowers • S. 'Vera Jameson' ♀ spreading, small, deep pink flowers

SIDALCEA
Malvaceae
PRAIRIE MALLOW

▲ ❀ ❦ SI summer
H 0.9–1.2m (3–4ft)
S 38–45cm (15–18in)
❄ -10°C (14°F)
Z 4–10

SIDALCEA 'LOVELINESS'

Delicate in appearance yet bold in effect, this member of the mallow family does not retain the sometimes hard appearance of its brothers and sisters. It does, however, have their lovely hollyhock-like flowers.

Soil Alkaline to acid, well drained but not dry
Aspect Full sun to very light shade
Habit Clump-forming, with foliage held close to the ground
Leaf Deciduous, light to mid-green, rounded to oval leaves, 5–8cm (2–3in) long and slightly less wide
Flower Deep saucer-shaped flowers, to 4cm (1½in) across and in shades of pink to red, are formed from 5 heart-shaped petals and borne in upright spikes, opening progressively from the base upwards
Use For the back or mid-point of mixed borders; good as a specimen plant; plant singly or in groups
Needs Propagate by division or from seed in spring. Dig up and divide every 5 years. May need support in windy areas
Varieties S. 'Brilliant' deep rose-pink flowers, to 75cm (30in) • S. 'Croftway Red' rich deep pink to red flowers, to 75cm (30in) • S. 'Elsie Heugh' clear pale pink flowers, to 1.2m (4ft) • S. 'Loveliness' compact habit, shell pink flowers, to 45cm (18in) • S. 'Mrs T. Anderson' good mid-pink flowers • S. 'Oberon' mid- to pale pink flowers, to 60cm (2ft) • S. 'Puck' good pink flowers, to 60cm (2ft) • S. 'Reverend Page Roberts' mid-pink flowers, to 1.2m (4ft) • S. 'Rose Queen' pink flowers, to 1.2m (4ft) • S. 'William Smith' ♀ salmon-pink flowers, to 75cm (30in)

SMILACINA
Convallariaceae/ Liliaceae
FALSE SOLOMON'S SEAL, SOLOMON'S PLUME

▲ ❀ ❦ SI spring SC
H 60–90cm (2–3ft)
S 60–90cm (2–3ft)
❊ -10°C (14°F)
Z 3–10

SMILACINA RACEMOSA

An interesting plant that is, as one of its common names would suggest, often mistaken for Solomon's seal (polygonatum). Appearing from nowhere in early spring, it rapidly grows to form an attractive clump, which is soon adorned with flowers.

Soil Moderately alkaline to acid, well fed and moist
Aspect Prefers light shade; will tolerate sun as long as soil is moist
Habit Clump-forming; upright shoots at first, quickly becoming more spreading when in flower
Leaf Deciduous, attractive, lance-shaped leaves, 8–9cm (3–3½in) long and 4.5–5cm (1¾–2in) wide, with dark green upper surface and grey-brown with brownish flecks on underside
Flower Fluffy panicles, to 8cm (3in) long, of creamy-white, scented flowers, borne at the ends of each leaf stalk in spring
Use Best as a specimen plant, singly or in a group; looks good in association with water or in a semi-woodland situation; will grow in a well-irrigated containers; can be used as a cut flower
Needs Propagate by division in spring. Looks small when purchased and may be difficult to find. Protect from slugs and snails
Species *S. racemosa* (false spikenard) ♀ the main form, as described above • *S. stellata* (star-flowered lily-of-the-valley) star-shaped white flowers, not as good as *S. racemosa*

SOLIDAGO
Asteraceae/Compositae
GOLDEN ROD

▲ ❀ ❦ SI late summer
H 0.6–1.2m (2–4ft)
S 38–60cm (15–24in)
❊ -15°C (4°F)
Z 3–9

SOLIDAGO 'LEMORE'

Old-fashioned and widely planted, yes, but still capable of providing a display of colour in the garden. Although the old, tall-growing varieties should not be completely overlooked, the newer, more compact varieties are well worth seeking out.

Soil Most
Aspect Full sun to light shade
Habit Clump-forming and upright
Leaf Deciduous, light green to grey-green, lance-shaped leaves, 8–10cm (3–4in) long and 5–10mm (¼–½in) wide, carried horizontally on stems
Flower Minute flowers in shades of yellow form feathery plumes, to 30cm (1ft) long, spreading horizontally outward from upright stems
Use Ideal, depending on height of variety, for the middle or back of mixed borders; spectacular when mass-planted
Needs Propagate by division in spring. Divide every 5 years
Varieties *S.* 'Cloth of Gold' deep yellow flowers, to 75cm (30in) • *S.* 'Crown of Rays' ('Strahlenkrone') clear yellow flowers, dense formation, to 60cm (2ft) • *S.* 'Golden Shower' bold yellow flower, to 75cm (30in) • *S.* 'Golden Thumb' yellow leaves, yellow flowers, to 30cm (1ft), good dwarf form with many uses • *S.* 'Goldenmosa' ♀ golden-yellow flowers, to 60cm (2ft), one of the best • *S.* 'Laurin' bushy habit, good yellow flowers, to 45cm (18in) • *S.* 'Lemore' cool lemon-yellow flowers, to 60cm (2ft) • *S.* 'Mimosa' mimosa-coloured flowers, to 1.8m (5ft 6in) • *S.* 'Queenie' yellow leaves, deep yellow flowers, to 30in (1ft)

STACHYS
Lamiaceae/Labiatae
BETONY, HEDGE
NETTLE, WOUNDWORT

▲ ❀ ❦ SI year round E
H 1–2 yrs 40cm (16in)
S 0.6–1m (2–3ft)
❄ -10°C (14°F)
Z 4–10

**STACHYS BYZANTINA
'SILVER CARPET'**

The silver leaves of the most often-seen form of this plant are always popular with children, but although the foliage is important, there are flowers, too, and when the green-leaved forms are grown, the flowers are the main attraction.

Soil Most; dislikes waterlogging or dry conditions
Aspect Prefers full sun but tolerates light shade
Habit Silver-leaved forms spreading; green-leaved forms clump-forming
Leaf Deciduous, silver or mid- to deep green, oval leaves, 13–15cm (5–6in) long and 5–6cm (2–2½in) wide, tapering to a point
Flower Mauve or pink, hooded, tubular flowers, 2.5cm (1in) long, form spikes to 20cm (8in) tall and 8cm (3in) wide
Use Silver-leaved varieties ideal for ground cover or edging; all forms suitable for the front of mixed borders; all forms good planted singly or in groups
Needs Propagate by division in spring. Lift and divide every 4 years to keep plants in good condition
Varieties *S. byzantina* (syn. *S. olympica*, *S. lanata*; lamb's tongue, lamb's ears, woolly betony) silver foliage, magenta flowers covered in silvery down, to 40cm (16in) • *S. b.* 'Cotton Boll' silver foliage, flower buds do not open, thereby producing silver-coloured cottonbud-like balls up the flower spike • *S. b.* 'Silver Carpet' silver-leaved variety, no flowers, ideal ground cover for a sunny place • *S. macrantha* (syn. *Betonica grandiflora*, *S. grandiflora*) dark green leaves, pink to mauve flowers, to 60cm (2ft), will tolerate shade

SYMPHYTUM
Boraginaceae
COMFREY

▲ ❀ ❦ SI spring
H 30–75cm (12–30in)
S 60–90cm (2–3ft)
❄ -15°C (4°F)
Z 4–10

**SYMPHYTUM
GRANDIFLORUM**

This strong-growing plant is ideal for difficult places where most other plants might fail. Do not attempt to grow it where it does not have room to spread. The green-leaved forms are attractive, but the variegated forms are really eye-catching.

Soil Most; dislikes very dry conditions
Aspect Full shade to full sun
Habit Clump-forming, spreading by underground roots
Leaf Deciduous, rich green or cream-variegated, oval to lance-shaped leaves, 10–15cm (4–6in) long and 4–5cm (1½–1in) wide, rough and deeply veined
Flower Bell-shaped flowers, 1cm (½in) long, in a range of colours, including cream, blue, red and pink, borne in small hanging clusters
Use Ideal for large-scale naturalizing; for colonizing difficult soil conditions; for the back of mixed borders
Needs Propagate by division. May require support
Varieties *S. azureum* green leaves, blue flowers • *S. caucasicum* green leaves, blue flowers, to 75cm (30in) • *S. grandiflorum* creamy-white flowers, green leaves, to 20–60cm (8–24in) • *S.* 'Hidcote Blue' green leaves, good blue flowers, to 60cm (2ft) • *S.* 'Hidcote Pink' pale blue to pinkish-blue flowers, to 60cm (2ft) • *S.* 'Hidcote Variegated' cream-variegated leaves, blue flowers, to (60cm (2ft) • *S.* 'Rubrum' green foliage, deep red flowers, to 40cm (16in) • *S.* × *uplandicum* green leaves, pink buds opening to blue flowers, to 1.2m (4ft) tall and wide • *S.* × *u.* 'Variegatum' ♀ variegated leaves, lilac-blue flowers, to 1m (3ft)

PERENNIALS

TELLIMA GRANDIFLORA
Saxifragaceae
FRINGECUPS

▲ ❀ ❦ SI all year E
H 45–60cm (18–24in)
S 45–60cm (18–24in)
❅ -10°C (14°F)
Z 4–10

This useful and easy-going plant not only bears welcome spring flowers but has attractive foliage all year round. Although it can be grown as a single specimen plant, it looks even better in large groups, and it is the perfect plant for gardens with woodland areas.

Soil Acid to alkaline; likes moisture but dislikes extremely dry conditions
Aspect Prefers light shade but tolerates full sun
Habit Neat and compact, clump-forming
Leaf Evergreen, light green or dull purple, round to oval leaves, 15–23cm (6–9in) long and 8–10cm (3–4in) wide; orange-red autumn colour
Flower Attractive, small, nodding, bell-shaped flowers, in green-yellow, carried on upright spikes, to 17cm (7in) long, above foliage in spring
Use For the front of mixed borders of all sizes both as a solo plant or in groups; ideal for woodland planting as long as moisture is available; good for ground cover and edging borders; can be grown in containers to good effect both for summer and winter displays
Needs Propagate by division in spring. Lift and divide every 4 years. Remove dead leaves as they occur
Varieties *T. grandiflora* the type species as described • *T. g.* Rubra Group (syn. *T. g.* 'Purpurea') dull purple foliage, slightly darker flowers

TELLIMA GRANDIFLORA

THALICTRUM
Ranunculaceae
MEADOW RUE

▲ ❀ ❦ SI summer
H 0.6–1.5m (2–5ft)
S 60–75cm (24–30in)
❅ -10°C (14°F)
Z 4–10

This is a lovely group of plants, but the variety *T. delavayi* 'Hewitt's Double' is outstanding. They are all upright, with interesting foliage and flowers, and the only drawback is that they need moisture at all times during the growing season.

Soil Moderately alkaline to acid, deep, moist and well fed
Aspect Full sun to light shade
Habit Clump-forming, upright (with support)
Leaf Deciduous, light green, divided, pinnate leaves, 15–17cm (6–7in) long and 4–6cm (1½–2½in) wide; some very feathery and attractive
Flower Very small flowers, borne in fluffy clusters on tall, upright flower spikes, in shades of pink, lilac, purple and white in mid- to late summer
Use For the back of mixed borders; ideal in association with water; good when mass-planted as a specimen planting
Needs Propagate from seed or by division in spring or from cuttings in summer. Needs support
Varieties *T. aquilegifolium* glaucous-blue leaves, greenish-white flowers • *T. a.* var. *album* tall growing, white flowers • *T. a.* 'Thundercloud' ('Purple Cloud') deep lilac-purple flowers • *T. delavayi* ♀ large panicles of single, lilac-blue flowers with bold cream stamens • *T. d.* 'Album' small, double, white flowers • *T. d.* 'Hewitt's Double' very small, double, flowers but giving a good overall display • *T. flavum* grey foliage, fluffy, yellow stamens • *T. flavum* ssp. *glaucum* ♀ blue-green leaves, larger flowers • *T. minus* grey-green leaves, pale green flowers, to 30–60cm (12–2ft)

THALICTRUM FLAVUM

TRADESCANTIA
Commelinaceae
SPIDERWORT

▲ ✿ ❦ SI summer
H 45–60cm (18–24in)
S 45–60cm (18–24in)
❄ -10°C (14°F)
Z 4–10

TRADESCANTIA 'ISIS'

This plant is not grown as often as it deserves, possibly because, unlike many perennials, it does not display its flowers boldly and because it normally requires support. However, it is certainly worthy of consideration.

Soil Moderately alkaline to acid, moist and well fed
Aspect Full sun to light shade
Habit Clump-forming, somewhat open, sprawling habit
Leaf Deciduous, dark green with light grey-green reverse, lance-shaped leaves, 15–30cm (6–12in) long and 1–2cm (½–¾in) wide, carried on arched, rigidly jointed stems
Flower Saucer-shaped flowers, 2.5–4cm (1–1½in) across, in blue, purple, pink or white, with central stamen cluster, borne in clusters amid foliage at irregular intervals; mostly single but some double forms
Use Ideal for the background or mid-ground of mixed borders of all sizes, either singly or in groups; looks spectacular mass-planted; good in association with water
Needs Propagate by division in spring or from cuttings in summer
Varieties *T.* × *andersoniana* 'Innocence' white flowers • *T.* × *a.* 'Iris Prichard' white, purple-tinged flowers • *T.* × *a.* 'Isis' ♀ deep blue flowers • *T.* × *a.* 'J.C. Weguelin' ♀ china blue flowers • *T.* × *a.* 'Osprey' ♀ pure white flowers • *T.* × *a.* 'Pauline' mauve-pink flowers • *T.* × *a.* 'Purewell Giant' carmine-purple flowers • *T.* × *a.* 'Purple Dome' purple, velvety flowers • *T.* × *a.* 'Rubra' purple flowers • *T.* × *a.* 'Zwanenburg Blue' royal blue flowers

VERBASCUM
Scrophulariaceae
MULLEIN

▲ ✿ ❦ SI summer–autumn
E
H 0.6–2m (2–6ft)
S 60–90cm (2–3ft)
❄ -10°C (14°F)
Z 4–10

**VERBASCUM
'HELEN JOHNSON'**

The large leaves, tall flower spikes and elegant shape all commend this plant to garden use. Most of the species are perennial, and a few are biennial.

Soil Alkaline to acid, well drained and well fed
Aspect Full sun
Habit Clump-forming; upright flower spikes
Leaf Evergreen, downy, silver-white, oval leaves, 60–90cm (2–3ft) long and 23–30cm (9–12in) wide, tapering and incurving, sometimes twisted
Flower Saucer-shaped flowers, borne on spikes 0.9–1.2m (3–4ft) tall, in yellow, pink, apricot or bronze in summer
Use As specimen plants; for the back or mid-point in borders
Needs Propagate from seed or by root cuttings or division in spring. Biennial species are self-seeding. Protect from slugs
Varieties *V. bombyciferum* ♀ biennial, very silver leaves, yellow flowers, to 1.2m (4ft) • *V. chaixii* yellow flowers in early summer, to 1m (3ft) • *V. c.* 'Album' white flowers with blue eye • *V.* Cotswold Group 'Cotswold Beauty' ♀ orange, yellow and purple flowers, to 1.2m (4ft) • *V.* Cotswold Group 'Cotswold Queen' orange, yellow and purple flowers, to 1.2m (4ft) • *V.* Cotswold Group 'Gainsborough' ♀ very silver foliage, bright yellow flowers, to 1m (3ft) • *V.* Cotswold Group 'Pink Domino' ♀ biscuit-yellow and mauve flowers, to 2m (6ft) • *V. densiflorum* many silver leaves, yellow flowers, to 1.2m (4ft) • *V.* 'Helen Johnson' ♀ copper-orange flowers, to 75cm (30in) • *V. phoeniceum* white, pink or purple flowers, to 1m (3ft)

VERONICA
Scrophulariaceae
VERONICA, SPIKED
SPEEDWELL

▲ ❀ ❦ SI summer–autumn
SC E
H 45–60cm (18–24in)
S 38cm (15in)
❋ -10°C (14°F)
Z 4–9

For intensity of flower colour, veronica has few rivals. It is also neat in habit, has attractive foliage and is adaptable.

Soil Alkaline to acid; dislikes very dry conditions
Aspect Full sun to light shade
Habit Clump-forming and upright
Leaf Evergreen, dark green or grey with silver reverse, oval to lance-shaped leaves, 5–13cm (2–5in) long and 2–2.5cm (¾–1in) wide
Flower Blue or pink flowers, borne on spikes 15–30cm (6–12in) long
Use For mixed borders; spectacular when planted *en masse*; good in large containers; a good cut flower
Needs Propagate by division in spring. Divide every 4 years
Varieties *V. austriaca* ssp. *teucrium* 'Blue Fountain' blue flowers, to 60cm (2ft) • *V. a.* ssp. *t.* 'Crater Lake Blue' ♀ deep blue flowers, to 30cm (1ft) • *V. a.* ssp. *t.* 'Royal Blue' ♀ deep blue flowers • *V. a.* ssp. *t.* 'Shirley Blue' light blue flowers, to 20cm (8in) • *V. gentianoides* ♀ dark green leaves, pale blue flowers, to 45cm (18in) • *V. g.* 'Alba' white flowers • *V. g.* 'Variegata' cream-splashed variegated leaves, blue flowers, to 40cm (16in) • *V. prostrata* 'Trehane' ♀ golden foliage, blue flowers, to 15cm (6in) • *V. spicata* green foliage, blue flowers, to 30–60cm (1–2ft) • *V. s.* 'Alba' pure white flowers • *V. s.* 'Barcarolle' green leaves, pink flowers • *V. s.* ssp. *incana* ♀ very silver-grey leaves , blue flowers, to 30cm (1ft)• *V. s.* ssp. *i.* 'Wendy' grey leaves, blue flowers • *V. s.* 'Minuet' pink flowers

**VERONICA AUSTRIACA ssp.
TEUCRIUM 'CRATER LAKE BLUE'**

VIOLA
Violaceae
VIOLET

❀ ❦ SI spring SC E
H 15–30cm (6–12in)
S 30–40cm (12–16in)
❋ -10°C (14°F)
Z 4–9

Fragrance, perpetual flowering, attractive foliage and useful growth habits are just a few of the violet family's good qualities, and they never fail to enchant.

Soil Acid to alkaline; dislikes extremely dry or extremely wet conditions
Aspect Light shade to full sun; does best in light shade
Habit Clump-forming, low and carpeting
Leaf Evergreen, glossy, dark green, oval leaves, 2.5–3cm (1–1¼in) long and wide, with silvery undersides
Flower Forward-facing, miniature, scented, pansy flowers, in shades of blue, violet, mauve, lavender, purple and yellow, made up of 5 oval petals, held singly on slender stalks above the foliage
Use At the front of mixed borders, singly or in groups; good as specimen plantings in their own right; can be grown in large containers to good effect
Needs Propagate by division or from seed in spring
Varieties *V.* 'Blue Carpet' mid-blue flowers • *V. cornuta* (horned pansy) ♀ deep violet flowers • *V. c.* Alba Group ♀ flowers pure white or white suffused with lime green • *V. c.* Lilacina Group lilac-blue flowers • *V. c.* 'Minor' ♀ lower growing and with smaller leaves • *V. c.* Purpurea Group deep blue flowers • *V.* 'Irish Molly' darkest purple flowers • *V.* 'Jackanapes' yellow-magenta flowers • *V.* 'Molly Sanderson' almost black flowers • *V.* 'Moonlight' pale yellow flowers • *V.* 'Norah Leigh' violet-blue flowers • *V. odorata* (common violet) purple-blue flowers

VIOLA 'JACKANAPES'

ARUNDO DONAX
Poaceae/Gramineae
GIANT REED

▲ ❀ ❦ SI all year E
H 2 yrs 3m (10ft)
S 2 yrs 1m (3ft)
❄ -10°C (4°F)
Z 3–9

Of all the grasses grown in gardens, this is the giant. Tall yet elegant, it will adapt to most conditions, and there are some interesting varieties, all with a clump-forming habit, which gives them potential as feature plants. Even though its winter hardiness cannot be relied upon in very cold areas, it is worth attempting for its height and foliage effect.

Soil Most; does best on moist soils with a high organic content
Aspect Full sun to very light shade; may need protection in very cold areas or cold winters
Habit Very upright, clump-forming; its width is half to one-third of its height
Leaf Narrow, grey-green, lance-shaped leaves emerge from central flower spikes, to 25cm (10in) long; they have a downward-bending habit; some variegated forms
Flower Good-sized, silver-green, plumes, often to 23cm (9in) long, ageing to light brownish-yellow in late summer to autumn; not always reliably produced
Use As solo feature plants or in clumps; spectacular *en masse* but individual specimens can be grown in mixed borders; can be container-grown if well watered
Needs Propagate from seed or by division in spring
Varieties *A. donax* the type species, mid-green to grey-blue leaves, light green to purple flowerheads • *A. d.* var. *versicolor* (syn. *A. d.* 'Variegata') very attractive, grey-green leaves with striped and white margins

ARUNDO DONAX VAR. VERSICOLOR

CAREX
Cyperaceae
SEDGE

▲ ❀ ❦ SI summer–autumn E
H 2 yrs 60cm (2ft)
S 2 yrs 60cm (2ft)
❄ -18°C (0°F)
Z 3–9

Whether in the variegated or green form, this is one of the most attractive of garden plants. The graceful, arching habit alone is reason enough to grow the plant.

Soil Moist and high in organic material; must be moisture retentive but not waterlogged
Aspect Full sun for golden-leaved forms; green types will tolerate deep shade
Habit Clump-forming; graceful arching foliage; medium rate of growth
Leaf Narrow, lance-shaped leaves, to 50cm (20in) long, green, green-gold or bronze
Flower Catkin-like, hanging flower- and seedheads in late summer
Use Solo or in groups, single or *en masse*; for mixed borders or by water; will grow in large containers
Needs Propagate by division in spring
Varieties *C. elata* 'Aurea' (syn. *C. stricta* 'Aurea'; Bowles' golden sedge) ♀ narrow, lime green to yellow-gold leaves, green-yellow flower- and seedheads carried close to the plant • *C. flagellifera* very attractive, arching, bronze foliage • *C. hachijoensis* 'Evergold' ♀ dark green leaves with bold cream-yellow bands • *C. pendula* (drooping sedge, weeping sedge) long, narrow, green foliage, hanging, catkin-like, green-brown flower- and seedheads, to 1.5m (5ft) • *C. siderosticha* 'Variegata' broad foliage by grass standards, with a pair of bold cream to pale yellow bands running the length of the leaf

CAREX ELATA 'AUREA'

CORTADERIA
Poaceae-Bambusoideae /Gramineae
PAMPAS GRASS

▲ ❀ ✇ SI late summer–autumn E
H 5 yrs 3.5m (12ft)
S 1m (3ft)
H 10 yrs 3.5m (12ft)
S 2m (6ft)
❄ -15°C (4°F)
Z 8–10

CORTADERIA SELLOANA 'PUMILA'

This well-known and rightly much used sentinel of the plant world has a role to play in many gardens. The diversity of varieties is not always appreciated, and the dwarf form can be used to good effect in a range of situations.

Soil Any; good, well-fed soil produces best plumes
Aspect Full sun; tolerates shade but plumes may be smaller
Habit Narrow base, spreading top, upright foliage and flower spikes; fast to establish
Leaf Evergreen, dark to olive green, lance-shaped grass spears, 1–2m (3–6ft) long, with very sharp serrated edges; some silver- and gold-variegated forms
Flower Large silver-white or off-pink plumes, 50cm (20in) or more long
Use As feature plant in a large lawn or the end of a shrub border; mass-planted
Needs Propagate from seed or by division. Remove dead flower shoots
Varieties *C. selloana* (syn. *C. argentea*) large silver-white plumes • *C. s.* 'Gold Band' arching habit, gold-striped leaves, small, limited flower spikes • *C. s.* 'Pumila' ♀ large white plumes, dwarf form, 2 × 1.5m (6 × 1.5ft) after 10 yrs • *C. s.* 'Rendatleri' large, open, feathery, hanging, pink-tinged plumes • *C. s.* 'Silver Cornet' silver-white leaves, creamy-white plumes • *C. s.* 'Sunningdale Silver' ♀ very large, silvery to pure white, fluffy, open plumes

FESTUCA
Poaceae/Gramineae
FESCUE

▲ ❀ ✇ SI summer–autumn E
H 2 yrs 23–50cm (9–20in)
S 2 yrs 30cm (1ft)
❄ -18°C (0°F)
Z 3–9

FESTUCA GLAUCA

These charmers of the grass family grow as tight blue mounds of foliage and flowers, which are retained as seedheads in autumn.

Soil Acid to alkaline, well drained but moisture retentive
Aspect Full sun; dislikes shade
Habit Compact clumps with spiky, attractive upright to slightly spreading leaves
Leaf Evergreen, spreading at maturity, very thin, pointed leaves, 10–17cm (4–7in) long, growing from central crown
Flower Small, off-white, fluffy plumes of flower spikes borne on long, wispy stems above foliage
Use In isolation or groups; in mixed or perennial borders; good in containers
Needs Propagate by division of clumps; trim tufts in early spring to encourage new growth
Varieties *F. amethystina* (tufted fescue, large blue fescue) grey-blue foliage, violet- to purple-green flower- and seedheads, to 50cm (20in) • *F. glacialis* (ice fescue) blue-green to grey foliage, violet flower- and seedheads, to 10cm (4in) • *F. glauca* (blue fescue) bright blue foliage, ageing to grey-blue, silver-grey to silvery-blue flowers, to 30cm (1ft) • *F. g.* 'Blaufuchs' ('Blue Fox') ♀ very bright blue foliage • *F. g.* 'Harz' blue to olive green, purple-tipped foliage • *F. g.* 'Seeigel' ('Sea Urchin') blue-green hair-like, small mounds • *F. valesiaca* blue-green, soft, hair-like, green to purple-maroon flower- and seedheads, to 50cm (20in) • *F. v.* 'Silbersee' ('Silver Sea') compact habit, silver-blue foliage

HAKONECHLOA MACRA 'AUREOLA' ♔
Gramineae
JAPANESE MOUNTAIN GRASS

▲ ❀ ❦ SI spring–autumn
H 2 yrs 75cm (30in)
S 2 yrs 75cm (30in)
❄ -18°C (0°F)
Z 3–9

The display of this golden-variegated variety is one of the best in the grass world and maybe better than of any other plant. The graceful, arching habit is pleasing, and when it is planted near water, the effect is startling. Take care with the soil and make sure it is in sun to get the best results.

Soil Moist and high in organic materials; moisture retentive but not waterlogged
Aspect Requires full sun to maintain the best golden colour
Habit Clump-forming, graceful, arching foliage; medium to fast growth rate
Leaf Narrow, lance-shaped leaves, to 50cm (20in) long; gold with a bold green band down the centre of each leaf and central bronze-brown markings close to central leaf becoming more marked throughout summer
Flower Spikes of green to yellow grass flower- and seedheads in late summer to autumn
Use Single or mass-planted; looks best by water; good in large, well-watered containers
Needs Propagate by division of root clumps in early spring
Varieties None

HAKONECHLOA MACRA 'AUREOLA'

HELICTOTRICHON SEMPERVIRENS
Poaceae/Gramineae
BLUE OAK GRASS

▲ ❀ ❦ SI summer–autumn
E
H 2 yrs 1.5m (5ft)
S 2 yrs 60cm (2ft)
❄ -18°C (0°F)
Z 3–9

A tall-growing, evergreen grass of great value in the garden. Over the years it has had several names, including *Avena candida* and *A. sempervirens*, some of which are still used today. Its common name well describes its appearance. The thin blue to grey-blue leaves are arranged in a clump and resemble a spiky, regular, ball-shaped mound, which is very useful in garden design. Against this blue background, the greenish-white flowers turn to darker seedheads.

Soil Tolerates all well-drained soils; does best in alkaline soil
Aspect Full sun to very light shade
Habit Clump-forming; moderate rate of growth
Leaf Thin, narrow and upright when young, slowly spreading and drooping as it ages; evergreen and blue to blue-grey all year round
Flower Soft, greenish-white flowerheads; followed by slightly darker seedheads
Use Solo or in groups; looks effective planted *en masse*; for mixed borders; good in association with water features; will grow in large, well-watered containers
Needs Propagate by division of root clump in autumn or spring
Varieties *H. sempervirens* ♔ type species as described • *H. s.* var. *pendulum* slightly more pendulous leaves and flowerheads

HELICTOTRICHON SEMPERVIRENS

MILIUM EFFUSUM 'AUREUM'

Poaceae/Gramineae
BOWLES' GOLDEN
GRASS, GOLDEN WOOD
MILLET

▲ ❀ ☙ S summer–autumn
E (semi)
H 2 yrs 40–60cm (16–24in)
S 40cm (16in)
❄ -15°C (4°F)
Z 3–9

MILIUM EFFUSUM 'AUREUM'

A bright, colourful grass with golden summer and autumn foliage, it can be grown in a container or in the open garden. It works particularly well near water, but has specific requirements when it comes to soil.

Soil Alkaline to acid and high in organic material; moisture retentive but well drained
Aspect Full sun
Habit Upright and loose clump-forming, often with no real structure; can be slow to become established
Leaf Semi-evergreen, soft-textured, typical grass-like leaves, 23–40cm (9–16in) long and to 5mm (¼in) wide
Flower Typical, small, broad, yellowish-green grass flower- and seedheads, yellowish-green, produced in late summer and carried on into autumn
Use As solo or group planting for foliage effect; good in association with water features
Needs Propagate by dividing established clumps. Remove dead stems and leaves in spring. Can seed itself but not invasively
Varieties *M. effusum* 'Aureum' lime green foliage ageing to golden-yellow

MISCANTHUS

Poaceae/Gramineae
SILVER GRASS

▲ ❀ ☙ SI summer–autumn
E (some)
H 2 yrs *see below*
S 2 yrs *see below*
❄ -18°C (0°F)
Z 4–10

MISCANTHUS SINENSIS 'ZEBRINUS'

Tall yet elegant, miscanthus adapts to a range of conditions.

Soil Most; does best on moist soils with high organic content
Aspect Full sun to light shade
Habit Upright; clump-forming; to a width of half the height
Leaf Narrow, grey-green, lance-shaped leaves off flower spikes, 25cm (10in) long, with a downward-bending habit; variegated forms are also available
Flower Good-sized, silver-green plumes, often to 23cm (9in) tall, ageing to light brownish-yellow in late summer to autumn
Use Solo or in groups; spectacular when mass-planted; individual specimens in mixed borders; will grow in containers
Needs Propagate from seed or by division in spring
Varieties *M. floridulus* ♀ deciduous or evergreen, pale green leaves with bold silver midrib, 2.5 × 1.2m (8 × 4ft) • *M. sacchariflorus* (Amur silver grass, silver banner grass) deciduous, rigid, blue-green leaves, fan-shaped, silver-white flower and seed plumes, to 1.5m (5ft) • *M. sinensis* ♀ arching, blue-green leaves, 1.2m (4ft) long, silky pale green seedheads, purple and maroon tints in autumn, to 4m (13ft) • *M. s.* 'Cabaret' white stripe up centre of mid-green leaves, to 2m (6ft) • *M. s.* 'Gracillimus' thin, mid-green, white midrib, to 1.2m (4ft) tall • *M. s.* var. *purpurascens* purplish-green leaves with pink midrib, orange-red in autumn, to 1.2m (4ft) • *M. s.* 'Silberfeder' ('Silver Feather') narrow mid-green, pale pink to brown flower- and seedheads, to 2.5m (8ft) • *M. s.* 'Zebrinus' (zebra grass) cream or yellow bands on mid-green leaves, to 1.2m (4ft)

MOLINIA
Poaceae/Gramineae
MOOR GRASS

▲ ❀ ❦ SI spring–autumn
H 2 yrs *see below*
S 2 yrs *see below*
❋ -18°C (0°F)
Z 2–9

**MOLINIA CAERULEA ssp.
CAERULEA 'VARIEGATA'**

This is an appealing group of grasses, mainly because of their foliage, but they need moist conditions to do well.Interesting as individuals, in a massed group they are spectacular.

Soil Acid to neutral; moist and high in organic material
Aspect Does best in sun but will tolerate light shade
Habit Clump-forming, dense; foliage upright when young, bending in midsummer; flower shoots upright, then spreading
Leaf Deciduous, mid-green, flat, lance-shaped leaves, bending from midsummer onwards; yellow in autumn; variegated forms available
Flower Purple to yellow flowerheads on upright, yellowish-purple shoots
Use In mixed borders or *en masse*; possibly does best as a woodland plant
Needs Propagate from seed in spring and varieties by division in spring. Grow new plants in containers before planting out
Varieties *M. caerulea* (purple moor grass) dense growth, mid-green foliage, purple at the base, narrow, purple flower spikes, turning yellow in autumn • *M. c.* ssp. *arundinacea* 'Karl Foerster' purple leaves, to 75cm (30in), arching seedheads • *M. c.* ssp. *a.* 'Sky Racer' green foliage turning bright yellow in autumn, to 2.2m (7ft) • *M. caerulea* ssp. *caerulea* 'Moorhexe' upright, dark purple flower spikes, to 50cm (20in) • *M. c.* ssp. *c.* 'Variegata' ♀ compact habit, cream-striped dark green foliage, purple-flowering shoots and flowers, to 60cm (2ft)

PHALARIS
Poaceae/Gramineae
RIBBON GRASS

▲ ❀ ❦ SI summer–autumn
H 2 yrs 0.6–2m (2–6ft)
S 2 yrs 0.6–1m (2–3ft)
❋ -18°C (0°F)
Z 3–10

**PHALARIS ARUNDINACEA VAR.
PICTA 'AUREOVARIEGATA'**

Care needs to be taken when planting these attractive grasses, because they can be invasive if they are planted in the wrong place.

Soil Alkaline to acid; does best in very moist ground but will tolerate drier conditions if necessary
Aspect Full sun to light shade
Habit Upright in spring and early summer, spreading, sometimes unattractively, towards autumn; fast spreading by underground shoots
Leaf Deciduous, grey-green, strap-shaped leaves, 30–50cm (12–20in) long and to 1cm (½in) wide in clumps and colonies; some forms with white-variegated leaves, others with pink bases to leaves
Flower Typical grass-type flowerheads, to 8cm (3in) long, on long wispy shoots, whitish-green in summer and retained into autumn
Use As foliage plant for large, mixed or perennial borders; planted in isolation, grouped or massed; good in association with water features; will tolerate growing in large containers
Needs Propagate by dividing clumps. Control growth by cutting back and removing plant material from the outer edges with a spade
Varieties *P. arundinacea* (reed canary grass, gardener's garter) grey-green leaves, to 2m (6ft) when in flower • *P. a.* var. *picta* 'Aureovariegata' white-variegated foliage, to 1m (3ft) • *P. a.* var. *p.* 'Feesey' bases of leaves flushed pink, to 1m (3ft)

SPARTINA PECTINATA 'AUREO-MARGINATA'
Poaceae/Gramineae
PRAIRIE CORD, FRESH-WATER CORD GRASS

▲ ❀ ❦ SI summer–autumn
E (semi)
H 2 yrs 60cm (2ft)
S 2 yrs 75cm (30in)
❊ -15°C (4°F) Z 3–9

A beautiful and bold golden-coloured grass to fill a specific planting role close to a slow-flowing stream or pond, but that is suitable only for those gardens where there is room for it to grow vigorously and spread beyond its original position. It is especially attractive when mass-planted and grown in association with *Iris sibirica* (Siberian iris).

Soil Tolerates acid to alkaline, wet to waterlogged soil, with a high organic content; resents any drying out
Aspect Full sun to very light shade; grows open and straggly in deeper shade
Habit Seedhead spikes erect, with 10–30 to each clump; foliage upright when young, becoming spreading outwards in midsummer
Leaf Spear-shaped, thin, grey-green leaves, with bold gold longitudinal stripes
Flower Upright, pale green, flat, grass-like flowers, ageing to yellow; followed by pale yellow grass seedheads
Use As marginal planting for wet areas such as streams and ponds where it has room to develop fully
Needs Propagate by division or from seed in spring
Varieties None

SPARTINA PECTINATA 'AUREOMARGINATA'

STIPA
Poaceae/Gramineae
FEATHER GRASS, NEEDLE GRASS, SPEAR GRASS, GIANT OAT

▲ ❀ ❦ SI summer–autumn
E
H 2 yrs 1–2.5m (3–8ft)
S 2 yrs 1–1.5m (3–5ft)
❊ -18°C (0°F)
Z 3–9

Wherever a striking feature plant is required, these elegant grasses can fill the role. The shape and colour are interesting, but the height is especially valuable because it adds an extra dimension to a planting without bulk. The tall seedhead stems turn golden-yellow in autumn, reflecting sunlight.

Soil Well-drained soils, high in organic material
Aspect Full sun to very light shade
Habit Upright; seedheads and stems spread gracefully in autumn; replaced each summer with a new crop
Leaf Evergreen, light grey-green, narrow, lance-shaped leaves, 1–1.4m (3ft–4ft 6in) long and 1cm (½in) wide; turning yellow in autumn; some forms with orange-brown shading
Flower Large, silver-green, wheat-like seedheads in large, loose panicles, 30cm (1ft) long, turning golden-yellow in autumn; some forms with coloured tints
Use As an individual feature plant; well-spaced in groups; as a seedhead for flower arranging
Needs Propagate by dividing clumps or from seed in spring
Varieties *S. arundinacea* (pheasant grass, New Zealand wind grass) dark-green leaves, streaked orange-brown, orange-brown in winter, hanging purplish seedheads, to 1m (3ft) • *S. calamagrostis* blue-green foliage, purple-tinted, broader seedheads in summer, to 1m (3ft) • *S. gigantea* (giant oat) ♀ the principal species, tall grey-green foliage, silver-green seedheads turning yellow-gold in autumn, to 2.5m (8ft) tall • *S. splendens* (chee grass) dark green foliage, purple green with white flecking to seedheads, to 2.5m (8ft)

STIPA GIGANTEA

ASPLENIUM SCOLOPENDRIUM
Aspleniaceae
HART'S TONGUE FERN

▲ ❦ SI all year E
H 2 yrs 50cm (20in)
S 2 yrs 60–75cm (24–30in)
❋ -15°C (4°F)
Z 9–10

ASPLENIUM SCOLOPENDRIUM

Its solid, non-indented fronds distinguish the hart's tongue fern from all other ferns. The glossy green, long, broad fronds point skywards from a central clump or rosette. Although its needs are specific if it is to do well, if you can provide the right conditions it will repay you with a fine display of foliage. In addition to the forms described, a number of variations in frond growth might be encountered.

Soil Alkaline to acid; does best on continuously moist soil but dislikes waterlogging
Aspect Prefers deep shade but tolerates sun as long as moisture is available
Habit Shuttlecock formation, with upright fronds becoming a little more spreading with age
Leaf Evergreen, glossy, mid-green, lance-shaped leaves, 40–53cm (16–21in) long and 5–6cm (2–2½in) wide, some twisted and wavy
Flower None of interest
Use For shady positions and woodland plantings; will grow in regularly watered containers; can be grown successfully indoors as well as out
Needs Propagate by division of established clumps in spring. remove dead or damaged leaves in spring and apply general fertilizer. Re-pot any that are grown in containers and are becoming pot-bound, using a good quality potting compost
Varieties *Asplenium scolopendrium* (syn. *Phyllitis scolopendrium*) ♀ the type species as described • *A. s.* Crispum Group twisted and wavy fronds

DRYOPTERIS
Dryopteridaceae
BUCKLER FERN, WOOD FERN, SHIELD FERN

▲ ❦ SI spring–summer
H 2 yrs *see below*
S 2 yrs *see below*
❋ -15°C (4°F)
Z 3–6

DRYOPTERIS FILIX-MAS 'CRISPA'

This is one of the most elegant of woodland plants, and it is found in a wide range of foliage forms. The planting site needs to be carefully selected, but it is otherwise trouble free.

Soil Acid or alkaline; requires soil that is high in organic material to ensure constant moisture without waterlogging
Aspect Shade
Habit Upright in spring, spreading outwards in summer
Leaf Mid-green fronds, indented as typical pinnate fern foliage; yellow-brown autumn colours
Flower Brown spores on undersides of leaves in late summer
Use For woodland or shady position; can be grown in large containers with some success
Needs Propagate by taking and sowing spores as they appear ripe, providing protection with bottom heat
Varieties *D. affinis* (golden male fern) ♀ semi-evergreen, lance-shaped, pale green with brown scaly midrib 1m (3ft) • *D. a.* 'Crispa Gracilis' low growing, fully evergreen, fronds congested and twisted at the ends, to 60cm (2ft) • *D. a.* 'Cristata The King' fronds arching and crested at the ends • *D. carthusiana* (narrow buckler fern) deciduous, narrow, pale green fronds, to 60cm (2ft) long • *D. c.* 'Cristata' crested form • *D. dilatata* (broad buckler fern) very broad tall fronds, to 1.5m (5ft) tall and 40cm (16in) wide, spread to 1.2m (4ft) • *D. filix-mas* (male fern) ♀ deciduous, attractive, mid-green, lance-shaped, fronds, to 1.2m (4ft) • *D. f.-m.* 'Crispa' crisped fronds, 50cm (20in) long • *D. f.-m.* 'Crispa Cristata' crested and twisted ends to fronds, to 60cm (2ft)

MATTEUCCIA STRUTHIOPTERIS
Dryopteridaceae
OSTRICH FERN,
SHUTTLECOCK FERN

▲ ❀ ❦ SI spring–autumn
H 2 yrs 0.6–1m (2–3ft)
S 2 yrs 0.6–1m (2–3ft)
❋ -15°C (4°F)
Z 3–8

The common names well describe the beautiful form and appearance of this fern, whose graceful, feather-like foliage emerges from a central crown. The mid-green colouring gives way to yellow-brown in autumn, and the spore spikes are also charming. If it is to be grown successfully, however, it must be provided with the correct conditions.

Soil Moderately alkaline to acid, deep, moisture-retentive, woodland-type soil; dislikes waterlogging and dryness, both of which will kill it
Aspect Light to deep shade; dislikes any sun
Habit Upright and graceful, like a shuttlecock
Leaf Deciduous, upright fronds, 0.75–1.2m (30–48in) long and 15–20cm (6–8in) wide
Flower Upright, bold, spear-like, brown spore heads produced from the centre of the plant in midsummer and retained into winter
Use In woodland and shady areas; attractive in association with water features
Needs Propagate by dividing established clumps in mid-autumn or early spring
Varieties None of garden interest

MATTEUCCIA STRUTHIOPTERIS

OSMUNDA REGALIS
Osmundaceae
ROYAL FERN,
FLOWERING FERN

▲ ❦ SI spring–autumn
H 2yrs 0.6–2m (2–6ft)
S 0.6–2m (2–6ft)
❋ -15°C (4°F)
Z 4–8

This elegant fern has giant, wand-like leaves that start as curled, unfolding, almost snake-like, brown leaf fronds in mid-spring. These turn mid-green in summer and in autumn sunlight look bronze-gold. All fronds emerge from a central crown, giving a fountain effect to the overall shape. In a well-thought-out planting, this is a jewel of a plant.

Soil Slightly alkaline to acid, deep, wet and boggy
Aspect Full sun to light shade
Habit Upright, majestic and elegant
Leaf Deciduous, large, green, broadly pinnate, multi-lobed fronds in summer, turning brown-gold in autumn
Flower Small brown spore cases, clustered together on attractive, upright, bold spikes in mid- to late summer, are retained in autumn
Use As an architectural plant if its size and need for water can be accommodated; good in association with water features
Needs Propagate by removing spores when spore cases open in green stage and sow within a few days; may produce side growth that can be removed with roots attached. Cover crowns with dead fronds throughout winter
Varieties *O. regalis* ♀ the main form planted • *O. r.* Cristata Group crested edges to fronds • *O. r.* 'Purpurascens' purple new fronds in spring • *O. r.* 'Undulata' wavy individual segments to each frond

OSMUNDA REGALIS

POLYPODIUM VULGARE
Polypodiaceae
COMMON POLPODY

▲ ❦ SI spring–summer E
some
H 2 yrs 60cm (2ft)
S 2 yrs 60cm (2ft)
H 5 yrs 75cm (30in)
S 5 yrs 1.2m (4ft)
❋ -15°C (4°F)
Z 5–10

POLYPODIUM VULGARE

There are about 75 ferns within the genus *Polypodium*, and most of them have thick, broad fern-like leaves. Most hardy polypodies come from North and Central America, although a few come from western Europe.

Soil Dry and well drained; polypodies can grow in small pockets of soil on banks and so forth; high levels of organic material in the soil will aid growth
Aspect Full sun to medium shade in a sheltered corner
Habit Creeping roots throw up leaf fronds in groups of, normally, 2 at each joint, forming an interlocking carpet of roots and foliage
Leaf Dark green, deciduous or evergreen, typical fern fronds, 60cm (2ft) long
Flower None; small, brown spore cases appear on underside of fronds in summer
Use As a foliage plant where dark green foliage and carpeting habit are needed
Needs Propagate by division. Remove old leaves as seen
Varieties *P. cambricum* (syn. *P. australe*; Welsh polypody, southern polypody) deciduous, lance-shaped, traditional dark-green fern fronds produced in late summer and dying in spring, yellow winter foliage • *P. c.* 'Cristatum' crested tips to edges of fronds • *P. glycyrrhiza* (liquorice fern) lance-shaped, mid-green fronds • *P. virginianum* (rock polypody, American wall fern) evergreen, lance-shaped, leathery fronds • *P. vulgare* (common polypody, adder's fern) evergreen, lance-shaped to oblong, dark green fronds

---

POLYSTICHUM
Dryopteridacae
HOLLY FERN,
SHIELD FERN

▲ ❦ SI all year E
H 2 yrs 75cm (30in)
S 2 yrs 1m (3ft)
❋ -15°C (4°F)
Z 3–8

POLYSTICHUM SETIFERUM

This is a most attractive group of ferns that have all the attributes expected from this category of plants. They need careful positioning within the garden and attention must be paid to the soil.

Soil Moist and high in organic material; dislikes high levels of alkalinity
Aspect Prefers shade but will tolerate some sun if moisture is present
Habit Upward-facing shuttlecocks of foliage, narrow at base, spreading at the top; ends of leaves droop
Leaf Mid- to dark green, feather-shaped leaves with deeply marked veins, to 1m (3ft) long and 30cm (1ft) wide; some forms have curled or plumed ends
Flower None of interest
Use For solo or group planting; will mix with other ferns but is perhaps best in isolation; ideal in a woodland setting
Needs Propagate by careful division of clumps in spring, making sure that there are roots on each division. Remove dead or very old leaves as seen
Varieties *P. aculeatum* (hard shield fern, prickly shield fern) ♀ leathery, dark green leaves, fronds wider than most ferns, spiny • *P. setiferum* (soft shield fern) ♀ soft, mid-green, lance- to feather-shaped fronds, each leaflet lobed and dissected • *P. s.* 'Plumosomultilobum' leaflets overlap, giving a thicker attractive appearance • *P. tsussimense* (Korean rock fern) lance-shaped leaves, oval, spiny pointed dark green leaflets

CORDYLINE
Agavaceae
CABBAGE TREE

▲ ❦ SI all year E
H 5 yrs 1m (3ft)
S 5 yrs 1m (3ft)
H 10 yrs 2m (6ft)
S 10 yrs 2m (6ft)
❄ -5°C (23°F)
Z 6–11

CORDYLINE AUSTRALIS

Lack of hardiness can be a problem with cordylines. In protected, coastal areas they will probably survive unscathed through the winter, but inland and in exposed areas they will need protection. One solution is to grow cordylines in containers so that they can be taken under cover in winter.

Soil Tolerates well-drained and dry soils; when grown in containers, attention must be given to watering because waterlogging at the roots can kill
Aspect Full sun to very light shade; in a sheltered area or under protection away from the coast and warmer areas
Habit Upright; leaves bend outwards with age
Leaf Evergreen, dark to greyish-green, sword-like leaves, 1m (3ft) or more long; some purple and variegated varieties
Flower Creamy-white, small, fragrant flowers borne in clusters on mature plants only
Use As a specimen or feature plant in the garden; good in containers
Needs Propagate from seed. Remove dead outer leaves as seen; leaves are pointed so take care when handling. Consider protection in winter
Varieties *C. australis* (New Zealand cabbage tree) ♀ green leaves • *C. a.* 'Albertii' ♀ yellow stripes and red midrib on grey-green background • *C. a.* 'Atropurpurea' purple leaves • *C. a.* 'Torbay Dazzler' cream stripes on green background • *C. a.* 'Variegata' creamy-white stripes

TRACHYCARPUS FORTUNEI
Arecaceae/Palmae
FAN PALM, CHUSAN PALM

▲ ❦ SI all year E
H 5 yrs 1.5m (5ft)
S 2 yrs 1.5m (8ft)
H 10 yrs 3m (10ft)
S 5 yrs 2m (6ft)
❄ -15°C (4°F)
Z 6–11

TRACHYCARPUS FORTUNEI

This is a giant among hardy palms that after about 50 years can reach the proportions of a tree but without the branch framework. It is just a little susceptible to winter cold, particularly until it grows to more than about 1m (3ft). However, it is often seen in some unexpected places where it has survived for many winters.

Soil Dry and well drained; high levels of organic material in the soil will aid establishment
Aspect Full sun to medium shade in a sheltered corner out of cold winds
Habit Very upright with a medium growth rate; lower leaves drop away over the years to reveal a straight, not unattractive, grey stem, topped with large foliage
Leaf Evergreen, dark green, palm-like fronds, to 1m (3ft) wide and deep, with dull grey reverse; growing as large fans reaching for light in all directions
Flower Mature plants bear pendent chains of small, yellow flowers but only following hot summer sunshine; bears fruit but not reliably
Use As a foliage plant for the dark green foliage and architectural effect
Needs Propagate from seed sown in autumn under protection and with the aid of a heated propagator or purchase new plants in spring, after winter cold has finished, and the new plant has time to establish. Remove old leaves as seen
Varieties *T. fortunei* ♀ the type species as described • *T. f.* 'Nanus' smaller foliage, shorter

ARUNDINARIA
**Poaceae-Bambusoideae
/Gramineae**
BAMBOO, JAPANESE
BAMBOO

▲ ❦ SI all year E
H 5 yrs 2m (6ft)
S 5 yrs 1m (3ft)
H 10 yrs 2.5m (8ft)
S 10 yrs 2m (6ft)
✻ -15°C (4°F)
Z 6–10

ARUNDINARIA MURIELIAE

Bamboos always attract interest in the garden. They are versatile and can be used as screens or windbreaks. If you have a smaller garden, look for some of the lower-growing, more controllable varieties. These bamboos are sometimes included in the genera *Pleioblastus, Pseudosasa* and *Fargesia*.

Soil Good, moist and well drained; resents dry and severely alkaline soil
Aspect Light to quite deep shade
Habit Upright, shoots branching from base, fast growing
Leaf Evergreen, glossy, dark green leaves, 17–20cm (7–8in) long and 2.5–5cm (1–2in) wide, with grey undersides
Flower Large, open, fluffy plumes of sulphur yellow flowers in very hot summers; the appearance of flowers may indicate the imminent death of the plant, however
Use As an individual or feature plant; good for screening; particularly good near water; can be grown in large containers but purchase large plants as they do not increase in size in such conditions
Needs Propagate by dividing mature clumps. No pruning
Varieties *A. humilis* (syn. *Pleioblastus humilis*) narrow, light green • *A. murieliae* (syn. *Fargesia murieliae*) mid-green • *A. nitida* (syn. *Fargesia nitida*) mid-green, dark purple stems • *A. pumila* (syn. *Pleioblastus humilis* var. *pumilus*) dwarf species, bright glossy green, to 75cm (30in) • *P. pygmaea* (syn. *Pleioblastus pygmaeus*) very dwarf variety, to no more than 25cm (10in) slightly glaucous leaves

---

CHUSQUEA
CULEOU ♛
**Poaceae-Bambusoideae
/Gramineae**
CHILEAN BAMBOO

▲ ❦ SI all year E
H 5 yrs 2m (6ft)
S 5 yrs 2m (6ft)
H 10 yrs 4m (13ft)
S 10 yrs 3m (10m)
✻ -15 (4°F) Z 6–10

CHUSQUEA CULEOU

The light green foliage of this fascinating bamboo is carried in regularly spaced whorls around the central bamboo cane, in a manner quite unlike that of most other plants of its size. It may be difficult to obtain, but where the right conditions can be provided it is worth making an effort to track down.

Soil Acid to neutral, moist soil; dislikes alkalinity mainly because this type of soil dries out too much; it is important to add large quantities of organic material to the soil at planting time and around the plant each spring as a mulch
Aspect Prefers light shade but will tolerate slightly more shade and a little sun
Habit Upright when young, becoming more spreading after 5–6 years
Leaf Evergreen, light green, narrow, lance-shaped leaves, produced in whorls at regular intervals up the bamboo canes, giving the plant a striking appearance
Flower May produce feather-like, off-white to cream flowers in clusters at the ends of the canes; these may signal the imminent death of the plant, and if so, there is little that can be done beyond identifying a non-flowering shoot and attempting to remove it from the parent plant and grow a new one
Use As a free-standing, specimen plant; looks good in association with water
Needs Propagate by division in spring. Tidy as required
Varieties None

PLEIOBLASTUS
Poaceae-Bambusoideae /Gramineae
VARIEGATED BAMBOO

▲ ❦ SI all year E
H 5 yrs 75cm (30in)
S 5 yrs 1m (3ft)
H 10 yrs 1–1.5m (3–5ft)
S 10 yrs 2m (6ft)
❊ -15°C (4°F)
Z 6–10

PLEIOBLASTUS AURICOMUS

Here is a group of foliage plants for all year round. Some forms have gold or white variegation. They are ideal for large-scale ground cover or spot planting, and they can also be grown in containers for limited periods. They are especially attractive when planted close to water features, although in ideal conditions they become invasive.

Soil Good, moist but well drained; resents very dry and severely alkaline soil
Aspect Light to quite deep shade, although may become more open and straggly in deep shade
Habit Low growing and carpeting; medium growth rate; spreads by underground shoots
Leaf Attractive evergreen, mid-green, leaves striped gold or white on a grey-green background, 13–17cm (5–7in) long
Flower Not grown for its flowers; if it does flower cut to ground level at once or it may die
Use For mass-planting; good near water features and for naturalizing; can be grown in containers in the short term
Needs Propagate by dividing mature clumps in spring. If looking shabby, cut down to ground level in early spring; it will grow a new crop of attractive foliage
Varieties *Pleioblastus auricomus* (syn. *Arundinaria auricoma, Arundinaria viridistriata*; kamuro-zasa) very attractive golden-yellow striped foliage, low growing, carpet-forming • *Pleioblastus variegatus* (syn. *Arundinaria variegata*; dwarf white-striped bamboo, chigo-zasa) white-striped variegation, to 1.2m (4ft)

SASA VEITCHII
Poaceae-Bambusoideae /Gramineae
BAMBOO

▲ ❦ SI all year E
H 5 yrs 1m (3ft)
S 5 yrs 1m (3ft)
H 10 yrs 1.2m (4ft)
S 10 yrs 3m (10ft) min
❊ -18°C (0°F)
Z 6–10

SASA VEITCHII

Formerly known as *Arundinaria veitchii*, this is a useful plant for colonizing very large areas of moist ground, for it is able to spread over many square metres. In gardens where limited room is available it can become invasive.

Soil Moist and high in organic material
Aspect Prefers light to moderate shade; will tolerate full sun as long as moisture is present in the soil to sustain the size of the leaves
Habit Upright stems; fast rate of growth, spreading by underground shoots, sometimes invasively
Leaf Large, dark green leaves, to 25cm (10in) long, each with an attractive white dead margin around the edges in autumn and winter
Flower None; flowering is rare and can lead to death of plant
Use For large-scale ground cover in large, moist, shady areas
Needs Propagate by division in spring. Remove dead shoots when no longer attractive
Varieties None

ALLIUM
Alliaceae/Liliaceae
FLOWERING ONIONS

▲ ❀ SI spring–summer
H 1 yr *see below*
S 1 yr 20 per cent of height
shown
❄ -18°C (0°F)
Z 4–10

ALLIUM CHRISTOPHII

Some onions are grown specifically for their flowers and the range is as varied as with any other bulb.

Soil Alkaline to acid, well prepared and with good drainage
Aspect Full sun to partial shade
Habit Upright
Leaf Deciduous, grey-green, lance- or strap-shaped leaves, 10–30cm (4–12in) long; onion-scented when crushed
Flower Star-shaped flowers in shades of white, pink, yellow or purple; in some varieties the flowers form ball-shapes, 15cm (6in) across, on stems to 1m (3ft); other varieties have small, open flowers on short stems
Use In rock gardens; in mixed planting schemes; in containers
Needs Propagate by dividing established clumps in autumn after foliage as died. Purchase new bulbs in autumn or spring and plant at a depth twice the bulbs' length
Varieties *A. beesianum* ♀ ball-shaped blue or white flowers, to 20cm (8in) • *A. caeruleum* ♀ ball-shaped, light blue flowers, to 60cm (2ft) • *A. christophii* ♀ (syn. *A. albopilosum*; star of Persia) ♀ large, purple, ball-shaped flowers with metallic sheen, attractive seedheads, to 50cm (20in) • *A.* 'Globemaster' giant, ball-shaped flowers, 20cm (8in) across, to 1m (3ft) tall • *A. h.* 'Purple Sensation' ♀ deep purple, ball-shaped flowers, to 1.2m (4ft) • *A. karataviense* ♀ metallic sheen to leaves, lilac-tinged white flowers, to 30cm (1ft) • *A. moly* ♀ small, star-shaped, open, yellow flowers, to 20cm (8in) tall • *A. sphaerocephalon* purple-lilac, oval flowers, to 50–75cm (20–30in)

AMARYLLIS BELLADONNA
Amaryllidaceae/ Liliaceae
BELLADONNA LILY, JERSEY LILY

▲ ❀ ❦ SI autumn
H 1 yr 75cm (30in)
S 1 yr 30cm (1ft)
❄ -10°C (14°F)
Z 5–10

AMARYLLIS BELLADONNA

One of the most magnificent of autumn-flowering bulbs, its giant tubular flowers are presented at the top of a strong flower stalk before the leaves appear. A native of South Africa, this lily requires the warmth of a wall if it is to flower. Without this additional warmth, the bulbs do not ripen enough to trigger the formation of the flower buds. One word of caution: the plant is poisonous.

Soil Well drained
Aspect Warm, sheltered and sunny
Habit Upright, with leaves appearing after flowering
Leaf Deciduous, lance-shaped, dark green leaves, 50cm (20in) long and 2.5cm (1in) wide
Flower 2, sometimes 3, large, tubular flowers, each up to 20cm (8in) long, off-white at the base and pink and purple at the mouth, are produced in autumn
Use As an autumn-flowering bulb; best planted in groups in front of a wall
Needs Propagate by division of the bulb clump on established plants after flowering. Purchase new bulbs in autumn; plant so that the necks of the bulbs are just below surface of soil
Varieties *A. belladonna* the type species as described above • *A. b.* 'Hathor' pink buds opening to white

ANEMONE
Ranunculaceae
ANEMONE,
WINDFLOWER

▲ ❀ ❦ SI spring SC E
H 1 yr 15–120cm (6–48in)
S 10 60cm (2ft)
❊ -18°C (0°F)
Z 3–7

ANEMONE BLANDA

This large group of flowering corms offers a wide range of interest in spring. Their foliage is shown as evergreen because it is produced in winter and dies off in early summer, to reappear the following winter.

Soil Acid to alkaline; resents excessively wet or dry soils
Aspect Full sun to light shade
Habit Basal leaves, surmounted by flowers, appear in spring
Leaf Evergreen, glossy, dark green or grey-green, trifoliate leaves, 5–13cm (2–5in) long and 8–9cm (3–3½in) wide
Flower Single or semi-double, daisy-shaped flowers, 5–6cm (2–2½in) across, in loose clusters in white or shades of red, purple, blue or pink
Use In woodland areas, rock gardens, wild gardens and containers; ideal for naturalizing; some varieties good as cut flowers
Needs Propagate by dividing established clumps of corms or purchase new ones in spring or autumn; soak newly purchased corms in water for 36 hours before planting. Protect from rodent attack
Varieties *A. blanda* single, mid-blue flowers • *A. b.* 'Blue Pearl' single, blue flowers • *A. b.* 'Radar' ♀ single, red flowers with white eye • *A. b.* 'White Splendour' ♀ single, large, pure white flowers • *A. coronaria* collectively named De Caen Hybrids single, mixed or in single colours, good as cut flowers • *A. c.* St Brigid Group double, mixed or single colours, good as cut flowers

---

BEGONIA
Begoniaceae
TUBEROUS BEGONIA

▲ ❀ ❦ SI summer
H 1 yr 23–30cm (9–12in)
S 30–50cm (12–20in)
❊ Not winter hardy
Z 2–10

BEGONIA × CARRIEREI

The startling colours of tuberous begonias will set the summer garden alight.

Soil Moderately alkaline to acid; soil must be well prepared, deep and moist but not waterlogged; use a peat-based compost for containers
Aspect Full sun to light shade
Habit Bushy annual growth
Leaf Deciduous, fleshy, glossy, dark or bright green, heart-shaped or round leaves, 5–13cm (2–5in) long and wide, wine-red or purple flushed
Flower Rounded petals form double or wing-shaped flowers, in colours from white, through pink and orange to red, with some bicoloured varieties
Use For mass-planting in the border; good in containers
Needs Propagate from seed or purchase new corms in spring and plant just at soil level. Remove dead flowers as seen. Lift corms and dry off before autumn frosts and store in a dry, frost-free place until spring. Buy *B. × carrierei* as ready-grown bedding plants when fear of spring frosts has passed
Varieties *B. × carrierei* (syn. *B. semperflorens*) bedding begonias • *B. × c.* 'Amber Scarlet' dark purple-red foliage, red flowers • *B. × c.* 'Aristo Mixed' mixed flower and leaf colours • *B. × c.* 'Linda' green foliage, rose-pink flowers tinged salmon pink • *B. × c.* 'Scarletta' green-bronze foliage, deep scarlet flowers • *B.* Tuberhybrida Hybrids (syn. *B. × multiflora* 'Non Stop' varieties) double flowers in various colours

CAMASSIA
**Hyacinthaceae/
Liliaceae**
QUAMASH, CAMASS,
CAMOSH

▲ ✿ ❦ SI summer
H 1 yr 1–1.2m (3–4ft)
S 23–30cm (9–12in)
✽ -15°C (4°F)
Z 3–9

CAMASSIA CUSICKII

This interesting group of early summer-flowering bulbs
deserves to be more widely planted in gardens of all sizes.
The erect flower spikes appear when most other spring bulbs
have finished, and the neat clumps of basal leaves make them
an important permanent feature of any planting scheme.

Soil Moderately alkaline to acid; deep, moist but well drained
Aspect Full sun to light shade
Habit Upright, clump-forming
Leaf Deciduous, glossy, mid- to dark green, strap-shaped
leaves, 30cm (1ft) long and 2.5–3cm (1–1¼in) wide
Flower Long, strap-like petals form open, star-shaped
flowers on tall spikes to 50cm (20in) long
Use As mid- to background planting in mixed or perennial
borders; as individual specimen planting; can be grown in
large containers to good effect
Needs Propagate by dividing established bulb clumps; do
this every 5–10 years in autumn to improve vigour and
numbers and size of flowers; cut all remaining growth to
ground level in autumn. Purchase new bulbs in autumn and
plant to twice depth of bulb. Alternatively, purchase pre-
grown plants in flower
Varieties *C. cusickii* leaves with wavy edges, deep blue
flowers • *C. leichtlinii* ♀ mauve-purple flowers • *C. l.*
'Semiplena' creamy-white flowers • *C. quamash* (syn.
C. esculenta) bright blue flowers, may be less hardy •
C. scilloides (syn. *C. fraseri*) violet-purple flowers, may
be less hardy

CANNA
Cannaceae
INDIAN LILY

▲ ✿ ❦ SI summer
H 1 yr 1.2m (4ft)
S 1 yr 60cm (2ft)
✽ Not winter hardy
Z 7–10

CANNA INDICA

This exotic-looking, tuberous plant is best used in any garden
where there is the slightest risk of frost as a tall spot bedding
plant or grown in a container, when it can easily be provided
with protection in winter. In summer the containers can, if
needed, be plunged into the garden soil to hide them in a
border, but if you do this, take extra care with watering.

Soil Well drained and high in organic material; use a good
quality compost in containers
Aspect Full sun
Habit Very upright
Leaf Large, green or purple, spear-shaped leaves, 50cm
(20in) long and 25cm (10in) wide, growing from the central
flower stalk
Flower Tubular flowers, with widely reflexed open ends,
grouped in clusters at the tops of the flower stalks, in a wide
range of colours, including bicolours
Use As a seasonal bedding plant to give height in the
garden or in containers; can be grown in greenhouses or
conservatories
Needs Winter protection. In exposed gardens support for
wind protection. Best purchased in spring and grown on in
pots under protection until all fear of frost has passed
Varieties Although there are named varieties, these are hard
to find and the plant is normally sold by illustrated colour
choice in early to mid-spring

CHIONODOXA
Hyacinthaceae/ Liliaceae
CHIONODOXA, GLORY OF THE SNOW

▲ ❀ ❦ SI spring
H 1 yr 13cm (5in)
S 13cm (5in)
❀ -15°C (4°F)
Z 3–9

CHIONODOXA FORBESII

A charming group of small, low-growing bulbs, many with an intensity of flower colour far beyond their size. They are ideal for planting in so many places within the garden, so it is surprising they are not more widely grown.

Soil Any as long as it is well drained
Aspect Full sun to light shade
Habit Small; flowers emerge at the same time as the leaves
Leaf Deciduous, dark green and very narrow, to 10–30cm (4–12in) long; erect at first, then spreading
Flower Small clusters of blue or pink star-shaped flowers in early spring, borne on stalks 10–20cm (4–8in) tall
Use For naturalizing in borders or at the base of trees; good in containers of all sizes; can be grown as a house plant in the short term
Needs Purchase new bulbs in autumn and plant at a depth twice their own length. Use good compost in containers
Varieties *C. forbesii* (syn. *C. luciliae*) blue flowers with white centres • *C. f.* 'Pink Giant' pink flowers with white centres • *C. luciliae* Gigantea Group (syn. *C. gigantea*) ♀ blue flowers with white centres, a slightly taller form • *C. nana* (syn. *C. cretica*) blue flowers with white centres, a slightly shorter form • *C. sardensis* ♀ deep blue flowers with blue centres

COLCHICUM
Colchicaceae/Liliaceae
AUTUMN CROCUS

▲ ❀ ❦ SI autumn
H 1 yr 15–25cm (6–10in)
S 25cm (10cm)
❀ -18°C (0°F)
Z 4–10

COLCHICUM AUTUMNALE

One of the stars of the late autumn garden, the foliage-free flowerheads seem to appear out of nowhere. The leaves follow later and stay through winter, dying down in late spring. Beware: all parts of the plant are poisonous if eaten.

Soil Alkaline to acid, light and well drained
Aspect Full sun to light shade
Habit Upright flowers appear before the leaves and are, sadly, often bent over in rain and wind. Supporting with small twigs may help. A layer of gravel over the soil surface helps the flowers to stay clean in bad weather
Leaf Deciduous, glossy, lance-shaped leaves, 20–40cm (8–16in) long and 5–6cm (2–2½in) wide
Flower Single or double, goblet-shaped flowers, 8–10cm (3–4in) long, reflexing when open to form a star-shape, in colours ranging from pure white to pink, blue and purple
Use For edging borders; in rock gardens; to grow through carpeting plants; good in containers; can be brought to flower on a window-sill without soil
Needs Propagate in spring by dividing corm clumps or from seed. Purchase new bulbs in autumn and plant just below the surface of the soil
Varieties *C.* 'Autumn Queen' ♀ white flowers overlaid with deep purple • *C. autumnale* (meadow saffron) purple, pink or white flowers • *C.* 'Lilac Wonder' amethyst blue flowers • *C. speciosum* purple flowers • *C. s.* 'Album' pure white flowers • *C.* 'Violet Queen' deep purple flowers • *C.* 'Water-lily' double, purple flowers

CONVALLARIA MAJALIS
Convallariaceae/ Liliaceae
LILY-OF-THE-VALLEY

▲ ❀ ❧ SI spring SC
H 1 yr 15cm (6in)
S 40–50cm (16–20in)
❋ -18°C (0°F)
Z 3–7

If only for the sake of the scent, this plant with its tuberous roots, which are called 'pips', is a must for every garden; it will grow in the smallest, darkest place. The attractive green leaves come first, then through them appear the clusters of small, scented flowers.

Soil Moderately alkaline to acid, moisture retentive but not waterlogged
Aspect Light to moderate shade
Habit Upright flowers and foliage; can be invasive if not contained
Leaf Deciduous, pointed oval leaves, 15–20cm (6–8in) long and 5–8cm (2–3in) wide, light green with darker linear veining and slightly curled
Flower Small bell-shaped, white or pink, highly scented flowers formed from 5 petals; 15 or more hang from slender upright stem
Use Best grown in isolation in shaded border; can be grown in large containers or annually planted in hanging baskets
Needs Propagate by dividing established clumps in autumn or spring. Purchase in early spring as 'pips' or pot-grown all year, including when in flower
Varieties *C. majalis* white flowers, the main form grown • *C. m.* var. *rosea* mother-of-pearl pink flowers, less vigorous in growth

CONVALLARIA MAJALIS

CRINUM × POWELLII
Amaryllidaceae/ Liliaceae
ELEPHANT LILY

▲ ❀ ❧ SI summer
H 1 yr 1m (3ft)
S 1m (3ft)
❋ -15°C (4°F)
Z 3–9

This giant of a plant can have bulbs over 50cm (20in) long, so a good, well-prepared soil is important. The lily-like summer flowers are valuable at a time when many other bulbs have finished flowering. The pink-flowering forms are very attractive, but even better are those with white flowers, although the bulbs may be difficult to find. Both the pink- and white-flowering types need plenty of room if they are to do well.

Soil Any deep, well-prepared soil
Aspect Full sun to very light shade or it may not flower
Habit Clump-forming, fast to grow once established
Leaf Deciduous, mid- to dark green, sword-shaped leaves, to 1m (3ft) long and 8cm (3in) wide, upright when young, bending downwards for about half their length at about flowering time
Flower Large pink or white trumpet-shaped, open-mouthed flowers borne in summer at the tops of stiff upright flower stalks; up to 10 buds to each stalk, opening in turn
Use As a specimen plant; normally grown in isolation to show off to full effect
Needs Propagate by lifting bulbs in early spring (which can be difficult as they are so large). Purchase new bulbs in early spring. Plant with top of bulb just below soil level. Pre-grown plants in pots may be available in summer
Varieties *C. × powellii* ♀ pink flowers • *C. × p.* 'Album' white flowers

CRINUM × POWELLII

CROCUS
Iridaceae
CROCUS

▲ ❀ 🐝 SI spring
H 1 yr 5–10cm (2–4in)
S 10–13cm (4–5in)
✳ -18°C (0°F)
Z 3–10

**CROCUS TOMMASINIANUS
'WHITEWELL PURPLE'**

Said by many to be the herald of spring, there are dozens of varieties to choose from, with a wide range of colours.

Soil Alkaline to acid, well fed, well prepared, well drained; dislikes waterlogging
Aspect Full sun to light or deep shade, according to variety
Habit Upright
Leaf Deciduous, very narrow, grass-like, dark green leaves, some with silver veining
Flower Goblet- to bowl-shaped flowers in colours from white to yellow, mauve, blue and purple, some striped varieties
Use For rock gardens; good in containers outside and indoors; will naturalize, often increasing by self-sown seed
Needs Allow leaves to die down naturally. Propagate by dividing established corm clumps in autumn. Buy corms in autumn and plant to a depth of twice the corms' length
Varieties <u>Early-flowering</u>: *C. chrysanthus* 'Blue Pearl' ♀ light blue flowers • *C. c.* 'Cream Beauty' ♀ creamy-white flowers • *C. c.* 'E. A. Bowles' ♀ deep yellow flowers • *C. c.* 'Snow Bunting' ♀ white and cream flowers, lilac feathering in bud • *C. c.* 'Zwanenburg Bronze' ♀ golden-yellow flowers, edged with bronze • *C. tommasinianus* 'Ruby' ♀ deep violet flowers • *C. t.* 'Whitewell Purple' purple flowers <u>Large-flowering hybrids (Dutch crocus)</u>: *C.* 'Golden Mammoth' golden-yellow flowers • *C. vernus* 'Flower Record' pale violet flowers • *C. v.* 'Jeanne d'Arc' white flowers with purple base • *C. v.* 'Pickwick' purple and white striped flowers • *C. v.* 'Queen of the Blues' lilac-blue flowers

CYCLAMEN
Primulaceae
HARDY CYCLAMEN

▲ ❀ 🐝 SI winter–spring E some
H 1 yr 15cm (6in)
S 30cm (1ft)
✳ -10°C (14°F)
Z 5–9

CYCLAMEN HEDERIFOLIUM

These fairies of the plant world have the daintiest of flowers standing above the attractive foliage. There are many varieties but some are more reliable and easier to grow than others. All require care with planting, especially with the choice of planting site and the preparation of the soil.

Soil Acid to neutral; soil must have a high organic content, including large amounts of leaf mould
Aspect Light to medium shade
Habit Spreading and forming low clumps
Leaf Wintergreen, deciduous in summer, dark green, rounded leaves, 5–6cm (2–2½in) long and wide, sometimes with silvery veins
Flower Shuttlecock-shaped flowers, 2cm (¾in) long and wide, with 5 oval petals, appear in autumn or early spring
Use In shady woodland sites or rock gardens; can be grown in containers as alpine pots outdoors or indoors; as pot plants or part of a collection
Needs Propagate from seed in spring. Purchase corms in autumn or spring, plant just on or below the soil surface. For best results, purchase pre-grown plants in pots
Species *C. cilicium* ♀ deciduous, strong leaf colour, pink or white flowers in autumn • *C. coum* ♀ magenta, pink or white flowers in winter and spring • *C. hederifolium* (syn. *C. neapolitanum*) pink and white flowers in autumn

DAHLIA
Asteraceae/Compositae
DAHLIA

▲ ❀ ❦ SI summer–autumn
H 1 yr 1m (3ft)
S same as heights
❅ Not winter hardy
Z 9–10

DAHLIA 'MAJESTIC KERKRADE'

These well-known plants are found in a range of colours and flower shapes. They are grown as an annuals.

Soil Most provided the soil is well prepared and well fed, containing high levels of organic material
Aspect Full sun
Habit Bushy and clump-forming
Leaf Deciduous, mid- to dark green, large, hand-shaped leaves
Flower Double, large or small flowers, some reflexed, others incurved or with petals in balls, in many different colours, appearing in late summer to autumn
Use For spot planting or growing *en masse*; an enthusiast's plant for collecting; a good cut flower
Needs Best to purchase new tubers or young plants each spring. Tubers can be lifted and stored in a frost-free place over winter. Propagate from new shoots appearing on tubers saved from previous year's plantings
Varieties <u>Cactus-flowered</u>: *D.* 'Apple Blossom' pale pink flowers • *D.* 'Autumn Fire' orange-red flowers • *D.* 'Majestic Kerkrade' pink flowers with orange centre • *D.* 'Purple Gem' purple flowers • *D.* 'White Kerkrade' white flowers <u>Decorative-flowered</u>: *D.* 'Arabian Nights' maroon flowers • *D.* 'Diamond' orange flowers • *D.* 'Edinburgh' purple flowers with white tips • *D.* 'Golden Emblem' golden-yellow flowers • *D.* 'Lavender Perfection' lavender flowers <u>Pompon-flowered</u>: *D.* 'Brilliant Eye' red flowers • *D.* 'Pot-gieter' yellow flowers • *D.* 'Willo's Violet' white-violet flowers

ERANTHIS
Ranunculaceae
WINTER ACONITE

▲ ❀ ❦ SI spring
H 1 yr 10–15cm (4–6in)
S 1 yr 15–20cm (6–8in)
❅ -18°C (0°F)
Z 4–9

ERANTHIS HYEMALIS

This is one of the oldest known plants, existing at the same time as, or even before, dinosaurs. The bright yellow flowers are, in fact, formed from sepals, not petals, and its close relatives are clematis and buttercups. This is a 'must' for anywhere that needs an early-flowering, low-growing plant, and, left undisturbed, it will thrive in deep shade.

Soil Alkaline or acid
Aspect Full sun to shade
Habit Small, upright flower stalks appear in late winter with a ring of leaves surmounted by a single flower bud; soon after flowering the plant turns yellow and dies away
Leaf Deciduous, glossy yellow to deep green, umbrella-shaped leaves, 8cm (3in) wide, divided into narrow segments; 2 only to each flower stalk
Flower Cup-shaped flowers, 3.5cm (1¼in) across, formed from 6 almost round petals in shades of yellow
Use Ideal for naturalizing in woodland gardens or rock gardens; will grow in containers
Needs Propagate from seed or divide mature tuber clumps in early to late autumn; can be dug up and moved just as the flowers are dying in spring; soak tubers in water for at least 36 hours before planting and plant at twice their own depth or they will fail. Protect from rodents
Varieties *E. hyemalis* ♀ the main form planted, bright lemon-yellow flowers • *E. h.* Cilicica Group similar to type species but with bronze leaves • *E. h.* Tubergenii Group golden-yellow flowers

ERYTHRONIUM
Liliaceae/Liliaceae
DOG'S TOOTH VIOLET,
ADDER'S TONGUE

▲ ❀ ✾ SI spring
H 1 yr 15cm (6in)
S 23–30cm (9–12in)
❄ -5°C (23°F)
Z 3–9

It is almost impossible to describe the beauty of these
charming flowers, which stand proudly above the attractive
foliage. Unfortunately, however, they have specific cultural
requirements, which must be met if they are to bear flowers.

Soil Moderately alkaline to acid; well-drained and open but
moisture-retentive soil that is high in organic material,
especially leaf mould
Aspect Light shade; sheltered from cold winds
Habit Flat, spreading, basal leaves; upright flower stalks
Leaf Attractive, deciduous, purple-green, narrowly oval,
tapering leaves 8cm (3in) long and 2cm (⅜in) wide, with white
marbling
Flower Star-shaped flowers, 5cm (2in) across, hanging from
graceful stems; white to pale pink with red markings at petal
bases or all yellow
Use For rock gardens or inter-planting in woodland areas;
good in containers
Needs Propagate by removing small offsets in early spring;
collect and sow seed; avoid purchasing pre-packed tubers in
favour of pre-grown plants
Varieties *E. californicum* 'White Beauty' ♀ cream flowers
with darker centre • *E. dens-canis* ♀ purple-mauve flowers,
possibly the easiest and best to grow • *E. hendersonii* purple
to light mauve flowers • *E.* 'Pagoda' ♀ yellow flowers, a
taller form

ERYTHRONIUM DENS-CANIS

FRITILLARIA
Liliaceae/Liliaceae
FRITILLARY

▲ ❀ ✾ SI spring
H 1 yr 0.3–1.2m (1–4ft)
S 10cm–1m (4–36in)
❄ -10°C (14°F)
Z 3–10

Two distinct species are commonly grown: the tall, elegant
Fritillaria imperialis (crown imperial) and the smaller
Fritillaria meleagris (snake's head fritillary). Both types are
of true garden value and each performs a different role.

Soil Alkaline to neutral, light and well drained
Aspect Full sun to light shade
Habit Upright
Leaf *F. imperialis*: light green, wide, strap-like leaves, to
25cm (10in) long, from the upright flower spike, pendulous in
habit; *F. meleagris*: light to olive green, strap-shaped or
lance-shaped leaves, from 8–20cm (3–8in) long and 5–25mm
(¼–1in) wide, from leaf stalk and bulb
Flower *F. imperialis*: bell-shaped flowers, hanging from the
crown of tall spikes in yellow, orange or red; *F. meleagris*:
hanging monk's cap flowers in shades of purple or white
Use *F. imperialis*: for large-scale or spot planting; isolated or
in groups; will grow in containers; *F. meleagris*: for rock
gardens; as naturalized feature planting; in containers
Needs Allow foliage to die down naturally. Propagate from
offsets or bulblets in summer. Purchase new bulbs in autumn
and plant bulbs to a depth twice their own length
Varieties *F. imperialis* (crown imperial) orange flowers •
F. i. 'Aurora' orange-red flowers • *F. i.* 'Maxima Lutea'
yellow flowers • *F. i.* 'Rubra Maxima' deep red flowers •
F. meleagris (snake's head fritillary, chequered lily) ♀
mottled silver over shades of purple with snakeskin effect •
F. m. var. *alba* ♀ white flowers

**FRITILLARIA IMPERIALIS
'LUTEA MAXIMA'**

GALANTHUS
Amaryllidaceae/ Liliaceae
SNOWDROP

▲ ❀ ☙ SI spring
H 1 yr 10–15cm (4–6in)
S 23–30cm (9–12in)
❊ -15°C (4°F)
Z 3–9

GALANTHUS NIVALIS

Still one of the favourite spring-flowering bulbs and rightly so. Few other spring plants signal the end of winter and the beginning of spring as emphatically as snowdrops. They are usually naturalized in borders and around trees.

Soil Alkaline or acid, moisture retentive
Aspect No preference
Habit Upright
Leaf Deciduous, strap-shaped, grey-green leaves, 20–23cm (8–9in) long and 3–5mm (⅛–¼in) wide
Flower Bell-shaped, pendant flowers in shades of white, formed from 3 large and 3 small petals in early spring; some double forms
Use For the rock garden; grouped in beds or naturalized in wild gardens; grown in containers both indoors and out
Needs Propagate by dividing established bulb clumps when foliage has died down; alternatively, just as flowers have died, lift bulbs and foliage and divide and replant (planting in the green). Sometimes snowdrops are offered for sale for planting in the green. Bulbs bought in autumn should be planted to a depth twice the bulbs' length. Pre-grown plants in pots available in spring when in flower
Varieties *G.* 'Atkinsii' ♀ double, white flowers, to 20cm (8in) high • *G. elwesii* ♀ white flowers with large green markings • *G.* 'Lady Beatrix Stanley' double, white flowers, to 13cm (5in) high • *G. nivalis* (common snowdrop) ♀ white flowers with green markings • *G. n.* 'Flore Pleno' ♀ double, white flowers

GALTONIA CANDICANS
Hyacinthaceae/ Liliaceae
SUMMER HYACINTH

▲ ❀ ☙ SI late summer SC
H 1 yr 0.6–1m (2–3ft)
S 1 yr 20–30cm (8–12in)
❊ -15°C (4°F)
Z 5–10

GALTONIA CANDICANS

One of the most underrated of late-summer-flowering bulbs and not widely planted, probably because the individual bulbs appear expensive. However, when you consider the flowers and the scent, they are seen to be good value. Plant them in groups of three or more to create the greatest impact.

Soil Alkaline to acid, moist but well drained; dislikes waterlogging
Aspect Full sun to light shade
Habit Upright leaves, becoming spreading
Leaf Deciduous, light green to grey-green, strap-shaped leaves, 30–40cm (12–16in) long and 2–3.5cm (¾–1¼in) wide
Flower Bell-shaped, white shaded green flowers, 4cm (1½in) long, carried in groups of 12 or more along upright stems; hyacinth scented
Use For mid- to background planting in mixed or perennial borders; can be grown in containers
Needs Propagate by removing and replanting bulblets every 5 years; alternatively purchase new bulbs in spring and plant at twice the depth of the bulb
Varieties None

GLADIOLUS
Iridaceae
GLADIOLUS

▲ ❀ ❦ SI summer
H 1 yr 50–60cm (20–24in)
S 1 yr 8–15cm (3–6in)
❄ 0°C (32°F)
Z 5–10

GLADIOLUS COMMUNIS ssp. BYZANTINUS

The summer-flowering form of the gladiolus is, sadly, not winter hardy and must be planted annually. The corms are lifted in autumn and stored over winter. The Nanus Hybrids and varieties of *G. communis* ssp. *byzantinus* are hardier and can be left in the ground over winter.

Soil Acid to alkaline, well drained and well fed
Aspect Full sun to light shade
Habit Upright
Leaf Deciduous, mid-green, pointed, lance-shaped leaves, 40–50cm (16–20in) long and 2–2.5cm (¾–1in) wide
Flower Lipped, trumpet-shaped flowers, 2.5–4cm (1–1½in) long, borne on flower spikes, which normally face in one direction (towards sun)
Use In isolation; in mixed or perennial borders
Needs Propagate by lifting and dividing hardy forms every 5–7 years. Lift non-hardy forms when foliage dies in autumn, store in a frost-free place to following mid-spring, then replant. Stake tall varieties. Purchase new corms in spring
Varieties *G. communis* ssp. *byzantinus* (syn. *G. byzantinus*) ♀ purple-red flowers, hardy, to 1m (3ft) <u>Nanus Hybrids</u>: *G.* 'Nymph' white flowers with red markings • *G.* 'Prins Claus' white flowers with bold red markings • *G.* 'The Bride' ♀ white flowers with yellow markings <u>Grandiflorus Group</u>: range of varieties in many colour combinations; available in large, medium and small flowering varieties <u>Primulinus Group (butterfly gladiolus)</u>: in a wide range of colours, edges of petals frilled

HYACINTHOIDES
**Hyacinthaceae/
Liliaceae**
ENGLISH BLUEBELL

▲ ❀ ❦ SI spring SC
H 1 yr 30–50cm (12–20in)
S 1 yr 23cm (9in)
❄ -18°C (0°F)
Z 2–10

HYACINTHOIDES NON-SCRIPTA

There is almost nothing to compare with a planting of bluebells, especially when they are growing in a woodland. No matter how many bulbs are planted initially, it takes several years before they begin to look natural.

Soil Alkaline to acid, moist, well drained and with a high organic content
Aspect Light to full shade
Habit Emerging in early spring, leafing, flowering and disappearing below the soil by midsummer
Leaf Deciduous, dark glossy green, strap-shaped, incurving leaves, 15–20cm (6–8in) long and wide
Flower Bell-shaped, single, flowers, 2cm (⅘in) long, in groups of 10 or more at the top of the flower spike, in blue or white in mid-spring
Use Best in wild or woodland gardens; plant 3–5 bulbs in each hole, with planting holes about 50cm (20in) apart, or 7 in each hole with 60cm (2ft) between groups
Needs Propagate by dividing established clumps in summer as leaves turn yellow. Protect newly planted bulbs from rodents. Purchase new bulbs in autumn and plant at twice the depth of the bulb
Species *H. non-scripta* (syn. *Scilla non-scripta*, *S. nutans*) blue or white forms

HYACINTHUS ORIENTALIS
Hyacinthaceae/ Liliaceae
COMMON HYACINTH

▲ ❀ 🦋 S winter–spring SC E
H 1 yr 15–30cm (6–12in)
S 15–20cm (6–8in)
❄ -10°C (14°F)
Z 4–7

HYACINTHUS ORIENTALIS 'DELFT BLUE'

These well-established winter- or spring-flowering bulbs can be planted outdoors or forced to give flowers and fragrance for indoors. The cultivation of each kind is different.

Soil In gardens: moderately alkaline to acid, well drained and well fed; in containers: bulb fibre
Aspect Full sun
Habit Upright, normally one large flower per bulb
Leaf Deciduous, but with winter leaf if forced; leaves strap-like, 23–40cm (9–16in) long and to 2cm (¾in) wide
Flower Bell-shaped, highly scented flowers, 2.5cm (1in) long, formed from 6 lance-shaped petals, borne in groups of 30 or more on flower spike in colours ranging from white to yellow, pink, red or blue; some double-flowered forms
Use For spot planting, in small groups, for massed bedding; can be grown in containers both indoors and out
Needs Buy new bulbs in autumn. If forced, allow 14 weeks to flower and grow in a cool, dark, frost-free, rodent-free place
Varieties *H. o.* 'Amethyst' mauve flowers • *H. o.* 'Amsterdam' dark red flowers • *H. o.* 'Ben Nevis' double, white flowers • *H. o.* 'Blue Giant' light blue flowers • *H. o.* 'City of Haarlem' ♀ primrose-yellow flowers • *H. o.* 'Carnegie' pure white flowers in dense spikes • *H. o.* 'Delft Blue' ♀ porcelain blue flowers • *H. o.* 'Gipsy Queen' ♀ salmon-orange flowers • *H. o.* 'Jan Bos' red flowers • *H. o.* 'Lady Derby' bright pink flowers • *H. o.* 'L'Innocence' pure white flowers • *H. o.* 'Ostara' ♀ dark blue flowers • *H. o.* 'Pink Pearl' ♀ deep pink flowers in large spikes

---

IRIS
Iridaceae
DUTCH IRIS

▲ ❀ 🦋 SI late spring–early summer
H 1 yr 50cm (20in)
S 8–10cm (3–4in)
❄ -15°C (4°F)
Z 5–10

DUTCH IRISES

An interesting group of bulbous irises that, because of their breeding, seem to have lost all trace of their botanical origin or name – *Iris × hollandia, I. xiphium* and *I. tingitana.* They are, however, among the most useful of bulbs, largely because they flower after the main rush of other spring-flowering plants.

Soil Alkaline or acid, well drained
Aspect Full sun to light shade
Habit Upright; foliage at same time as the flowers
Leaf Deciduous, dark green, cylindrical, angled leaves 60–75cm (24–30in) long
Flower Flowers formed of 6 narrow petals, the outer 3 with petal-like branches attached, the inner 3 more or less erect, in shades of brown, blue, purple or yellow, some bi-colour forms, in late spring to early summer
Use For the front of borders; can be grown in containers; good among roses in borders to give early colour; a good cut flower
Needs Protect from rodents. Propagate by lifting in early to mid-autumn and replant bulbs and bulblets separately. Purchase new bulbs in autumn and plant at two and a half times their own depth
Varieties Named varieties can be purchased from specialist bulb suppliers but are normally sold by colour rather than name

IRIS
Iridaceae
DWARF IRIS

▲ ❀ ☙ SI late winter–early spring)
H 1 yr 25cm (9in)
S 8–10cm (3–4in)
✳ -15°C (4°F)
Z 5–10

IRIS RETICULATA

These irises form a very attractive group of dwarf bulbs, and their flowers are often regarded as harbingers of spring. Because they never reach any great size, they are ideal for a wide range of positions in the garden. The main colours are blue to purple, but a yellow form also exists.

Soil Alkaline or acid, well drained
Aspect Full sun to deep shade
Habit Short and upright; with foliage following the flowers
Leaf Deciduous, dark green, cylindrical, angled leaves, 30–40cm (12–16in) long
Flower Flowers formed of 6 narrow petals, the outer 3 with petal-like style branches attached, the inner 3 more or less erect, in shades of blue to purple or yellow in late winter to early spring
Use For rock gardens or the front of borders; can be grown in containers indoors and out
Needs Protect from rodents. Propagate by lifting in early to mid-autumn and replant bulbs and bulblets separately. Purchase new bulbs in autumn and plant at two and a half times their own depth. Pre-grown plants available in pots in early spring
Varieties *I. danfordiae* similar to *I. reticulata* but with yellow petals, flowering earlier • *I. histrioides* 'Major' ♀ deep blue flowers, shorter • *I. reticulata* ♀ deep blue flowers • *I. r.* 'Cantab' light blue flowers • *I. r.* 'Joyce' sky blue flowers with orange markings • *I. r.* 'J.S. Dift' scented, red-purple flowers

LEUCOJUM
**Amaryllidaceae/
Liliaceae**
SNOWFLAKE

▲ ❀ ☙ SI late spring
H 1 yr 60cm (2ft)
S 23cm (9in)
✳ -15°C (4°F)
Z 4–8

LEUCOJUM AESTIVUM

A delightful group of clump-forming bulbs with a distinctive shape and form. The foliage sets off the nodding white flowers to perfection. They are a delight anywhere in the garden, but planted near water they have a particular charm.

Soil Neutral to acid and moist; loamy texture preferred
Aspect Light shade to full sun
Habit Upright, clump-forming
Leaf Attractive, deciduous, sea-green, lance-shaped, narrow leaves 25–30cm (10–12in) long, produced with flowers
Flower Hanging, bell-shaped flowers formed from 6 oval, 1cm (½in) long, pointed petals borne on upright stiff stem
Use For spot planting; mass-planted in shady or sunny areas; attractive near water features
Needs Divide established bulb clumps after foliage has died down to propagate or every 5–8 yrs to give space for re-growth. Purchase new bulbs in autumn and plant at two and a half times their own depth
Varieties *L. aestivum* (summer snowflake, loddon lily) white flowers tipped with green, the main form planted • *L. a.* 'Gravetye Giant' ♀ stronger growing variety • *L. vernum* (spring snowflake) ♀ similar species but less than half as tall

LILIUM
Liliaceae/Liliaceae
LILY

▲ ❀ ❦ SI summer SC some
H 1 yr 0.6–2m (2–6ft)
S 23–40cm (9–16in)
❄ -18°C (0°F)
Z 4–8

LILIUM REGALE

Rightly loved for their flowers and, sometimes, their scent, these lilies are completely hardy and have a range of uses.

Soil Moderately alkaline to acid, deep, rich and well prepared, well drained but moisture retentive
Aspect Full sun to very light shade
Habit Upright
Leaf Deciduous, mid- to dark green, lance- or spade-shaped leaves, to 60cm (2ft) long, borne on full length of flower stem
Flower Up to 30 funnel-shaped flowers, in yellows, golds, oranges, reds or white, carried in clusters on long spikes
Use For planting singly or in groups; in mixed or perennial borders; good in containers
Needs Propagate by removing and replanting side bulblets. Purchase new bulbs in autumn and early spring and plant at two and a half times their own depth
Varieties *L.* African Queen Group burnt orange flowers • *L. auratum* (golden ray lily, mountain lily) strongly scented, bowl-shaped flowers, creamy-white with central yellow bars and brown speckling • *L.* 'Connecticut King' clear yellow flowers • *L.* 'Côte d'Azur' deep pink flowers • *L.* 'Enchantment' ♀ orange flowers • *L.* 'Fire King' deep orange flowers • *L.* 'Grand Paradiso' orange-red flowers • *L.* Golden Splendor Group golden-yellow flowers • *L.* 'Orchid Beauty' orange-yellow flowers • *L. regale* ♀ (regal lily) highly scented, white flowers with yellow centres • *L.* 'Rosita' grey-purple flowers with dark spots and red anthers • *L.* 'Sterling Silver' ivory-white flowers spotted with wine-red

---

MUSCARI
Hyacinthaceae/ Liliaceae
GRAPE HYACINTH

▲ ❀ ❦ SI spring
H 1 yr 20cm (8in)
S 10–15cm (4–6in)
❄ -18°C (0°F)
Z 3–9

MUSCARI ARMENIACUM

Although it is often regarded as a common plant, the main variety, *Muscari armeniacum*, has many roles to play, and there are several varieties that merit garden space. A little care is needed, because some can be invasive in too small a space.

Soil Alkaline to acid
Aspect Sun to moderate shade
Habit Upright, leaves becoming arching with age
Leaf Deciduous, dark green, strap-shaped, pointed leaves, 10–20cm (4–8in) long and 5mm (⅕in) wide
Flower Numerous, tiny, rounded flowers, in shades of blue or white, packed tightly together in a uniform pattern form a thimble-shaped flowerhead, 2.5–4cm (1–1½in) long, carried on a stout, upright stem; some varieties have open, fluffy plumes
Use For spot planting or edging; in massed groups or rock gardens; can be grown in containers indoors or out
Needs Propagate by lifting and dividing established bulb clumps after flowering. Every 4–7 years lift and divide clumps to give space. Purchase new bulbs in autumn and plant at twice their own depth
Varieties *M. armeniacum* ♀ deep blue flowers • *M. a.* 'Blue Spike' large, double, deep blue flowers • *M. a.* 'Saffier' deep blue flowers with white rims • *M. aucheri* (*M. tubergenianum*; Oxford and Cambridge grape hyacinth) similar species with two-tone blue flowers • *M. botryoides* 'Album' similar to *M. armeniacum* but with pure white flowers • *M. comosum* 'Plumosum' feathery, open, large pale blue flowers

NARCISSUS
**Amaryllidaceae/
Liliaceae**
DWARF DAFFODILS

▲ ✼ ☙ SI spring SC
H 1 yr *see below*
S 20 per cent of height
✼ -15°C (4°F)
Z 4–10

**NARCISSUS
'GOLDEN HARVEST'**

These delightful plants have won the hearts of all gardeners.

Soil Most but dislikes very wet soil
Aspect Sun to light shade
Habit Upright
Leaf Deciduous, grey-green, strap-like, to 30cm (1ft) long
Flower Trumpet-shaped in shades of yellow or white
Use In containers; for mass-planting or in small groups
Needs Propagate by dividing established clumps in autumn.
Buy bulbs in autumn and plant at twice their own depth
Varieties *N. canaliculatis* multi-headed, white reflexed back
petals, yellow centre, to 10cm (4in) • *N.* 'February Gold'
trumpet-flowered, bright yellow, to 25cm (10in) • *N.* 'Golden
Harvest' (dwarf form) trumpet-flowered, to 20cm (8in) • *N.*
'Hawera' trumpet-flowered, yellow, outer petals reflexed, to
20cm (8in) • *N.* 'Jack Snipe' trumpet-flowered, white outer
and yellow inner petals, to 20cm (8in) • *N.* 'Jenny' ♀
trumpet-flowered, white flowers, to 25cm (10in) • *N.* 'Minnow'
cream outer, lemon-yellow centre, round petals, to 20cm (8in)
• *N.* 'Peeping Tom' trumpet-flowered, yellow, back petals
reflexed, to 40cm (16in) • *N. pseudonarcissus* 'Lobularis'
(syn. *N. lobularis*; Lent lily) trumpet-flowered, yellow, to
20cm (8in) • *N.* 'Rippling Waters' trumpet-flowered, white,
scented, to 30cm (1ft) • *N.* 'Rip van Winkle' strap-like
petals, yellow, to 20cm (8in) • *N.* 'Silver Chimes' trumpet-
headed, creamy-white, to 30cm (1ft) • *N.* 'Thalia, trumpet-
flowered, white, one of the best 30cm (1ft) • *N.* 'Waterperry'
trumpet-flowered, white with yellow centre, to 30cm (1ft)

NARCISSUS
**Amaryllidaceae/
Liliaceae**
TALL-GROWING
DAFFODILS

▲ ✼ ☙ SI spring SC some
H 1 yr 60cm (2ft)
S 8–30cm (3–12in)
✼ -15°C (4°F)
Z 4–10

**NARCISSUS
'FEBRUARY GOLD'**

There is little more to be written about the virtues of
Narcissus. They should be in every garden.

Soil Alkaline to acid; tolerates all but very wet soils
Aspect Full sun to light shade
Habit Upright
Leaf Deciduous, strap-like leaves, to 60cm (2ft) long and
2cm (¾in) wide
Flower Trumpet-shaped, double or single flowers in colours
according to variety
Use In small groupings or mass-plantings; will grow in
containers indoors or out
Needs Propagate by dividing established bulb clumps after
leaves die. Purchase new bulbs in autumn and plant at two
and a half times the depth of the bulb
Varieties (H, unless otherwise indicated, to 42cm/16in) *N.*
'Actaea' ♀ yellow outer, red centre, fragrant • *N.* 'Carlton'
♀ large lemon cup • *N.* 'February Gold' early flowering,
clear golden, to 30cm (1ft) • *N.* 'Flower Drift' double, white
outer petals, red centre, fragrant • *N.* 'Flower Record' large
cup, bright orange centre, to 30cm (1ft) • *N.* 'Fortune' large
orange cup, to 50cm (20in) • *N.* 'Geranium' ♀ multi-headed
red centre, fragrant • *N.* 'Golden Harvest' lemon, early
flowering • *N.* 'Ice Follies' ♀ large cup, lemon-yellow centre
• *N.* 'Mount Hood' ♀ pure white trumpet, to 39cm (14in) •
N. 'Sempre Avanti' large creamy-white cup, orange centre •
N. 'White Cheerfulness' creamy-white multi-headed, fragrant
• *N.* 'Yellow Cheerfulness' yellow, multi-headed, fragrant

NERINE
**Amaryllidaceae/
Liliaceae**
NERINE

▲ ✱ ✿ SI autumn SC some
H 1 yr 50–60cm (20–24in)
S 8–15cm (3–6in)
✱ -15°C (4°F)
Z 8–10

NERINE BOWDENII

The intense pink autumn flowers of these South African plants never fails to please, but if they are to achieve their full potential, the correct conditions are required. The bulbs should be planted close to a wall to provide the heat needed to trigger them to make flowers for the coming season. The flowers come first and no sign of foliage is seen until they have finished. Hardiness with all but *Nerine bowdenii* can be suspect.

Soil Well drained and prepared; close to a wall for warmth
Aspect Full sun
Habit Upright flowers and foliage
Leaf Deciduous, dark to mid-green, strap-shaped leaves, 50–53cm (20–21in) long and 1–2cm (½–¾in) wide; appear after the flowers
Flower Slightly scented, narrow petals form trumpets, 10–13cm (4–5in) wide, borne in clusters, in intense shades of pink or white
Use Grown in isolation along the base of sunny walls; will grow in large containers indoors or out
Needs Propagate by lifting and dividing established bulb clumps in early summer. Purchase new bulbs in spring or pre-grown plants in pots when in flower or just after. Plant with necks of bulbs just below the soil surface with a little sharp sand below the bulb to help drainage
Varieties *N. bowdenii* ♀ principal variety • *N. b.* 'Alba' white flowers, tender • *N. b.* 'Pink Triumph' silver-pink flowers, open shape • *N. undulata* (syn. *N. crispa*) open, pale pink flowers, crinkled effect, tender

---

ORNITHOGALUM
**Hyacinthaceae/
Liliaceae**
STAR OF BETHLEHEM

▲ ✱ ✿ SI spring
H 1 yr 23cm (9in)
S 15cm (6in)
✱ -15°C (4°F)
Z 7–10

**ORNITHOGALUM
UMBELLATUM**

There are a number of species in this genus, but only one is hardy for growing outdoors in all but the most sheltered of gardens and that is *Ornithogalum umbellatum*, the true star of Bethlehem. The others species listed are worth growing as pot plants indoors, where they can be protected from frost.

Soil Alkaline to acid; dislikes extremely wet conditions
Aspect Full sun to light shade
Habit Untidy and spreading but charming
Leaf Deciduous, dark glossy green, lance-shaped leaves, 2.5–4cm (1–1½in) long and wide
Flower Attractive, white, star-shaped flowers, formed of 6 oval to lance-shaped petals 1cm (½in) wide, borne in open clusters in late spring
Use For group plantings; in rock gardens; in containers indoors or out
Needs Propagate by lifting and dividing established bulb clumps after leaves die. Purchase new bulbs in autumn and plant at two and a half times their own depth
Varieties *O. lanceolatum* very short growing, clusters of large, thick flowers and foliage • *O. narbonense* upright habit, pyramidal white flowers, to 1m (3ft) • *O. nutans* ♀ upright habit, green-white, drooping flowers • *O. oligophyllum* (syn. *O. balansae*) dwarf species, spreading • *O. thyrsoides* (chincherinchee, wonder flower) tall growing, larger, cupped-shaped flowers borne in clusters, to 60cm (2ft), a good cut flower • *O. umbellatum* (star of Bethlehem) pure white flowers, the principal hardy species (spreading)

OXALIS
Oxalidaceae
OXALIS

▲ ❀ ☙ SI spring–summer
H 1 yr 10–15cm (4–6in)
S 23–30cm (9–12in)
❋ -15°C (4°F)
Z 6–10

OXALIS ADENOPHYLLA

Given the right planting conditions, this group of plants can be very attractive; if they are in the wrong place, they will almost certainly fail and die. They originate from the wild forms that flourished in woodland soils, and their roots need to be in soil that contains a high degree of organic material.

Soil Moderately alkaline to acid, light, open and sandy; the soil must be rich in organic material, especially leaf mould
Aspect Light shade; tolerates some sun
Habit Clump-forming and spreading
Leaf Deciduous, grey to grey-green, V-shaped leaflets radiate from the stalks in a parasol-like arrangement; they are attractive in their own right
Flower Saucer-shaped, upward-facing, flowers 1cm (½in) across, in shades of pink or white in late spring to early summer
Use For edging borders or paths; for rock gardens; naturalized in woodland settings; can be grown in containers indoors or out
Needs Propagate by lifting and dividing rhizomes after leaves have died back. Purchase new bulbs in autumn and plant just below soil surface. Protect from rodents
Varieties *O. adenophylla* ♀ flowers with light pink centres, shading to lavender-pink, the principal variety planted • *O. articulata* (syn *O. floribunda*) clusters of smaller shamrock leaves, pink flowers, less hardy • *O. enneaphylla* purple-veined flowers, less hardy • *O. magellanica* bronze leaves, white flowers, less hardy

PUSCHKINIA
Hyacinthaceae/
Liliaceae
STRIPED SQUILL

▲ ❀ ☙ SI spring
H 1 yr 20cm (8in)
S 8–10cm (3–4in)
❋ -15°C (4°F)
Z 4–8

PUSCHKINIA SCILLOIDES

A charming, spring-flowering bulb of real beauty. It can be used in almost every situation a flowering bulb is needed. There are no real problems, and it is surprising that it is not more widely planted.

Soil Moderately alkaline to acid; light and sandy in texture
Aspect Full sun to very light shade
Habit Upright foliage and flower stalks with nodding flowerheads; appears in mid-spring, disappears by mid-summer and returns the following spring
Leaf Deciduous, glossy, dark green, strap-shaped leaves, 5–8cm (2–3in) long and 5mm (¼in) wide
Flower Star-shaped flowers, 2cm (¾in) wide, 5–10 per stem, borne in late spring; white with pale blue shading and a bold mid-blue bar down the centre of each petal
Use As edging for borders and for ground cover; ideal on rock gardens; can be grown in containers and indoors as a pot plant
Needs Propagate by dividing established bulb clumps after foliage has died down. Purchase new bulbs in autumn and plant to twice the depth of the bulb
Varieties *P. scilloides* light blue flowers with darker blue central stripe on each petal • *P. s.* var. *libanotica* (syn. *P. libanotica*) almost all white flowers, sometimes with blue stripes

RANUNCULUS
Ranunculaceae
RANUNCULUS GARDEN
HYBRIDS

▲ ✿ ❦ SI spring
H 1 yr 25cm (10in)
S 15cm (6in)
✳ -5°C (23°F)
Z 8–10

This hybrid form of the buttercup is bright and colourful, almost flamboyant, and it in no way resembles its more lowly cousin. It needs careful siting if the flowers are to blend with other garden plants, but if care is taken in choosing its position, it can be a very worthwhile and colourful addition to the spring garden.

Soil Any well-drained and prepared soil; the addition of organic material helps
Aspect Full sun to very light shade
Habit Upright at first, spreading when in flower
Leaf Very dissected, deciduous, mid- to light green, hand-shaped leaves, appearing in spring and dying away in early to midsummer
Flower Very double, flat-topped balls of numerous sepals, to 8cm (3in) wide
Use A spot plant for spring colour in the garden; will grow in containers
Needs Propagate by division of the tubers in early summer after the foliage has died down. Purchase and plant new tubers in autumn or spring, soaking them in water for 36 hours before planting. Can be purchased in spring pre-grown in pots and in or about to come into flower
Varieties *R.* 'Carnival Mixed' the plants available may not carry the full name; they are often offered only as mixed colours and cannot be selected by colour unless bought as pre-grown plants

**RANUNCULUS
'CARNIVAL MIXED'**

SCILLA
**Hyacinthaceae/
Liliaceae**
SIBERIAN SQUILL,
SPRING SQUILL

▲ ✿ ❦ SI spring
H 1 yr 20cm (8in)
S 15cm (6in)
✳ -18°C (0°F)
Z 1–10

This little relative of the bluebell brings to the spring garden the most intense blue of any flower. The attractive dark foliage is followed by the short-stalked bluebell-like flowers. In the ideal conditions, it can become invasive, seeding itself freely and spreading over a wide area, making it an ideal plant for spring ground cover.

Soil Most, if well-drained
Aspect Light shade to full sun; does best in shade
Habit Upright, short and neat in growth
Leaf Deciduous, mid- to dark green, strap-shaped, pointed-tipped leaves, 8–10cm (3–4in) long and 5mm (¼in) wide, produced just before the flowers in early spring; dying away by early summer to reappear the following spring
Flower Slightly open, bell-shaped flowers, 2cm (¾in) wide, borne in groups of 4–5 on short stems in spring just after the leaves have developed
Use For underplanting other plants, such as roses; good for naturalizing; can be grown in containers outdoors and indoors as a spring pot plant
Needs Propagate by dividing established bulb clumps every 5–8 years. Can be lifted just after the flowers have died and divided and transplanted. Will self-seed. Purchase new bulbs in autumn and plant at twice the depth of the bulb
Varieties *S. sibirica* mid- to dark blue flowers with a darker central band • *S. s.* var. *alba* white flowers • *S. s.* 'Spring Beauty' larger and deeper blue flowers, probably the best blue

**SCILLA SIBIRICA
'SPRING BEAUTY'**

TULIPA
Liliaceae
DWARF TULIPS

▲ ✿ ❦ SI spring
H 1 yr *see below*
S 25 per cent of height
✾ -15°C (4°F)
Z 3–7

TULIPA 'RED RIDING HOOD'

The colour, shape and height of these dwarf tulips make them suitable for planting in dozens of positions in the garden.

Soil Most, as long as the soil is well prepared and well fed
Aspect Full sun to light shade
Habit Upright, spreading leaves
Leaf Wide, grey-green, lance-shaped leaves, 23cm (9in) long, some with markings
Flower Typical tulip flowers in a wide range of colours
Use For containers inside or out; for spot planting or *en masse*
Needs Bulbs can be left planted all year round. Purchase new plants in autumn and plant at twice the bulbs' own depth
Varieties *T.* 'Cape Cod', orange-red flowers, 25cm (10in) • *T.* 'Chopin' yellow flowers with red shading, to 13cm (5in) • *T.* 'Fritz Kreisler' flowers with rose base, sulphur yellow tips, to 15cm (6in) • *T.* 'Gaiety' white flowers, yellow centre, with pink on the outside, to 13cm (5in) • *T.* 'Heart's Delight' deep pink outside, paler on inside, to 25cm (10in) • *T.* 'Johann Strauss' creamy-yellow flowers with red stripes on outside, to 25cm (10in) • *T.* 'Lady Diana' red flowers with lemon stripes, to 25cm (10in) • *T.* 'Pandour' red flowers flushed with yellow, to 25cm (10in) • *T.* 'Plaisir' peachy pink, white-flushed flowers, to 13cm (5in) • *T.* 'Red Riding Hood' ♀ good leaf markings, bright red flowers, to 30cm (1ft) • *T.* 'Stresa' ♀ yellow flowers with red flashes, to 13cm (10in) • *T.* 'Toronto' ♀ peach-pink, multi-headed flowers, to 25cm (10in) • *T.* 'Water Lily' creamy-yellow flowers with flushes of red on outside, to 13cm (5in)

TULIPA
Liliaceae
TALL-GROWING TULIPS

▲ ✿ ❦ SI spring
H 1 yr *see below*
S 20cm (8in)
✾ -15°C (4°F)
Z 3–7

TULIPA 'APELDOORN ELITE'

Spectacular is the only word that can be used to introduce this group of bulbs.

Soil Acid to alkaline, well cultivated and well fed
Aspect Full sun to light shade
Habit Upright
Leaf Light olive green, lance-shaped, 23cm (9in) long and to 7cm (2¾in) wide
Flower Typically tulip-shaped in a wide colour range; parrot type tulips have frilled or fringed petals
Use For mass-planting or spot plantings; will grow in containers
Needs Lift every year and store dry until replanting in autumn. Purchase new bulbs in late autumn and plant at twice the depth of the bulb
Varieties <u>Parrot type:</u> to 60cm (2ft): *T.* 'Estella Rijnveld' white flowers with deep red stripes • *T.* 'Fantasy' ♀ pink flowers, flushed with cream and green • *T.* 'Texas Flame' pale yellow flowers with deep red stripes • *T.* 'White Parrot' white flowers <u>Double, early:</u> to 25cm (10in): *T.* 'Electra' deep pink flowers • *T.* 'Engelenburcht' white flowers • *T.* 'Monte Carlo' deep yellow flowers • *T.* 'Peach Blossom' silver-pink flowers <u>Lily-flowered:</u> 65–70cm (26–28in): *T.* 'Mariette' deep pink flowers • *T.* 'Maytime' white-edged lilac flowers • *T.* 'West Point' bright yellow flowers • *T.* 'White Triumphator' clear white flowers <u>Single, tall:</u> 60–70cm (24–28in): *T.* 'Abu Hassan' maroon and deep yellow flowers • *T.* 'Apeldoorn' red flowers • *T.* 'Apeldoorn Elite' red and yellow flowers

ACAENA
Rosaceae
NEW ZEALAND BURR

▲ ✤ ✌ SI all year E
H 2 yrs 15cm (6in)
S 50cm (20in)
✳ -15°C (4°F)
Z 4–9

**ACAENA SACCATICUPULA
'BLUE HAZE'**

The foliage of this group of plants is only slightly more attractive than the flowers, burr-like seedheads and overall shape. They form flat carpets, reliably evergreen in all but the very coldest of winters.

Soil Alkaline to acid; tolerates dryness but not full drought
Aspect Full sun to very light shade
Habit Spreading and carpeting
Leaf Evergreen, grey to blue-green or bronze, pinnate leaves, formed from 7–11 oval leaflets and 5–10cm (2–4in) long and wide
Flower Tight ball-shaped flowers, green but ageing to purple-brown, are held in spikes above foliage; followed by maroon-brown, burr-shaped seedheads in late summer which are retained into autumn
Use Grow in isolation for best effect on rock gardens, screes or between paving; good for underplanting or ground cover
Needs Propagate from cuttings in summer. No pruning required but trim lightly around edges in mid- to late spring
Varieties *A. adscendens* bronze foliage • *A. caesiiglauca* (syn. *A. caerulea*) blue-green foliage, red-brown flowers and burrs • *A. magellanica* ssp. *magellanica* (syn. *A. glauco-phylla*) grey foliage, purplish burrs • *A. microphylla* ♀ bronze-green foliage, crimson spines and burrs • *A. m.* 'Kupferteppich' ('Copper Carpet') bronze foliage, red flowerheads and burrs • *A. saccaticupula* 'Blue Haze' (syn. *A.* 'Pewter') blue-bronze foliage, red-stemmed brown burrs follow flowers

---

ARABIS
Brassicaceae/Cruciferae
WALL CRESS,
ROCK CRESS

▲ ✤ ✌ SI spring E
H 2 yrs 15cm (6in)
S 60cm (2ft)
✳ -15°C (4°F)
Z 3–9

**ARABIS ALPINA ssp.
CAUCASICA 'VARIEGATA'**

The pink and white forms of this well-known garden plant are often seen tumbling over garden walls or being used as small-scale carpeting, but the variegated forms are less well known and even more interesting. They are all trouble free and easy going and can be used in a variety of ways in the garden.

Soil Acid or alkaline; dislikes very wet winter conditions
Aspect Full sun to very light shade
Habit Spreading
Leaf Semi-evergreen to evergreen, grey-green, pointed, oval leaves 5–10cm (2–4in) long
Flower Small, oval, white or cerise flowers, borne in profusion over plant surface in spring
Use For rock gardens or banks; as ground cover or under-planting; grown singly or mass-planted
Needs Propagate by separating small self-rooted sections or from seed. Cut back all shoots by 20 per cent to encourage new flowering shoots for following year
Varieties *A. alpina* ssp. *caucasica* 'Flore Plena' (syn. *A. caucasica* 'Flore Pleno') ♀ double, white flowers, fast-spreading • *A. a.* ssp. *c.* 'Variegata' (syn. *A. caucasica* 'Variegata') silver- and gold-variegated foliage, single, white flowers • *A. androsacea* 'Rosabella' tight habit of growth, single, cerise-pink flowers • *A. blepharophylla* 'Frühlings-zauber' ('Spring Charm') ♀ cerise-pink flowers • *A. procurrens* 'Variegata' (syn. *A. ferdinandi-coburgi* 'Variegata') ♀ evergreen, bright green foliage with ivory-white margins, single, white flowers

ARMERIA
Plumbaginaceae
THRIFT, SEA PINK

▲ ❀ ❦ SI spring–summer E
H 2 yrs 15–20cm (6–8in)
S 30–50cm (12–20in)
❄ -15°C (4°F)
Z 5–9

These tight, compact little plants are much more robust than their size would suggest. In the wild they grow on the tops of chalk cliffs, often exposed to all the worst elements a plant could experience. The flowers stand like beacons above the foliage in shades of pink, red and white, attracting bees, butterflies and other beneficial insects. When they are grown in the garden on rock gardens, screes or in containers, they increase in size and are even more attractive.

Soil Alkaline to acid, well-drained soil; they do particularly well on alkaline soils
Aspect Full sun
Habit Carpeting and low mound-forming
Leaf Evergreen, glossy dark green, grass-like leaves, 8–10cm (3–4in) long, borne in dense, overlapping rosettes; some leaves die in winter and turn brown
Flower Small, tight, globular heads in shades of pink or white, carried on stiff stems
Use In rock gardens, between paving, or in troughs and large containers
Needs Propagate by dividing clumps or from seeds in spring
Varieties *A.* 'Bee's Ruby' ♀ deep pink flowers • *A. juniperifolia* 'Bevan's Variety' ♀ deep rose-pink flowers on short stems • *A. maritima* mid-pink flowers • *A. m.* 'Alba' white flowers • *A. m.* 'Bloodstone' very deep pink flowers • *A. m.* 'Düsseldorfer Stolz' ('Düsseldorf Pride') dark pink, almost red flowers • *A. m.* 'Ruby Glow' dark pink flowers • *A. m.* 'Vindictive' ♀ red-pink flowers

ARMERIA MARITIMA

AUBRIETA
Brassicaceae/Cruciferae
AUBRIETA

▲ ❀ ❦ SI spring E (semi)
H 2 yrs 15–20cm (6–8in)
S 60cm–1m (2–3ft)
❄ -10°C (14°F)
Z 4–9

Aubrietas are known by almost every gardener and planted in almost every garden, but it is just possible that this familiarity prevents their being used to the full potential and that, properly managed, they could offer even more.

Soil All, except very wet
Aspect Full sun or very light shade
Habit Spreading or falling downwards over a wall
Leaf Semi-evergreen to evergreen, grey-green, pointed, oval leaves, 1–2cm (½–¾in) long; can be damaged by cold and become unattractive for a short period in winter
Flower Small single or double flowers formed from 4 heart-shaped petals, in shades of blue, mauve, pink, red or purple, in early to mid-spring
Use For rock gardens or walls; between paving; as ground cover or underplanting; can be grown in containers and hanging baskets
Needs Propagate by division or cuttings or from seed in spring. Cut back all shoots by 20 per cent after flowering
Varieties *A.* 'Argenteovariegata' white-edged, mid-green foliage, single, pink-mauve flowers • *A.* 'Aureovariegata' gold-edged leaves, single, mauve-pink flowers • *A.* 'Bob Saunders' large, double, purple-red flowers • *A.* 'Bressingham Pink' large, double, pink flowers • *A. deltoidea* ssp. *rosea* deep pink flowers • *A.* 'Doctor Mules' ♀ single, deep violet-purple flowers • *A.* 'Maurice Prichard' single, light pink flowers • *A.* 'Red Carpet' single, deep red flowers

**AUBRIETA DELTOIDEA ssp.
ROSEA**

AURINIA
Brassicaceae/Cruciferae
YELLOW ALYSSUM

▲ ✿ ❦ SI spring
H 2 yrs 15–25cm (6–10in)
S 0.6–1m (2–3ft)
✳ -15°C (4°F)
Z 4–10

This reliable plant was formerly classified in the genus *Alyssum*, but the name change has not changed the bright golden display of flowers that cascades down a low wall or clambers over a rock garden each spring. Perhaps the only danger is that it is regarded as such a common plant that it is passed over in favour of something less often seen – and that would be a mistake.

Soil Most, except very dry or wet
Aspect Full sun
Habit Carpet-forming and spreading
Leaf Deciduous, grey to silver-grey, oval to lance-shaped, round-ended leaves, 4–5cm (1½–2in) long
Flower Many tiny, 4-petalled flowers in closely bunched clusters in shades of yellow spread over the whole plant in spring
Use For the edges of borders, between paving, tumbling over walls; good in large containers
Needs Propagate from seed or replant rooted side growths. Trim lightly over top and sides after flowering to induce new flowering shoots for the following year
Varieties *A. saxatilis* (syn. *Alyssum saxitile*) ♀ golden-yellow flowers • *A. s.* 'Citrina' ♀ slightly taller growing, primrose-yellow flowers • *A. s.* 'Compacta' compact habit, very showy yellow flowers • *A. s.* 'Dudley Nevill' warm yellow flowers • *A. s.* 'Flore Pleno' double, golden-yellow flowers • *A. s.* 'Gold Dust' golden-yellow flowers

AURINIA SAXATILIS

CAMPANULA
Campanulaceae
BELL FLOWER

▲ ✿ ❦ SI spring or summer
SC some E
H 2 yrs 8–12cm (3–30in)
S 30–75cm (12–30in)
✳ -15°C (4°F)
Z 3–10

The plants in this large genus produce wonderful displays of cup- or bell-shaped flowers. They are almost all reliably hardy, and they have many uses in the garden.

Soil Alkaline to acid, well drained
Aspect Full sun to light shade
Habit Creeping and spreading; some clump-forming
Leaf Deciduous, light green, soft-textured, pointed, oval leaves, 2.5–4cm (1–1⅛in) long and wide with toothed edges
Flower Cup-, saucer-, star- or bell-shaped flowers in blues, white and pinks; some double forms
Use For the front of borders or as edging for rose beds; in rock gardens; some may self-seed; good in containers
Needs Propagate from seed or by division of clumps in spring
Varieties <u>Dwarf, clump-forming, less hardy</u>: to 50cm (20in): *C. carpatica* 'Blaue Clips' ('Blue Clips') light sky blue flowers • *C. c.* 'Blue Moonlight' china blue flowers • *C. c.* 'Chewton Joy' light-blue flowers • *C. c.* var. *turbinata* 'Hannah' pure white flowers • *C. c.* var. *t.* 'Isabel' deep blue flowers • *C.* 'Constellation' lavender-blue flowers <u>Creeping, hardy</u>: *C. cochleariifolia* ♀ dainty blue flowers • *C. c.* 'Elizabeth Oliver' double, powder-blue flowers • *C. c.* 'Oakington Blue' deep blue flowers • *C.* 'Covadonga' deep blue flowers • *C.* 'G.F. Wilson' large violet-blue flowers • *C. portenschlagiana* (syn. *C. muralis*) ♀ very strong growing, deep blue flowers • *C. poscharskyana* vigorous grower, star-shaped pale blue flowers • *C. pulla* dangling purple-blue bells • *C. rotundifolia* (harebell) pale blue flowers

CAMPANULA CARPATICA 'BLAUE CLIPS'

CERASTIUM TOMENTOSUM
Caryophyllaea
SNOW IN SUMMER

▲ ❀ ❦ SI spring SC
H 2 yrs 15cm (6in)
S 1m (3ft)
❋ -15°C (4°F)
Z 3–10

CERASTIUM TOMENTOSUM

The common name of this fast-growing alpine describes it perfectly when it is in flower, although it should, accurately, be 'snow in late spring'. It is an invasive plant and far too strong for all but the largest rock gardens. However, if a fast-growing, spreading plant is required for ground cover in the sun, this is the plant to choose. In addition to the flowers, there is the attractive silver-grey foliage, which holds its interest until the winter frosts, when it is killed off, reappearing the following spring.

Soil Any
Aspect Full sun
Habit Spreading, can be invasive
Leaf Deciduous, silver-grey, downy, oval leaves, 2.5–5cm (1–2in) long and 2–2.5cm (¾–1in) wide
Flower Tiny, white, oval, indented petals form round, reflexed flowers borne in small clusters in late spring
Use For ground cover; over banks; will grow in large containers
Needs Propagate by replanting rooted side-growths. Cut all growth that may have overwintered back almost to ground level in early spring after it has protected the plant through winter
Varieties *C. tomentosum* (syn. *C. biebersteinii*) woolly grey leaves, white flowers • *C. tomentosum* var. *columnae* compact habit, silver foliage, white flowers, less invasive • *C. t.* 'Silberteppich' ('Silver Carpet') silver foliage, white flowers, possibly the best form

DIANTHUS
Caryophyllaceae
ALPINE PINKS

▲ ❀ ❦ SI summer SC E
H 2 yrs 6–20cm (2½–8in)
S 30cm (1ft)
❋ -10°C (14°F)
Z 3–10

DIANTHUS ALPINUS

Scent, dainty habit, fascinating flowers and a wide range of colours contribute to making the dianthus a very useful garden plant and one of the most popular alpines.

Soil Alkaline to acid, well drained
Aspect Full sun to very light shade
Habit Clump-forming, slightly spreading with age
Leaf Very narrow, grey-green to silver-grey, lance-shaped leaves
Flower Single or double, typical carnation-shaped flowers; smaller in size than those of taller growing types but otherwise the same; in a wide range of colours and mostly scented
Use For rock gardens and screes; good for edging borders and paths; ideal for containers, especially trough gardens
Needs Propagate in early summer from leaf or stem cuttings. Remove dead flowerheads as seen. Lightly trim over in spring before growth starts
Varieties *D. alpinus* ♀ slow growing, mat-forming, large, single rosy-red flowers • *D.* × *arvernensis* ♀ silvery mat-forming foliage, smallish, single, pink flowers • *D. deltoides* ♀ trailing bright green carpet, single flowers, white or shades of pink, sometimes with dark central eye • *D.* 'Inshriach Dazzler' ♀ single, carmine flowers with fringed edge • *D.* 'La Bourboule' ♀ single flowers, clear pink fringed petals • *D.* 'Little Jock' double, pale pink flowers with maroon central eye • *D. microlepis* var. *musalae* cushion-forming, single, pink or purple flowers • *D. pavonius* (syn. *D. neglectus*) ♀ very large, single flowers in shades of pink

DIASCIA
Scrophulariaceae
DIASCIA

▲ ❀ ♥ SI summer
E (in shelter)
H 2 yrs 30cm (1ft)
S 40–50cm (16–20in)
❄ 0°C (32°F)
Z 8–10

DIASCIA 'RUBY FIELD'

Sadly, unless they are in a very sheltered warm garden, these plants may not be winter hardy. However, if they do survive the winter, that is a bonus, for they are worth growing for a single season for the bold display of flowers.

Soil Moderately alkaline to acid, light textured and well drained
Aspect Full sun to very light shade; more shade will stop it from flowering although it will continue to grow; not reliably winter hardy
Habit Upright, spreading as it comes into flower; fast growing
Leaf Deciduous or evergreen, light to mid-green, broadly oval, toothed leaves, to 2cm (¾in) long and wide
Flower Numerous 5-petalled, cup-shaped, 2-spurred flowers, dark rose to purple-pink, borne in upright sprays in summer
Use As foreground planting for mixed and perennial borders; for rock gardens or isolated plantings; will grow in containers
Needs Propagate by cuttings both in spring or late autumn in case plants are lost in cold weather; protect resulting plants under glass until planted out when all spring frosts have passed. Trim lightly in spring those that survive winter
Varieties *D. cordata* dark rose-pink flowers • *D. elegans* mat-forming, mid-pink flowers • *D. rigescens* ♀ evergreen, rose-pink flowers, less hardy • *D.* 'Ruby Field' (× *stachyoides*) ♀ dark pink-red flowers • *D. vigilis* ♀ arching sprays of light pink flowers

---

DRABA
Brassicaceae/Cruciferae
WHITLOW GRASS

▲ ❀ ♥ SI spring E
H 2 yrs 2.5–8cm (1–3in)
S 40cm (16in)
❄ -10°C (14°F)
Z 8–10

DRABA LONGISILIQUA

These charming, mound-forming evergreen plants look like flowering hummocks in spring when they are covered with white or yellow flowers.

Soil Most; must be well drained
Aspect Full sun to very light shade
Habit Hummock, mound or carpet-forming; compact in overall shape
Leaf Rosettes of dark green, lance-shaped leaves, 1cm (½in) long
Flower Racemes densely covered with bright yellow or white flowers in late spring; each open cup-shaped flower formed from 4 petals
Use For rock gardens and containers, especially sink gardens
Needs Propagate by cuttings taken in early summer
Varieties *D. aizoides* (yellow whitlow grass) cushion- or mat-forming, woody plant, deep-green rosettes, bold yellow flowers • *D. bruniifolia* quickly spreading, carpeting habit, yellow flowers • *D. dedeana* cushion-forming, more woody, grey-green foliage, white, blue to violet towards the base of the flowers • *D. longisiliqua* ♀ oval, grey-green leaves, yellow flowers • *D. molissima* hummock-forming, grey-green foliage, yellow flowers • *D. repens* quickly spreading, carpeting habit, yellow flowers • *D. rigida* hummock-forming, dark green foliage, yellow flowers , slower growing, may need protection in winter • *D. rigida* var. *imbricata* (syn. *D. imbricata*) slower growing, low hummock-forming, yellow flowers • *D.* × *salomonii* green foliage, white flowers

ALPINES

DRYAS
Rosaceae
MOUNTAIN AVENS

▲ ❀ ✿ all year E
H 2 yrs 10cm (4in)
S 1m (3ft)
❊ -15°C (4°F)
Z 2–8

This delightful and interesting alpine plant produces thick carpets of dark green evergreen foliage followed by cup-shaped flowers and unusual tufted seedheads. As it ages, its form becomes woody and almost shrub-like in character.

Soil Most, even quite dry
Aspect Full sun; dislikes shade
Habit Clump-forming yet spreading and growing as a flattish carpet; woody
Leaf Oblong with pointed ends, dark green with silver reverse, deeply veined leaves; some turn brown in winter
Flower Cup-shaped, pale yellow flowers, to 2.5cm (1in) across, with deeper yellow centres borne in late spring and summer; followed by attractive fluffy white seedheads, which are kept well into winter
Use For the rock garden or edging borders; as small areas of ground cover; will grown in containers
Needs Propagate from seed in spring or from cuttings in early summer. Remove old brown leaves when they are no longer attractive
Varieties *D. drummondii* the species as described • *D. d.* 'Grandiflora' larger flowers • *D. octopetala* (mountain avens) ♀ paler flowers • *D.* × *suendermannii* ♀ nodding flowers

DRYAS × *SUENDERMANNII*

ERINUS
Scrophulariaceae
SUMMER STARWORT,
ALPINE BALSAM

▲ ❀ ✿ SI spring–summer
H 2 yrs 8cm (3in)
S 10cm (4in)
❊ -10°C (14°F)
Z 2–7

A small, rather underrated plant, erinus has much to offer, even though, in plant terms, it can be short-lived. Make sure that it is positioned where it will not be swamped by other plants so that the neat little bush has room to display its flowers from spring to summer.

Soil Best in poor soil but will tolerate most
Aspect Full sun to light shade
Habit Compact, non-spreading, tufted formation
Leaf Dark grey-green, lance- or wedge-shaped leaves, to 2.5cm (1in) long and covered in a sticky resin
Flower Small flowers, mainly pink-crimson, borne in profusion on short racemes from spring to summer; a white-flowered form is available
Use As a low alpine plant for rock gardens and scree beds; good in containers including sink gardens
Needs Propagate from seed in spring. Lightly trim after flowering to encourage new growth for the next year
Varieties *E. alpinus* ♀ not always long lived, pink-purple flowers • *E. a.* var. *albus* white flowers • *E. a.* 'Dr Hähnle' rosy-pink to crimson flowers, good for poor soil • *E. a.* 'Mrs Charles Boyle' pink flowers

ERINUS ALPINUS

GENTIANA
Gentianaceae
GENTIAN

▲ ❀ ❦ SI spring–summer
H 2 yrs 10cm (4in)
S 40cm (16in)
❄ -10°C (14°F)
Z 3–9

GENTIANA SINO-ORNATA

The upturned trumpet-like flowers are the most intense blue, and they are perfectly set off by the dark green foliage. These are alpine plants, but hardiness can be suspect, although dampness, rather than cold, is the problem. Most forms also require acid soil.

Soil Neutral to acid, open and well drained but not over-dry; dislikes extremely alkaline soil
Aspect Full sun
Habit Foliage as a carpet with flowers above
Leaf Evergreen, light green, ovate leaves, 5–6cm (2–2½in) long and 1–2cm (½–¾in) wide, with silver undersides
Flower Trumpet-shaped flowers, over 2.5cm (1in) wide and 5cm (2in) long, in brilliant blue in spring or summer
Use For rock gardens; as isolated feature plants; good in containers such as a sink garden
Needs Propagate from seed or by division of clumps after flowering. Protect in very cold, wet winters
Varieties *G. acaulis* (syn. *G. kochiana*; trumpet gentian) ♀ deep blue flowers with some green spots in spring • *G. farreri* electric blue flowers in autumn, tolerates alkaline soil • *G.* 'Inverleith' ♀ pale blue flowers in autumn • *G.* × *macaulayi* 'Kingfisher' bright blue flowers in spring, dislikes lime • *G. septemfida* ♀ blue flowers in late summer, dislikes lime • *G. sino-ornata* ♀ bright blue flowers striped dark blue with green stripes in autumn, dislikes lime • *G. verna* soft blue flowers in spring, tolerates some lime

HELIANTHEMUM
Cistaceae
ROCK ROSE, SUN ROSE

▲ ❀ ❦ SI spring–early summer E
H 2 yrs 10cm (4in)
S 2 yrs 75cm (30in)
❄ -15°C (4°F)
Z 5–10

**HELIANTHEMUM
'RHODANTHE CARNEUM'**

Technically a low-growing shrub, helianthemum is regarded by most gardeners as an alpine plant in its use within the garden. The flowers are borne in spring and early summer, and there is a wide range to chose from.

Soil Acid to mildly alkaline, well drained and open
Aspect Full sun but tolerates very light shade
Habit Upright at first, becoming spreading with age
Leaf Evergreen, dark glossy green or grey-green, ovate leaves, 2.5–5cm (1–2in) long
Flower In a range of colours from white, through yellow to pink, orange and red
Use As a low, ground-covering, carpeting flowering shrub; as an alpine shrub in rock gardens; for cascading over short walls; will grow in containers
Needs Propagate from cuttings in early summer. Trim lightly with hedging shears after flowering
Varieties *H.* 'Ben Afflick' deep orange flowers with darker centre • *H.* 'Ben Hope' carmine flowers with deep orange centre • *H.* 'Ben Ledi' bright deep rose to pink flowers • *H.* 'Fireball' deep orange flowers • *H.* 'Fire Dragon' (syn. *H. n.* 'Mrs Clay') ♀ flame-orange flowers • *H.* 'Henfield Brilliant' ♀ double, dark red flowers • *H.* 'Jubilee' primrose-yellow flowers • *H.* 'Mrs C.W. Earle' deep orange flowers • *H.* 'Raspberry Ripple' rose-pink flowers with white tips • *H.* 'Rhodanthe Carneum' (syn. *H.* 'Wisley Pink') pink flowers with orange centre • *H.* 'Wisley Primrose' ♀ primrose-yellow flowers • *H.* 'Wisley White' white flowers

ALPINES

IBERIS
Brassicaceae/Cruciferae
CANDYTUFT

▲ ❀ ❦ SI spring E
H 2 yrs 15–23cm (6–9in)
S 50–60cm (20–24in)
❊ -18°C (0°F)
Z 3–10

**IBERIS SEMPERVIRENS
'SCHNEEFLOCKE'**

Looking as if it is covered by snow when it is in flower, this spreading alpine plant is one of the first to flower. Neat in growth, non-invasive and easy to manage, it is suitable for all gardens, and it is especially attractive when it is grown with yellow daffodils.

Soil Moderately alkaline to acid, well drained and light in texture
Aspect Full sun to very light shade
Habit Carpeting, spreading, not invasive
Leaf Evergreen, dark green, lance-shaped leaves, 5–8cm (2–3in) long and 5mm (¼in) wide, with grey underside
Flower. Dome-shaped white flowers, formed from many small round petals and to 2.5cm (1in) wide, appear in mid-spring; often a repeat flowering in midsummer
Use In rock gardens, between paving and over walls; for ground cover or border edging
Needs Propagate by removing and replanting small, self-rooted side-growths or from cuttings in spring. Trim all over to reduce the length of the shoots by 20 per cent after the last flowering in summer to encourage new foliage and flowers the next year
Varieties *I. saxatilis* low growing, pink-tinged white flowers, to 15cm (6in) • *I. sempervirens* (syn. *I. commutata*) ♀ the basic white-flowered form • *I. s.* 'Schneeflocke' ('Snowflake') ♀ woody habit, white flowers • *I. s.* 'Weisser Zwerg' ('Little Gem') compact habit, white flowers

---

LEONTOPODIUM ALPINUM
Asteraceae/Compositae
EDELWEISS

▲ ❀ ❦ SI summer
H 2 yrs 23cm (9in)
S 23–30cm (9–12in)
❊ -15°C (4°F)
Z 4–9

LEONTOPODIUM ALPINUM

A plant that always conjures up visions of the Austrian Alps and *The Sound of Music*, the flowers look as if they are wrapped in woolly scarves to beat off the worst of winter's cold. The long flowering period and silver foliage make them attractive and interesting plants, but they are susceptible to cold, wet winters.

Soil Moderately alkaline to acid, well drained and sandy
Aspect Full sun
Habit Clump-forming basal foliage
Leaf Very attractive, deciduous, felty, grey-green, narrowly lance-shaped leaves, 4–6cm (1½–2½in) long
Flower Lance-shaped, woolly bracts surround brownish flowers to form an attractive head, 5–8cm (2–3in) across, on upright stems
Use For rock gardens, solo or grouped; good in containers indoors or out
Needs Propagate from seed sown in spring. Keep rain off in winter in a wet area
Varieties None of garden interest

LEWISIA
Portulacaceae
BITTERWOOD

▲ ❀ ❦ SI summer E
H 2 yrs 23cm (9in)
S 30cm (1ft)
❄ -5°C (23°F)
Z 3–9

It is almost impossible not to fall in love with this beautiful alpine plant. The bold ring of pastel, often shaded, multi-coloured flowers is held against an almost perfect ring of foliage. Unfortunately, it is not always winter hardy and must be planted in a protected place in very well-drained soil – a specially prepared planting niche in a dry stone wall, for example. Growing it in an alpine house is the ideal and certain way to enjoy this plant.

Soil Alkaline to moderately acid, light, well drained
Aspect Full sun to very light shade
Habit Flat topped, mound-forming
Leaf Evergreen, light silver-grey, lance-shaped, lobed leaves, 5–10cm (2–4in) long and 4cm (1½in) wide, radiating from a low central mound and often with red-orange shading
Flower Narrow, strap-like petals with notched ends form small, saucer-shaped flowers, which are borne in small clusters, in pastel shades of pink; some purple and silver-lined forms
Use For alpine or rock gardens; good when planted in niches in walls; will grow in containers both indoors and out
Needs Propagate from seed in spring. Protect in winter
Varieties *L. columbiana* pale pink to deep magenta flowers • *L. cotyledon* ♀ hybrids in a wide range of flower colours, the main forms planted • *L. rediviva* deciduous, pink or white flowers • *L. tweedyi* ♀ purple-tinged foliage, white to peach flowers

LEWISIA COTYLEDON

LITHODORA
Boraginaceae
LITHODORA

▲ ❀ ❦ SI summer E
H 2 yrs 15cm (6in)
S 75cm (30in)
❄ -10°C (14°F)
Z 3–9

The intense blue of this creeping carpeting plant, which used to be classified in the genus *Lithospermum*, catches the eye the moment it is seen. The colour is intensified by the dark evergreen foliage, over which the flowers stand, proud and erect. In addition to not being reliably hardy in very cold winters, these plants must have acid soil.

Soil Acid; dislikes any alkalinity; requires a high level of organic material in the soil
Aspect Prefers very light shade but will tolerate full sun as long as the soil is moist
Habit Spreading and moderately fast growing
Leaf Evergreen, dark green, narrow, lance-shaped leaves, to 5cm (2in) long, with silver underside
Flower Star-shaped flowers, 1cm (½in) across, formed from 6 small petals and produced in a mass over the surface of the plant in spring and summer; a white form is available and worth growing
Use As a spreading plant for rock gardens and screes. Can be grown in a large container with lime-free compost
Needs Propagate from cuttings in spring. Protect from cold in hard winters. Trim back shoots from the outside after flowering by 20 per cent of their length
Varieties *L. diffusa* 'Grace Ward' ♀ dark green foliage, bright blue flowers • *L. d.* 'Heavenly Blue' ♀ intense blue flowers, the main variety • *L. oleifolia* ♀ grey foliage, light blue flowers

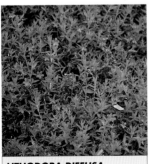

**LITHODORA DIFFUSA
'HEAVENLY BLUE'**

PHLOX
Polemoniaceae
ALPINE PHLOX

▲ ❀ ♥ SI spring E (semi)
H 2 yrs 8cm (3in)
S 60cm (2ft)
❄ -15°C (4°F)
Z 3–8

This low-carpeting alpine has a density of flowers almost without equal. From late spring to early summer it is covered in a mass of star-shaped flowers in a wide range of colours.

Soil Moderately alkaline to acid, open, light, well drained
Aspect Full sun
Habit Carpeting and creeping
Leaf Semi-evergreen, dark green, lance-shaped leaves, 3.5–4cm (1¼–1½in) long and 5mm (¼in) wide
Flower Flat or reflexed, saucer- and star-shaped flowers, to 1cm (½in) across, in a range of colours from white to pink, red, purple and blue; some bicoloured forms
Use For rock gardens, between paving, as front edging of borders or tumbling over walls; will grow in containers
Needs Propagate by division. Trim back from outer edges and top by 20 per cent of length after flowering to encourage new growth and flowers the following year
Varieties *P. adsurgens* ♀ small, leathery leaves, soft pink flowers • *P. douglasii* 'Boothman's Variety' ♀ violet-pink flowers with dark eye • *P. d.* 'Crackerjack' ♀ compact habit, red to magenta flowers • *P. d.* 'Iceberg' ♀ white, blue-tinged flowers • *P. d.* 'Red Admiral' ♀ crimson flowers • *P. × procumbens* (syn. *P. amoena*) more tufted, magenta-pink flowers • *P. stolonifera* (creeping phlox) quick spreading, blue, pink or white flowers • *P. subulata* 'Amazing Grace' pale pink flowers with deep pink centre • *P. s.* 'G.F. Wilson' deep lavender-blue flowers • *P. s.* 'Marjorie' deep pink flowers • *P. s.* 'McDaniel's Cushion' ♀ deep pink flowers

PHLOX DOUGLASII 'BOOTHMAN'S VARIETY'

SAXIFRAGA
Saxifragaceae
SAXIFRAGE

▲ ❀ ♥ SI all year E
H 2 yrs 5–30cm (2–12in)
S 15–60cm (6–24in)
❄ -15°C (4°F)
Z 6–9

The genus represents a large group of alpine-type plants, from the very low growing to those that are almost the size of a perennial plant. Some of the larger-growing forms can be used for small areas of ground cover.

Soil Moderately alkaline to acid, light and well drained
Aspect Full sun to very light shade
Habit Spreading and carpet-forming
Leaf Evergreen, small, lance-shaped or round leaves, borne in small rosettes, ranging in colour from white to silvery grey, light, mid, dark or red-green or yellow according to variety
Flower Star- or saucer-shaped flowers in shades of pink, red or yellow
Use For edging, underplanting or rock gardens; in containers; may tolerate being grown as a house plant in a cool room
Needs Propagate from cuttings in summer. Remove flower spikes when faded
Varieties *S.* 'Cloth of Gold' golden foliage, saucer-shaped, white flowers • *S.* 'Pearly King' mid-green foliage, saucer-shaped, white flowers, • *S.* 'Pixie' dark green foliage, saucer-shaped, rose-red flowers • *S.* 'Schwefelblüte' ('Flowers of Sulphur') green foliage, saucer-shaped, sulphur-yellow flowers • *S.* 'Triumph' mid-green foliage, saucer-shaped, blood-red flowers, • *S. umbrosa* light green foliage, star-shaped, pale pink flowers • *S. u.* 'Variegata' foliage splashed with yellow variegation, star-shaped, pale pink flowers • *S. × urbium* (London pride) green foliage, tiny, star-shaped, pink flowers

SAXIFRAGA × URBIUM

SEDUM
Crassulaceae
STONECROP

▲ ❀ ❦ SI all year E
H 2 yrs 8–10cm (3–4in)
S 30–50cm (12–20in)
❄ -15°C (4°F)
Z 4–10

**SEDUM SPATHULIFOLIUM
'CAPE BLANCO'**

Neat, carefree and colourful, these charming plants have many uses in the garden – there are so many species and varieties that you are sure to find room for at least one.

Soil Alkaline or acid, light and well drained
Aspect Full sun
Habit Carpet- and mat-forming with a medium growth rate
Leaf Evergreen, white to silver-white, green or purple-red, round leaves, 1cm (½in) across, in rosettes to 5cm (2in) wide
Flower Star-shaped, pink, red or bright yellow flowers, 5–10mm (¼–½in) across, in clusters
Use As carpeting plants for all areas including dry places; good on rock gardens and in containers; some can be used for ground cover
Needs Propagate by removing foliage rosettes and treating as cuttings
Varieties *S. acre* (biting stonecrop, wall pepper) pale green foliage, many small yellow flowers • *S. a.* 'Aureum' bright yellow flowers • *S. lydium* green, red-tipped foliage, white flowers • *S. obtusatum* green foliage, yellow flowers • *S. rupestre* (syn. *S. reflexum*) grey-green leaves, yellow flowers • *S. spathulifolium* bright yellow flowers • *S. s.* 'Cape Blanco' ♀ silvery-white foliage, yellow flowers • *S. s.* var. *majus* slightly larger leaves, yellow flowers • *S. s.* 'Purpureum' ♀ purple foliage, golden-yellow flowers

SEMPERVIVUM
Crassulaceae
HOUSELEEK

▲ ❀ ❦ SI all year E
H 2 yrs 13cm (5in)
S 50cm (20in)
❄ -15°C (4°F)
Z 5–10

**SEMPERVIVUM
'COMMANDER HAY'**

This hardy succulent always has attractive foliage, but when the foliage is topped by the arching, upright flower spikes it is even more eye-catching. Growing in a wide range of conditions, being relatively small and with a wide range of uses, it is a favourite with gardeners all over the world.

Soil Most, except very wet
Aspect Full sun to light shade
Habit Many single plants make up a mounded carpet
Leaf Numerous green to purple, pointed, rigid leaves form a rosette to 13cm (5in) across, which grows in ever-expanding carpets; some forms change to red in winter
Flower Upright flower stalks, nodding at the tops, the spikes covered with masses of pink flowers in summer
Use For rock gardens or containers; they even grow on old tiled roofs
Needs Propagate by removing leaves and treating as cuttings in spring
Varieties *S. arachnoideum* (cobweb houseleek) ♀ green to red foliage with fine white hairs between tips, pink flowers • *S.* 'Commander Hay' ♀ large green rosettes with red tips, green to red flowers, • *S. giuseppii* pea green foliage, pink flowers • *S.* 'Jubilee' mid-green foliage, pink flowers • *S.* 'Mahogany' mahogany-red foliage • *S. marmoreum* ssp. *marmoreum* 'Rubrifolium' red-purple foliage • *S. montanum* dark green foliage, purple flowers • *S.* 'Othello' brown-purple rosettes

THYMUS
Lamiaceae/Labiatae
THYME

▲ ✤ ❦ SI spring–summer
SC foliage E
H 2 yrs 5–8cm (2–3in)
S 30–60cm (1–2ft)
✳ -15°C (4°F)
Z 4–10

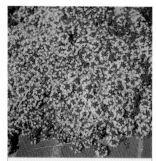

**THYMUS × SERPYLLUM
'ROSY CUSHION'**

This low-growing, aromatic plant has long been a favourite with gardeners, and not just for the pleasant scent that is released when the leaves are crushed.

Soil Tolerates high alkalinity; soil should be well drained because dislikes waterlogging
Aspect Full sun to light shade
Habit Creeping, carpet-forming, forming low mounds
Leaf Evergreen, light to dark green, aromatic, oval leaves, to 5mm (¼in) long and wide; some forms with grey or silver foliage, others silver- or gold-variegated
Flower Masses of small, star-shaped, tight clusters of flowers in white to shades of pink and red
Use For rock gardens; ideal for patios between paving; good in containers; some types can be used as culinary herbs
Needs Propagate from cuttings or by division in spring. Trim lightly in early spring, removing up to 9cm (3in) of growth
Varieties *T. × citriodorus* 'Archer's Gold' bright gold foliage • *T. × c.* 'Aureus' ♀ deep gold foliage • *T. × c.* 'Bertram Anderson' ♀ grey-green foliage shaded yellow • *T. × c.* 'Silver Queen' silver-variegated foliage • *T.* 'Doone Valley' gold-speckled, deep green foliage • *T. polytrichus* 'Porlock' bright pink flowers • *T. richardii* ssp. *nitudus* 'Peter Davis' green-grey foliage, pink flowers • *T. serpyllum* var. *albus* white flowers • *T. s.* 'Annie Hall' green foliage, flesh pink flowers • *T. s.* 'Pink Chintz' ♀ grey-green foliage, clear pink flowers

TRIFOLIUM
**Leguminosae/
Papilionaceae**
ORNAMENTAL CLOVER

▲ ✤ ❦ SI spring–autumn
E (semi)
H 2 yrs 8–15cm (3–6in)
S 50cm–1m (20–36in)
✳ -18°C (0°F)
Z 6–9

**TRIFOLIUM REPENS 'PURPUR-
ASCENS QUADRIFOLIUM'**

The purple, clover-like foliage, the white to yellow pea-shaped flowers and its ability to grow almost anywhere make this a very useful plant. It can be persistent in its colonization, but only rarely does it become invasive. It is often used to fill small, difficult spaces, but it is also useful as ground cover for underplanting roses or dwarf azaleas, which are difficult areas to cover without creating competition for the main planting.

Soil Most; very tolerant of dry areas once established
Aspect Full sun to light shade
Habit Spreading; may become invasive on, say, a rock garden, but is otherwise useful
Leaf Semi-evergreen, deep purple, green- or gold-margined divided leaves, 2–2.5cm (¾–1in) across, formed from 4 or more round leaflets
Flower Tiny, narrow pea flowers in summer borne in dense spikes in typical clover heads; red, pink or white, ageing to yellow, followed by small brown seedheads
Use For carpeting, ground cover or rock gardens, or between paving
Needs Propagate by division at almost any time
Varieties *T. pratense* 'Susan Smith' (syn. *T. p.* 'Dolly North', *T. repens* 'Gold Net') gold-edged green foliage, pink flowers • *T. repens* 'Purpurascens Quadrifolium' maroon leaves with bright green edges, white flowers ageing to yellow

ALCEA ROSEA
Malvaceae
HOLLYHOCK

▲ ❀ ❦ SI late spring–early summer E
H 1 yr 2m (6ft)
S 1 yr 50cm (20in)
❄ -10°C (14°F)
Z 2–10

ALCEA ROSEA CHATER'S DOUBLE GROUP

This cottage-garden plant never fails to attract attention with its upright flower spikes, which are festooned with single or double flowers in summer. The flowers open progressively from the bottom of the spike to the top, and the strong yet soft colours add to the dramatic effect. Hollyhocks may become perennial, and in many gardens they will self-seed freely but never to the extent of overstaying their welcome.

Soil Most; dislikes very wet or dry soil
Aspect Full sun
Habit Basal rosette of main leaves; flowers borne on strong upright spikes to the height indicated; a few may reach 2.5m (8ft)
Leaf Basal rosette formed of oval, mid-green leaves, 50cm (20in) long and half this in width with a dull light grey sheen; leaves on the flower spike are smaller
Flower Single or double flowers, 8cm (3in) across, in a range of colours; petals often with frilly edges, flowers at bottom of spike open first
Use As a feature plant; in mixed plantings
Needs Propagate by sowing seed in early summer
Varieties *A. rosea* Chater's Double Group pink, apricot, red, white, lavender, blue or yellow flowers • *A. r.* 'Indian Spring' white, pink or yellow single flowers, to 2.5m (8ft) • *A. r.* Majorette Group semi-double, mixed soft colours, to 1m (3ft) • *A. r.* 'Nigra' single, deep brown-maroon flowers, to 2m (6ft) • *A. r.* Summer Carnival Group double, wide range of colours, for annual growing only

BELLIS PERENNIS
Asteraceae/Compositae
DOUBLE DAISY

▲ ❀ ❦ SI late winter–spring E
H 1yr 60cm (2ft)
S 1yr 15–23cm (6–9in)
❄ -10°C (14°F)
Z 3–10

BELLIS PERENNIS

A reliable winter bedding plant, this daisy was widely used in the early 1900s and is now regaining its popularity and taking its rightful place among the plants used to brighten our gardens in early spring. Whether the small- or giant-flowered form is used, it mixes well with other spring plants, especially early bulbs.

Soil Moderately alkaline to acid, well-drained soil; apply generous amounts of plant food; if grown in a container, use good quality compost
Aspect Full sun to light shade; frost hardy
Habit Clump-forming
Leaf Evergreen, light green, oval, thick, fleshy, rough-edged leaves, 8–10cm (3–4in) long and 2.5–5cm (1–2in) wide, slightly indented and coated with soft hairs
Flower Narrow, round-ended petals form small or large, ball-shaped flowers, borne singly on slender stems above the foliage, ranging in colour from white, through pink to red, depending on the variety
Use For bedding, solo or *en masse* in gardens; good in containers, including hanging baskets
Needs Propagate from seed or by dividing mature clumps in late summer. Remove spent blooms to encourage second flowering
Varieties *B. perennis* 'Alba Plena' white petals with pink-red tips • *B. p.* 'Goliath' large flowers, mixed colours • *B. p.* 'Monstrosa' very large, pink, red and white flowers • *B. p.* 'Pomponette' small pink to red flowers

BIENNIALS

BRASSICA
Brassicaceae/Cruciferae
ORNAMENTAL CABBAGE

▲ ✔ SI autumn–winter E
H 1 yr 30cm (1ft)
S 1 yr 30cm (1ft)
❋ -5°C (23°F)
Z 4–8

BRASSICA OLERACEA

Grown as ornamental plants since the mid-nineteenth century, the worth of these brassicas as winter foliage plants is again being appreciated and they are coming once more into their own. Two types are available: the open-leaved kales and the true, close-leaved cabbage types. Both will stand a degree of cold, but very wet weather can cause rotting. Even so, they are very useful winter bedding plants.

Soil Most, except very wet or dry; when growing in containers use good quality compost
Aspect Full sun to light shade
Habit Cabbage- or kale-like foliage and growth
Leaf Open, lacerated, kale- or round-cabbage shaped foliage; colours include cream, white, pink and purple, either singly or in combinations of three colours
Flower None; flowering denotes the end of their useful lives
Use As ornamental foliage plants for the garden or containers; small plants can be used in hanging baskets
Needs Propagate by seed sown in early summer. Try to grow or buy plants in large containers; those grown in small pots do not increase in size when planted into their final growing positions. It is important to remove dead lower leaves as they show to prevent further rotting
Varieties *B. japonica* var. *crispifolia* generic name for kale group • *B. oleracea* generic name for cabbage group

---

DIGITALIS
Scrophulariaceae
FOXGLOVE

▲ ❀ ✔ SI spring–early summer E (semi)
H 1–2 yrs 0.5–1.5m (20in–5ft)
S 1 yr 30–50cm (12–20in)
❋ -10°C (14°F)
Z 3–10

DIGITALIS PURPUREA

Elegant, statuesque, colourful and, above all, easy to grow foxgloves that are planted or sown can, after flowering in the second year, turn biennial. There is a white form of garden merit that, unfortunately, does not stay true and in the second and third generation of plants almost always turns purple in flower.

Soil Alkaline to acid, moisture retentive
Aspect Full sun to light shade
Habit Upright
Leaf Semi-evergreen, light green to light grey-green, oval to lance-shaped leaves 6–20cm (2½–8in) long and 1–15cm (½–6in) wide
Flower Lipped, tubular, nodding flowers, hanging from upright stems, in shades of rose, purple, white or yellow, often with darker internal throat markings, in spring
Use For mid- or background planting in mixed or perennial borders or a in wild garden
Needs Propagate from seed. Cut to ground level in autumn. Apply a general fertilizer in spring or replace plants annually by self-sown seedlings, sown seed or purchased pre-grown plants in autumn
Varieties *D. grandiflora* (yellow foxglove) ♀ yellow flowers with brownish throat markings • *D. purpurea* rose-purple flowers with darker throat markings • *D. p.* f. *albiflora* ♀ white flowers, but not stable, turning purple in second generation • *D. p.* Foxy Group good pink flowers facing both ways on flower spikes

ERYSIMUM
Brassicaceae/Cruciferae
WALLFLOWER

▲ ✿ ❦ SI spring SC E
H 1 yr 30–50cm (12–20in)
S 1 yr 25–40cm (10–16in)
❄ -10°C (14°F)
Z 3–10

**ERYSIMUM CHEIRI
'PERSIAN CARPET'**

This plant, formerly classified in the genus *Cheiranthus*, has always held the affection of gardeners and is still planted widely for its bold flower display. There are many individual straight-coloured varieties but not all are grown by commercial horticulture. Mixed colour selections have become the norm, planted on their own or with tulips.

Soil Most well-drained and well-fed soils
Aspect Full sun to light shade
Habit Upright, becoming more bushy just before flowering; in very sheltered areas may become perennial, particularly the Siberian wallflower (*E. × allionii*)
Leaf Evergreen, light grey-green, lance-shaped leaves, 8–9cm (3–3½in) long and 1–2cm (½–¾in) wide
Flower Unmistakably scented flowers, 2.5cm (1in) across, borne in open clusters of 25 or more in spring; each flower formed of 4 round petals; colours range from white to pink, red, purple, yellow or orange, according to variety
Use As grouped or massed spring bedding; can be grown in the garden or in containers; good in combination with other spring-flowering plants and bulbs
Needs Propagate from seed in summer
Varieties *E. × allionii* (Siberian wallflower) bright orange flowers • *E. × a.* 'Golden Bedder' deep golden-yellow flowers • *E. cheiri* 'Persian Carpet' (wallflower, gillyflower) flowers in mixed pastel colours • *E. c.* 'Vulcan' deep red flowers • *E. c.* 'Eastern Queen' flowers in shades of pink • *E. c.* 'Tom Thumb Mixed' dwarf variety, flowers in mixed colours

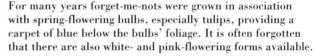

MYOSOTIS
Boraginaceae
FORGET-ME-NOT

▲ ✿ ❦ SI spring E
H 1 yr 15–20cm (6–8in)
S 1 yr 20–30cm (8–12in)
❄ -10°C (14°F)
Z 3–10

MYOSOTIS ALPESTRIS

For many years forget-me-nots were grown in association with spring-flowering bulbs, especially tulips, providing a carpet of blue below the bulbs' foliage. It is often forgotten that there are also white- and pink-flowering forms available.

Soil Alkaline to acid; feed well for good flowering
Aspect Full sun to light shade
Habit Spreading; self-seeding after flowering; they germinate and continue to grow this way for many years
Leaf Evergreen, light grey-green, oval to lance-shaped leaves, 8–9cm (3–3½in) long and 1cm (½in) wide, with pointed end
Flower Small, square, saucer-shaped flowers, borne in clusters 1–2.5cm (½–1in) across above foliage, in early to late spring; colours range from white, pale to deep blue and pink
Use For mixed borders, edging or underplanting of spring-flowering bulbs. Good in the open garden and containers
Needs Allow to seed after flowering to ensure self-sown plants for the future. Attacked by a symbiotic fungus that shows up about 4 weeks before the plants flower and clears up just in time before flowering
Varieties *M. alpestris* (alpine forget-me-not) bright blue flowers with creamy-white eyes • *M. a.* 'Alba' white flowers • *M. a.* 'Indigo' deep blue flowers • *M. a.* 'Ultramarine' ultramarine blue flowers • *M. sylvatica* (garden forget-me-not) similar species, true biennial and taller, blue flowers • *M. s.* 'Rosea' pink flowers look good with red tulips both tall and dwarf

PRIMULA
Primulaceae
POLYANTHA

▲ ❀ ✇ SI late winter–early spring SC E
H 1 yr 20–30cm (8–12in)
S 1 yr 30cm (1ft)
❄ -10°C (14°F)
Z 3–9

PRIMULA CRESCENDO SERIES

This versatile spring-flowering plant is, rightly, loved by all gardeners. Usually planted in autumn to flower in the following spring, they can also be grown on as perennial plants for many years, bringing colour and interest to the spring garden for years to come.

Soil Most well-prepared and moisture-retentive soils
Aspect Full sun to light shade
Habit Clump-forming, evergreen and almost dormant in winter; coming into life and flower in early spring
Leaf Oval to lance-shaped, deeply veined, dark green leaves, often to 25cm (10in) long; frost-resistant and attractive
Flower Typical primrose-shaped flowers, in a wide range of single and bicoloured shades, are borne in clusters on long, upright flower stalks, to 30cm (1ft) tall, from late winter to early summer
Use For solo or mass-planting in the garden or containers, including hanging baskets; mixes well with other spring-flowering bedding plants and bulbs
Needs Propagate by division or seed in early summer. Remove dead flowerheads and leaves
Varieties *P.* Cowichan Series bronze-green foliage, velvet-textured petals • *P.* Crescendo Series wide range of flower colour all with bold, yellow central spot • *P.* Rainbow Series wide range of flower colour on shorter stems

VIOLA ×
WITTROCKIANA
Violaceae
WINTER-FLOWERING
PANSY

▲ ❀ ✇ SI winter–spring E
H 1 yr 20–25cm (8–10in)
S 1 yr 25–40cm (10–16in)
❄ -10°C (14°F)
Z 4–8

VIOLA WINTER FLOWERING MIXED

The range of colours and winter hardiness of this group of plants continues to grow, and they rank among the best biennials for winter and early spring flower displays. Very cold weather can set them back but only rarely kills them. The main flowering time is early spring, but, depending on the weather, intermittent flowering at other times is possible.

Soil Alkaline to acid, well fed
Aspect Full sun to medium shade
Habit Short and clump-forming; although mainly grown as biennials, they will often turn into perennial plants and grow for several years
Leaf Evergreen, dark glossy green, oval leaves 4.5–8cm (1¾–3in) long, rounded and toothed, with duller underside
Flower Rounded, flat-faced, forward-looking flowers, 5–8cm (2–3in) across, formed from 5 fan-shaped petals, mono- or multicoloured with dark shading, colours depending on variety; flowers appear in winter and spring, but sometimes year round
Use As winter and spring bedding for containers, including hanging baskets, or the open garden
Needs Propagate from seed in midsummer. Remove dead flowers as seen. Trim lightly in spring if grown for a second year
Varieties *V.* 'Chantreyland' large, bright apricot-orange flowers • *V.* Winter Flowering Mixed hybrids in mixed colours • *V.* × *wittrockiana* commercial hybrids • *V.* 'Yellow Queen' large, deep golden-yellow flowers

ABIES
Pinaceae
SILVER FIR

▲ ❦ SI all year SC foliage
pine-scented E
H 10 yrs *see below*
S 10 yrs *see below*
❄ -15°C (4°F)
Z 4–7

**ABIES LASIOCARPA
'ARIZONICA COMPACTA'**

These slow-growing firs are miniature versions of their big brothers. The needles, which are dark green or blue, are tightly packed around the branches, and, as with all conifers, the scent of the foliage is pleasing. In addition, at maturity they produce cones.

Soil Most
Aspect Full sun to very light shade
Habit Mound-forming or spreading
Leaf Evergreen, short, green or glaucous-green needles
Flower None; cones produced at maturity
Use For specimen planting on rock gardens; ideal as specimens in lawns and open areas; can be grown in large containers with success as long as good quality compost is used
Needs Propagate from cuttings in summer or by commercial grafting. No pruning required but can be lightly trimmed to shape if necessary
Varieties (Treble H and S for dimensions at maturity)
A. balsamea f. *hudsonia* ♀ slow growing, glossy green foliage, 30 × 60cm (1 × 2ft) • *A. concolor* 'Compacta' (syn. *A. c.* 'Glauca Compacta') slow growing, glaucous tinge to foliage, irregular shape, 3 × 3m (10 × 10ft) • *A. lasiocarpa* 'Arizonica Compacta' ♀ slow growing, greyish-green foliage, irregular shape, 1 × 1m (3 × 3ft)

ARAUCARIA ARAUCANA
Araucariaceae
CHILE PINE, MONKEY PUZZLE TREE

▲ ❦ SI all year SC foliage
pine-scented E
H 10 yrs 8m (26ft)
S 10 yrs 4m (13ft)
❄ -15°C (4°F) Z 3–9

ARAUCARIA ARAUCANA

The rigid, scale-like needles that hug the branches make this tree almost impossible to climb – no doubt the source of one of its common names. Araucarias have been known since the dinosaurs, and they were widely planted in Victorian times, which means that many are seen in gardens today. If you have the space, plant one now so that it will be enjoyed in the year 2100.

Soil Most; dislikes very wet soil
Aspect Full sun; shade leads to distorted shape
Habit Open and upright, becoming more round-topped in time; slow to establish but growing faster in the third or forth year after planting, but slowing down after 20 years; will reach 25m (80ft) at maturity (80 years)
Leaf Evergreen, dark glossy green, short, flat and sharp needles borne in spirals along branches
Flower None; cones produced at maturity
Use As a specimen for open areas or as a sentinel; can be planted as an avenue at distances of 14m (46ft)
Needs Propagate from seed in spring; plant out when 60–75cm (24–30in) tall and purchase only container-grown (for preference) or root-balled plants
Varieties None

CALOCEDRUS
Cupressaceae
INCENSE CEDAR

▲ ❦ SI all year SC foliage
pine-scented E
H 10 yrs *see below*
S 10 yrs *see below*
❋ -18°C (0°F)
Z 2–9

This attractive conifer was once called *Libocedrus decurrens* and under that name was widely planted by the Victorians in almost every garden of any importance. Today these plantings still exist, although some are now beginning to show their age. Only recently has its value been appreciated by today's gardeners, and it is being planted again, although this means that only relatively young or very old plants are seen.

Soil Most
Aspect Full sun
Habit Upright, columnar and tight, strict regimented formation
Leaf Evergreen fronds, mid- to dark green or splashed pale yellow to gold, all facing upwards and overlapping to form a column of foliage
Flower Red bud-like flowers and cones produced on very mature plants
Use For specimen planting; ideal as a feature to mark, say, an entrance or gateway; good in the winter garden landscape, standing out boldly in colour and shape
Needs Propagate from cuttings in summer or by commercial grafting. No pruning required but can be lightly trimmed. May be damaged by heavy snow
Varieties (Quadruple H and S for dimensions at maturity) *C. decurrens* ♀ broad column of flattened, rich green, fan-shaped foliage, 2 × 0.75m (6ft × 30in) • *C. d.* 'Aureovariegata' mid-green, gold-splashed foliage, 2 × 0.75m (6ft × 30in)

CALOCEDRUS DECURRENS

CEDRUS
Pinaceae
CEDAR

▲ ❦ SI all year SC foliage
pine-scented E
H 10 yrs *see below*
S 10 yrs *see below*
❋ -18°C (0°F)
Z 2–8

One of the most admired of large conifers, with a number of dwarf forms worth consideration.

Soil Most
Aspect Full sun
Habit Upright, pendulous or prostrate, or mound-forming
Leaf Evergreen, tufted fronds of green, glaucous-green, gold or grey
Flower Red 'buds' followed by grey-blue cones, ageing to brown, produced only at maturity
Use For specimen planting where space allows
Needs Propagate from seed or by commercial grafting
Varieties (Quadruple H and S for dimensions at maturity) *C. deodara* (Himalayan cedar, deodar cedar) drooping tips to greyish-green foliage, 3 × 2m (10 × 6ft) • *C. d.* 'Aurea' (golden deodar cedar) ♀ drooping tips to golden-yellow foliage, 3 × 2m (10 × 6ft) • *C. d.* 'Golden Horizon' spreading but bushy, soft yellow foliage, 2 × 3m (6 × 10ft) • *C. libani* (cedar of Lebanon) conical habit becoming flat-topped with age, bright to dark green foliage, 2 × 1.5m (6 × 5ft) • *C. l.* ssp. *atlantica* 'Aurea' (syn. *C. atlantica* 'Aurea'; Blue Atlas cedar) upright, golden-yellow foliage, 2 × 1m (6 × 3ft) • *C. l.* ssp. *atlantica* Glauca Group (syn. *C. atlantica* f. *glauca*; blue cedar, Atlas cedar) upright, glaucous-green foliage, 4 × 2m (16 × 6ft) • *C. l.* ssp. *atlantica* 'Glauca Pendula' pendulous, bluish-white foliage, 3 × 2m (10 × 6ft) • *C. l.* ssp. *libani* 'Sargentii' slow growing, weeping, prostrate, dark foliage, 1 × 1.2m (3 × 4ft)

**CEDRUS LIBANI ssp.
ATLANTICA GLAUCA GROUP**

CHAMAECYPARIS
Cupressaceae
FALSE CYPRESS – SLOW
GROWING

▲ ꙮ SI all year SC foliage
pine-scented E
H 10 yrs *see below*
S 10 yrs *see below*
❄ -18°C (0°F)   Z 2–9

**CHAMAECYPARIS LAWSONI-
ANA 'ELLWOOD'S GOLD'**

The mainstay of collections of dwarf conifers, and there are
many interesting forms. Beware the word 'dwarf': many can
reach substantial size.

Soil Most
Aspect Full sun
Habit Upright, pyramidal or round
Leaf Evergreen fronds of green, blue, gold, grey or variegated
Flower Red 'buds' and brown cones produced at maturity
Use As specimens wherever a small, neat feature plant is
required
Needs Propagate from cuttings in summer or by commercial
grafting. Can be lightly trimmed in spring to improve shape
Varieties (Treble H and S for dimensions at maturity)
C. lawsoniana 'Ellwoodii' ♀ slow growing, upright, close,
grey foliage, 2 × 0.75m (6ft × 30in) • *C. l.* 'Ellwood's Gold'
♀ slow growing, upright, green, gold-tipped foliage, 1.5 ×
0.75m (5ft × 30in) • *C. l.* 'Minima Aurea' ♀ slow growing,
tightly packed, bright yellow foliage, 1 × 0.75m (3ft × 30in) •
C. l. 'Minima Glauca' ♀ slow growing, rounded, bushy, sea
green foliage, 1.2 × 1m (4 × 3ft) • *C. l.* 'Pygmaea Argentea'
♀ slow growing, mound-forming, bluish-green foliage with
silvery-white tips, 60 × 50cm (24 × 20in) • *C. obtusa* 'Kosteri'
slow growing, flattened sprays of bright green foliage, bronze
in winter, 1.2 × 1m (4 × 3ft) • *C. pisifera* 'Boulevard' ♀ slow
growing, silvery-blue foliage, 1.5 × 1m (5 × 3ft) • *C. p.*
'Filifera Aurea' ♀ slow growing, broadly conical, bright
yellow, thin, thread-like foliage, 1.2 × 1m (4 × 3ft)

CHAMAECYPARIS
Cupressaceae
FALSE CYPRESS –
SPECIMEN TREES

▲ ꙮ SI all year SC foliage
pine-scented E
H 10 yrs *see below*
S 10 yrs *see below*
❄ -18°C (0°F)   Z 2–9

**CHAMAECYPARIS
LAWSONIANA 'LANE'**

These are among the most important groups of garden-sized
specimens, offering much in diversity of colour and shape.

Soil Most
Aspect Full sun
Habit Upright, pyramidal, conical or pendulous
Leaf Evergreen fronds of green, glaucous-green, gold or grey
Flower Red or blue 'buds' and small brown cones produced
at maturity
Use As specimen planting; if planted at distances of 1m (3ft)
those indicated will produce a formal or informal hedge
Needs Propagate from cuttings in summer or by commercial
grafting. Can be trimmed
Varieties (Treble H and S for dimensions at maturity)
C. lawsoniana 'Allumii' compact, bluish foliage, 2 × 1.2m
(6 × 4ft), hedge • *C. l.* 'Columnaris' narrow pillar, bluish-
grey foliage, H 2 × 0.75m (6ft × 30in) • *C. l.* 'Erecta' upright,
deep green foliage, 2 × 1.2m (6 × 4ft), hedge • *C. l.* 'Fletcheri'
♀ columnar, soft grey-green foliage, 1.5 × 1m (5 × 3ft) •
C. l. 'Green Pillar' upright, green foliage, 2 × 0.75m (6ft ×
30in) • *C. l.* 'Lane' (syn. *C. l.* 'Lanei') conical, golden foliage,
2 × 1m (6 × 3ft), hedge • *C. l.* 'Pembury Blue' ♀ conical,
blue foliage, 2 × 1.2m (6 × 4ft), hedge • *C. l.* 'Pottenii'
pyramidal, feathery, light green foliage, 2 × 1m (6 × 3ft) •
C. l. 'Stewartii' conical, golden foliage 2 × 1.2m (6 × 4ft),
hedge • *C. l.* 'Wissellii' ♀ twisting branches, blue-green
foliage, 1.5 × 0.75m (5ft × 30in) • *C. pisifera* 'Plumosa Aurea'
conical, feathery light golden foliage, 1.5 × 1m (5 × 3ft)

CRYPTOMERIA
Taxodiaceae
JAPANESE CEDAR

▲ ❦ SI all year SC foliage
pine-scented E
H 10 yrs *see below*
S 10 yrs *see below*
❄ -15°C (4°F)
Z 3–8

**CRYPTOMERIA JAPONICA
'ELEGANS COMPACTA'**

This is an interesting group of conifers but one that is not
widely planted. There is a good range of heights, colours and
foliage textures within the genus, and all the plants establish
themselves quickly.

Soil Most
Aspect Full sun
Habit Upright, pyramidal, mound-forming and spreading
Leaf Evergreen, short or long needles, green, glaucous-
green, gold or grey
Flower None; fir cones produced at maturity
Use For specimen planting on rock gardens
Needs Propagate from cuttings in summer or by commercial
grafting. No pruning required but can be lightly trimmed
Varieties (Treble H and S for dimensions at maturity)
C. japonica (Japanese cedar) fast growing, tall, upright, with
attractive thick green foliage with an orange tinge, attractive
orange-red bark on trunks, 5 × 3m (16 × 10ft) • *C. j.*
'Elegans' broadly conical habit, brown-green foliage turning
to copper-bronze, 3 × 3m (10 × 10ft) • *C. j.* 'Elegans
Compacta' (syn. C. j. 'Elegans Nana') soft, fluffy, light
green foliage, turning bronze in winter, 1 × 1m (3 × 3ft) •
C. j. 'Globosa Nana' slow growing, neat rounded bush,
yellowish-green foliage turning bluish in winter, 1.2 × 1.2m (4
× 4ft) • *C. j.* 'Spiralis' slow growing, twisted branches, green
foliage, 1 × 1m (3 × 3ft) • *C. j.* 'Vilmoriniana' ♀ slow
growing, tight congested bush, rich red-purple winter colour,
1 × 1m (3 × 3ft)

× CUPRESSOCYPARIS LEYLANDII
Cupressaceae
LEYLAND CYPRESS

▲ ❦ SI all year SC foliage
pine-scented E
H 10 yrs *see below*
S 10 yrs *see below*
❄ -18°C (0°F)   Z 3–8

**× CUPRESSOCYPARIS
LEYLANDII**

A group of conifers that has achieve a certain degree of
notoriety, because once they are established, they just grow
and grow. They do make good hedges where there is space to
accommodate them.

Soil Most deep, well-prepared soils; dislikes very alkaline or
wet soil
Aspect Full sun
Habit Upright, pyramidal
Leaf Evergreen fronds of green, gold- or white-splashed
variegated
Flower None
Use As specimen planting; good as a windbreak, especially
in seaside areas; a good formal or informal hedge if planted
at distances of 1m (3ft)
Needs Propagate from cuttings in summer. No pruning
required but will need trimming 2–3 times a year in this form
Varieties (Treble H and S for dimensions at maturity)
× *C. leylandii* very fast and large growing, broad, columnar,
graceful habit, bright green foliage, 6 × 2m (21 × 6ft) •
× *C. l.* 'Castlewellan' fast growing, pyramidal, golden-yellow
foliage, 4 × 2m (13 × 6ft) • × *C. l.* 'Harlequin' fast growing,
white-splashed variegation, 3 × 2m (13 × 6ft) • × *C. l.*
'Naylor's Blue' dark blue sheen to foliage, 3 × 1.5m (13 × 5ft)
• × *C. l.* 'Robinson's Gold' ♀ slightly fuller and slower than
× *C. l.* 'Castlewellan', yellow foliage, 4 × 2m (13 × 6ft)

CUPRESSUS
Cupressaceae
CYPRESS

▲ ✿ SI all year SC foliage
pine-scented E
H 10 yrs *see below*
S 10 yrs *see below*
✳ -15°C (4°F)
Z 3–9

**CUPRESSUS ARIZONICA
'PYRAMIDALIS'**

This group of conifers represents the extremes of hardiness. Some of the species are among the hardiest of plants, but others are comparatively tender. This latter group, however, includes cypresses that are excellent for maritime areas and for city gardens, where they appreciate the extra protection afforded by the buildings.

Soil Most
Aspect Full sun
Habit Upright, pyramidal specimens; all are very fast growing
Leaf Evergreen, long, open fronds of green, gold or blue
Flower None; fir cones produced at maturity
Use For specimen planting; hardy forms good for screening; all good in coastal areas
Needs Propagate from cuttings in summer. No pruning required but can be lightly trimmed in spring to improve shape. May require protection in winter
Varieties (Triple H and S for dimensions at maturity)
C. arizonica 'Pyramidalis' ♀ upright, wide column, intense bright blue, very hardy, 5 × 2m (16 × 6ft) • *C. macrocarpa* (Monterey cypress) conical when young, becoming broad-topped with age, bright green foliage, tender, 4 × 1.5m (13 × 5ft) • *C. m.* 'Goldcrest' ♀ upright habit, bright golden-yellow foliage if planted in full sun, can be tender, H 3 × 1.2m (10 × 4ft) • *C. sempervirens* 'Stricta' (Italian cypress) ♀ narrow, columnar habit, dark green foliage, tender, H 2.5 × 0.6m (8 × 2ft)

GINKGO
Ginkgoaceae
MAIDENHAIR TREE

▲ ✿ SI summer–autumn
H 10 yrs *see below*
S 10 yrs *see below*
✳ -18°C (0°F)
Z 3–5

GINKGO BILOBA

This deciduous conifer, with its unusually shaped foliage, provides some of the finest autumn colour. When it is used as a specimen tree, there is little that can compare with it.

Soil Most
Aspect Full sun
Habit Upright male forms, spreading forms female; a rare pendulous form exists, as does a rather poor variegated variety; slow to establish, it gains height between 3 and 20 years, after which it slows down until, in 50 years, reaching a height of 18m (60ft) with a spread of 9m (30ft)
Leaf Deciduous, fan-shaped, light grey-green foliage; good yellow autumn colour
Flower Inconspicuous, small, soft, round sulphur yellow, plum-like fruits produced in warm gardens in hot summers
Use As a specimen tree for medium to large gardens; good as avenue planted at distances of 14m (46ft); can be fan-trained on a large wall
Needs Propagate from seed sown in spring or by commercial grafting. No pruning required
Varieties (Treble H and S for dimensions at maturity)
G. biloba ♀ pale green, fan-shaped leaves turning yellow in autumn, the main form, 2 × 1m (6 × 3ft) • *G. b.* 'Fastigiata' male, fastigiate form, 1.5 × 0.6m (5 × 2ft) • *G. b.* 'Pendula' a rare form for its weeping habit, 1.5 × 1m (5 × 3ft) • *G. b.* 'Variegata' leaves splashed white mainly in spring and early summer, 1.5 × 1m (5 × 3ft)

CONIFERS

JUNIPERUS
Cupressaceae
JUNIPER – SLOW GROWING

▲ ♦ SI all year SC foliage
juniper-scented E
H 10 yrs *see below*
S 10 yrs *see below*
❄ -18°C (0°F)   Z 3–8

JUNIPERUS COMMUNIS 'COMPRESSA'

There are many charming and useful dwarf conifers in this genus, all of value in providing specimen feature plants. When buying, take care, for there is a wide range of sizes; all those listed here are moderately slow growing.

Soil Most
Aspect Full sun to very light shade
Habit Upright, spreading, pyramidal and mound-forming
Leaf Evergreen fronds of needles, green, glaucous-green, gold or grey
Flower None
Use As specimens; good in large containers
Needs Propagate from cuttings in summer or by grafting
Varieties (Double H and S for dimensions at maturity)
J. chinensis 'Aurea' ♀ conical, gold foliage, 1 × 0.6m (3 × 2ft) • *J. c.* 'Pyramidalis' ♀ pyramidal, blue foliage, 1.2 × 0.75m (4ft × 30in) • *J. c.* 'Compressa' ♀ tight conical bush, light green foliage, possibly the most dwarf conifer in gardens, H 30 × 13cm (12 × 5in) • *J. c.* 'Hibernica' (Irish juniper) ♀ narrow column, grey foliage, 1.5 × 0.3m (5 × 1ft) • *J. × media* 'Blaauw' branches turn outwards at tips, scale-like, upright, becoming spreading, deep grey-green foliage, 1.2 × 1.2m (4 × 4ft) • *J. procumbens* 'Nana' ♀ ground-hugging habit, bright apple-green foliage, 40 × 60cm (16 × 24in) • *J. scopulorum* 'Skyrocket' narrow column, blue-grey foliage, 2.5 × 0.3m (8 × 1ft) • *J. squamata* 'Blue Star' ♀ dense, bushy, steel-blue foliage, 0.75 × 1m (30in × 3ft) • *J. s.* 'Meyeri' dense, block-forming, steel-blue foliage, 1.5 × 1.5m (5 × 5ft)

JUNIPERUS
Cupressaceae
JUNIPER – SPREADING

▲ ♦ SI all year SC foliage
juniper-scented E
H 10 yrs *see below*
S 10 yrs *see below*
❄ -18°C (0°F)
Z 3–9

JUNIPERUS × MEDIA 'OLD GOLD'

A very large group of conifers, invaluable for ground cover.

Soil Most
Aspect Full sun to very light shade
Habit Upright, spreading, pyramidal, mound-forming, pendulous
Leaf Evergreen fronds of green, glaucous-green, gold, grey or variegated
Flower None; berries may be produced at maturity
Use For ground cover, hanging over banks or walls; as specimens; smaller varieties can be grown in containers
Needs Propagate from cuttings in summer or by commercial grafting. No pruning required
Varieties (Double H and S for dimensions at maturity)
J. communis 'Depressa Aurea' golden in summer, bronze in winter, 0.75 × 1.2m (30in × 4ft) • *J. c.* 'Repanda' ♀ carpet-forming, dull green foliage, 0.6 × 2m (2 × 6ft) • *J. horizontalis* (creeping juniper) prostrate, blue-green foliage, 0.3 × 1.5m (1 × 5ft) • *J. × media* 'Old Gold' ♀ fast growing, prostrate, golden foliage, 1 × 2m (3 × 6ft) • *J. × m.* 'Pfitzeriana' (Pfitzer juniper) ♀ semi-prostrate, vigorous, dark green foliage with drooping tips, 1.2 × 2m (4 × 6ft) • *J. × m.* 'Pfizeriana Aurea' (golden Pfitzer) semi-prostrate, gold-tipped foliage, 1.5 × 2m (5 × 6ft) • *J. sabina* 'Blau Donau' ('Blue Danube') prostrate, grey-green foliage, 1 × 1.2m (3 × 4ft) • *J. s.* 'Tamariscifolia' prostrate, grey-blue foliage, 0.6 × 1.5m (2 × 5ft) • *J. virginiana* 'Grey Owl' ♀ semi-prostrate, vigorous, grey-blue, 1.2 × 2m (4 × 6ft)

LARIX
Pinaceae
LARCH
▲ ✿ SI spring–autumn SC
foliage pine-scented
H 10 yrs *see below*
S 10 yrs *see below*
❄ -15°C (4°F)
Z 3–8

LARIX KAEMPFERI

A group of deciduous conifers which has many attractive features. The weeping form makes one of the most graceful of trees if there is space for it to grow to its full size.

Soil Most; prefers sandy, light-textured soil
Aspect Full sun
Habit Upright or pendulous; very fast growing
Leaf Deciduous, bunches of light green, soft needles in spring, turning bright yellow to gold in autumn; spectacular in both seasons
Flower Very small flowers, yellow (male) and red (female); small brown cones produced in quantity at maturity
Use For specimen planting singly or in groups; useful for forming windbreaks and screens; planted *en masse* as a small wood or larger plantation
Needs Propagate from seed sown in spring or, for the weeping form, by commercial grafting on to stems of *L. decidua*. No pruning required. Apart from weeping form, plant small trees at distances of about 50cm (20in); both bare-rooted or container- grown plants can be found
Varieties (Quadruple H and S for dimensions at maturity) *L. decidua* (European larch, common larch) ♀ conical habit, light green foliage, ageing to yellow, 5 × 2m (16 × 6ft) • *L. kaempferi* (Japanese larch) ♀ conical habit, bright green foliage, ageing to yellow, 5 × 2m (16 × 6ft) • *L. k.* 'Pendula' (weeping Japanese larch) wide-spreading weeping habit, 4 × 5m (13 × 16ft) • *L.* × *marschlinsii* new yellow shoots, otherwise as *L. decidua*

METASEQUOIA, TAXODIUM
Taxodiaceae
REDWOOD, SWAMP
CYPRESS

▲ ✿ SI summer–autumn
H 10 yrs *see below*
S 10 yrs *see below*
-15°C (4°F)   Z 3–8

**METASEQUOIA
GLYPTOSTROBOIDES**

These two genera are grouped as their characteristics and needs are very similar, although the swamp cypresses (as their name suggests) tolerate slightly wetter growing conditions and can, in fact, be planted right at the water's edge. They overcome root suffocation by slowly sending up strange nodules or breathing roots.

Soil Moist to wet, tolerating averagely moist conditions
Aspect Full sun
Habit Upright columns, producing specimen trees; trees in both genera have interesting and attractive trunks and stems
Leaf Deciduous fronds of bright green, feather-like foliage with good yellow-bronze autumn colour
Flower None; small cones produced at maturity after a hot summer
Use As a specimen plant, near or away from a water feature
Needs Propagate from cuttings in summer or seed in spring. No pruning required
Varieties (Quadruple H and S for ultimate dimensions) *Metasequoia glyptostroboides* ♀ conical, open, strong-growing, flattened, feathery, bright green foliage, ageing to bronze, then golden, 4 × 1.5m (13 × 5ft) • *Taxodium distichum* ♀ column shaped, feathery, light green foliage, yellow-bronze autumn colour • *T. d.* var. *imbricarium* (syn. *T. d.* var. *ascendens*) branchlets are drooping, 3 × 1.2m (10 × 4ft) • *T. d.* var. *i.* 'Nutans' ♀ leaves narrower, drooping and giving the appearance of many thin ropes, 2.5 × 1.2m (8 × 4ft)

CONIFERS

PICEA
Pinaceae
SPRUCE

▲ ❦ SI all year SC foliage
pine-scented E
H 10 yrs *see below*
S 10 yrs *see below*
❄ -18°C (0°F)
Z 2–8

PICEA PUNGENS 'KOSTER'

It is hard not to think of Christmas when describing this group of plants. The genus includes a far wider range of useful garden plants than this seasonal symbol might suggest.

Soil Most, except very wet
Aspect Full sun
Habit Spreading, pyramidal, mound-forming
Leaf Evergreen, short or long needles, green, glaucous-green, gold or grey
Flower None; cones produced at maturity
Use For specimen planting
Needs Propagate from seed. No pruning required
Varieties (Treble H and S for ultimate dimensions) *P. abies* (common spruce, Norway spruce, Christmas tree) conical habit, mid-green foliage, short needles, 2 × 1.2m (6 × 4ft) • *P. a.* 'Nidiformis' ♀ slow-growing, flat-topped, spreading habit, dark green foliage, 1 × 1m (3 × 3ft) • *P. breweriana* (Brewer's weeping spruce) ♀ conical, weeping habit, long, pendulous branchlets, dark blue-green foliage, 2 × 1.2m (6 × 4ft) • *P. glauca* var. *albertiana* 'Conica' ♀ slow growing, conical habit, dense bright-green foliage, 1.2 × 0.75m (4ft × 30in) • *P. mariana* 'Nana' ♀ slow growing, very tight, congested ball, grey-blue foliage, 1 × 1m (3 × 3ft) • *P. omorika* 'Pendula' ♀ narrow, conical habit, drooping branches, dark green foliage, 1.5 × 1m (5 × 3ft) • *P. pungens* 'Globosa' ♀ slow growing, irregular bushy habit, dense blue foliage, 1 × 1m (3 × 3ft) • *P. p.* 'Koster' (Koster spruce) ♀ silver-blue foliage, 1.2 × 1m (4 × 3ft)

PINUS
Pinaceae
PINE

▲ ❦ SI all year SC foliage
pine-scented E
H 10 yrs *see below*
S 10 yrs *see below*
❄ -18°C (0°F)
Z 2–8

PINUS SYLVESTRIS

With so many variations in form, colour and size, it is no wonder that pines are so often used in gardens.

Soil Most
Aspect Sun
Habit Upright, spreading, pyramidal or mound-forming
Leaf Evergreen, long needles, green, glaucous-green, gold or grey
Flower None; fir cones produced at maturity
Use As a specimen plant
Needs Propagate from seed or by commercial grafting. No pruning required
Varieties (Treble H and S all for dimensions at maturity) *P. densiflora* 'Umbraculifera' umbrella-shaped habit, dense, dark green foliage, 0.7–3 × 3m (27–36 × 36in) • *P. mugo* (mountain pine) dark green foliage, 1.2 × 2m (4 × 6ft) • *P. m.* 'Gnom' slow-growing, compact, dark green foliage, 1 × 1m (3 × 3ft) • *P. strobus* (Weymouth pine) pyramidal, becoming umbrella-shaped, long bluish-green needles, 5 × 4m (16 × 13ft) • *P. sylvestris* (Scots pine) ♀ conical when young, flat-topped with age, grey or blue-green foliage, 4 × 2m (13 × 6ft) • *P. s.* 'Aurea' ♀ conical habit, good golden-yellow winter foliage, 1.5 × 1.2m (5 × 4ft) • *P. s.* 'Beuvronensis' ♀ compact, densely branched, green foliage, 2 × 2m (6 × 6ft) • *P. s.* 'Watereri' conical habit when young, rounded with age, blue-green foliage, 3 × 1.5m (10 × 5ft) • *P. wallichiana* (syn. *P. griffithii*; Himalayan pine, Bhutan pine) light bluish-green long needles, giant blue-brown cones, 4 × 2m (13 × 6ft)

TAXUS
Taxaceae
YEW

▲ ❦ SI all year E
H 10 yrs *see below*
S 10 yrs *see below*
❊ -18°C (0°F)
Z 2–8

TAXUS BACCATA 'FASTIGIATA AUREOMARGINATA'

Among the hardiest of plants, with a very wide range of habit and colour differences, from upright pillars to spreading or weeping, yews can even be used as a formal hedge.

Soil Most
Aspect Full sun to moderate shade; the deeper the shade, the more open the habit
Habit Upright, spreading, pendulous; good as specimen trees
Leaf Evergreen, short fronds of foliage, green, gold or gold-variegated
Flower Small sulphur-yellow flowers, followed by small poisonous red fruits
Use Specimen planting and screening; if planted at distances of 1m (3ft) those indicated will produce a formal hedge
Needs Propagate from cuttings in summer or by commercial grafting. No pruning required but can be trimmed
Varieties (Treble H and S for ultimate dimensions) *T. baccata* (English yew, common yew) ♀ dark green, 2 × 1.5m (6 × 5ft), ultimately 9 × 10m (30 × 32ft), hedge • *T. b.* 'Dovastonii Aurea' ♀ weeping habit, green foliage with gold edges to leaves, 2 × 2m (6 × 6ft) • *T. b.* 'Fastigiata' ♀ upright, dark green, 2 × 0.6m (6 × 2ft) • *T. b.* 'Fastigiata Aureomarginata' ♀ upright habit, deep yellow margins to green foliage, 1.5 × 0.6m (5 × 2ft) • *T. b.* 'Repandens' ♀ prostrate habit, shiny green, drooping at tips, 1 × 4m (3 × 13ft), double for ultimate dimensions • *T. b.* 'Semperaurea' ♀ semi-erect shoots, golden foliage, 2 × 3m (6 × 10ft)

THUJA
Cupressaceae
WESTERN RED CEDAR –
SLOW GROWING

▲ ❦ SI all year SC foliage pine-scented E
H 5 yrs *see below*
S 5 yrs *see below*
-15°C (4°F)   Z 3–9

THUJA OCCIDENTALIS 'RHEINGOLD'

A large group of ornamental conifers with many interesting characteristics. The varieties listed are slow growing.

Soil Most; tolerates reasonably damp areas
Aspect Full sun
Habit Upright, pyramidal
Leaf Evergreen fronds of green, gold or grey
Flower None; cones produced at maturity
Use As a specimen plant
Needs Propagate from cuttings in summer or by commercial grafting. No pruning required but can be lightly trimmed in spring to shape
Varieties (Double H and S for ultimate dimensions) *T. occidentalis* 'Hetz Midget' green-blue foliage, 60 × 75cm (24 × 30in) • *T. o.* 'Holmstrup' ('Holmstrupensis') ♀ neat, conical, bushy habit, tightly packed rich green foliage, 4 × 2m (13 × 6ft) • *T. o.* 'Lutea Nana' ♀ erect habit, golden-yellow foliage, 2 × 1m (6 × 3ft) • *T. o.* 'Rheingold' ♀ bushy to conical habit, old-gold foliage in summer turning rich copper-gold in winter, 1.5 × 1m (5 × 3ft) • *T. orientalis* 'Aurea Nana' ♀ globose habit, erect, flattened foliage sprays, golden-yellow in summer, yellow or bronze-green in winter, 1.5 × 0.75m (5ft × 30in) • *T. o.* 'Elegantissima' ♀ golden, compact, 3 × 1.2m (10 × 4ft) • *T. o.* 'Rosedalis' soft feathery foliage, purple-brown in winter, bright butter-yellow in spring, turning light green, 1 × 0.75m (3ft × 30in) • *T. p.* 'Stoneham Gold' ♀ erect to conical, orange-yellow foliage tinged bronze at tips, 1.5 × 1m (5 × 3ft)

THUJA
Cupressaceae
WESTERN RED CEDAR –
SPECIMEN PLANTS

▲ 🌣 SI all year SC foliage
pine-scented E
H 10 yrs *see below*
S 10 yrs *see below*
-15°C (4°F)   Z 3–9

THUJA PLICATA

All these trees have aromatic foliage with a range of colours
and sizes. They are very reliable and undemanding.

Soil Most
Aspect Full sun to very light shade
Habit Upright, pyramidal; medium to fast rate of growth
Leaf Evergreen fronds of green, gold or yellow-splashed
variegated
Flower None; cones produced at maturity
Use As specimen trees; if planted at distances of 1m (3ft)
those indicated will produce a formal hedge; if planted at
distances of 2m (6ft) can be used for informal screening
Needs Propagate from cuttings in summer. Can be lightly
trimmed as a hedge
Varieties (Treble H and S for ultimate dimensions unless
otherwise indicated) *T. occidentalis* 'Wareana Lutescens' conical, flattened sprays of light yellow-green, 3×1.2m ($10 \times$
4ft), double for ultimate dimensions • *T. o.* 'Pyramidalis'
narrowly pyramidal, mid-green 3×1m (10×3ft), double for
ultimate dimensions • *T. o.* 'Smaragd' neat pyramidal, bright
green, 1.5×1m (5×3ft) • *T. plicata* (western red cedar)
pyramidal, shiny mid-green foliage in large flattened sprays,
fragrant in summer, 4×2m (13×6ft) • *T. plicata*
'Atrovirens' ♀ conical, dark glossy green, 10×4m (32×3ft)
• *T. p.* 'Zebrina' conical habit, light green foliage striped
with greeny-yellow, 8×3m (26×10ft)

TSUGA
Pinaceae
HEMLOCK,
HEMLOCK SPRUCE

▲ 🌣 SI all year SC foliage
pine-scented E
H 10 yrs *see below*
S 10 yrs *see below*
❋ -15°C (4°F)
Z 4–8

TSUGA HETEROPHYLLA

These are among the aristocrats of the conifer world for their
shape and the softness of the foliage effect. Whatever their
size, all make specimen trees of real value.

Soil Most
Aspect Full sun to very light shade
Habit Upright, spreading, mound-forming and pendulous
forms
Leaf Evergreen fronds of glaucous-green, with silver-white
undersides
Flower None; cones produced at maturity
Use Use slow-growing forms for specimens; put spreading
and taller types in a large space where they can fully develop;
for screening and as a timber tree grown in woods
Needs Propagate from cuttings in summer or by commercial
grafting. No pruning required but can be lightly trimmed
Varieties (Treble H and S for ultimate dimensions unless
otherwise stated) *T. canadensis* (eastern hemlock) pyramidal
habit, light green foliage with two whitish bands beneath,
10×3m (32×10ft) • *T. c.* 'Bennett' slow growing, semi-
prostrate, flat-topped, light to mid-green foliage with branchlets drooping at tips, 0.5×1m (20in $\times$ 3ft), double for
ultimate dimensions • *T. c.* 'Pendula' ♀ slow growing, low,
pendulous, bushy, with overlapping drooping branches, mid-
green foliage with silver-white undersides, 2×4m (6×13ft),
double for ultimate dimensions • *T. heterophylla* (western
hemlock) ♀ large, graceful, conical form, grey-green foliage
with silver reverse, 7×3m (23×10ft)

INDEX

Abelia 40
Abies 225
Abutilon 40
Acaena 209
Acanthus 130
Acer
   Japanese maple 41
   negundo 24
   platanoides 24
   pseudoplatanus 25
   rubrum 25
   snake-bark maple 26
Achillea 130
Actinidia 98
Aesculus 26
African lily 131
Agapanthus 131
Akebia quinata 98
Alcea rosea 221
Alchemilla 131
alder 27
Allium 191
Alnus 27
Alstroemeria 132
Amaryllis belladonna 191
Amelanchier 41
Ampelopsis glandulosa 99
Anaphalis 132
Anemone 133, 192
angel's fishing rods 143
Anthemis tinctoria 133
Aquilegia 134
Arabis 209
Aralia elata 42
aralia ivy 105
Araucaria araucana 225
Arbutus 27
Aristolochia macrophylla 99
Armeria 210
Artemisia 134
Arum italicum 135

Aruncus 135
Arundinaria 189
Arundo donax 179
ash 32
Asplenium scolopendrium 185
Aster 136
Astilbe 136
Astrantia major 137
Aubrieta 210
Aucuba japonica 42
Aurinia 211
Australian bluebell 113
autumn crocus 194
avens 149
Azalea 43
Azara 43

barberry 44
bay 73
bean tree 33
bear's breeches 130
beauty berry 46
beauty bush 72
beech 32
Begonia 192
belladonna lily 191
Bellis perennis 221
Berberidopsis corallina 100
Berberis 44
bergamot 161
Bergenia 137
Betula 28
Billardiera longiflora 100
birch 28
birthwort 99
bishop's mitre 145
bitterwood 217
bladdernut 94
bleeding heart 142
blue spiraea 48
bluebell creeper 113

bluebells 200
Boston ivy 109
bottlebrush 46
box 45
Brachyglottis 44
bramble 89, 111
Brassica 222
broom 55–6, 64, 92
brush bush 60
Buddleja 45
burning bush 143
butterflies 10
butterfly bush 45
Buxus 45

calico bush 71
California beauty 63
California lilac 49
Californian tree poppy 88
Callicarpa 46
Callistemon 46
Calluna 47
Calocedrus 226
Caltha 138
Camassia 193
Camellia 47
camomile 133
Campanula 138, 211
Campsis 101
candytuft 216
Canna 193
Caragana 28
Carex 179
Carpenteria californica 48
Carpinus 29
Caryopteris 48
Catalpa 29
catnip 162
Ceanothus 49
Cedrus 226
Celastrus orbiculatus 101
Centranthus ruber 139

Cerastium tomentosum 212
Ceratostigma 49
Cercis 30
Chaenomeles 50
Chamaecyparis 227
cherry, flowering 36
chestnut 26
Chilean bellflower 107
Chilean firebush 58
Chilean glory flower 104
Chimonanthus praecox 50
Chinese holly 79
Chinese lantern 166
Chionodoxa 194
chocolate vine 98
Choisya ternata 51
choosing plants 19
Christmas berry 82
Christmas box 91
Chusquea culeou 189
Cistus 51
Clematis 102, 103
climbing bittersweet 101
climbing cathedral bells 103
climbing plants 13, 14
climbing vibernum 110
Cobaea scandens 103
Colchicum 194
colour 7, 9–11
columbine 134
comfrey 175
conifers 7, 13, 14
Convallaria majalis 195
Convolvulus cneorum 52
coral bells 152
coral plant 100
Cordyline 188
Coreopsis 139
cornel 52
Cornus 52
Cortaderia 180
Corydalis 140
Corylopsis 53
Corylus 53
Cotinus 54
Cotoneaster 54
cottage gardens 8
cotton lavender 90
cowslip bush 53
crab apple 35
Crambe 140
cranesbill 148
Crataegus 30
Crinodendron 55
Crinum × powellii 195
Crocosmia 141
Crocus 196

Cryptomeria 228
Cupressocyparis leylandii 228
Cupressus 229
cutting back 22
Cyclamen 196
Cytisus 55
  battandieri 56

daffodils 204
Dahlia 197
daisy bush 78
Daphne 56
Darmera 141
Davidia involucrata 31
day lily 151
Delphinium 142
Deutzia 57
devil's walking stick 42
Dianthus 212
Diascia 213
Dicentra 142
Dictamnus 143
Dierama 143
Digitalis 222
Dodecatheon 144
dogwood 52
Doronicum 144
Draba 213
dropwort 148
Dryas 214
Dryopteris 185
Dutchman's pipe 99

Eccremocarpus 104
Echinops 145
edelweiss 216
Elaeagnus 57
elder 90
elephant lily 195
elephant's ear 137
Embothrium coccineum 58
Enkianthus 58
Epimedium 145
Eranthis 197
Erica 59
Erigeron 146
Erinus 214
Eryngium 146
Erysimum 147, 223
Erythronium 198
Escallonia 59
Eucalyptus 31
Eucryphia 60
Euonymus 60
Euphorbia 147
evening primrose 162

evergreen foliage 14
Exochorda 61

Fagus 32
Fallopia baldschuanica 104
false acacia 38
Fatshedera lizei 105
Fatsia 61
feeding 22
fertilizers 22
Festuca 180
fetterbush 74
Filipendula 148
firethorn 86
flannel bush 63
flax lily 82
fleabane 146
flowering cherry 36
flowering currant 87
forget-me-not 223
formal gardens 6–7
Forsythia 62
Fothergilla 62
foxglove 222
Fraxinus 32
Fremontodendron 63
fringecups 176
Fritillaria 198
Fuchsia 63
fumitory 140

Galanthus 199
Galtonia candicans 199
Garrya 64
gas plant 143
Genista 64
Gentiana 215
Geranium 148
Geum 149
Ginkgo 229
Gladiolus 200
Gleditsia 33
globe thistle 145
goat's beard 135
golden rod 174
granny's bonnet 134
grape hyacinth 203
greater masterwort 137
Griselinia 65
growth rates 12
gum tree 31
Gypsophila 149

hairy canary clover 76
Hakonechloa macra
  'Aureola' 181
Halesia 65

Hamamelis 66
handkerchief tree 31
hawthorn 30
hazel 53
heathers 47, 59
Hebe 66
Hedera 105
height of plants 11, 13
Helenium 150
Helianthemum 215
Helianthus 150
Helictotrichon sempervirens 181
Helleborus 151
Hemerocallis 151
Heuchera 152
Hibiscus syriacus 67
Himalayan honeysuckle 75
Hippophae rhamnoides 67
Hoheria 68
holly 69
holly grape 77
hollyhock 221
honeylocust 33
honeysuckle 76, 109
hop 106
hornbeam 29
Hosta 152
Houttuynia 153
Humulus lupulus 106
Hyacinthoides 200
Hyacinthus orientalis 201
Hydrangea 68
Hypericum 69

Iberis 216
Ilex 69
Incarvillea 153
Indian bean tree 29
Indian lily 193
indigo bush 70
Indigofera 70
informal gardens 7
insects 10–11
Ipomoea hederacea 106
Iris
   Dutch 201
   dwarf 202
   flag 154
Italian buckthorn 86
Itea 70
ivy 105

Jacob's ladder 167
Japanese anemone 133
Japanese angelica tree 42
Japanese aralia 61

Japanese bitter orange 84
Jasminum 71, 107
Jersey lily 191
Jew's mallow 72
Judas tree 30
juneberry 41
Juniperus
   slow growing 230
   spreading 230
jupiter's beard 139

Kalmia latifolia 71
Kerria 72
king cup 138
Kniphofia 154
Kolkwitzia 72

Laburnum 33
lace bark 68
lady's mantle 131
Lamium 155
Lapageria rosea 107
Larix 231
Lathyrus
   everlasting pea 108
   odoratus 108
Laurus 73
Lavandula 73
Lavatera 74
lavender 73
Leontopodium alpinum 216
leopard plant 156
leopard's bane 144
Leucanthemum 155
Leucojum 202
Leucothoe 74
Lewisia 217
Leycesteria formosa 75
leyland cypress 228
Liatris 156
Ligularia 156
Ligustrum 75
lilac 95
Lilium 203
lily of the Incas 132
lily-of-the-valley 195
lilyturf 157
lime 39
linden 39
ling 47
Linum 157
Liquidambar 34
Liriodendron 34
Liriope 157
Lithodora 217
Lobelia 158
Lonicera

honeysuckle 109
   shrubby honeysuckle 76
Lotus hirsutus 76
lungwort 169
Lupinus 158
Lychnis 159
Lysimachia 159

Macleaya 160
Magnolia 77
Mahonia 77
maintenance of plants 19–22
mallow 67
Malus 35
maples 24–6, 40–1
marsh marigold 138
Matteuccia struthiopteris 186
meadow bright 138
meadowsweet 148
Meconopsis 160
Metasequoia taxodium 231
Mexican orange blossom 51
michaelmas daisy 136
mile-a-minute vine 104
milfoil 130
Milium effusum 'Aureum' 182
Mimulus 161
Miscanthus 182
mock orange 81
Molinia 183
Monarda 161
monkey flower 161
monkey puzzle tree 225
montbretia 141
morning glory 106
Morus 35
moths 10
mountain ash 39
mountain avens 214
mountain laurel 71
mountain spurge 79
mugwort 134
mulberry 35
mullein 177
Muscari 203
Myosotis 223
Myrtus 78

Narcissus 204
nasturtium 114
Nepeta 162
Nerine 205
ninebark 83
nutrients 20, 22

Oenothera 162
Olearia 78
Oregon grape 77
oriental poppy 163
ornamental cabbage 222
ornamental pear 37
ornamental tickseed 139
Ornithogalum 205
Osmanthus 79
Osmunda regalis 186
Oxalis 206

Pachysandra 79
Paeonia 80, 163
pampas grass 180
pansy, winter-flowering 224
Papaver orientale 163
Parthenocissus 109
Passiflora 110
passion flower 110
pea tree/shrub 28
pear trees 37
pearly everlasting 132
Penstemon 164
Perovskia 80
Persicaria 164
Peruvian lily 132
Phalaris 183
pheasant berry 75
Philadelphus 81
Phlomis 81
Phlox 218
    paniculata 165
Phormium 82
Photinia 82
Phygelius 165
Physalis alkekengi 166
Physocarpus opulifolius 83
Physostegia 166
Picea 232
Pieris 83
Pileostegia viburnoides 110
Pinus 232
Pittosporum 84
planning gardens 16
planting 20–1
Platycodon 167
Pleioblastus 190
Polemonium 167
polyantha 224
Polygonatum 168
Polypodium vulgare 187
Polystichum 187
Poncirus trifoliata 84
poplar 36
Populus 36

Potentilla 85, 168
Primula 169, 224
privet 75
protecting plants 17–18
pruning 12, 21, 22
Prunus
    flowering cherry 36
    shrubby 85
Pulmonaria 169
Pulsatilla vulgaris 170
purple bells 111
Puschkinia 206
Pyracantha 86
Pyrus 37

quince 50

ragwort 44
Ranunculus 207
red hot poker 154
red valerian 139
Rhamnus alaternus 86
Rheum 170
Rhodochiton atrosanguineus 111
Rhododendron 87
Rhus 37
Ribes 87
Robinia 38
rock cress 209
rock rose 51, 215
Rodgersia 171
Romneya coulteri 88
Rosa
    alba 124
    Bourbon 125
    Burnet 129
    centifolia 125
    China 126
    climbing roses 117, 123
    cluster 116
    Damask 126
    eglanteria 127
    floribunda 116
    gallica 127
    ground-cover 119
    hip 128
    hybrid tea bush 116
    miniature 118
    musk rose 128
       climbing 23
       Himalayan 123
    patio 118
    pillar 117
    rambling 117
    rugosa 129
    Scotch 129

shrub roses
    county series 120
    modern hybrid 124
    Old English 119
    old fashioned hybrid 123
    standard 121
single-flowered 116
spring-flowering species 122
standard roses
    floribunda 120
    hybrid tea 120
    shrub 121
    weeping 121
summer flowering species 122
sweet briar 127
Rosmarinus 88
rowan 39
Rubus
    bramble 89
    fruiting bramble 111
Rudbeckia 171
Russian sage 80
Russian vine 104

sage brush 134
sailor's button 72
St John's wort 69
Salix 38, 89
salt cedar 96
Salvia 172
Sambucus 90
Santolina 90
Sarcococca 91
Sasa veitchii 190
Saxifraga 218
Scabiosa 172
scent 15
Schisandra rubriflora 112
Schizophragma 112
Scilla 207
Scots heather 47
sea buckthorn 67
sea holly 146
seasons 14–15
sedge 179
Sedum 173, 219
Sempervivum 219
senecio 44
serviceberry 41
shadbush 41
shape of plants 11–14
shooting star 144
shrubby cinquefoil 85
shrubby prunus 85
shrubby ragwort 44

shrubs 21–2
Sidalcea 173
silk tassel 64
silverbell tree 65
silverbush 52
site 17–18
size of plants 11–14
Skimmia 91
Smilacina 174
smoke tree 54
sneezeweed 150
snow in summer 212
snowberry 95
snowdrop 199
snowdrop tree 65
snowflake 202
soil 4, 11–12, 18–19
  preparation 20–1
Solanum 113
Solidago 174
Sollya heterophylla 113
Sorbaria 92
Sorbus 39
Spartina pectinata
  'Aureomarginata' 184
Spartium junceum 92
spiderwort 177
Spiraea 93
  blue spiraea 48
spoon wood 71
spotted laurel 42
spread of plants 11, 13
spruce 232
spurge 147
squill 206, 207
Stachys 175

Stachyurus 93
staff vine 101
Staphylea 94
Stephanandra 94
Stipa 184
stonecrop 219
strawberry tree 27
sumach 37
summer hyacinth 199
sweet box 91
sweet gum 34
sweet olive 79
sweet peas 108
sweetspire 70
Symphoricarpos 95
Symphytum 175
Syringa 95

Tamarix 96
tassel tree 64
Taxus 233
Tellima grandiflora 176
Thalictrum 176
thrift 210
Thuja 233, 234
Thymus 220
Tilia 39
Trachelospermum 114
Trachycarpus fortunei
  188
Tradescantia 177
tree mallow 74
tree peony 80
tree spiraea 92
trees 21
Trifolium 220

Tropaeolum 114
trumpet creeper 101
trumpet flower 153
Tsuga 234
tulip tree 34
Tulipa 208

umbrella plant 141

Verbascum 177
Veronica 66, 178
Viburnum 96
Viola 178
Viola × *wittrockiana* 224
virginia creeper 109
Vitis 115

wall cress 209
wallflower 223
watering 22
Weigela 97
whitebeam 39
wild gardens 8
willow 38, 89
windflower 133
winter flowers 14, 15
winter hazel 53
winter-flowering pansy 224
wintersweet 50
Wisteria 115
witch-hazel 66
wormwood 134

yarrow 130
yew 233
Yucca 97